D1288156

# EARLY TOURS
## IN
## DEVON AND CORNWALL

# EARLY TOURS

## IN

# DEVON AND CORNWALL

A reprint with a new introduction by

### ALAN GIBSON

of the volume edited by
R. PEARSE CHOPE, B.A.
first published in 1918

REPRINTS OF ECONOMIC CLASSICS

AUGUSTUS M. KELLEY • PUBLISHERS
NEW YORK • 1968

Published in the U. S. A. by
AUGUSTUS M. KELLEY, PUBLISHERS
New York, New York

Printed in Great Britain by
Latimer Trend & Co Ltd Whitstable
for David & Charles (Publishers) Limited
South Devon House Railway Station
Newton Abbot Devon

# CONTENTS

# INTRODUCTION TO THE NEW EDITION

Mr Pearse Chope was a careful, deeply-read antiquarian, with a devotion to Devon and Cornwall, and especially to the Hartland district—of which his knowledge was incomparable. He took what might be called a perverse pride in the fact that Hartland was farther from a railway head than anywhere else in the country. Indeed he called one of his books *Farthest from Railways*, proudly beginning: 'If you will take any general railway map of England, such as "Bradshaw" or the "ABC", and try with a compass to draw the largest circle without crossing a railway line, you will, after many trials, fix its centre at Hartland Point, North Devon, for

> "When you have sought all England round
> Farthest from railways this will be found" '

—lines which could have come from Tennyson in an off moment, but which I suspect were written, despite the quotation marks, by Pearse Chope himself. Hartland Point is fourteen miles from Bude, and sixteen from Bideford. He could not have envisaged the savage demolition of the country railway system in the sixties, and the country towns which now count themselves fortunate if they are within thirty miles of a railway line. My edition of *Farthest From Railways: an Unknown Corner of Devon*, dates from 1947, by which time it had already sold thirty-four thousand copies. He had similar successes with other relatively brief sketches.

Nevertheless, *Early Tours in Devon and Cornwall* is unquestionably his major work. It was first published in 1916–17, as an appendix to successive editions of *Devon and Cornwall Notes and Queries*. To set a proper value on the book, it is necessary to remember that a great deal of writing on local history at that period was casual and inaccurate. The average local 'guide-book' was a rehash of legend and half-truth, if it existed at all. Here and there an enthusiastic parson such as Coope at Thurlestone and Warner at Yealmpton, would use his parish records to write a useful parish history, but there were few authoritative background histories on which such men could draw —nothing comparable with Hoskins's *Devon*, for instance— and furthermore the author would almost certainly have to pay for the publication himself. Local history did not arouse even local interest. There were such things as WEA classes in 1916, but they spent their time studying Tom Paine and Marx, or possibly Lecky and Macaulay. Local history was usually regarded as a trivial subject, unworthy of the attention of those who were setting out to put the world right. It was only after the second war, when the world had proved more difficult to set right than we had expected, that the surge of interest in local history began. One could draw some hefty but vague conclusions on this—Britain's withdrawal from an imperial role, and so on—but I am sure Pearse Chope would have had none of that. He would simply have said that knowledge is always precious, and that a perfectly good place to start acquiring knowledge is your own doorstep—and then work slowly outwards.

In 1916, therefore, he had a much smaller public than that which makes possible the re-publication of his book today. A small public, but determined: a band of brothers (more often sisters, perhaps) who maintained a scholarly interest in the history of their own villages, towns, and counties. These were the people whose paragraphs and questions made up the bulk of *Devon and Cornwall Notes and Queries* every quarter. The same names, or initials, or pseudonyms occur again and again—but they were Pearse Chope's public, they were the people for whom he was writing, and they watched him like so many hawks. For instance, he quoted Leland, enumerating the bridges of the Tamar, as referring to 'Hawte Bridge', and had confirmed the spelling himself in a marginal note. This produced, in the next issue, a comment from 'AC': 'This should probably be Hawse Bridge, the name by which it is now known being Horse Bridge. Horse Bridge is quite close to Hingston Down, and some connection with Hengst and Horsa has often been suggested, probably without warrant in the latter case.'

This comment was very typical of the local historians of that era: a proper correction made from local observation, followed by an imaginative flight into non-history ('probably without warrant in the latter case' does, after all, imply, 'possibly *with* warrant in the former'—and here we are back with our old friends Hengist and Horsa). These were people who would be careful in their recording of churchwardens' accounts, but who were still reluctant to discard the legends with which they had grown up. They clung to such characters as Brutus the Trojan, who, you will remember, founded the British race by the simple process of landing a few miles up the Dart and declaring

'Here I stand and here I rest
And this place shall be called Totnes'

which proved him a rotten poet, if nothing else.

I suppose, if anyone had asked Pearse Chope, 'Why do you take such trouble with a book, which is going to appeal to only a handful of folk, and many of them only half-historians?'—I suppose that his answer would have been, however diffidently expressed, that he was writing for posterity. The gratifying thing is that posterity has come so soon. For now local history is very much one of the OK subjects, at university and WEA class alike, and it is an easy bet to say that this new edition will sell far more copies than the original. A vast and, on the whole, responsible literature has grown up around local history in the last twenty years. A new generation of readers, more numerous, better informed, await this book.

Well, here it is. And the new generation will find that this, a forgotten book, is one of their best guides to the history of the South West. They will find that Pearse Chope's editing was meticulous, and that his choice of authors was well balanced. Anyone would have put in Leland and Defoe, and even Celia Fiennes. It took a thoughtful and enquiring mind to include the lieutenant from Norwich, the Duke of Tuscany, and Dr William Stukeley.

It is a book that needs to be read twice. First it should be read slowly, taking the footnotes as they come, and gradually digested. (It must be admitted that Pearse Chope was rather lavish in his footnotes, but that was a good fault in his day.) Then put the book away for a fortnight or so, and read it again: text only, ignoring the most tempting footnote. What a panorama of the development of Devon and Cornwall then reveals itself! The rise and fall of great industries, the roads contracting and widening, new towns growing, old towns declining, castles and cottages, enclosures and invasions—they are all there, a speaking history of a part of England which has none the less refused to surrender its identity to England (sometimes we are well ahead of the rest of the country, sometimes well behind—you will find some interesting examples of this in the book, and you would have found even more had it been continued into the nineteenth century).

This, indeed, is my only complaint. Pearse Chope stops too soon. There is room for another volume describing the experiences of the successors of his pioneering heroes—especially since, in the first quarter of the nineteenth century, the fashion of a West Country holiday began to be established: maybe the present publishers will be encouraged to produce such a work.

Finally, I must confess that *Early Tours in Devon and Cornwall* had lain unread for many years upon my shelves, until the invitation to write this introduction prompted me to take it up again. I had always remembered it as a book of charm and delight. Upon re-reading, after a long interval, I find these qualities even more evident. I do not doubt that this is an enjoyment which you will share.

ALAN GIBSON

# INTRODUCTION

Books of travel have a peculiar fascination which it is difficult to resist. They mostly consist of elaborate descriptions of foreign lands and are adapted to excite our admiration and wonder, but the more modest records of journeys in our homeland amid familiar scenes call up pleasant memories of the past and prove even more entrancing. Such journeys in our own counties of Devon and Cornwall generally form parts of more extended tours, and are recorded in large or many-volumed books that, though well-known, are not readily accessible. It has, therefore, been thought desirable to make a collection of the records of some of the earlier of these journeys, and to issue them as a separate volume.

The selected tours were all made before the coming of the railways, and have been chosen for their interest and variety. They range in time from John Leland the antiquary, who travelled throughout England between the years 1534 and 1543, to Don Manuel Alvarez Espriella, the alleged author of some fanciful " Letters from England " written by Robert Southey in 1802. Their interest in the case of Leland is mainly historical and archæological, of the Norwich Lieutenant ecclesiological, of Stukeley antiquarian, of Duke Cosmo ceremonial, of Celia Fiennes, Defoe, and Don Espriella social, of Pococke and Shaw topographical, of Maton scientific, and of Marshall agricultural.

Leland's Itinerary is of great value and interest, but, as originally written and as edited by Thomas Hearne, it consists merely of rough notes without any attempt at forming a connected narrative. There are several repetitions, and two separate accounts of Cornwall are given. The text has, therefore, been re-arranged in the form of a continuous narrative, incorporating the marginal and other notes, and the two Cornish accounts have been dovetailed together, making one Itinerary of what were two or more separate tours. The tedious tables of distances, most of which are incorrect, have been omitted, but notices of bridges and such like have been retained. It is hoped that no fact of importance or interest has been overlooked. The place names and personal names have, as far as possible, been identified in marginal notes, and copious foot-notes have been added in explanation or illustration of the text. The whole of the text of Leland's Itinerary has been published in a similar form by Miss Lucy Toulmin-Smith, but the version here given was made quite independently and before the writer had an opportunity of consulting Miss Toulmin-Smith's excellent work.

The Norwich Lieutenant's Survey is chiefly interesting from the list it gives of the monuments in Exeter Cathedral. It is taken from the Lansdowne MSS. in the British Museum, and has not, so far as is known, been hitherto published *in extenso*, although it has been occasionally quoted. It is, therefore, considered advisable to print verbatim the whole of the matter relating to Devonshire. Nothing more is known about the author than appears in the title of his Survey.

The next of the selected tours is the official record of the travels of Cosmo III, Grand Duke of Tuscany, who passed through Devonshire on his way to the court of Charles II. It gives a vivid picture of the ceremonies observed at that time, not only by the officials in their reception of the Grand Duke himself, but also by the cathedral clergy and the corporation of Exeter in the performance of their ordinary functions.

The most valuable of all from the social and economic point of view is the diary of a lady, Celia Fiennes, who travelled through England on a side saddle in the time of William and Mary. This lady was daughter of Colonel Nathaniel Fiennes, a Parliamentarian officer, and sister of the third Viscount Saye and Sele. Her powers of observation were remarkable, and all her information is given at first hand. She gives a vivid account of the operations of fulling and dyeing cloth at Exeter, and of tin mining and blowing at St. Austell; she complains of the narrowness and dirtiness of the roads, requiring all goods to be carried on the backs of horses, by means of so-called " crooks "; she describes the spinning of straw " to form a caul or

network to lay over their thatch on their ricks and houses,"
and the burning of turves for fuel, which "makes one smell
as if smoked like bacon"; she expresses surprise that there
were no windmills in such a windy district; and she alludes
to a curious "custom of the country" at St. Austell, viz.,
"a universal smoking—men, women, and children have all
their pipes of tobacco in their mouths and so sit round the
fire smoking." This curious diary was published verbatim
in 1888, but, as the original spelling and punctuation are
rather confusing, they have been to some extent modernized.
Thanks are due to the editor, the Hon. Mrs. Griffiths, and
to the publishers, the Leadenhall Press, Ltd., for permission
to include this record in the series.

Next come two records of the same date (1724) but of
very different character. The first is an account of a visit
to Exeter by the well-known antiquary, Dr. William
Stukeley, whose speculations must be taken with some
reserve; the other is from an anonymous description of a
tour through the whole island of Great Britain, which was
really written by Daniel Defoe, the author of "Robinson
Crusoe." The latter account is full of interest and would
be of far greater value if it could be held to be wholly
reliable, but parts of it are so inaccurate that it is obvious
the writer, when at a loss for facts, did not hesitate to
draw upon his imagination, and thus other parts are unfortunately rendered liable to suspicion, though there can
be no doubt of the substantial accuracy of the work as a
whole. Among the most striking statements are that
20,000 hogsheads of cider were sent from the South Hams
every year to London for mixing with wines; that at
Totnes salmon peal were caught with the aid of a dog
and could be bought for twopence each; that at Dartmouth
seventeen pilchards were bought for a halfpenny, and the
two tourists and their servant were able to dine at a cost
of three farthings; that at Bideford herrings were cured by
salt obtained by dissolving rock-salt in sea-water and
evaporating the brine thus produced. A description of a
storm witnessed by the writer, and some second-hand stories
from Carew's *Survey of Cornwall*, have been omitted.

The next two narratives are by clergymen, the Rev.
Dr. Richard Pococke, afterwards bishop successively of

Ossory and of Meath, and the Rev. Stebbing Shaw, afterwards rector of Hartshorn. They are similar in character, and contain much second-hand information which is of little value. Some of this matter has been abbreviated, but it has not been found desirable to make any extensive alterations. The former was first published in 1888 by the Camden Society, and permission to include it in the series has been kindly given by the present owners of the copyright, the Royal Historical Society, through Mr. Hubert Hall, the director of the Society's publications.

The observations of Dr. W. G. Maton and of William Marshall are of a more scientific nature. Dr. Maton, then a young man from Oxford, was particularly interested in botany and geology, as was Marshall in agriculture and rural economy, but both narratives are full of topographical interest. Extracts only are given from the original works, and, in the case of Marshall's, the matter has been selected to give a continuous itinerary. The absence of wheeled vehicles is still remarkable: Marshall did not "meet a pair of wheels" between Bideford and Swimbridge, although he passed through Barnstaple, and he remarks "a somewhat freer use of wheeled carriages in this part of the county than in the South Hams and West Devonshire."

Finally, we have the above-mentioned letters of Don Espriella, which, although pseudonymous, no doubt represent in the main the first-hand observations of the writer, Robert Southey, and describe the features most likely to attract the attention of an intelligent foreigner. They are more literary in style than any of the others, and fitly conclude the series.

# THE ITINERARY OF JOHN LELAND
# THE ANTIQUARY 1534-43

THE Boundes of Somerseteshire go to a place caullid the Spånne, and the Tourres; for ther be Hillokkes of Yerth cast up of auncient tyme for Markes and Limites betwixt Somersetshir and Devonshire, and here about is the Limes and Boundes of Exmore forest. Span Head.
Five Barrows (?).

From Simonsbath Bridge I rode upon an high Morisch Hylle, and so passing by 2. Myles in lyke Ground, the soyle began to be sumwhat fruteful, and the Hilles to be ful of Enclosures, ontylle I cam a 3. Miles farther to a poore Village caullid Brayforde. Simonsbath.

From Braiford to Berstaple an 8. Miles by hilly ground, having much Enclosures for Pasture and Corne. Brayford.

The Toune of Berdenestaple[1] hath be[en] waullid, and the Waulle was in compace by Estimation half a Myle. It is now almost clene faullen. The names of the 4. Gates by Est, West, North, and South, yet remain, and manifest Tokens of them. Barnstaple.

I think that the olde Name of the Toune was in Britanne Tunge Abertaw, bycause it stode toward the Mouth of Taw Ryver. Berdenes shortely or corruptly spoking, as I thinke, or Abernesse.[2] Staple is an addition for a Market.

The Suburbes be now more then the Toun.

The Houses be of Stone, as al Houses in good Tounes there aboute be.

There be manifest Ruines of a great Castelle at the North West side of the Towne a litle beneth the Toun Bridge, and a Peace of the Dungeon yet standith. One

---

[1] The earliest documentary form of the name, in or about the year 1018, is "Beardastapole," and among the abbreviated forms on the coins of Ethelred II. (979-1016) struck at that mint are BEARDA, BARDA, BARDAN, BEAR, BAR (A. J. V. Radford, "Coins and Tokens of Devon," *Trans. Devon. Assoc.*, xxxix., 349-50). "Staple," as Leland says, is an addition for market.

[2] There does not appear to be any authority for Abertaw, or Abernesse.

*Juhel of Totnes.* Johelus de Totenes,[1] filius Aluredi, was the first that I can reade of that lay yn this Castelle.

There is but one Paroche Chirch in the Town. There hath beene 4. Chapelles, of the which one was at the Est End of the Bridge dedicate to Thomas Beket, now profanid.[2] The other 3. yet stande, one of Alhalowes, at the North Gate, [and] another of S. Nicolas, at the West Gate, as I remember.[3]

*John Holman.* One Holman, Vicar of the Paroche Chirch in Berstaple, made a fair Chapelle, and foundid a Cantuarie in it in the Paroche Chirch Yard in Berstaple.[4]

Barnstaple Priory. The Priorie of Blake Monkes[5] at the Northe Ende the Towne was foundid by Johelus de Totenes, that was Lorde of the Toun and Castelle of Berstaple.

*Henry de Tracy.* One Tracy[6] was after Lorde of the Castelle and Toun, and taken as founder of the Priorie.

Barnstaple Br. Sum say that one of the Tracys made the right great and sumptuus Bridge of Stone having 16. high Arches

---

1 Juhel of Totnes was one of the largest tenants-in-chief at the time of the Domesday Survey (1087), but the earliest record of his connection with the Honour of Barnstaple is in 1113. (*Victoria History of Devon*, i., 557, 559.)

2 There was a Chantry Chapel by the Bridge before 1312, for on 29 Feb., 1311-12, Sir Thomas de Tottonia, priest, was collated by lapse, discord having arisen between Sir Wm. Martyn, Knt., and the Prior and Monks of the Blessed Mary Magdalen, of Barum. On 19 Dec., 1319, Sir Richard de Scottescombe, priest, was instituted to the "Perpetua Cantaria *facienda* in Capella Beati Thome, juxta Pontem Barnastapolie, pro animabus Domini Henrici Traci, progenitorum et successorum suorum, et pro animabus omnium Fidelium defunctorum"—patron, Sir William Martyn, Knt. (Stapeldon's *Register*, ed. Hingeston-Randolph, 188.)

3 This one was dedicated to the Blessed Mary and St. Nicholas. It is mentioned in Bishop Grandisson's *Register*, 24 May, 1332, as being near the Strand; and it was in 1844 a warehouse. Dr. Oliver believed the third to have been dedicated to St. Sabinus, the bishop. (Oliver, *Monasticon Exon.*, 198.)

4 St. Anne's, recently the Grammar School. Oliver doubts this statement, because Bishop Lacy in 1444 granted an indulgence to al sincere penitents who would contribute to its maintenance, and John Holman did not become vicar until 1461. (Oliver, *Monasticon Exon.*, 198.)

5 A Cluniac priory, dedicated to St. Mary Magdalen, and made dependent on the abbey of St. Martin's in the Fields at Paris. (Oliver, *Monasticon Exon.*, 196.) The exact date of the foundation is uncertain.

6 Henry de Tracy confirmed the founder's grants to the priory in 1146, and was succeeded by his son Oliver in 1165. (Oliver, *Monasticon Exon.*, 199; *Victoria History of Devon*, i., 557.)

at Berstaple; there be Landes gyven to the Maintenaunce of this Bridge.[1]

One Philippus de Columbariis[2] was after Lord of Berstaple; and this Philip died circa annum Dñi. 1344. or 47. He and his Wife lay booth buried in the Priory of Berstaple, [where also] lay summe of the Barons of Slane[3] yn Ireland.

*Philip de Columbers.*

There was one William Mertun, a Knight, Lord of Berstaple, [and] of late Dayes the Duke of Excester.[4] The Countes of Richemont,[5] grand Dame to Henry the 8, was Lady of Berstaple; [and] Henry, late Duke of Richmont and Somersete,[6] was Lord of [it].

*William, Lord Martin. Henry Holland, Duke of Exeter. Margaret, Countess of Richmond. Henry Fitzroy, Duke of Richmond.*

There is a Mair in Berstaple, and the Burgesses take King Ethelstan as chief of Privileges to the Toun. [There is] a Fair at the Nativite of our Lady.

Plimtoun is devided from the North Suburbe and the Priory only by a grete Causey of Stone, having an archid Bridge at eche Ende of it. This Bridge was made long sins by a Merchaunt of London caullid Stawford[7] by this occasion: He chauncid to be at Berstaple to by Cloth, and saw a Woman ryding to cum over by the low salte Marsch from Plymtun towarde Berstaple, and the tyde cam so sore yn by a gutte, that brekith yn there from the Haven shore to the Marsch, that she could not passe; and, crying for Help, no man durst cum to her, and so she was drownid.

*Pilton.*

*Sir John Stowford.*

---

[1] "Tradition delivers that it was begun by two maiden sisters, who by spinning and teaching young children their skill finished the two first piers." (Westcote, *View of Devon*, 295.)

[2] From the Tracy family the barony descended to the Martins. "The elder co-heiress of the last Baron Martin brought it to Philip de Columbers, who died without issue. The barony of Barnstaple passed in consequence to the Lords Audley, descended from the other co-heiress." (Lysons, *Devon*, 35.) Philip, Lord Columbers, died 1341; his wife's name was Alienora.

[3] Members of the family of Flemyng.

[4] Richard II. gave it to his half-brother, John Holland, Earl of Huntingdon. After the death of Henry Holland, Duke of Exeter, it came again to the Crown. (Lysons, *Devon*, 36.)

[5] Margaret, Countess of Richmond, had a grant of it for life in 1487. (Lysons, *Devon*, 36.)

[6] Henry Fitzroy, natural son of Henry VIII. Lysons does not mention his connection with Barnstaple.

[7] Westcote (*View of Devon*, 295) and Risdon (*Survey of Devon*, 334) attribute this to Sir John Stowford, Lord Chief Baron, a native of Stowford in the parish of West Down.

Then Stawford toke the Prior of Berstaple a certen summe of Money to begyn this Causey, chekid on eche side, and the Bridgges, and after payid for the performing of it.

There cummith a praty Broke from the Hilles at Berstaple by Est and rennith along by the Priorye Waulle and so goith thorowgh the Bridge at the Ende of the Causey, and strayte dryvith a Mille and so ynto the Haven. Picartes[1] and other smaul Vessels cum up by a gut out of the Haven to the other Bridge on the Causey at Plymtun Townes Ende.

Plymtun is but one fair long streate, and is mainteynid by Clothe making.[2] The West North West side of the Toun for the more part longid to the Priory of Berstaple.

The Est side of the Toune longid to th'abbay of Clif for the more part. King Athelstan gave fair Landes in and by Plymtun to th'abbay of Malmesbyri,[3] [which] had also the Personage of Plymtun impropriatid.

The Bisshop of Excestre hath an auncient Maner Place a Mile above Berstaple-Bridg, caullid Tawton, on the Est part of the Haven. Bisshop Veysy[4] of late made this House sumwhat lesse then it was but more handsum.[5]

The Erle of Bathe[6] hath a right goodly Maner and Place at Tawstoke on the West side of the Haven, a mile above Berstaple Bridge; [and he] hath a goodly Maner Place toward Tiverton caullid Bampton.

Moulton [is] a good Market Town a 7. Miles by Est from Berstaple.

---

1 *Picard.* A large sailing-boat or barge formerly used for coast or river traffic. (*New Eng. Dict.*)

2 In Westcote's time (1630) this had a bad reputation, for he says: "Pilton vents cottons for lining; so coarse a stuff as there was a *væ* or woe pronounced against them in these words—'Woe unto you Piltonians, that make cloth without wool.'" (*View of Devon*, 61.)

3 There was a Benedictine priory at Pilton, which was a cell to Malmesbury Abbey, and the priors "performed the duty of the ordinary parish priest of Pilton." (Oliver, *Monasticon Exon.*, 244.)

4 John Veysey was bishop of Exeter 1519-51 and 1553-4. He alienated the manor of Bishop's Tawton from the See in 1550, and conveyed it, by royal requisition, to John, Lord Russell, afterwards Earl of Bedford. (Lysons, *Devon*, 479.)

5 In 1822 ruins of it were still to be seen. (Lysons, *Devon*, 479.)

6 John Bourchier, Lord Fitzwarren, was created Earl of Bath in 1536, and died about 1540. He was succeeded by his son John, who died 1560. (Vivian, *Visitations of Devon*.)

The King gave of late to the Erle of Hampton[1] a great Lordship caullid Fremingtun; it lyith from byneth Berstaple Bridge on the West side of the Haven to the Nesse.

The Ryver of Taw is no very mayne streame at the Ebbe as it apperith at Berstaple. From Berstaple to the very Haven Mouth a v. Miles, and the very Mouth of it is no large thing; and a litle without is a barre. There rennith a shore on the West side of the Haven a 3. Miles byneth Berstaple to this Nesse or Point [where] metith the Ryver of Turege and Taw togither, making a brode Water, and go to the Severn Se.

From this Nesse up to Bedeford Bridge apon Turege a 4. Miles, wher is a praty quik[2] Streate of Smithes and other Occupiers for Ship crafte *cis pontem*.

The Bridge at Bedeforde is a very notable Worke, and hath xxiiij. Arches of Stone, and is fairly wauliid on eche side; but the Arches be not so high as the Arches of Berstaple Bridge be. A poore Preste[3] began thys Bridge; and, as it is saide, he was animatid so to do by a Vision. Then al the Cuntery about sette their Handes onto the performing of it, and sins Landes hath bene gyven to the maintenaunce of it. Ther standith a fair Chapelle of our Lady *trans pontem* at the very ende of it, and there is a fraternite in the Town for perservation of this Bridge; and one waitith continually to kepe the Bridge clene from al Ordure.

The greatest part of the Toune is *ultra pontem*, and ther is a fair Paroch Chirch.

Ther is no wekely Market[4] at a sette day at Bedeforde.

*Wm. Fitz-william, Earl of Southampton.*
*Fremington.*
*Taw R.*

*Torridge R.*

*Bideford.*

*East-the-Water.*

*Bideford Br.*

---

[1] Presumably William Fitzwilliam, Earl of Southampton (d. 1542), lord high admiral, and an intimate friend of Henry VIII. from childhood.

[2] Lively, stirring.

[3] Richard Gourney (Westcote, *View of Devon*, 337); Richard Gornard (Risdon, *Survey of Devon*, 281-2). The name does not appear in the Episcopal Registers, but these only date back to 1257, and it is almost certain that the bridge was in existence before that date.

[4] A market on Monday and a fair for five days at the festival of St. Margaret were granted, in 1271, to Richard de Grenville, and these were confirmed, and two other fairs granted, by the borough charter procured in 1574 by Sir Richard Grenville. (Lysons, *Devon*, 48.) The present market-day is Tuesday.

Appledore.

There is a good Village[1] *ulteriori ripa* a 2. Miles byneth Bedeford, caullid Apledour, and thens about a Mile is the Haven Mouth, a smaul Thing at Ebbe of Water. The Haven Entery is barrid with Sande, and the Enterie into it is daungerus.

*Coffin.*
Portledge.
Hartland.
Hartland
Point.

Mr. Cophin[2] dwellith a 3. Miles by [South] West from Bedeford.

Hertland is x. Miles from Bedeford, much by Morische Ground but very good for Broode of Catelle. Hertey point lyith North [West] 3. Miles nerer to the Mouth of Taw then Hertlande. From the very Point of the Haven Mouth of Taw to cut strait over to Hertey Point is a 6. or 7.

Hartland
Abbey.

Miles; and Hertland Priory[3] [is] a 3. Miles above Hertey Point, and standith not a Mile from the Se; but bytwix the Mouth of Tawe and Hertey Point lyith a very cumpasid Bay, and almost in the midle thereof is a Place caullid

Clovelly.
*Robert Cary.*

Clovelle, wherabout Caryl[4] dwellith; and here is the nerest *Trajectus* into Lundey Isle.

Newton
Tracey.

Alverdiscott.
*Henry Bellew.*

From Berstaple to Newtoun, a poore Village, by stony and hille and sum enclosid Ground a 3. Miles; and thens to Alscote by much like Ground a 3. Miles. Master Bedlow dwellith at Alscote; [he] hath recoverid two Lordshippes that were the Baron of Slane's.[5] I left his House hard by on the lift Hand; and thens I cam to Toringtun a 2. Miles of.

Torrington.

Torington is a great large Toune, and stondith on the brow of an Hille, and hath a 3. fair Streates yn it, and a good Market[6] every weke, and ons a Yere upon S. Michael's day the best Fayr in al those Quarters.

---

[1] Westcote, writing in 1630, says: "In the memory of man, at a place called Appledore, stood but two poor houses." (*View of Devon*, 342.)

[2] The Coffin family had been at Portledge ever since the reign of Henry II. The representative at this time was probably Richard, who died in 1555.

[3] Hartland Abbey, of Augustinian Canons, founded about 1170 by Geoffrey de Dynham.

[4] Robert Cary, died 1540.

[5] The Bellew at this time was Henry. His father, Patrick, died in 1533. His grandfather, John Bellew, mar. Anne, dau. and co-heir of John Fleming, the representative of the Flemings, Barons of Slane. (Vivian, *Visitations of Devon*, 68.)

[6] "Much frequented, and for abundance and good victuals few markets in this country or elsewhere better furnished." (*View of Devon*, 327.)

In the Town is but one Paroch Chirch. Dr. Chaumbre persone therof.

The most parte lyvith there by making of Cloth.[1]

There is a Mair, and the Toun is privilegid with Libertees.

The Ryver of Torege rennith under the rootes of the Hille, on the which the Town stondith, and apon Turege at Torington be 2. Bridgges of Stone, one caullid the South Brid[ge] of 3. Arches of Stone, and another half a Mile lower, caullid the West Bridge, the which is the greater of the 2., and by this Weste Bridge the way lyith to Hertland, that is xij. Miles of.

A litle above the South Bridge stoode a fair Castelle[2] apon the Brow of the Hille hangging over Torege Ripe, of the which at this present tyme nothing remainith stonding but a neglect Chapelle.[3]

I lernid that one Sir Wyllyam of Torington[4] was Lord of this Castel and the Town, for whom and for his Sunne they pray in the Paroche Chirch. The King of late tyme gave the Lordship of Torington onto Fitzwilliams, Erle of Hamptun.[5]

Litle-Tarington is on an Hille beyond Turege Water a Mile by South, and therby dwellith one Mr. Monk,[6] a Gentilman.

There is an Hamlet longging to Tarington Toun, not a Mile by Est from Tarington, caullid S. Gilys, wher George Rolles hath builded a right fair House of Bryke.[7]

Fristok Priory[8] is aboute a Mile from Tarington.

*Dr. Chamber.*

Taddiport Br.

Rothern Br.

*William de Toriton.*

*Wm. Fitz-william, Earl of Southampton.*
Little Torrington.
*Anthony Monk.*
St. Giles in the Wood.
*George Rolle.*
Frithelstock.

---

[1] "Barnstable and Torrington furnish us with bays, single and double; frizados, and such like." (Westcote, *View of Devon*, 61.)

[2] Built by Richard de Merton in 1340. (Lysons, *Devon*, 529.)

[3] This Chapel of St. James was in existence before 1278, when William de Mertone, deacon, was appointed chaplain on the presentation of Thomas de Mertone. (Bronescombe's *Register*, ed. Hingeston-Randolph, 187.) It was afterwards converted into a school-house and taken down before 1780. (Risdon, *Survey of Devon*, 273; Lysons, *Devon*, 529.)

[4] William de Toriton was in possession in 1166, and was succeeded by his two sons John and Mathew, with a childless son of John, called William, between them. (*Victoria History of Devon*, i., 566.)

[5] See note 1 on p. 5.

[6] Anthony Monk, ancestor of the famous George Monk, Baron Monk of Potheridge, Earl of Torrington, and Duke of Albemarle.

[7] George Rolle of Stevenstone, died 1552.

[8] Of Augustinian Canons, founded by Robert Beauchamp, about 1220, by canons from Hartland Abbey. (Oliver, *Monasticon Exon.*, 219.)

Torridge R.

The Ryver of Turege risith in a Morisch Ground a 3. Miles by [South] Est from Herteland, almost by the principale Hedde of Tamar.[1] The first notable Bridge on Turege is Kissington Bridg; thens half a Mile to Pulford Bridg; thens a 2. Miles to Woddeford Bridge; thens a 2. Miles to Depeford Bridge of 3. Arches; thens to the South Bridge of Torington; thens to the West Bridge of Torington; thens to Bedeford Bridge about a 4. Miles; and a 2. Miles lower is the Confluence of Turege and Taw, and so strait into Severn by the Haven Mouth.

Woolley Moor.
Kismeldon Br,
Putford Br.
Woodford Br.
Bradford Br.
Taddiport Br.
Rothern Br.
Bideford Br.

From Tarington over the South Bridg to Depeford by hilly and much enclosid Ground and sum wood, an 8. Miles of. From Depeford to Lanstoun (Fanum Stephani) a xij. Miles by Hilly and much Morische Ground baren of Wodde.

Bradford.

Launceston.

Or ever I cam to Lanstoun by a Mile I passid over a Bridge of Stone having 3. Arches, and a smaul, caullid New Bridge, thorough the which the Ryver of Tamar rennith, that almost from the Hed of it to the Mouth devidith Devonshir from Cornewaule. This New Bridge was of the making of the Abbates of Tavestok and mainteinyd by them; for Tavestoke Abbay had fair Possessions thereaboute.

New Br.

The Ryver of Tamar risith a 3. Miles by [South] Est from Hertelande, and thens cummith to Tamertun, and ther is a Bridg over Tamar of Stone; Yalme Bridge of Stone 2. Miles lower; New Bridg 2. Miles lower; Polstun Bridge 2. Miles lower; Greistoun Bridge a 2. Miles or more lower; Tavestoke about a 4. miles from Greston Bridg, and Grestoun Bridg being about a 3. Miles from Launston is the way from Launston to Tavestok; Hawte Bridg; another Bridg caullid New Bridg; Caulstoke Bridg next the Se begon by Sir Perse Eggecumbe.[2] Lideford Bridge is not on Tamar. By the Ryver of Tamar from the Hedde, yssuying owt towarde the Sowthe, the Contery being Hilly, ys fertile of Corne and Gresse with sum Tynne Warkes wrought by Violens of Water.

Tamar R.
N. Tamerton.
Yalm Br.
New Br.
Polston Br.
Greystone Br.

Hawte Br.
New Br.
Calstock Br.
*Sir Piers
Edgcumbe.*
Lydford Br.

After that I had enterid a litle into the Suburbe of

---

[1] Woolley Moor, in Morwenstow parish.

[2] Sir Piers Edgcumbe (d. 1539), K.B., sheriff of Devon, 1493, 1494, and 1497; made Knight-banneret for his service at the battle of Spurs, 1513.

Launstoun, I passid over a Brooke caullid Aterey, that rennith    Ottery R.
yn the Botom of the stepe Hil that Launstoun stondith
on.   After that I had passid over Aterey I went up by
the Hille through the long Suburbe ontylle I cam to the
Toun Waul and Gate, and so passid thorough the Toun,
conscending the Hille ontylle I cam to the very Toppe of
it, wher the Market Place and the Paroche Chirch of
S. Stephane, lately re-edified, be.

Launston, otherwys cawled Lostephan, yn old tyme
cawlled Duneuet,[1] stondith ii. Myles beyownd Powlston
Bridge on Tamar Westward.   The sayde Town Duneuet,
otherwise Lawnston, is a walled Towne ny yn Cumpas a
Myle, [and] the Wall ys hy, larg and strong, and defensably
set, but now ruinus.[2]   On the North side of the Towne a
Castel stonding on a hye Hille within the sayd Towne hath
iii. rowndes Wardes.   The Moles that the Kepe standeth
on is large and of a terrible highth, and the Arx of it is
the strongest, but not the biggist, that ever I saw in any
aunciient Worke in Englande.   Part of the Castel stonding
North West ys Parcel of the Walle of the Town.   Ther be
withyn this Town iii. Gates and a Postern; also a Gate to
go owt of the Castel ynto the old Parke.   Sum Gentelmen
of Cornewal hold ther Landes by Castelgard, that ys to say
for Reparation of this Castel and Towne;[3] and withyn this
Castel ys a Chapel, and a Hawle for Syses and Sessions,
for a commune Gayle for al Cornwayle is yn this Castel.

Withyn this Towne is a Market,[4] a Mayre and

---

[1] Launston, now spelt Launceston, is said to be a corruption of
Lanstephan, i.e., Stephen's Church, and was previously called Dunheved or Dunhevet.   The earliest forms of the name of the priory
and church in the Episcopal Registers are "Lanscevatone" and
"Lanstavetone."

[2] An official survey, taken in the year 1337, speaks of it as being
even then in a very ruinous state. (Lysons, *Cornwall*, 188.)

[3] The manor and honor of Launceston, which had a very extensive
jurisdiction, belonged from time immemorial to the Earls of Cornwall,
who had their chief seat at Launceston Castle.   It was taken from
the native Earls by William the Conqueror, and given to his half-
brother Robert, Earl of Moreton, whom he made Earl of Cornwall.
It passed with the earldom; and when Cornwall was erected into a
duchy, was annexed to it by Act of Parliament. (Lysons, *Cornwall*,
187.)

[4] The market is held by prescription.   In the reign of King John
the burgesses gave five marks for the King's licence to change their
market-day from Sunday to Thursday. (Lysons, *Cornwall*, 189.)

Burgesses,[1] with a Chapel of Mary Magdalen[2] to theyr Uses.
Ther is a litle Pirle of Water that servith the high Parte
of Lanstoun, [and there] be ii. Conduites of derived Water.
In a Vale at the Foote of the Hil of the sayd Town,
abowt an Arow Shot fro the Castel Northward, is a Priory
of Chanons Regular,[3] dedicate to S. Stephan. It stondith
by a fair Wood side, and thorowgh this Wood rennith a
Pirle of Water cumming out of an Hil therby, and [it]
servith al the Offices of the Place. In the Chirch I markid
2. notable Tumbes, one of Prior Horton[4] and another of
Prior Stephane.[5] One also told me that one Mabilia, a
Countes, was buried ther in the Chapitre House. One
William Warwist, Bisshop of Excestre, erectid this Priorie,
and was after buried at Plymtoun Priory that he also erectid.
Warwist, for erection of Launston Priory, suppressid a
Collegiate Chirch of S. Stephan, having Prebendaries, and
gave the best part of the Landes of it to Launstoun Priory,
and took the Residew hymself.[6]    There yet standith a Chirch
of S. Stephan[7] about half a Mile from Launstoun on a

*Roger de Horton. Stephen Tredydan. Wm. Warelwast.*

St. Stephen's Church, Newport.

[1] The town of Dunhevet (now Launceston) was made a free borough in the reign of Henry III., by Richard, Earl of Cornwall, who granted various privileges to the burgesses, and a piece of ground to build their guildhall upon, to be held of him and his heirs, by the annual render of a pound of pepper. (Lysons, *Cornwall*, 189.)

[2] The chapel of St. Mary Magdalen has become the parish-church of Launceston. (Lysons, *Cornwall*, 190.) It is entirely constructed of granite, and was erected in 1524 by Sir Henry Trecarrel, of Trecarrel. (Murray's *Handbook for Devon and Cornwall*, 5th ed., 187.)

[3] Augustinian canons; refounded by Bishop William Warelwast in 1126. "No remains of the priory buildings are known to exist, unless the Norman arch, preserved at the White Hart inn, be part of them." (Oliver, *Monasticon Exon.*, 21-2.)

[4] Roger de Horton became prior in 1308. Growing blind and feeble, he was in 1316 provided with a coadjutor, but the date of his death is not known. (Oliver, *Monasticon Exon.*, 22.)

[5] Stephen Tredydan occurs as prior in 1379, and died in office, 403. (Oliver, *Monasticon Exon.*, 22.)

[6] The church of St. Stephen was collegiate before the Conquest, and filled with secular canons. King Henry I. gave this church to the church of Exeter. William Warelwast, bishop of Exeter, 1107-1137, suppressed the college of secular canons, and in its stead founded a priory of Austin monks in the parish of St. Thomas, about half-way between St. Stephen's and the castle. (Lysons, *Cornwall*, 191.)

[7] The parochial church of St. Stephen was dedicated by Bishop Bronescombe in 1259. (Oliver, *Monasticon Exon.*, 22.) The parish is now known as Newport, but was formerly called Launceston, while the present Launceston was called Dunheved. (Lysons, *Cornwall*, 192.)

Hille, wher the Collegiate Chirch was.  The Opinion is that
the Chanons first dwelled on this Hille, and cam thens
downe to a better and a warmer Site.  In the Priory
Chirche Yarde standeth also a Paroche Chyrche.[1]  Gawen
Carow hath the Custody of the Priory.

St. Thomas's Church.
*Gawen Carew.*

There is a Chapelle by West North West a litle without
Launstowne, dedicate to S. Catarine ; it is now prophanid.[2]

Trecarelle [lives] at Trecareile by Launston.

*Trecarrel, in Lezant.*
*Boscastle.*

From Launston to Botreaux Castelle, vulgo Boscastel,
first a 2. Miles by enclosid Ground having sum Woodde
and good Corne.  Thens an 8. Miles by Morisch and Hilly
Ground and great scarsite of Wod, insomuch that al the
Countery therabout brennith Firres and Hethe.  And thens
a 2. Miles to Boscastle by enclosid Ground metely fruteful
of Corne but exceding baren of Wood, to the which the
Bleke Northen Se is not there of Nature favorable.

The Myddel of Cornewale to the Est Part [is]  Hy
Montaynes rochel Ground, very baren, with sum Tynne
Warkes yn them.  Cornewal thorough owt from the East
Part to the West, nerer to the North Part then to the
Sowth, ys Hy Montaynes baren Ground.

The Toun of Boscastelle[3] lyith apon the Brow of a
rokky Hille by South Est, and so goith doun by lenght to
the Northe toward the Se, but not even ful hard to it.  It
is a very filthy Toun and il kept.[4]  There is a Chirch in
it, as I remembre, of S. Simpherian.[5]  The Lorde Botreaux was Lord of this Toun, a man of an old Cornish
Linage, and had a Maner Place, a Thing, as far as I
could heare, of smaul Reputation, as it is now, far onworthe
the name of a Castel.  The People ther caulle it the
Courte.[6]  Ther cummith down  a litle broke from South

*Lord Botreaux.*

---

[1] St. Thomas's.

[2] In Bishop Lacy's Register is an indulgence in favour of the
chapel of St. Catharine, adjoining Launceston Priory.  (Oliver,
*Monasticon Exon.*, 22.)

[3] Boscastle is derived from Bottreaux Castle.

[4] Carew says : " Bottreaux Castle [is] seated on a bad harbour of
the North sea, suburbed with a poore market town." (*Survey of
Cornwall*, ed. 1769, 120.)

[5] Forrabury Church, dedicated to St. Symphorian, a native of
Autun, in Burgundy, and beheaded there in A.D. 178.

[6] " The diversified roomes of a prison, in the Castle, for both
sexes, better preserved by the Inhabitants' memorie, than descerneable
by their owne endurance, shew the same, heeretofore to have exercised
some large jurisdiction." (Carew, *Survey of Cornwall*, 120 *d*.)

Est out of the Hilles therby, and so renning by the West side of the Towne goith into Severn Se betwixt 2. Hylles, and ther maketh a pore Havenet, but of no certaine salvegarde.

*Lord Hungerford.*

One of the Hungrefordes married with one of the Heires generale of Botreaux, and so Boscastel cam to Hungreford. Then cam Boscastelle by an Heir Generale of the Hungrefordes onto the Lord Hastinges. Hastinges Erle of Huntendune and the late Lord Hungreford had a Lordship of the Botreaux in partition, caullid Parke, and ther is a Manor Place or Castelet[1]; it is a vj. Miles from Botreaux by South.

*Lord Hastings. Hastings, Earl of Huntingdon. Park, in Egloshayle.*

Ther is no very notable Toun or Building from Botreaux along apon the Shore upper on Severn to Hertland point but Strettoun, and that is xij. Miles from Botreaux, and ther is a praty Market; it stondith about a Mile from the Se. There is a Place nere to Stretton caullid Ebbingford, but now communely Efford, wher John Arundale of Trerise[2] was borne, and hath a fair Maner Place; in the which Syr John Chaumon[3] now dwellith, that maried the Mother yet lyving of John Arundale of Trerise. Old Treviliane, a man of pratie Land but cumming of a Youngger Brother of the chife House of that Name, dwellith toward Stretton at a place caullid . . .

*Stratton.
Efford.
Sir John Arundell.*

*Sir John Chamond.
Trevelyan.*

*? Basill, in St. Clether.*

Fro Stratton to Padstow the Contery by the North Se ys rather Hylle then Montaynenius, and ys very fertyle of Gras and Corne; and the Clives of the sayd Northe Se betwne the Places aforesayd hath good fyne blew Slates,

---

[1] The manor of Park, in Egloshayle, was the property and seat of the Peverells, whose co-heiresses brought it to the families of Basset and Bottreaux. In Lysons' time (1814) a farm-house occupied the site of the barton, and part of the remains of the old mansion had been converted into stables. (Lysons, *Cornwall*, 81-2.)

[2] This was Sir John Arundell of Trerice, the celebrated "Jack of Tilbury" or "Jack for the King." He was born about 1494, was Esquire of the Body to Henry VIII., knighted at the battle of Spurs, and Vice-Admiral of the West. He lived at Gwarnack (see p. 19) and died in 1561. Monument in Stratton Church. (Vivian, *Visitations of Cornwall.*)

[3] The house of the Chamond family was in the adjoining parish of Launcels, "so called for that it was sometimes a Cell appertaining to the Abbot of Hartlond." Sir John Chamond, "a man learned in the common lawes, was knighted at the Sepulchre," and married, as his second wife, Jane, daughter of Sir Thomas Grenvile, and widow of Sir John Arundell of Trerice. He died in 1544, and his widow in 1552. (Carew, *Survey of Cornwall*, 118.)

apte for Howse Kyveryng, and also hath diverse Vaynes of Leade and other Metalles not yet knowen.

From Botreaux to Tredewy Village on the Shore [is]        Tredewy.
about a Myle, and ther cummith downe a Broke rising in
the gret rokky Hilles therby.   From Tredewi to Bossinny        Bossiney.
on the Shore [is] about a Mile.

This Bosseny hath beene a bygge thing for a Fischar
Town, and hath great Privileges grauntid onto it.[1]   A Man
may se there the Ruines of a gret numbre of Houses.   Here
also cummith down a Broke, and this Brook and Tredewy
Water resort to the Se at one Mouth bytwixt ij. Hilles,
wherof that that is on the Est side lyith out lyke an Arme,
or Cape, and makith the Fascion of an Havenet, or Pere,
whither Shippelettes sumtime resorte for socour.   A Frere
of late dayes toke apon hym to make an Haven at this
Place, but he litle prevailid theryn.

There ly 2. blake Rokkes as Islettes at the West North        The Sisters.
West point or side of this Creeke, the one, saving a Gut
of Water, joyning to the other; and yn these brede Gulles
be al lykelihod.

From Bossinny to Tintagel Castle[2] on the Shore [is] a        Tintagel.
Mile.   This Castelle hath bene a marvelus strong and notable
forteres, and almost *situ loci inexpugnabile*, especially for the
Dungeon that is on a great and high terrible cragge environid with the Se, but having a Draw Bridge from the
Residew of the Castelle onto it.   The Residew of the
Buildinges of the Castel be sore wether beten and yn Ruine,
but it hath bene a large thinge.   The Castel had be lykehod
iii. Wardes, wherof ii. be woren away with gulfyng yn of
the Se, yn so much that yt hathe made ther almost an Isle,
and no way ys to enter ynto hyt now but by long Elme
Trees layde for a Bryge.   So that now withowte the Isle
renneth alonly a Gate Howse, a Walle, and a fals Braye
dyged and walled.   In the Isle remayne old Walles, and
yn the Est Part of the same, the Grownd beyng lower,
remayneth a Walle embateled, and Men alyve saw theryn a

---

[1] Bossiney did not become a parliamentary borough until the reign
of Edward VI., but, though not incorporated, it probably had a mayor
before that time.   (Lysons, *Cornwall*, xxxvii., 306.)

[2] This castle is of great antiquity, and is said to have been the
birth-place of King Arthur; but its first mention in actual history is
in 1245.  (Lysons, *Cornwall*, 304.)

Postern Dore of Yren. Ther is yn the Isle a prety Chapel of S. Ulette *alias* Uliane, with a Tumbe on the left side. There ys also yn the Isle a Welle, and ny by the same ys a Place hewen owt of the Stony Grownd to the Length and Brede of a Man. Also ther remayneth yn the Isle a Grownd quadrant walled as yt were a Garden Plot; and by this Walle appere the Ruines of a Vault. The Grownd of this Isle now nuryshyth Shepe and Conys.

**Trevena.**

The Castel stondith in the Paroche of Trevenny, and the Paroch [Church] thereof is of S. Symphorian, ther caullid Simiferian.[1]

**Camelford.**

Wythyn iiii. Myles of the sayde Tintagel ys Camylford, abowt [which] ar certen old Mynes, wrought yn tymes past, but of what Metall yt ys now onknowen. Wythyn a Myle above that poore Village Sowth runneth the Ryver that goyth ynto the Severn Se at Paddistow, and yt is the greatest Ryver on the North Syde of Cornewale, and ys

**Camel R.**

cawled yn the commune Spech there, Dunmere,[2] and yn the Kyngges Grawnt of Privilege to the Chanons of Bodmynne, and the Burgesses of the same Towne, Alan, yt may fortune for Alaune. Sum Historyes cawl it Cablan. By this Ryver Arture fought his last Feld, yn token wherof the People fynd there yn plowing Bones and Harneys.[3]

Passing a Mile from the Chirch of S. Symphorian by Hilly and Hethy Ground I cam over a Brooke that ran from South Est North to Severn Se, and about half a Myle

**Gull Rock.**

beyound the Mouth of this Brook lay a great Blak rok lyke an Islet yn the Se not far from the Shore.

**Port Isaac.**

Porthissek, a praty Fisschar Village, lyith about a 3. Miles from the Mouth of th'afore sayd Brook lower by West on Severn Shore. There resortith a Broke to Porthissek; and there is a Pere and sum socour for Fisschar Botes.

---

1 The parish is now called Tintagel. Its church is dedicated to St. Marcelliana. St. Symphorian is the saint of the parish church of Bottreaux, or Forrabury. (See note 5 on p. 11.)

2 Now called Camel. The chief tributary is called Allen.

3 " Upon the river of Camel, neere to Camelford, was that last dismal battel strooken betweene the noble king Arthur and his treacherous nephew Mordred, wherein the one took his death, and the other his death's wound. For testimony whereof, the olde folke thereabouts will shew you a stone, bearing Arthur's name, though now depraved to Atry." (Carew, *Survey of Cornwall*, 122 d.)

Porthguin, a Fisschar Village, lyith a 2. Miles lower on the Shore, and there is the Issue of a Broke and a Pere. And a 3. Miles lower is the Mouth of Padestow Haven.

From Dindagelle to S. Esse Village [is] a 4. Miles, [and there is] meately good Ground about S. Esse's selfe. From S. Esse to Trelille Village [is] 2. Miles, [and] from Trelille [I went] to (S. Cua), wher Master Carniovies, *alias* Carnsey (Carnsew) hath a praty House (Bokelley), fair Ground, and praty Wood about it. Cauelle [also lives] in S. Cua Paroch at Trearach,[1] [and] Nicolle in S. Tedy Paroch[2] by Bokelly. Thens 3. Miles by good Corne Grounde, but no Wood, to Wadebridge.

Wher as now Wadebridge is there was a Fery a 80. Yeres syns, and Menne sumtyme passing over by Horse stoode often in great Jeopardie. Then one Lovebone, Vicar of Wadebridge, movid with pitie began the Bridge, and with great Paine and Studie, good People putting their Help therto, finishid it with xvij. fair and great uniforme Arches of Stone.[3] One told me that the Fundation of certein of th'arches was first sette on so quik sandy Ground that Lovebone almost despairid to performe the Bridg ontyl such tyme as he layed Pakkes of Wolle for Fundation.[4] ·

The Ryver of Alawne rennith thorough Wadebridge, evidentely seen at lower. The first memorable Bridge on Alane is caullid Helham Bridge; Dunmere Bridge of 3. Arches a 2. Miles lower; Wadebrid[ge] a 3. Miles lower by Land and 4. by Water. In the way passing from Dunmere Bridge toward Bodmyn there rennith a praty Broket thoroug a Bridge of one Stone Arche, a very litle

*Portquin*

*St. Teath.*

*Trelill.*
*St. Kew.*
*Carnsew.*
*Bekelly.*
*Cavall.*
*Treharrock.*
*Nicoll.*
*St. Tudy.*
*Wadebridge.*

*John Lovibond.*

*Camel R.*

*Helland Br.*
*Dunmere Br.*

---

[1] The manor of Treharrick, in St. Kew, belonged to a family of that name, whose heiress brought it to the Cavalls in the reign of Henry VII. (Lysons, *Cornwall*, 162.)

[2] The manor of St. Tudy and Trelil belonged to the family of Nicoll. (Lysons, *Cornwall*, 314.)

[3] "The longest, strongest, and fayrest that the Shire can muster." (Carew, *Survey of Cornwall*, 143 d.) The bridge connects the parishes of Egloshayle and St. Breock, and is nearly 320 feet in length. It was built in the reign of Edward IV., by public contributions set on foot by John Lovibond, then vicar of Egloshayle, who, according to Hals, gave lands then worth 20*l.* per annum for its support. (Lysons, *Cornwall*, 83.)

[4] This tradition, which is attached to other bridges, is without evidence to support it; the bed of the river is of rock. (Maclean, *Trigg Minor*, i., 401.)

St. Lawrence.

Mitchell.

Padstow.

Bodmin.

Bodmin Priory.

way beyond Dunmer Bridge; this litle Broke servith the Milles and rennith by the Est Ende of the Town of Bodmyn. There cummith a Brooke into Alaune about a 2. Miles byneth Dunmere Bridge, and at S. Laurence, scant a Mile owte of Bodmyn, I passid over a Bridge on this Water in the way to Michale.

From Wade Bridge to Padestow, a good quik Fisschar Toun but onclenly kepte, [is] a 4. Miles. This Toun is auncient, being the Name of Lodenek in Cornische, and yn Englisch, after the trew and old Writinges, Adelstow—*Latine Athelstian locus*; and the Toune there takith King Adelstane for the chief Gever of Privileges onto it.[1]

Shyppes cum not yn but at the Flowyng Water, [but] there use many Britons with smaul Shippes to resorte to Padestow with Commoditees of their Countery and to by Fische. The Toun is ful of Irisch Men.[2]

From Wadebridge to Dunmere [is] a 3. Miles, and thens a Mile to Bodymn. Bodmyn hath a Market on every Saturday lyke a Fair for the Confluence of People.[3] The Showe and the Principale of the Toun is from West to Est along in one Streate. There is a Chapel at the West Ende of the Toun. The Paroçh Chirch standith at the Est End of the Town, and is a fair large Thyng; there is a Cantuarie Chapel[4] at th'est Ende of it.

The late Priory of Blake Chanons[5] stoode at the Est Ende of the Paroch Chirch Yarde. S. Petrocus was Patrone

---

[1] As the termination is evidently Saxon, it is more likely to be a corruption of Ealde-stowe: it does not appear that Athelstan had ever any connection with Padstow. (Lysons, *Cornwall*, 251). In the Episcopal Registers the earliest forms seem to be Lelestou, Allestou, and Allestowe. (Bronescombe's *Register*, ed. Hingeston-Randolph, 161.)

[2] "It reapeth greatest thrift by traffiking with Ireland, for which it commodiously lieth." (Carew, *Survey of Cornwall*, 143.)

[3] "The greatest of Cornwall." (Carew, *Survey of Cornwall*, 123d.)

[4] St. Thomas. (Oliver, *Monasticon Exon.*, 15.)

[5] Augustinian canons; refounded by Bishop William Warelwast. It was originally Benedictine, and is reputed to have been founded by King Athelstan in 936. Under Warelwast's auspices, Algarus, a nobleman, is said to have erected the conventual church, and assisted in the endowment of the establishment. (Oliver, *Monasticon Exon.*, 15).

of this, and sumtyme dwellyd ther.[1] [His] Shrine and
Tumbe yet stondith in th'est Part of the Chirche. There
hath bene Monkes, then Nunnys, then Seculare Prestes,
then Monkes agayn, and last Canons Regular in S. Petroke's
Chirch[2] yn Bodmyne. Willyam Warlewist, Bisshop of
Excestre, erectid the last Fundation of this Priory, and
had to hymself part of th'auncient Landes of Bodmyn
Monasterie. Ther lay buryed before the High Altare in
a High Tumbe of a very Darkesche gray Marble, one
Thomas Viviane,[3] Prior of Bodmyn, and Suffragane by
the Title of the Bishoprike of Megarense; he dyed not long
sins. I saw no [other] Tumbes in the Priory very notable.

*Wm. Warel-
wast.*

*Thomas
Vivyan.*

Ther was a good Place of Gray Freres in the South
side of Bodmyn Town.[4] One John of London, a Merchaunt, was the Beginner of this House, [and] Edmund,
Erle of Cornewaul, augmentid it. There lay buried in the
Gray Freres Sir Hugh and Sir Thomas Peverelle, Knightes,[5]
and Benefactors to the House.

*Franciscan
Convent.
John Fitzralph.
Edmund, Earl
of Cornwall.
Sir Hugh
Peverelle.
Sir Thomas
Peverelle.*

There is another Chapel in Bodmyn beside that in the

---

[1] St. Petrock, according to the best authorities, was a native
of Wales, crossed over to Padstow (Petrockstow) in the year 518,
and afterwards settled at Bodmin, where he died in 564. His body
reposed in a beautiful shrine before the chapel of St. Mary, at the
east end of the conventual church. (Oliver, *Monasticon Exon.*, 15.)
The remains were stolen by one of the canons and taken to Brittany,
but they were recovered by Prior Roger, in 1177, and brought back in
a beautiful ivory casket, which is still preserved at Bodmin. (Maclean,
*Trigg Minor*, i., 231-2).

[2] Oliver supposes that the choir was appropriated to the convent,
and the nave was used by the parishioners (*Monasticon Exon.*, 15);
but Maclean is of opinion that there is sufficient evidence to prove
that the parish church and the conventual church were quite distinct
(*Trigg Minor*, i., 150).

[3] Thomas Vivyan became prior in 1508, and shortly afterwards
he was consecrated bishop of Megara in Greece, to act as suffragan
to Bishop Oldham, of Exeter. He died in 1533. The tomb, which
was originally in the priory church, was probably removed into the
parish church for preservation, and in 1819 was placed in the north
chancel aisle. (Oliver, *Monasticon Exon.*, 17; Maclean, *Trigg Minor*,
i., 158).

[4] The Franciscan convent of St. Nicholas was situated on the
south side of the market-place. It was begun by a London merchant, John Fitzralph, and completed 1239 by Richard, Earl of
Cornwall, brother to King Henry III. (Oliver, *Monasticon Exon.*,
17, 18.)

[5] Of Park, in Egloshayle.

West Ende of the Toune, and an Almose House, but not endowid with Landes.[1]

**King Athelstan.**

The Toune of Bodmyn takith King Edelstane for the chief Erector and Gyver of Privileges onto it.

[The land is] fruteful from Launston (otherwise cawled Donnevet) to Bodman, [and] yn a dry Somer good for

**Dozmary Pool.**

Pasturage for Catel, wyth sum Tynnes Werke. Dosmery Poole is of Lenght by Estimation ii. Arow Shottes, and of Bredth one, stonding on a Hille, yn the Est Part of the which Poole ys a Vale of xiiii. or xv. Fadome depe by Estimation; and owt of thys Poole issueth a Ryver, the which runnyng by the Space of a Myle and a *dim.* ys of ii. Fadome depe, and ys cawled Depe Hatche.[2] Also, yn

**St. Neot R.**

the sayd Hilly Grownd and Mooresch be redde Deere, the wich, when they be schafed, take the sayde Poole for Soyle.

From Bodman to Redruth Village, nerer to the North Se then to the Sowth be by Montaynes, baren also, yelding bare Pasture and Tynne. From Redruth to Carne Godolghan the Contery ys Hylly, very baren of Gresse and plenteful of Tynne.

**St. Lawrence.**

From Bodmyn to S. Laurence, wher is a pore Hospital or Lazar House[3] beyond the Bridge, [is] about a Mile. Thens a 5. Miles by Hilly and Mory Ground, and so ther left an Hille caullid Castelle Endinas scant a Mile of on

**Castle-an-Dinas.**

[1] Two hospitals, dedicated to St. Anthony and St. George, are mentioned in the will of Thomas Killegrew, 1500. St. George's was licensed by Bishop Stafford in 1405, and by Bishop Lacy in 1432; St. Margaret's also is often mentioned in the episcopal registers. (Oliver, *Monasticon Exon.*, 15.)

[2] Carew asserts that it is "a mile or better in compasse, fed by no perceyved spring, neither having any avoydance, untill (of late) certaine Tynners brought an Audit therefrom"; and, again, "more than a mile about, no streames it empt, nor any fill." (*Survey of Cornwall*, 122.) However, he is clearly mistaken, and James Michell, in his parochial history of St. Neot's, says:—"It is situate on a small stream called St. Neot's River, a branch of the Fowey, which rises in Dosmare Pool." (Hunt, *Popular Romances of the West of England*, 3rd ed., 142.)

[3] Bishop Stafford, in 1395, granted an indulgence for the support of the poor lepers of St. Laurence, near Bodmin, and Bishop Lacy, in 1435, granted a similar indulgence. The house was refounded by Queen Elizabeth in 1582, who recites in her charter that there had for a long time been a great company of lazar people in it, known by the name of a prior, brethren, and sisters. Under a decree of Chancery the lands are now settled in trust towards the support of the Cornwall Infirmary; but lepers are admitted. (Oliver, *Monasticon Exon.*, 15.)

the Right Hond; I saw no Building on it, but an Hille bering that Name.[1] Thens to Michal, a poore thorougfare, a 4. Miles by Hilly and much Morisch Grounde and no Wood. Thens to Alaine Paroche a 6. Miles; the Ground about Alein berith good Corne and Grasse. Thens a Mile to Guernek; there is very good Corne and Pasture about Guernek.

    Guernek a late was one of the Maner Places of Boville, *alias* Beville. This Name cam out of Base Normandy, and long continuid ther ontylle of late tyme it felle onto 2. Doughters of Boville, wherof the one was maryed onto Arundale of Trerise, now lyving, [and] the other to Graneville[2] : and so they devide almost 300. (litle lak of 400) Markes of Lande.

    This Arundale gyvith no part of the Armes of great Arundale of Lanheran by S. Columbes.[3] But he told me that he thought that he cam of the Arundales in Base Normandy that were Lordes of Culy Castelle, that now is descendid to one Mounseir de la Fontaine, a French Man, by Heire Generale.[4] This Arundale ys caullid Arundale of Trerise by a difference from Arundale of Lanheron. Trerise is a Lordship of his a 3. or 4. Miles from Alein Chirch. The House that John Arundale of Trerise dwellith yn [i.e. Guernek] was Boville's; and this Boville gave the Ox in Gules in his Armes.[5] There ys yet one of the Name of the Beviles, a Man of a C. *li.* land.[6]

    The Grownd by the Se Cost from Paddestow to Saynct

*Marginal notes:* Mitchell. — St. Allen. — Gwarnack. — Lanherne. — Trerice.

---

    [1] Carew says the top of the hill is "environed with deep treble trenches, which leave a large playne space in the midst; they call it Castellan Danis, and it seemeth (in times past) to have bin a matter of moment, the rather, for that a great cawsey (now covered with grasse) doth lead unto it." (*Survey of Cornwall*, 143 *d.*)

    [2] John Bevill mar. Elinor, dau. and heir of John Petit, and their daughters Marie and Matilda mar. respectively Sir John Arundell of Trerice and Sir Richard Grenvile.

    [3] "The Country people entitle them, The great Arundels : and greatest stroke, for love, living, and respect, in the Countrey heretofore they bare." (Carew, *Survey of Cornwall*, 144.)

    [4] "Precisely to rip up the whole pedigree were more tedious then behoovefull." (Carew, *Survey of Cornwall*, 145 *d.*)

    [5] According to Vivian (*Visitations of Cornwall*), the arms are : *Ermine, a bull passant, sable.*

    [6] Probably Peter Bevill, half brother of John Bevill.

St. Agnes
Beacon.

Anne's Hille (i.e. *super montem Annæ*), wheron ys no maner of Buylding, [is] sumwhat Hilly [and] ys fruteful of Corne and Gresse, but wyth lytle Tynne.[1]  Apon an viii. Myles from Paddestou ys a lytle house of Canons Secular, cawled

Crantock.

Crantoke.[2]  From Saynct Anne's Hil to Lanant, a Village, the Contery by the North Se ys sumwhat Hylly, Sanday, and Baren, and yn sundery Places of the same wel re-

Connerton.

plenyshed with Tynne.  By Conarton cummith a River, cawllid Dour Conor, and goith into the Se not far from Lanant Ryver Mouth.  In the Mouth of the Ryver that

Godrevy Is.

cummith by Lanant ys the Rokket Godryve, wheryn bredeth Se Fowle.

Lelant
(Hayle.)

The Toune of Lannant is praty; the Church therof is of S. Vnine,[3] [and] the Personage is impropriate to Heyles in Glocestreshir.  [There is] passage at Ebbe over a great Strond, and then over Heyle Ryver.  Ther cam to this Place ons, the Haven beyng onbarrid and syns chokid with Tynne Workes, good talle Shippes.

St. Erth.

St. Erth Bridge, a good Mile from Lannante, [is] of 3. Archis, a litle byneth the Paroche [Church], that stondith on the Est side of the Haven.  This Bridge was made a 200. Yers syns; afore ther was a Fery.  There was a Castel caullid Carnhangives,[4] as apperith, or Maner Place now clene doun, not far from the Bridg.  Dinham, as sum say, was Lord of this Place, and to the Court therof be longging many Knightes' and Gentilmen's services.  Mr. Mohun hath

*Trewinnard.*

a fair Lordship by S. Erth's caullyd . . .  Trewinard,

---

1 " Saint Agnes, one of the high hils, by his entrailes (like Prometheus) feedeth the Tynners pecking, or picking bils, with a long lived profit, albeit, their scarcle Eagle eyes sometimes mistake the shadow for the substance, and so offer up degenerate teares, as a late sacrifice to repentance." (Carew, *Survey of Cornwall*, 148 *d.*)

2 The collegiate church of Crantock was in existence before the Conquest.  It was probably refounded by Bishop William Brewer in the reign of Henry III., and in 1283 the church of St. Columb Minor was certainly appropriated to it.  The establishment consisted of a dean, eight canons, and seven vicars, but the number of vicars was subsequently reduced to four.

3 Uni was a brother of Ia.  (See note 3 on p. 22.)

4 " A little above the vicarage-house is a circular double entrenchment, called Carhangives, said to have belonged to the Dinham family; it is still held under the manor of Cardinham." (Lysons, *Cornwall*, 94.)

a Gentilman, [has a] dwelling at Trewinard yn S. Erth       Trewinnard.
Paroch.[1]

Ryvier Castel, almost at the Est Part of the Mouth of       Rivier.
Hayle Ryver on the North Se, [is] now, as sum think,
drounid with Sand; this was Theodore's Castelle.[2]

Combe Castelle, *ubi tm loci vestigia*, and Pencombe, a
litle Foreland about a Mile upper than Kenor on Severn.
Basset hath a right goodly Lordship called Treheddy[3] by       *Bassett.*
this Cumb. Ther cummith a good Brooke down by Combe.       Tehidy.
Cayle Castelle, a Mile by Est from River, [is] in S. Filake's       Phillack.
Paroche.[4]

Nikenor, a 2. Miles from Ryvier, [was] sumtyme a great       Conarton.
Toun [but is] now gone; 2. Paroche Chirchis, yet [to be]
seene a good deal several on from the other, [were] sumtyme
in the Towne, but it is now communely taken to be in
S. Guivian's Paroch,[5] and ther cummith a Broket to the Sea.       Gwithian.

Carnbray, on an Hil, [is] a Castelet or Pile of Basset's,       Carnbrea.
a Mile West of Revier Toun.[6] There was sumtyme a Park,
now defacid.

---

[1] The barton of Trewinnard, in St. Erth parish, belonged to an
ancient family of that name, two of whom were successively members
for the county in the reign of Edward III. The last who appears
to have possessed this barton was William Trewinnard, one of the
members for Helston in the reign of Henry VIII. From the
Trewinnards it passed to the Mohuns, who some time resided at
Trewinnard. (Lysons, *Cornwall*, 93.) This seems to have happened
before Leland wrote his account.

[2] The site of Rivier or Theodore's Castle had, in 1814, been
buried by the sands; the Riviere estate then belonged to the Cornish
Copper Company. (Lysons, *Cornwall*, 266.)

[3] The manor of Tehidy, in Illogan parish, belonged, at a very
early period, to a branch of the baronial family of Dunstanville, from
whom, about the year 1200, it passed in marriage to the Bassets of
Ipsden in Oxfordshire, descended from a younger son of Ralph
Basset, the justiciary, in the reign of Henry I. In the year 1330,
William Basset, Esq., had the King's licence to fortify his mansion
of Tehidy. (Lysons, *Cornwall*, 143.)

[4] Cayle-Castle, Castle-Cayle or Kayel, with a moat and keep,
belonged, in 1814, to the heirs of John Curnow, Esq.; there was
then a farm-house within the moat. No intimation is given of the
ancient proprietors of this castle. (Lysons, *Cornwall*, 266.)

[5] This must refer to the great manor of Conarton, parcel of the
honor of Gloucester. The site of the manor, which anciently gave
name to the parish, is said to have been formerly occupied by a large
town, which had two parish churches. (Lysons, *Cornwall*, 129.)

[6] On the summit of a steep hill, in Illogan parish, 697 feet above
the level of the sea, called Carnbrea, are the remains of a castle,
which is mentioned by William of Worcester in his Itinerary, written in
the reign of Edward IV., as then the property of Sir John Basset, Knt.

St. Just.

From Lanant by the North Se to S. Just, *alias* Justini, beyng the very West Poynt of al Cornewayle, and wher ys no thing but a Paroch Chyrch of [? and] divers sparkeled Howses, the North Part ys Montaynes and Baren Growne, but plenteful of Tynne. The very West Poynt, as yt ys

Pedn an Laaz, i.e. Land's End.

cawled now yn Cornysch, ys Penwolase, id est, *infimum caput*.

By al the North Se yn Cornewale be sundry Crekes, wher as smawle Fissher's Bootes be drawn up to dry Land, and yn fayr Wether the Inhabitans fysche with the same. At Paddestow Haven, Lanant, and S. Yes, the Balinggars[1] and Shyppes are saved and kept fro al Weders with Keyes or Peres.

St. Ives.

S. Jës [is] a 2. Miles or more from Lannant. The Place that the chief of the Toun hath and partely dooth stonde yn is a very Peninsula, and is extendid into the Se of Severn as a Cape. Most Part of the Houses in the Peninsula be sore oppressid or overcoverid with Sandes that the stormy Windes and Rages castith up there; this Calamite hath continuid ther litle above 20. Yeres. The best part of the Toun now standith in the South Part of the Peninsula, up toward another Hille, for Defence from the Sandes. There is a Blok House and a fair Pere in the Est side of the Peninsula, but the Pere is sore chokid with Sande.[2]

The Paroch Chirch is of Jä, a noble Man's Doughter of Ireland and Disciple of S. Barricus. Jä and Elwine with many others cam into Cornewaul and landid at Pendinas. This Pendinas is the Peninsula and stony Rock wher now the Toun of S. Jës stondith. One Dinan, a Great Lord in Cornewaul, made a Chirch at Pendinas[3] at the Request of Jä, as it is written yn S. Jës Legende. Ther is now at the very Point of Pendinas a Chapel of

---

1 *Balinger.* A small and light sea-going vessel, apparently a kind of sloop, much used in the 15th and 16th centuries, but its nature was already forgotten in 1670. (*New Eng. Dict.*)

2 Carew (1602) says: "Order hath bene taken, and attempts made, for bettering the Road, with a Peere, but eyther want, or slacknesse, or impossibilitie, hitherto withhold the effect." (*Survey of Cornwall*, 154.)

3 The present church is not on Pendinas, and was originally a mere chapel to the neighbouring church of Lelant, of which Ia's brother Uni is the patron saint. (Smith and Wace, *Dict. of Christian Biography*, HIA.) This chapel was built by virtue of a bull from Pope Alexander I., 1410, and was consecrated by Bishop Edmund Lacy, 1434. (Lysons, *Cornwall*, 150.)

S. Nicolas,[1] and a Pharos for Lighte for Shippes sailing by Night in those Quarters.[2]

The Town of S. Jës is servid with fresch Water of Brokettes that rise in the Hilles therby.

The late Lorde Brooke was Lord of S. Jës, now Blunt, Lord Monjoy and young Poulet.[3]  There dwellith a Gentilman of a 50. Markes Land by Yere, caullid Glynne, yn S. Jës.

*Lord Brooke.*
*Charles Blount, 5th Baron Mountjoy.*
*Pawlet.*
*Glynn.*

S. Piranes in the Sandes is an xviij. Miles from S. Jës upward on Severne, and S. Carantokes is a 2. Miles above that on the shore; els litle or no notable Thing on the shore for so farre.  The shore from S. Jës is sore plagued to S. Carantokes with Sandes.

St. Piran's.
Crantock.

Scylley is a Kenning, that is to say, about an xx. (or 30) Miles from the very Westeste Pointe of Cornewaulle.

Ther be of the Isles of Scylley cxlvii. (or 140) that bere Gresse (besyde blynd Rokkettes), exceding good Pasture for Catail.[4]

Scilly.

S. Mary Isle is a 5. Miles or more in Cumpace; in it is a poore Toun and a meately strong Pile, but the Roues of the Buildings in it be sore defacid and woren.  The Ground of this Isle berith exceding good Corn, insomuch that, if a Man do but cast corn wher Hogges have rotid it wyl cum up.

St. Mary's.

Iniscaw longid to Tavestoke, and ther was a poore Celle

Trescow.

---

[1] Holinshed mentions this chapel as having belonged of late to Lord Brooke, and then to Lord Mountjoy.  It is also mentioned in the *Liber Regis*, and must have been appurtenant to the manor of Ludgvan-Lees.  There were still some remains in 1814. (Lysons, *Cornwall*, 151.)

[2] In 1814 there was still a battery (block house) on the eastern side, and the old pharos, which still existed, was used for depositing government stores.  A new and commodious pier was constructed, under the direction of Mr. Smeaton, between the years 1766 and 1770. (Lysons, *Cornwall*, 148.)

[3] These were Lords of the Manor of Ludgvan-Lees, which had an extensive jurisdiction in St. Ives parish.  This manor was granted by Richard, Earl of Cornwall, to the family of Ferrers, from whom it passed, by successive female heirs, to those of Champernowne and Willoughby (Lord Brooke).  The co-heiresses of the latter brought it to Pawlet and Blount (Lord Mountjoy). (Lysons, *Cornwall*, 150, 205.)

[4] Lysons gives the total as about 40, bearing grass. (Lysons, *Cornwall*, 330-1.)

of Monkes of Tavestoke.[1] Sum caulle this Trescaw (or S. Nicholas Isle). In [it] ys a lytle Pyle or Fortres,[2] and a Paroch Chyrche that a Monke of Tavestoke yn Peace[3] doth serve as a Membre to Tavestoke Abbey. Ther be yn that Paroch abowt a lx. Howseholdes.

St. Agnes.

S. Agnes Isle [is] so caullid of a Chapel theryn. [It] was desolatid by this Chaunce *in recenti hominum memoria:* The hole Numbre almost of v. Housoldes that were yn this Isle cam to a Mariage or a Fest into S. Mary's Isle, and goinge homewarde were al drownid.

Rat Is.

There is one Isle of the Scylleys cawled Rat Isle, yn the which be so many Rattes that, yf Horse or any other lyving Best be browght thyther, they devore hym.

Bovy Is.
St. Martin's.

Ther is a nother cawled Bovy Isle, [and another] S. Martine's Isle.

Inishaw.

Ther is a nother cawled Innisschawe, that ys to say, the Isle of Elder, by cawse yt bereth stynkkyng Elders. There be wild Bores or Swyne.

St. Helen's.

[Another is] Saynct Lides Isle, wher yn tymes Past at her Sepulchre was gret Superstition.

There appere tokens in diverse [of] the Islettes of Habitations now clene doun. Gulles and Puffinnes be taken in diverse of these Islettes, and plenty of Conyes be in diverse of [them.] Diverse [also] berith wyld Garlyk. Few Men be glad to inhabite these Islettes for al their Plenty, because of Sea Robbers that take away their Cattle by force; these Robbers be French Men and Spaniards.

*Davers.*
*Whittington.*

One Davers, a Gentilman of Wilshir, whos chief House is at Daundesey, and Whitington, a Gentilman of

---

[1] The cell or priory of St. Nicholas consisted of but two members, and it is not clear whether the house had a corporate character distinct from that of the mother abbey. As early as the reign of the Confessor the abbey of Tavistock had possessions in the Scilly Islands, and Henry I. confirmed to the abbey and to Turoldus, one of the monks of Scilly, all the churches and land of Scilly as they had heretofore held them, and granted them his special protection. (Oliver, *Monasticon Exon.*, 73.)

[2] Old-Castle, which appears to have been afterwards enlarged, as its ruins show it to have been a considerable building. (Lysons, *Cornwall*, 336.)

[3] During the wars with France, which rendered the continuance of a monastic establishment in the islands insecure, Edward III. authorised the parent abbey so far to deviate from the conditions of the endowment as to celebrate daily service there by secular instead of regular clergy. (Oliver, *Monasticon Exon.*, 73.)

Glocestreshire, be owners of Scylley,[1] but they have scant 40. Markes by Yere of Rentes and Commodities of it.

From S. Just to Newlin Estward the Grownd ys sumwhat Hilly and Fertyle of Gresse, with Tynne Werkes both weete and dry, without Havyn or Creeke, savyng yn dyver Places ther remayne Capstaynes like Engins as Shyppes doth way ther Ancres by, wherwith they draw the Bootes up to dry Land, and fisch but yn fayr Wether.

Also yn the South-West Poynt betwyxt S. Just and Newlyn ys nothyng but as yt wher a Hil enclustered with Rokkes as yt had bene yn tymes past a Castel (Castel Treuyne), and for the Declaration therof there remayne yet toward the Land ii. Wardes clene fawllen downe; but the Stone of them remayne ther very fayre and well quadrated.[2] The Ruine of the Fortelet yn the Poynt ys at thys day a Hold irrecuperable for the Fox.

*Treryn Castle.*

Ther lyith betwyxt the South-West and Newlyn a Myle or more of the Se S. Buryens, a Sanctuary, wherby, as nere to the Chyrch, be not above viii. dwellyng Howses. Ther longeth to S. Buryens a Deane and a few Prebendarys that almost be nether ther. King Ethelstan [was the]

*St. Buryan.*

*King Athelstan.*

---

[1] They were representatives of that branch of the Arundell family which inherited the estates of the Coleshills and Blanchminsters, previous owners of Scilly. In 1345 Ralph de Blanchminster held the isles of Scilly under the duchy of Cornwall, as of the honor of Launceston, by the annual render of 300 puffins. In the reign of Henry VI. the rent was only 50 puffins, or 6s. 8d., the islands being then the property of Sir John Coleshill, representative of the Blanchminsters: their annual value in 1484 was estimated at 40s. in time of peace; in time of war, nothing. (Lysons, *Cornwall*, 332.)

[2] Elsewhere Leland describes this as "Tredine Castel Ruines at the South West Point of Penwith. *Manifesta adhuc extant vestigia.* I hard say that one Mayendu was Lord of it." The so-called "castle" seems to be a purely natural formation, but the headland of Treryn is isolated by an entrenchment of earth and stones, forming a triple line of defence, of which the outer vallum is about 15 ft. high. Most of the Cornish headlands are cut off from the mainland by a sort of scarp and breastwork. At Treryn Castle (besides the three lines of fortifications) this scarp occurs faced with stones, and has an entrance with granite posts. These "cliff castles" have been assigned to Britons, Romans, Saxons, Danes, and Irish; but it seems quite impossible to determine by whom they were originally constructed. On Treryn Castle is the celebrated Logan Stone, which was overturned in 1824 by Lieut. Goldsmith. (Murray's *Handbook for Devon and Cornwall*, 5th ed., 321.)

Founder of S. Burien's College and Giver of the Privileges and Sanctuarii to it.[1]  S. Buriana, an Holy woman of Ireland, sumtyme dwellid in this Place, and there made an Oratory.[2]  King Ethelstane goyng hens, as it is said, and returning[3] made *ex voto* a College wher the Oratorie was.

*Thomas Levelis.*  Thomas Levelis [lives] about S. Buriane's.[4]

Newlyn.      Newlin ys a poore Fisschar Towne, and hath al only a Key for Shyppes and Bootes with a lytle Socur of Land Water.  Withyn a Arow Shot of the sayd Key or Pere lyith directly a lytle low Island with a Chapel yn yt,[5] and this lytle Islet bereth Gresse.

Mousehole.      Newlin is an Hamlet to Mousehole,[6] [which is] a mile lower.  Mousehole in Cornish [is] Portenis (Portus Insulæ).[7] [It] ys a praty Fysschar Town yn the West Part of Montesbay, lyyng hard by the Shoore, and hath no Savegarde for Shyppes but a forced Pere.[8]  Also yn the Bey be Est

---

[1] The collegiate church was certainly in existence before the Conquest, and is mentioned in Domesday Book.  St. Buryan's Church was dedicated by Bishop Brewer in 1238, the record of which includes also a *vidimus* of the original endowment by King Athelstan in 943, a date evidently incorrect.  The clergy were probably then seven in number.  (Oliver, *Monasticon Exon.*, 6, 8.)  An ancient building on an estate called Bosliven, of which the walls were remaining in 1814, about 12 ft. high, overgrown with ivy, was said, by what was most probably a groundless tradition, to have been the sanctuary, and was held in much veneration.  (Lysons, *Cornwall*, 49.)

[2] According to Lysons, she "received sepulture here." (*Cornwall*, 49.)

[3] "What time he had conquered the Sillane Islands." (Carew, *Survey of Cornwall*, 159.)

[4] At Trou or Trewoof. (Lysons, *Cornwall*, 50.)

[5] This seems to be confused with St. Clement's Isle, off Mousehole. (See p. 27.)

[6] Both Newlyn and Mousehole are in the parish of St. Paul, and both had chapels of ease: Mousehole chapel, which had been a sea-mark, was destroyed by the encroachments of the ocean before 1414, but was probably rebuilt and again destroyed by the Spaniards in 1595. (Lysons, *Cornwall*, 256.)

[7] "The Iland haven, so called through a little Iland placed before it." (Carew, *Survey of Cornwall*, 156.)

[8] It was formerly a market-town: the charter for a market on Tuesdays, with a fair for three days at the festival of St. Barnabas, was granted to Henry de Tyes, in 1292 ; the market was confirmed in 1313 to Alice de Lisle, with a fair for seven days at the festival of St. Bartholomew.  A new quay was constructed at Mousehole in or about the year 1392. (Lysons, *Cornwall*, 254.)

the same Towne ys a good Roode for Shyppes cawled Gnaves Lake. Kiwartun[1] [lives] at Newlin by Mousehole, [and] John Godolcan[2] at Mousehole.

A little beyond Mousehole [is] an Islet and a Chapel of S. Clementes in it.

There hath bene much Land devourid of the Sea betwixt Pensandes and Mousehole. There was found of late Yeres syns Spere Heddes, Axis for Warre, and Swerdes of Coper wrappid up in lynid scant perishid, nere the Mount in S. Hilaries Paroch in Tynne Works. There is an old Legend of S. Michael that speketh of a Townlet in this Part, now defaced and lying under the Water.

Pensants,[3] about a Myle (2. miles) fro Mowsehole, stonding fast in the Shore of Montbay, ys the Westest Market Towne[4] of al Cornwayle, and no Socur for Botes or Shyppes but a forsed Pere or Key. Ther is but a Chapel yn the sayd Towne, as ys yn Newlyn, for theyr Paroches Chyrches be more than a Myle of.[5]

Marhasdeythyou, *alias* forum Jovis,[6] ys a Fischar Towne with a Market, and standeth fast apon the Shore of the Bay directly agaynst the Foote of S. Michael's Mont

*Margin notes:*
Gwavas Lake.
*Chiverton.*
*John Godolphin*

St. Clement's Is.

Penzance.

Marazion.

---

[1] The barton of Kerris was some time a seat of the Chivertons. (Lysons, *Cornwall*, 255.)

[2] The barton of Trewarveneth came to the Godolphin family by the marriage of Sir David Godolphin with the daughter of John Cowling, of this place. (Lysons, *Cornwall*, 254.)

[3] "By Interpretation, The Saint's head." (Carew, *Survey of Cornwall*, 156.)

[4] A market, to be held on Wednesdays, was granted in 1332 to Alice de Lisle, with a fair for seven days at the festival of St. Peter *ad vincula:* this market was confirmed, in 1404, to Thomas Lord Berkeley, with three fairs of two days each; one at the Conception, another at the Nativity of the Virgin Mary, and a third at the festival of St. Peter *in cathedrâ.* (Lysons, *Cornwall*, 210.)

[5] The parish-church of Maddern.

[6] Thursday Market. In 1085 Robert, Earl of Moreton, granted to the monks of St. Michael a market on Thursday, and five fairs; but it is not expressed where they should be held. St. Michael's Mount and Marazion are both in the parish of St. Hilary. (Lysons, *Cornwall*, 135-6). It is probable that both "Marazion" and "Market-Jew" are derived from "marghas," "maras," a *market. Ion* and *iou* are both plural terminations; so that "marghas-ion" and "marghas-iou" both signify the "markets," and afford satisfactory etymologies for both names. (Murray's *Handbook for Devon and Cornwall*, 5th ed., 298.)

Northward. In Marhasdeythyow ys but a poore Chapel yn the Myddes of the poore Town,[1] and a lytle Chapel yn the Sand nere by the Towne toward the Mont,[2] [for] the Paroch Chirch of Markine[3] [is] a Mile of. Markesin, a great long Town, [was] burnid 3. and 4. anno Henr. 8. à Gallis.[4] Markine and the Mount be both in S. Hilarie's Paroche. Be the West End of the Towne ys a Lake, or a *rivulus*, the Hedde wherof risith withyn a Myle of Lanant Northwordde fro Marhesdeythyou; and the Grownd of bred [th] betwene the ful Se marke at *forum Jovis* and the ful Se marke of Lanant Ryver is not ii. Myles.

St. Michael's Mount.

The Cumpace of the Roote of the Mont of S. Michael is not *dim.* Myle abowt. The Sowth Sowth-Est Part of the Mont is pasturable and breedeth Conys. The Resydue [is] hy and rokky. To the North North-West is a Peere for Bootes and Shyppes. In the North North-Est ys a Garden with certen Howses with Shoppes for Fyschermen.[5] The way to the Chyrche enteryth at the North Syd fro half Heb to half Fludde to the Foote of the Mont, and so assendeth by Steppes and Greces Westward, and thens returneth Estward to the utterward of the Chyrch. Withyn the sayd Ward is a Cowrt stronly walled, wher yn on the South Syde is the Chapel of S. Michael, and yn the Est Syde a Chapel of our Lady. The Capytayne and Prestes Lodginges be yn the Sowth Syde and [to] the West of S. Mich. Chapel. Comes Moritaniæ & Cornubiæ[6] made a Celle of Monkes in S. Michel Mont; this Celle was ons gyven to a College in Cambridge, [and it was] syns given

---

[1] Dedicated to St. Ervat. (Lysons, *Cornwall*, 137.)

[2] Probably the same which Dr. Borlase speaks of, by the name of the chapel of St. Catherine, on the chapel-rock, near Marazion; of this there were no remains in 1814. (Lysons, *Cornwall*, 137.)

[3] St. Hilary.

[4] "At the beginning of K. H. the 8 raigne, it felt the Frenchmen's fiery indignation, who landed there with 30. sayle. But the smoke of those poore houses, calling in the country to the rescusse, made the place over hote for the enemies' any longer abode." (Carew, *Survey of Cornwall*, 156.)

[5] Before 1700 the place had become so far decayed, that there remained only one cottage, inhabited by a widow-woman. (Lysons, *Cornwall*, 138.)

[6] Robert, Earl of Moreton, apparently confirmed a previous grant by Edward the Confessor. (Oliver, *Monasticon Exon.*, 28.)

to Syon.[1]  [There is] a fair Spring in the Mount.[2]  The
Mont is enclosed with the Se fro *dim.* Flud to *dim.* Ebbe,
otherwyse Men may cum to the Mont a foote.

In the Bay betwyxt the Mont and Pensants be fownd
neere the lowe Water Marke Rootes of Trees yn dyvers
Places, as a Token of the Grownde wasted.

Ludewin, *alias* Ludevaulles, wher, as sum suppose, was
a Castel, [is] a Mile by West from Markesin; it longid to
the Lord Brooke.[3]

*Ludgvan.*

S. Germocus [is] a Chirch 3. Miles from S. Michael's
Mont by Est South Est, and a Mile from the Se.  S.
Germok [was] ther buried, [and] his Tumbe is yet [to be]
seene ther.[4]  S. Germoke's Chair [is] in the Chirch Yard,
[and] S. Germoke's Well a litle without the Chirch Yard.

*Lord Brooke.*
*Germoe.*

Garsike, *alias* Pengarsike, [is] nere the Shore a 3. Miles
by Est from S. Michaele's Mont.  One Henry Force was
Lord of it.  One of the Worthe's Wives gave a late this
Land with a Doughter of hers to one of the Milatuns of
Devonshir.[5]  Milatun hath Milatun yn Devonshire.

*Pengersick
Castle.*
*Henry Force.*
*Worth.*
*Militon.*

Cairdine [is] an old Mansion of the Cowlines, wher now
William Godolcan dwellith.[6]  Carne Godalcan [is] on the
Top of an Hille, wher is a Diche, and there was a Pile
and principal Habitation of the Godalcans.  The Diche yet

*Kerthen, in
Crowan.*
*Cowlin.*
*William
Godolphin.*
Godolphin Hill.

---

[1] It was transferred by Henry V. to the new monastery of Sion
under authority of Parliament, and the sanction of ecclesiastical
confirmation.  Conflicting grants of this property were afterwards
made both to Sion House and to King's College, Cambridge; but the
college relinquished its claim, and from the reign of Henry VI. to
that of Henry VIII. the ecclesiastical history of the mount is identified
with that of the monastery of Sion.  (Oliver, *Monasticon Exon.*, 28.)

[2] Carew calls it "a tye pit, not so much satisfying use, as relieving
necessitie."  (*Survey of Cornwall*, 154 *d.*)

[3] The manor of Ludgvan-Lees, in the parish of Ludgvan, was
granted by Richard, Earl of Cornwall, to the family of Ferrers,
from whom it passed, by successive female heirs, to those of
Champernowne and Willoughby, Lord Brooke.  (Lysons, *Cornwall*, 205.)

[4] St. Germochus was an Irish chief who accompanied St. Breaca
to Cornwall in the fifth century.  (Smith and Wace, *Dict. of Christian
Biography*.)

[5] According to Lysons, it was acquired by the Militon family by
purchase.  (Lysons, *Cornwall*, 42.)

[6] Kerthen, in the parish of Crowan, was formerly a seat of the
Cowlins, from whom it passed, by a female heir, to the Godolphins.
It was at this time the residence of William Godolphin (son of Sir
William), to whom, at this place, Leland was for some time a guest.
(Lysons, *Cornwall*, 72.)

apperith, and many Stones of late Time hath beene fetchid thens.[1]  It is a 3. Miles from S. Michael's Mont by Est North Est.

Cair Kenin, *alias* Gonyn & Conin, stood in the Hille of Pencair ; there yet apperith 2. Diches.   Sum say that Conan had a Sun caullid Tristrame.

From Mr. Godalcan's to Trewedenek [is] about a 4. Miles ; wher Thomas Godalcan, yonger sun to Sir Willyam buildith a praty House, and hath made an exceding fair blo House Mille in the Rokky Valley therby.   [There are] no greater Tynne Workes yn al Cornwal then be on Sir Wylliam Godalcan's Ground.

From Mr. Godalcan ['s] to Pembro, wher the Paroch Chirch is, [? belongs] to Mr. Godalcan.

Wythyn ii. Myles of the Hedde of the ful Se marke [in] Heyle Ryver ys Heylston (Hailstoun), *alias* Hellas, [which] stondith on an Hil [and is] a good Market Toun having a Mair and Privileges, [and] withyn the which ther is a Cowrt for the Coynage of Tynne kept twys yn the Yeer.[2]   Yn the Town is both a Chapel and a Paroch [Church] at the North West Ende of the Towne ; and yet appereth yn the Town *vestigia castelli* yn the West Part.[3] [There is also] an Hospital of S. John yet stonding at the West South West End of the Town, of the Foundation

of one Kylligrin.[4]   A Ryver runnyng under the same *vestigia* of the Castel yssueth toward the Sowthe Se, [and,] stopped ther with Sowth Est wyndes casting up Sandes, maketh a

Poole cawled Loo of an Arow Shot yn Breede and a ii.

---

[1] William of Worcester speaks of a castle at Godolphin, which he calls Godollen, and describes it as in a state of dilapidation. (Lysons, *Cornwall*, 42.)

[2] In the yere 1201, the men of Helston gave forty marks of silver, and a palfrey, to King John, that their town might be made a free borough, and have a mercatorial gild.   King Edward I. made it one of the coinage towns.   The borough of Helston has returned members to Parliament ever since the reign of Edward I.   A market on Saturday was granted to the burgesses of Helston in 1336, and four annual fairs for three days each. (Lysons, *Cornwall*, 132.)

[3] William of Worcester, in the reign of Edward IV., speaks of Helston Castle as being then in ruins.   There were in 1814 no remains of it ; the site was then a bowling-green. (Lysons, *Cornwall*, 133.)

[4] St. John the Baptist, but the earliest name was that of St. Mary Magdalen.   The valor of Henry VIII. attributes the foundation of it to an archdeacon of Cornwall. (Oliver, *Monasticon Exon.*, 72.)

Myle yn Cumpas yn the Somer. In the Wynter, by reason of Fluddes floweng to Heylston Town, wherby the Mylles nere Heylston beyng stopped, they be constrayned to cut the Sandy Banke betwyxt the Mowth of the Poole and the Se, wherby the Water may have Yssue, and the Mylles grynd[1]; by the which Gut so opened the Se floweth and ebbeth yn to the Poole, wherby Se Fysch enteryng with a Sowth Est Wynde ys closed yn the Poole, the Gut beyng agayn choked and fylled with Sand, and so after taken with Trowtes[2] and Eles drawen yn the same Poole. Ons in 3. or 4. Yeres, what by the wait of the fresch Water and Rage of the Se, it brekith out, and then the fresch and salt Water metyng makith a wonderful Noise; but sone after the Mouth is barrid again with Sande. At other Tymes the superfluite of the Water of Lo Poole drenith out through the sandy Barre into the Se. If this Barre might be alway kept open, it would be a goodly Haven up to Hailestoun.

The Cowntery fro Newlyn to Heylston ys meetely fertyle of Gresse and Corne, and plentuus of Tynne by the Sowth Se.[3] Wythyn iii. Myles of Lyzart Poynt ys a litle Isle withyn the Bay, cawled Inispriuen, and [it] conteyneth ii. Acres of Grownd, wheryn be Byrddes and Cones.

Inispriven.

Fro the Poynt of Lyzart to Hayleford Haven the Grownd is fertile of Corne and Gresse by the Sowth Se. Also, wythyn iii. Myles of the Sowth Se betwene Haylford and the Est Syde of Montesbay is a wyld Moore cawled Gunhilly, i.e. Hilly Hethe, wher ys Brood of Catayle.

Goonhilly Downs.

Also yn the West syde of the Poynt of Hayelford Haven, and withyn the Land of Meneke, or Menegland, is a Paroch Chirch of S. Keueryn, otherwis Piranus, and ther is a Sanctuary with x. or xii. dwelling Howses, and therby was a Sel of Monkes, but now goon home to ther Hed

Meneage.
St. Keverne.

---

[1] When the town-mills at St. John's bridge have their wheels stopped by the swelling of the lake, the mayor of Helston applies to the Lord of Penrose; and, on presenting him with a few half-pence in a leathern purse, has a right to cut through the bar and make a passage for the water. (Lysons, *Cornwall*, cxc.)

[2] Carew says: "It breedeth a peculiar kind of bastard Trought, in bignesse and goodnes exceeding such as live in the fresh water, but comming short of those that frequent the salt." (*Survey of Cornwall*, 152.)

[3] In another place: "Ys not very fertile, but hath good Tynne Workes."

Hows.[1] The Ruines of the Monastery yet remenith.[2]

Beaulieu Abbey. St. Anthony.

S. Keverin's longgid to Bewle Abbey in Hampshir.

S. Pirane's, *alias* Keuerine, [is] 2. Miles from S. Antonie's, and not a Mile from the Main Se. The patronage of S. Antonie's longid to Trewardreth.[3] St. Antonie's standith in the Point of the Land of Gilling Creke, and the Mouth of Hailford Haven.

Helford R.

Ther be 4. Crekes on the South side of the Haven thus namid: Pen Castel, a Mile from the Haven Mouth, whither Shipes do resorte, and here is a *trajectus* from the one side of the Haven to the other; Caullons, half a Mile

Mawgan.

upward; then Mogun a 2. Miles higher, wher the Bridge is with the Broken Stone, [and] S. Mogun's Chirch; [and then] Gaire, a flite shot beyond this Bridge, wher is a Causey of stone, in the midle wherof is a Bridge having but one Arche. These Bridges be a 4. Miles or more from the Mouth of Hailford Haven. A litle beside these Bridges

Gweek.

[is] the principal Arme of Hailford Haven, caullid Wike, the wich flowith about a 3. Miles upland by North to Wike Mille.

About a 2. Miles beneth this Confluence rennith up on the [North] side of the Haven a Creeke of Salt Water caullid Poulpere (Poole Penreth), and hemmith in a peace

*Reskymer.* Merthen.

of Mr. Reskymer's Parke at Merdon, so that with this Creke and the Main Se Water of the Haven apon a 3. Partes the Parke is strenkthyd. Morden [is] in Constantine Parish, [and] Mr. Reskimer hath [there] a Ruinus Maner Place and a fair Park well woddid. He hath [also] a Maner

---

1 The church at the time of the Domesday Survey seems to have been collegiate, but after the property had been granted by Richard, Earl of Cornwall, to his father's foundation at Beaulieu, Hants, it does not appear to have retained its collegiate character. Until the dissolution of religious houses, the vicars of St. Keverne were presented by the abbot and convent of that Cistercian abbey. (Oliver, *Monasticon Exon.*, 71).

2 At Tregoning, the immediate site of the priory, there were still some small remains of monastic buildings in 1814. (Lysons, *Cornwall*, 159).

3 The church of St. Anthony was appropriated to the priory of Tywardreth. Bishop Tanner says that there was at this place a cell of black monks of Angiers, belonging to this priory, which existed as early as the reign of Richard I.; its site is supposed to have been on an estate called Lantinny, adjoining the church-yard, where foundations of buildings and remains of human bodies have been found. (Lysons, *Cornwall*, 18-19).

caullid by his own Name a Mile from Moreden; there hath beene a fair House, but it felle to Ruine in tyme of Mynde. From Gaire Bridge to Tremain, wher Mr. Reskimer now dwellith, [is] a good Mile. This litle House longgid to Tremain, and in tyme of Mynde cam by Heire General to one Tretherde. This Trederth hath beside Landes and a praty Maner Place at . . . .[1] John Riskimer's Mother was Tretherth's Daughter.[2] There is in Devonshir one of the Tremayns, a Man of fayre Landes. Mr. Reskimer berith in his Armes a Wolphe.[3] One of the Reskimers gave land to S. Keverine's, for sustentation of certein poore folkes.

*Tremayne.*

*Tremayne.*
*Tretherffe.*

St. Keverne.

Paul Wheverel [is] about half a Mile lower, and there is on the same side a Mile lower another Creek callid Cheilow, *alias* Calmansake. S. Mawname Chirch [is] at the very Point of the Haven on the side toward Falmuth [and forms] a Se marke.

Polwheveral Cr.

Calamansack Cr.
St. Mawnan.

From Morden I rode by morey and rokky Ground to S. Budocus Chirch. This Budocus was an Irisch Man and cam into Cornewalle and ther dwellid.

Budock.

A litle from the Chirch there enterid betwixt ij. Hilles on the Shore a shorte Creke lyke an Havenet, [called] Levine Prisklo, *alias* Levine Pole, but it was barrid. And a Quarter of a Mile farther I cam to Arwennak,[4] Mr. Keligrewis Place, stonding on the Brimme or Shore within Falmouth Haven. This Place hath beene of Continuaunce the auncient House of the Killigrewes. There was another House of the Keligrewis descending out of this, and it was in the Toun of Penrine, [but] now both these Houses be joynid yn one.

Swan Pool.
Arwenack.
*Killigrew.*

---

[1] Query, Trethurfe, in the parish of Ladock.

[2] John Reskymer was the eldest son and heir of John Reskymer and Catherine, daughter of John Tretherffe. He died without issue. (Vivian, *Visitations of Cornwall.*)

[3] *Argent, three bends Gules, in chief a wolf courant Azure.*

[4] The manor of Arwenack was acquired by the Killigrew family in the reign of Richard II., by marriage with the heiress of Arwenack. The Killigrews, in consequence, removed their residence from Killigrew in St. Erme, the ancient seat of the family, to Arwenack. John Killigrew, Esq., who died in 1567, built at Arwenack what was then esteemed the finest and most costly house in the county. (Lysons, *Cornwall*, 102.)

Pendennis
Point.

The very Point of the Haven Mouth, being an Hille wheron the King hath buildid a Castel,[1] is caullid Pendinant, and longgith to Mr. Keligrewe. It is a Mile in Cumpace and is almost environid with the Se, and, where it is not, the Ground is so low, and the Cut to be made so litle, that it were insulatid. There lyith a litle Cape or Foreland within the Haven a Mile *dim.*, almost again[st]

Trefusis Point.

Mr. Kiligrewis House, caullid Penfusis. Bytwixt this Cape and Mr. Keligrew's House one great Arme of the Haven rennith up to Penrine Toun. There dwellith an auncient

*Trefusis.*

Gentilman caullid Trefusis at this Point of Penfusis.[2]

Falmouth
Haven.

Falemuth ys a Havyng very notable and famose, and yn a maner the most principale of al Britayne.[3] For the Chanel of the Entre hath be space of ii. Myles ynto the Land xiiii.

Carrick
Roads.

Fadum of Depes, wich communely ys cawllyd Caryk Rood by cawse yt ys a sure Herboro for the greatest Shyppes that travayle be the Ocean. At the Entre of the Haven lyith a blynd Roke covered at ful See, nerer the West Syde of the Haven then the East, cawled Caregroyne, i.e. *insula vel rupes potius vitulorum marinorum, alias Seeles.* Seles when they cast theyr Calves cum to Lond, and ley ther *fœtum* in a dry Banke, the which they may com to, and ther they suffer theyr *fœtum* to tary a whyle or the[y] bryng hym to the Se.

Penryn.

The first Creke or Arme that castith out on the North West side of Falemuth goith up Perin, and at the Ende it brekith into 2. Armes, the lesse to the College of Glasenith,

St. Gluvias.

i.e. *viridis nidus*, or Wag Mier at Perin, the other to S. Gluvias, the Paroch Chirch of Penrine therby. Peryn [is]

---

[1] Pendennis Castle, adjoining to Falmouth, but in the parish of Budock, was built by King Henry VIII. on the site of an ancient fortification. John Killigrew, Esq., on whose land the castle was erected, was appointed the first governor. (Lysons, *Cornwall*, 104.)

[2] Trefusis, the seat from time immemorial of this ancient family. (Lysons, *Cornwall*, 235-6.)

[3] It is noteworthy that no mention is made of any town. A manuscript history of the Killigrews says that there was only a single house there, besides Arwenack, when Sir Walter Ralegh, being homeward bound from the coast of Guinea (Guiana), put in there. It is probable that there were also a few fishers' cottages. The first attempt to enlarge this insignificant village, then called Smithick, was in 1613, when John (afterwards Sir John) Killigrew, to whom the site belonged, began to build several new houses, in face of much opposition from the corporations of Penryn, Truro, and Helston. (Lysons, *Cornwall*, 99-100.)

a prety Towne of Marchandyse and Vytayle Market.[1] Yn the Town ys a Chapel, and a Quarter of a Myle owt of the Town ys the Paroch Chyrch. Stakes and Foundation of Stone [are] sette yn the Creeke at Penrine afore the Toun, a little lower then wher it brekith into Armes, [and there is] a Gap in the Midle of the Stakes and a Chain.

One Water Good (Walter Brunscombe), Bisshop of Excestre, made yn a More, caullid Glesnith, in the Botom of a Park of his at Penrine, a Collegiate Church, cawled S. Thomas, wher be Secular Chanons with a Provost, xij. Prebendaries, and other Ministers.[2] This College is stron[g]ly wallid and incastellid, having 3. strong Towers and Gunnes at the But of the Creke.[3] [There is] good wood about the South and West syde of Penrith. *Glasney.*

Betwixt the Point of Land of Trefuses and the Point of Restronget Wood is Milor Creek, and ther is S. Milor's Chirch, and beyond the Chirch is a good Rode for Shippes. The next Creek is caullid Restronget, [and] betwixt Restrongith Creke and the Creeke of Truru be two Creekes. The Creke of Truru afore the very Toun is devidid into 2. Partes, and eche of them hath a Brook cumming doun, and a Bridge, and the Market Toun of Truru (Trureu) bytwixt them booth.[4] The White (Blake) Freres House[5] was on *Mylor.* *Truro.*

---

[1] " Rather passable, then noteable, for wealth, buildings, and Inhabitants." (Carew, *Survey of Cornwall*, 150 *d.*) A market on Mondays, and a fair at the festival of St. Thomas the Martyr, were granted to the Bishop of Exeter in 1258, and a fair at the festival of St. Vitalis in 1312. (Lysons, *Cornwall*, 120.)

[2] Walter Bronescombe in 1264 commenced, and in 1267 endowed, here a college for thirteen canons, one of whom was to be styled provost or president, and for thirteen vicars. Bishop Stapeldon annexed one of the prebends of this collegiate church to the office of archdeacon of Cornwall. (Oliver, *Monasticon Exon.*, 48.)

[3] Oliver, in 1846, says: "Scarcely a vestige now remains." A few years earlier a small portion of the fabric was discovered in a private garden at a short distance from Penryn, and on its south side, viz., the shaft and capital of a small column, and a portion of its pointed arch, both apparently standing on their original site, and clearly announcing an early style of pointed architecture. (*Monasticon Exon.*, 48.)

[4] The market is held by prescription, the claim to it having been certified and allowed in the reign of Edward I. (Lysons, *Cornwall*, 309.)

[5] This was a Dominican convent of Friars Preachers, or Black Friars, founded by the Reskymer family. Bishop Bronescombe dedicated their conventual church in 1259. (Oliver, *Monasticon Exon*, 67.) In 1814 the site was occupied by tan-pits. (Lysons, *Cornwall*, 311.)

the West Arme yn Kenwyn streate. Kenwen Streat is severid from Truru with this Arme; and Clementes Streat by Est is seperate on the Est side from Truru with the other Arme. [There is] one Paroch Chirch in Truru self, [and] Kenwen and Clementes Streates have several Chirchis, [which] bere the name of the Sainctes of the Paroch Chirchis. [There is] coynage of Tynne at Midsomer and Michelmas at Truru. [It] is a Borow Toun, whereyn is a Mayre, and privilegid. Ther is a Castelle a Quarter of a Mile by West out of Truru longging to the Erle of Cornwale, now clene doun. The site therof is now usid for a shoting and playing Place.[1]

*Earl of Cornwall.*

Out of the Body of Truro Creke on the Est side brekith a Crek Estwarde a Mile from Truru, and goith up to Tresilian Bridge. At the Entery and Mouth of this Creeke is a Rode for Shippes caullid Maples Rode, [where] faught a late xviij. Sail of Marchant Spaniardes and 4. Shippes of Warre of Depe. The Spaniardes chac'd hither the French Men.[2]

*Tresillian Br.*
*Malpas.*

A Mile and a half [below] the Mouth of Truru Creke [is a creek] caullid La Moran [Lan Moran] Creke, of the Chirch of S. Moran. The Mayne Stream goith up 2. Miles above Moran Creke, ebbing and flowing, and a Quarter of a Mile above is the market Toune of Tregony, *vulgo* Tregny,[3] [w]here is a Bridge of stone *aliquot arcuum* apon Fala Ryver.

*Lamorran.*

*Tregoney.*

---

[1] The scarped mound where it stood may be seen to this day, on the high ground at the top of Pydar-street, to the left. It is crowned by a modern circular wall, surrounded by a circular terrace, arrangements which render it probable that this castle resembled Launceston in plan. (Murray's *Handbook for Devon and Cornwall*, 5th ed., 197.)

[2] In January, 1536-7, Spanish ships chased French ones not merely into Falmouth Harbour but up the Truro river, and engaged them twice in Malpas Roads. When ordered to desist, the Spanish commander said that he would have them or die for it, and when, after a third attempt, he sailed away, it was probably because he had found himself too weak rather than becaues Sir John Arundel had threatened to raise the county upon him. (*Victoria History of Cornwall*, i., 485.)

[3] The market, which is on Saturday, is held by prescription. Henry de Pomeroi certified his right to it in the reign of Edward I.; King Henry III., in 1266, had granted to the said Henry a fair at the festival of St. Leonard. (Lysons, *Cornwall*, 73.)

[Here] is an old Castel[1] and a Paroch Chyrch of S. James[2] standing yn a More by the Castel; also a Ch . . . standing yn the Myddes of the Towne, and at the Est End of the Town a Paroch Chyrche.

Fala River risith a Mile or more of Rochehille, and goith by Granborow, wher is a Bridg of Stone over it. Grampound [is] a 4. Miles from Rac and 2. litle Mile from Tregony. Mr. Tregyon hath a Maner Place richely begon and amply, but not ended, caullid Wuluedon, *alias* Goldoun.[3]

At the Hed of Lanyhorne Creeke standith the Castelle of Lanyhorne, sumtyme a Castel of an 8. Tourres, now decaying for lak of Coverture.[4] It longgid as principal House to the Archdecons. This Landes descendid by Heires general to the best Corbetes of Shropshir, and to Vaulx[5] of Northamptonshir, [but] Vaulx' part [has been] syns bought by Tregyon of Cornewaul.

From Lanyhorne Pille is a Place or Point of Land of 40. Acres or therabout as a Peninsula, [which] is caullid Ardeuermeur. Petite's principal House was at Ardeuerauian in Falmouth Haven by the Peninsula caullid Ardeuerameur.

*Fal R.*
*Roche Rocks.*

*Grampound.*
*Tregian.*

*Wolveden,*
*alias Golden.*
*Lanihorne.*

*Archdeacon.*
*Corbett.*
*Vaux.*
*Tregian.*

*Ardevora.*
*Petit.*

[1] Tregony-Castle, of which there are no remains, is said to have been built by Henry de Pomeroy, on behalf of John, Earl of Cornwall, at the time that King Richard I. was in the Holy Land; it was standing, and was the seat of the Pomeroys, in the reign of Edward IV.: its site was at the lower end of the town, a little below the hospital. (Lysons, *Cornwall*, 74.)

[2] On the north side of the town stood what is called Old Tregony, where was a church dedicated to St. James; the walls of which were standing when Tonkin made his collections (about 1736); part of the tower remained many years later. (Lysons, *Cornwall*, 75.)

[3] This manor belonged to the ancient family of Wolvedon or Wulvedon, the last male heir of which died in 1512. The large estates passed by a female-heir to the Tregians or Tregyans, who built a magnificent mansion at Golden, of which the ruins still remained in 1814. (Lysons, *Cornwall*, 271.)

[4] William of Worcester speaks of it as standing, in his *Itinerary of Cornwall*, *temp.* Edward IV. Tonkin describes a large tower which was pulled down in 1718; and says that within 30 years of the time of his writing six out of eight towers of the castle had been standing: some cottages were built on the site, but there are now no remains of the castle itself. (Lysons, *Cornwall*, 279.)

[5] A co-heiress of Arcedekne married Lucy; and the co-heiresses of Sir William Lucy married into the families of Corbett and Vaux. One moiety of the manor of Lanihorne, being described as lately parcel of the possessions of Sir William Vaux attainted, was granted in 1462 to Avery Cornburgh: this moiety passed by purchase to the Tregians, and in 1620 belonged to Ezekiel Grosse; the other moiety was then vested in Sir Henry Wallop, Knt. (Lysons, *Cornwall*, 279.)

St. Just Cr.

St. Mawes Cr.

Castle Point.

St. Mawes.

St. Anthony.

Petite's Landes be now descendid to Arundale of Trerise, Granville Knight, and Killigrew.[1] From the Mouth of the West Creke of this Peninsula to S. Juste Creeke [is] a 4. Miles or more. From S. Juste Pille or Creke to S. Mauditus Creeke is a Mile *dim*. The Point of Land betwixt S. Just Cr. and S. Maws is of sum caullid Pendinas; on this Point stondith as yn the Entery of S. Maws Creek, wher is a Castelle or Forteres (Fortelet) late begon by the King (lately buylded by the Contery).[2] This Creke of S. Maws goith up a 2. Myles by Est North Est into the Land, and so far it ebbith and flowith, and ther is a Mylle dryven with a fresch Brook that resortith to the Creke.

Scant a Quarter of a Mile from the Castel, on the same side upper into the Land, is a Praty Village or Fischar Toun (a poor Fischar Village) with a Pere, cawllid S. Maws (S. Mausa, *alias* La Vausa); and ther is a Chapelle of hym, and his Chaire of Stone a litle without, and his Welle.[3] They caulle this Sainct there S. Maudite; he was a Bisshop in Britain and paintid as a Schole-Master.

Half a Mile from the Hedde of this downward to the Haven is a Creke in a Corner of a Poole, with a round marke made in charte, on the which is a Mille grinding with the tyde. Apon the Sowth Syde of this Creke [of S. Maws] ys a Celle of S. Antonie longging to Plymton

---

[1] The manor of Ardevro or Ardevora, said to comprise the manors of Treveneage and St. Mawes, belonged at an early period to the Petits, whose co-heiresses, in the reign of Henry VI., married Arundell of Tolverne and Sayer. In Carew's time it belonged to the Sayers; and the house, which had been the chief seat of the Petit family, was then occupied by Mr. Thomas Peyton. (Lysons, *Cornwall*, 106.)

[2] St. Mawes castle was built by King Henry VIII., for the protection of Falmouth harbour, in 1542, during the war with France. Mr. Trefry, of Fowey, had the superintendence of the work, and at his request Leland wrote some Latin inscriptions to be placed on the building. (Lysons, *Cornwall*, 153.)

[3] Mr. Whitaker speaks of St. Mawes'-well in this town, and says that there was a chapel close to it, turned into a dwelling-house, which, by its Gothic windows, exhibited some traces of its original use. This chapel was no doubt the same which, in the registers ot the See of Exeter, is called the chapel of St. Mauduit: the inhabitants of St. Just, in which parish St. Mawes is situated, had a licence to attend divine service in it. (Lysons, *Cornwall*, 153.)

Priory; and here of late dayes lay 2. Chanons of Plympton Priory.[1]

From S. Antonies Point at the Mayne Se to Penare Point [is] a 3. Miles *dim.* Grefe Islet lyith scant half a Mile Est of Penare, wherin breadeth Gulles and other Se foulles. This Gref lyith North from the Forne, a Point or Foreland in Britain, bytwene the wich is the Entery of the sleve of the Occean; and betwixt Forne and Grefe is a v. Kennynges, and here is *breviss. trajectus* by Estimation from Cornewaulle into Britaine Continentes.

About a Myle by West of Penare is a Force[2] nere the shore in the Paroch of S. Geron's; it is single dikyd, and within a But Shot of the North side of the same apperith an Hole of a vault broken up by a plough yn Tylling; this Vault hath an Issue from the Castelle to the Se. And a litle by North of the Castelle [are] a 4. or 5. Borowes or Cast Hilles.

Dudeman Foreland or Point is about v. Miles from Grefe. [There is] no Wood on the very Cost from S. Antonies Point to Dudeman, [but] inward yn the Land is some Woode.

Chapelle Land or Point is in the Park of Bodrugan; and yn this Park was the House of Sir Henry Bodrugan, a Man of Auncient stok, atteyntid for takyng Part with King Richard the 3. agayn[st] Henry the 7.[3]; and, after [his] flying into Ireland, Syr Richard Eggecomb, Father to Sir Pers Eggecombe, had Bodrigan and other Parcelles of Bodrigan's

*Side notes:*
Plympton Priory.
St. Anthony Head.
Nare Head.
Gull Rock.
Dingerein Cas. in Gerrans.
Dodman Point.
Chapel Point.
Bodrugan.
*Sir Hen. Bodrugan.*
*Sir Ric. Edgcumbe.*

---

[1] This church of St. Anthony was dedicated by Bishop Bronescombe in 1259. The cell was burnt down by the French in 1338. The property, after the dissolution of Plympton Priory, was leased, and afterwards granted in fee, as parcel of Plympton. (Oliver, *Monasticon Exon.*, 134.)

[2] Dingerein Castle, on an estate called Cargurrell. Whitaker supposes it to have been the residence of King Gerennius. (*Cathedral of Cornwall*, i., 294.) The name of the parish is supposed to be derived from the same king.

[3] The manor of Bodrugan or Bodrigan belonged to an ancient family of that name, who held it under the Champernowns. This family became extinct in the male line of its elder branch about the year 1330. Sir Henry Bodrugan is said to have been originally called Trenowth, and it does not appear how he was connected, or whether he was at all connected, with the ancient Bodrugan family. Borlase describes the remains of Bodrugan castle as very extensive, and says that there was nothing in Cornwall equal to it for magnificence. (Lysons, *Cornwall*, 123.)

40 EARLY TOURS IN DEVON AND CORNWALL

*Trevanion.*
*Restronguet.*
*Newham.*
*Pentewan Beach.*

Landes. And Trevagnon[1] had part of Bodrigan's Landes, as Restonget and Newham, both in Falamuth Haven.

From Chapel Land to Pentowen, a sandy Bay, witherto fischar Bootes repair for a Socour, [is] a 2. Myles. Here issuith a praty Ryver that cummith from S. Austelles; and there is a Bridge of stone of the Name of the Town. S.

St. Austell.

Austol's [is] a poore Village with nothing notable but the Paroch Chirch. S. Austol *erat heremita.*

Black Head.

From Pentowen to the Blake Hedd [is] a Mile. There is a fair Quarre of Whit Fre Stone on the Shore betwixt Pentowen and Blak-Hed, whereof sum be usid in the inward Partes of S. Maw's Forteresse. The Residew [is] of More-stone and slate; and Pendinas Castelle is of the same stone, except the Wallinge. And in the Cliffes between the Blak-

Tywardreath Bay.

Hed and Tywartraith Bay is a certeyn Cave, wheryn apperith Thinges lyke Images giltid. And also in the same Cliffes be vaynis of Metalles, as Coper and other.

There is a Mile from the Entery of Tywartraith Bay up yn the Land at the But Ende of it a Paroch Chirch of

St. Blazey.

S. Blase, and ther is a New Bridge of Stone of the Sainctes Name over a Broke that ther cummith into the Bay.

Tywardreath.

Tywardreth, a praty Toun (a poore Village) but no Market, lyith a Quarter of a Mile from the Est side of the Bay. Ther is a Paroch Chirch, and ther was a Priory of Blak Monkes (Cluny Monkes), [a] Celle sumtyme to a

*Champernowne.*
*Cardinham.*
*Arundell.*

House in Normandy.[2] Sum say Campernulphus was Founder of this Priory, sum say Cardinham, [but] Arundale of Lanhern was of late taken for Founder. I saw a Tumbe in the West Part of the Chirch of the Priori with this Inscription: " Hæc est Tumba Roberti filii Wilihelmi." This Robert Fitz Williams[3] was a Man of fair Landes *tempore Edwardi* 3. *reg. Ang.*

---

[1] William Trevanion, Esq. (Lysons, *Cornwall*, 235.)

[2] St. Andrew's Benedictine Priory was founded here by an ancestor of the Cardinham family, a contemporary of the Conqueror, and was made dependent on the great abbey of SS. Sergius and Bacchus at Angers. In the 13th century, Isolda de Cardinham, widow, conveyed the manors of Tywardreth and Ludgvan to Henry Champernowne, which may have led to the mistake that Champernowne was the founder of the priory. (Oliver, *Monasticon Exon.*, 33.) Arundell of Lanhern was one of the representatives of the Dynham family.

[3] In 1169 Robert Fitz-William and Agnes his wife, and Robert their son, granted the glebe of St. Austle to St. Andrew's Priory. (Oliver, *Monasticon Exon.*, 34.)

From Falemuth to Trewardreth by the Sowth Se the
Ground is metely fertyle of Corn and Gresse, and [there
are] no Tyn Werkes from Falemuth to Dudman Foreland.
From Dudman Foreland to Trewardreth the Contre [is]
sumwhat baren of Gresse and Corne, and replenishid with
Tynne Werkes, with Vaynes yn the Se Clyves of Coper.
From Trewardreth to Fowey Town ys ii. Myles, [and]
bytwene thes Townes by the Sowth Se ther is plenty of
Corn and Gresse, but no Tynne Werkes. The Point of
Land on the Est side of Tywardreth Bay is caullid
Penarth-Point.

? Gribbin Hd.

Ther is at the West Point of the Haven of Fawey
Mouth a Blok House devisid by one Thomas Treury, now
livinge,[1] and made partely by his Cost, partely by the Town
of Fawey. A litle higher on this Point of the Hille is a
Chapel of S. Catarine[2]; and hard under the Roote of this
Hille, a litle withyn the Haven Mouth, is a litle Bay or
Creke bering the Name of Catarine.

Fowey.
*Thomas
Trefry.*

About a Quarter of a Mile upper on this the West side
of Fawey Haven is a square Toure of Stone for Defence
of the Haven, made about King Edward the 4. Tym, and
a litle above this Tower on the same side is Fawey Town
lying alonge the shore and buildid on the side of a great
slatty rokkid Hille. In the Midle of the Toun apon the
shore self is a House buildid quadrantly in the Haven, which
shadowith the Shippes in the Haven above it from 3. Partes
of the Haven mouth and defendith them from Stormes.

The Town of Fowey ys a Market Town[3] walled defensably to the Se Cost, and hath Gates also. The Howses
of the Towne be well buylded of Stone, and yl enhabited.
The Name of the Toun of Fawey is in Cornisch Conwhath.
It is set on the North side of the Haven, and is set hangging
on a maine rokky Hille, and is in length about a Quarter
of a Mile.

---

[1] Thomas Trefry died 1563. The fort was still in use in 1814.
(Lysons, *Cornwall*, 109.)

[2] William de la Hay, prior of Tywardreth, was licensed, 1390, to
have divine service performed in St. Catharine's Chapel, Fowey.
(Oliver, *Monasticon Exon.*, 35.)

[3] The market was granted to the Prior of Tywardreth, in 1316, to
be held on Monday, together with two fairs, one for three days, at
the festival of St. Barre, and the other for the same duration at the
festival of St. Lucy. (Lysons, *Cornwall*, 107.)

*Cardinham*
Tywardreath
Priory.

*Champer-
nowne.*

The Towne longgid to one Caridinham, a Man of great
Fame, and he gave it to Tywartraith Priorie,[1] of the which
sum say that Cardinham was Founder, [and] sum say
Campernulph of Bere; but at this Gift Fawey was but a
smaul Fischar Toun.

The Paroch Chirch of Fawey is of S. Fimbarrus, and
was impropriate to the Priorie of Tywartraith.[2]

The Glorie of Fawey rose by the Warres in King Edward
the first and the thirde and Henry the v. Day, partely by
Feates of Warre, partely by Pyracie, and so waxing riche
felle al to Marchaundice; so that the Town was hauntid
with Shippes of diverse Nations, and their Shippes went to
al Nations.

The Shippes of Fawey sailing by Rhie and Winchelsey
about Edward the 3. tyme wold vale no bonet beying
requirid, wherapon Rhy and Winchelsey Men and they
faught, wher Fawey Men had victorie, and therapon bare
their Armes mixt with the Armes of Rhy and Winchelsey;
and then rose the Name of the Gallaunts of Fawey.[3]

The French-men diverse tymes assailed this Town, and
last most notably about Henry the vj. tyme, when the wife
of Thomas Treury the 2. with her Men repellid the French
out of her House in her Housebandes Absence. Wherapon
Thomas Treury buildid a right fair and stronge embatelid
Towr in his House, and embateling al the Waulles of the
House in a maner made it a Castelle; and onto this Day
it is the Glorie of the Town Building in Faweye.

---

[1] The manor of Fowey was held, at the time of the Domesday
Survey, under the Earl of Moreton, by Richard, ancestor of the
Fitz-Richards and Fitzwilliams, whose heiress married Robert de
Cardinham. This Robert, in the reign of Richard I., gave the church
of Fowey and certain lands which formed a manor to the prior and
convent of Tywardreth, who claimed manorial rights under this grant
in the reign of Edward I. The manor of Fowey, however, appears to
have been retained by Robert de Cardinham. (Lysons, *Cornwall*, 109-10.)

[2] The church was rebuilt in 1336, and dedicated to St. Nicholas.
The original patron saint was St. Barre, supposed to have been
St. Barrus or Fimbarrus, the first Bishop of Cork, who, according to
William of Worcester, was buried at Fowey. The church was again
rebuilt or much altered, and its present handsome tower erected, about
1466. (Lysons, *Cornwall*, 111.)

[3] As a proof of the importance of Fowey, it may be noted that it
contributed 47 ships to Edward III.'s great fleet against Calais, a
greater number than came from any other port in England. (Hakluyt,
*Voyages.*)

In Edwarde the 4. Day 2. stronge Towers were made a
litle beneth the Toun, one on eche side of the Haven, and
a Chayne to be drawen over. When Warre in Edward
the 4. Dayes seasid betwene the French Men and
Englisch, the Men of Fawey usid to pray, kept their
Shippes, and assailid the Frenchmen in the Sea agayn[st]
King Edwardes Commandement; wherapon the Capitaines
of the Shippes of Fawey were taken and sent to London,
and Dertemouth Men commaunded to fetche their Shippes
away, at which tyme Dertmouth Men toke their (*sic*) in Fawey,
and toke away, as it is said, the great Cheine that was
made to be drawen over the haven from Towr to Towre.

From Fowey Town End by North in the Haven is
Chagha Mille Pille, a litle uppeward on the same side, [and]
a good Mile above Chagha Mille Pille is on this West side
Bodmyn Pille having for Wares then to be caried to Bodmyn.
A Quarter of a Mile from Bodmyn Crek Mouth up into the
Haven on the same side is Gullant, a Fischar Tounlet | *Golant.*
(Towne).[1] From Gullant to Lantian Pille or Crek [is] | *Lantyan.*
about half a Mile; Barret, a Man of mene Landes, dwellith | *Barret.*
bytwixt Gullant and Lantient Pille, [and] Lantient Lord-
ship longid to the Erle of Saresbyri.[2] From Lantiant Pille | *Earl of*
to Bloughan Pille or Creke [is] nere a Mile; Carteis, a | *Salisbury.*
Gentilman of almost an 100. Mark Land dwellith bytwixt | *Carteis.*
Blowghan and Penknek by Lostwithiel. From Bloughan
to Lostwithiel [is] scant a Mile on the principal stream of
Fawey River. It hath ebbid and flowen above Lostwithiel,
but the Spuing of the Sandes of the Tynne Werkes hath
stoppe yt, [and] now it flowith not ful to the Toun.

At the Hedd of the ful Se Marke of this Haven, and a
Quarter of a Myle more is the Toune of Lost Whythyel, | *Lostwithiel.*
[which] ys the Shyre Towne of Cornewal, for ther the
Shyre is kept by the Shryfe ons yn the Moneth. Also at
this Toun is the Coynege Haul for Tynne, [and there] is

---

[1] Golant or Glant, the principal village in St. Sampson, formerly
gave name to the parish, which in 1814 was commonly known in the
neighbourhood by its ancient name of Glant. (Lysons, *Cornwall*,
280.)

[2] The manor or honour of Lantyan was among the ancient possessions of the Montacutes, Earls of Salisbury. On the attainder of
Margaret, Countess of Salisbury, who was beheaded in 1541, it fell
to the Crown. (Lysons, *Cornwall*, 280.)

Quynag of Tynne twys a Yere. And by the Shyre Hawle appere Ruines of auncyent Buildinges. [There is] a Howse of the Duke of Cornwal. The Towne is privilegid for a Borow, and there is Wekely a Market on Thursday.[1] Richardus Rex Ro. comes Cornubiæ privilegid this Toun.[2] The Paroche [Church] is of S. Barptolome.[3]

*Restormel.*

The Kinges Parke of Restormel [Rostormel] is hard by the North side of the Town of Lostwithiel.[4] [There are] Tynne Workes [and] Good Woode in this Parke. Ther is a litle rownd Castel on an Hil in this Parke, wher sumtymes the Erles of Cornewal lay. The Base Court is sore defacid, [but] the fair large Dungeon yet stondith.[5] A

*Earl of Cornwall.*

---

[1] In the reign of Richard I., Robert de Cardinham gave ten marks to the Crown for the privilege of establishing a market here. (Lysons, *Cornwall*, 203.)

[2] The present name, Lostwithiel, is a corruption of *Lestwithiel, the Supreme Court.* (Murray's *Handbook for Devon and Cornwall*, 5th ed., 234.) Richard, Earl of Cornwall and King of the Romans, made Lestwithiel, including Penkneth, a free borough. Edmund, Earl of Cornwall, his son, appears to have been the chief benefactor to this town; he erected handsome buildings, at a great charge, for his Exchequer, for a shire-hall, &c., ordaining that the coinage and sale of tin should be at Lostwithiel only, and that all county-meetings should be held there. It is probable that these exclusive privileges were of short duration, though the county-elections still continued to be held there until the Reform Act, as well as the Epiphany and Midsummer quarter-sessions. In the hall, which in 1814 was still standing, were held the Stannary parliaments, and here also was the Stannary court, with a prison adjoining, the only one in the county belonging to the Stannaries. (Lysons, *Cornwall*, 203.)

[3] St. Bartholomew.

[4] Restormell Park was disparked by King Henry VIII., together with other parks in Cornwall, at the instance of Sir Richard Pollard. (Lysons, *Cornwall*, 178; Carew, *Survey of Cornwall*, 22 d.)

[5] Restormell castle was a seat of the Cardinans, and was probably built by them. Edmund, Earl of Cornwall, died seised of the manor, castle, and park in 1300. So early as 1337 the castle is described in an official survey as considerably out of repair. (Lysons, *Cornwall*, 176-7.) Carew, writing in Elizabeth's reign, says: "His base court is rather to be conjectured than discerned by the remnant of some fewe ruines; amongst which an oven of 14. foot largenes, through his exceeding proportion, prooveth the like hospitality of those dayes. The inner court grounded upon an intrenched rocke, was formed round, had his utter wall thick, strong, and garretted; his flat roofe covered with lead, and his large windowes taking their light inwards. It consisted of two stories, besides the vaults, and admitted entrance and issue, by one onely gate, fenced with a Portcouliz." (*Survey of Cornwall*, 138.)

Chapel cast out of it [is] a newer Work then it, and [is] now onrofid. [There is] a Chapel of the Trinite in the Park not far from the Castelle.[1]

From Lostwithiel to Casteldour, now clene down, [is] 3. good Miles by plentiful Ground of Corn and Gresse. Caetledour longgid to the Erle of Saresbyri.[2] A Mile of is a broken Crosse thus inscribid: "Conomor et filius cum Domina Clusilla." [3]

*Castle Dour.*

*Earl of Salisbury.*

The Castel of Cardinham[4] [is] a 4. Miles or more by North from Lostwithiel. To this Castelle longith many Knightes services.[5] Arundale of Lanherno, The Lord Souch, Compton, and . . . partith Cairdinham's Landes.[6]

*Cardinham.*

The Ryver of Fawey risith in Fawey More about a 2. Miles from Camilford by South in a very Wagmore in the side of an Hil. Thens to Draynesbridge of flat More Stones; thens to Clobham Bridg drounid with sand ij. Miles and more; thens to Lergen Bridge of 2. or 3. Arches a Mile lower; thens to Newbridg of Stone archyd a 2. Miles; thence to Resprin Bridge of Stone arched, *alias* Laprin, about 2. Miles; thens to Lostwithiel Bridge of v. Arches ij. myles.

*Fowey R.*

[1] On or near the site of this chapel was in 1814 a house, previously called Trinity, but then Restormell House. (Lysons, *Cornwall*, 178.)

[2] The Earls of Salisbury had a castle here, the site of which is called Castle-Dore: William of Worcester, in his Itinerary (*temp.* Edw. IV.), speaks of it as a dilapidated castle, by the name of Ditford, near Golonant. (Lysons, *Cornwall*, 281.)

[3] This is apparently the monument described in the *Victoria History of Cornwall* (i., 416) as a "rude pillar stone now standing at Four Turnings, on the high road from Fowey to Lostwithiel. It was formerly called the Long Stone, and stood at Castle Dôr, in the parish of Tywardreath, two miles north of its present position. On the front of the stone is the inscription in two lines: CIRVSIUS HIC IACIT CVNOMORI FILIUS. On the back is a Tau cross in relief.

[4] There are no remains of Cardinham Castle, the seat of the Dinhams, but the site is still called the Castle. (Lysons, *Cornwall*, 57.)

[5] The Honor of Cardinham comprised 71 knights' fees.

[6] After the death of Lord Dynham in 1501 his estates were divided among the representatives of his four sisters, viz. (1) Margaret, mar. Nicholas, Baron Carew; (2) Elizabeth, mar. Fulk Bourchier, Lord Fitzwarren, from whom descended the Earls of Bath; (3) Joan, mar. John, Lord Zouch; and (4) Catherine, mar. Sir Thomas Arundell of Lanherne. The fourth part belonging to Carew passed to the family of Compton of Compton Winyats, Warwickshire.

A litle above Lostwithiel Bridge of Stone the Ryver of Fawey brekith into 2. Armes, wherof at this Day the lesse goith to the Ston Bridg, the bigger to a Wodde Bridge even again [st] and but a litle way of from the Stone Bridg, and after a praty way lower the Armes cum agayn to one Botom. The great Part of Fawey Water is by policie turnid from the Stone Bridg for [fear of] choking of it and for to put the sande of from the Botom of the Toun. The Stone Bridg in Tyme of memorie of Men lyving was of Arches very depe to the sight, [but] the Sande is now cum to within a 4. or 5. fote of the very Hedde of them. The Sande that cummith from Tynne Workes is a great Cause of this, and yn tyme to cum shaul be a sore Decay to the hole Haven of Fawey. Barges as yet cum with Marchanties within half a Mile of Lostwithiel.

*St. Winnow.*
*John de*
*St. Winnow.*
*Lord Hastings.*
*William*
*Lower.*
*Thomas*
*Trefry.*

From Lostwithiel doun along Fawey Ryver to S. Winnou's, an Abbate Chirch,[1] [is] a good Myle; by the wich Chirch of old tyme enhabited a Gentilman, Joannes de S. Winnoco. After the Lordes Hastinges wer Owners of it; and [it was] then sold to Guiliam Loures gret Grauntfather now lyving.[2] This Lower hath to wife one of the 2. Doughters of Thomas Treury. By this Chirch is a Warfe to make Shippes by. [There is] much good Wood at S. Ginokes and on the other side of the Haven agayn[st] it. From S. Guinow's Chirch to the Point of S. Winow's Wood [is] half a Mile.

*Lerryn.*

Here goith yn a salt Crek half a Mile on the Est side of the Haven, and at the Hed of it is a Bridge, caullid Lerine Bridge, and the Creke berith also the Name of Lerine. At the North side of this Lerine Creke, almost at the Hedd, is Teuthey, Laurence Courtineis House; it longgid ons to Stonard, sins to Cayle, and now last to the Courtineis of the Howse of Devonshir descendinge.

*Ethy.*
*Laurence*
*Courtenay.*
*Stonard.*
*Cayle.*

From Lerine Creke to S. Carac Pille or Creeke [is] about half a Mile; in Midle of this Creke on the North side was a litle Celle of Sainct Cyret and Julette, longging to Montegue Priory, (ys a Sel of ii. Blake Monkes of Montegu,

*Cell of*
*St. Cyrus.*

---

1 St. Winnocus, a native of Brittany, was first Abbot of Wormhoult, in Flanders, at the end of the seventh century. (Smith and Wace, *Dict. of Christian Biography.*)

2 It seems to have been this William Lower's grandfather, Nicholas, to whom the manor was sold, in 1470, by Margaret, Lady Huntingdon.

and is dedicat to S. Sirice and Julit).[1]  From the Mouth of
S. Carak Pille to Poul-Morlande Pille [is] about a Mile;
[and] from the Mouth of Poulmorland to Bodenek Village
(a Fischar Toun; a poore Fisshar Village) half a Mile, wher
the Passage or *trajectus* is to Fawey.  Mr. Mohun[2] hath a
Maner Place, caullid the Haul, on an Hil above this Village.

Penpoll Creek.
Bodinnick.

Hall.

From Bodenek to Pelene Point [is] a Quarter of a Mile,
and here entereth a Pille or Creek half a Mile up into the
Land; at the Hed of this Pille is a Chapel of St. Wilow,[3]
and by it is a place caullid Lamelin, lately longging to
Lamelin, now to Trelauny by Heir General.  Trelauny's
House is at Meneheneth by Liscard.

Lamelin.
*Lamelin.*
*Trelawney.*
Menheniot.

On the South side of this Creke is the Paroch Chirch
caullid Lanteglise juxta Fawey, being the Paroch Chirch
of Bodenek and Poulruan.

Lanteglos.

From the Mouth of this Creke to Poulruan, a good
Fischar Town (a Fisshar Village) [is] a Quarter of a Mile.
Here by on the Hill is a Chapell of S. Salvatir (Savyor),[4]
and at this Polruan Toun is a Tower of Force marching
again [st] the Tower on Fawey side.  Ther was ons, as is
said, a Chaine to go over the Haven from Tower to Toure.
The Haven Mouth of Fawey is 2. Bow Shottes of.  The
very Point of Land at the Est side of the Mouth of this
Haven is caullid Pontus Crosse, *vulgo* Paunch Crosse.

Polruan.

From Fowey Haven to Lowe Creeke the Grownd ny

---

[1] The first, and it is believed the only occasion, on which this
cell of St. Cyrus, Ciricus, or Ciricius is noticed in the episcopal
registers is in 1236, when Bishop Brewer charged the bishopric with
an annuity in its favour.  At an early period it was an appendage
to Montacute Priory in Somersetshire.  The prior had but two
religious persons under his government, and the sum total of the
rents was £11 1s.  The parish church of Vepe, in which this cell
was situate, was re-dedicated by Bishop Grandisson, in 1336, to
SS. Ciricius and Julitta.  The infant Cyrus and his mother, Julitta,
suffered martyrdom under Diocletian about the year 304.  The
churches of Newton St. Cyres and Luxulian, and a chapel at Calstock, were also dedicated to them. (Oliver, *Monasticon Exon.*, 69.)

[2] Sir Reginald Mohun, born about 1509, died 1556.

[3] William of Worcester says that St. Willow the Hermit and Martyr
was beheaded at Lanteglos, near the place where Walter Hart, Bishop
of Norwich, who was the son of a miller at this place, was born.
(Lysons, *Cornwall*, 185.)

[4] The ruins of this chapel, which was annexed to Lanteglos Church,
still remained in 1814 on a hill, which is called from it St. Saviour's
hill. (Lysons, *Cornwall*, 185.)

the See Syde ys very fertile of Corne and Gresse, and [there are] no Tynne Werkes.

By Est the Haven of Fowey apon a iiii. Myles ys a smawle Creke cawled Poul Pier, and a symple and poore Village (a litle fischar Toun) apon the Est Syde of the same of Fisshar Men, and the Bootes ther Fisshing be saved by a Peere or Key.[1]

In the Est Syde also of this Poul Pyrre, ii. Myles of, is another Creeke cawled Loow, being but a Tyde Creke. For at low Water benethe the Bridge a Man may both wade and ryde over yn the Somer. Ther is on eyther Side of this smawl Creke a smaule Fissher Villag, hard on the Se Shore, the one cawlled Est and the other West Loowe, Est Loowe being a praty Market Towne,[2] and yn eyther of them a Chapel.[3] Also yn the sayde Creekes Mouth neere sumwhat to the Sowthe West is a lowe Isle, cauled S. Nicholas Isle, not a Quarter of a Myle fro the mayn Shore, and [it] conteyneth a vj. or viij. Acres yn Cumpace, and fedeth Shepe and Cones, nurishing also Broode of Se Byrdes. Ther is a great Bridg sumwhat above these ii. Vyllages of x. or xij. Stones Arches, over the which Men passe when the Se ys yn.[4] [There is] good Wood about Low Creke, [and] Salmon [are] taken yn this Creke.

Ther is a Maner Place caullid Trelaun about this Low Creke, sumtyme Bonville's, now the Marquise of Dorsete's.[5]

*Polperro.*

*Looe.*

*? St. George's Isle.*

*Trelawne.*
*Bonville.*
*Marquis of Dorset.*

---

[1] "The poore harbour and village of Polpera coucheth betweene 2. steepe hils, where plenty of fish is vented to the fish drivers, whom we call Jowters." (Carew, *Survey of Cornwall*, 131 d.)

[2] A market and fair at East-Looe were granted by King Henry II. to Henry de Bodrugan, then lord of the manor, as appears by the *quo warranto* roll of King Edward I., when the claim to the market was certified, together with the right of a pillory, cucking-stool, and other manerial privileges. (Lysons, *Cornwall*, 216.)

[3] The chapel at East-Looe was dedicated to St. Mary; a deed of the reign of Henry IV. speaks of a spot of ground given to this chapel. That at West-Looe was dedicated to St. Nicholas, and in 1814 had been converted into a Guildhall. (Lysons, *Cornwall*, 217, 301.)

[4] The bridge, being 141 yards in length, only 6 feet 2 inches wide, and supported by 13 stone arches, was built about the year 1400. (Lysons, *Cornwall*, 216.)

Lord Bonvile was beheaded in 1461, and on the accession of Edward IV., Elizabeth, Lady Harrington, the widow of Lord Bonvile's grandson, had a large dower assigned her out of his estates in Cornwall; her only daughter, by Bonvile, brought Trelawne and other estates to Thomas Grey, Marquis of Dorset. (Lysons, *Cornwall*, 257.)

Kendale and Code, Gentilmen, dwelle in Morel Paroch on the Est side of this Creke.

*Kendall, Coode.*
Morval.

From Low Creeke to Seton Bridge of Stone of 2. Archis and Setoun Ryver [is] a 3. Miles, and from Seton to Ramehed about a 9. miles. From Low to Tamar by the Sowth Se the Ground is fertile of Corn and Gresse, but withowt Tynne Warkes.

Seaton Br.
Seaton R.
Rame Head.

[From Bodenek I went] a v. Miles by very plesaunt inclosid Ground prately woodid, plentiful of Corn and Gresse; then a 3. Miles by mory and hethy Ground; then 2. Miles by hilly and woddy Ground to Liscard. About half a Mile or I cam to Liskard I passid in a wood by a Chapel of owr Lady, caullid *our Lady in the Park*, wher was wont to be gret Pilgrimage; this Chapelle of Ease longgith to Liskard,[1] and so doth 2. or 3. more. Liskard stondith on Rokky Hilles, and is the best Market Toun at this day in Cornwaul, saving Bodmyn; in this toun the Market is kept on Monday. The Paroch Chirch is of S. Martine, stondith on an Hil, and is a fair large thing. There was a Castel on an Hille in the Toun side by North from S. Martin. It is now al in Ruine, [but] Fragments and Peaces of waulles yet stond. The site of it is magnificent and looketh over al the Toun. The Castelle was the Erles of Cornwall. It is now usyd somtym for a Pound for Cattell.[2] The Towne knowlegith Fredom and Privileges by the Gift of Richard King of Romanes and Erle of Cornewaul.[3] Ther is a goodly Conduct in the Midle of the Town, very plentiful of Water, to serve the Town.

Liskeard.

*Earl of Cornwall.*

---

1 It was determined in the reign of Edward II. that the incumbent of the parish-church had no right to the oblations made at this chapel. (Lysons, *Cornwall*, 202.)

2 It is not improbable that the manor-house or castle was built by Richard, King of the Romans, who occasionally resided in it. A survey of the year 1337 calls it a manor-house, and describes it as having a hall, chapel, and six chambers, all out of repair. William of Worcester, *temp*. Edward IV., speaks of Liskeard Castle as then standing, and one of the palaces of the Duke. (Lysons, *Cornwall*, 200.)

3 Liskeard was made a free borough in 1240 by Richard, Earl of Cornwall and King of the Romans, who bestowed on the burgesses the same privileges which he had already granted to those of Launceston and Helston. His son Edmund, in 1275, granted them the fee of the borough, with the profits arising from the markets, fairs, &c., subject to a rent of 18*l*. per annum. (Lysons, *Cornwall*, 199.)

Cartuther.

Menheniot.
*Trelawny.*
*Helligan.*

Notter Br.
Lynher R.
St. Germans.

Cumming out of Liskarde about half a Mile I left Cortyder, a goodly Lordship, and an old Maner Place, on the Right Hond; it is a Hunderith Pounde by the Yere. This is now fawllen onto Heir General in Partition.  Cotyder and the Lordship of Treegelly, now caullid Minheneth Lordship, longgid, as Mr. Trelawny told me, to one Heling or Eling,[1] &c. ; the Name [Tregelly] and sum Ruines yet remaine. Trelawney now lyving is the 4. of that Name that hath be[en] Lord of Minheneth. There was one Sir John Trelawney, an Auncient Gentilman, Father to the first Trelawney of Minheneth, but be likelihod he had an Elder Sun, for Trelawney now living hath none of the Landes, but it is descendid to Heires Generales.[2]

From Liskard to Minheneth [is] 2. Miles, wher is a fair large old Chirch; the Personage of it is impropriate to Excester Colledge in Oxon.[3]  From Mynhenet to the Ruines of Bodulcan's Place [is] a 2. Miles.

The Soile betwixt Minheneth and Natter Bridge of 2. or 3. Archis on Liner Ryver [is] very good, and enclosid, and metely wel woddyd.  From Natter Bridge to S. Germane's [is] about a 2. Miles.  S. Germane's is but a poor Fischar Town; the Glory of it stoode by the Priory of Blake Canons, and a Paroche Chirche yn the Body of the same.[4]  Beside the

---

[1] The same, probably, who from this their residence took the name of Cartuther, and became extinct about the year 1400; the heiress or co-heiress of this family brought Cartuther to the Beckets. (Lysons, *Cornwall*, 224.)

[2] Sir John Trelawny's second son, John Trelawny of Menheniot, married Joan, dau. and heir of Nicholas Helligan, and died 1509. Their son, Sir John, was succeeded by John, who married Florence, dau. and co-heir of Sir Hugh Courtenay, and died 1513, leaving a son Walter, who died 1518, and a grandson John, born about 1504 and died 1563. (Vivian, *Visitations of Cornwall.*) The family seat at Menheniot was called Pool, from whence they removed, in the reign of James I., to Trelawny in Pelynt. Their old mansion, which Carew speaks of as far beneath the worth and calling of its possessor, was in 1814 occupied as the parish poor-house. (Lysons, *Cornwall*, 223-4.)

[3] The vicarage, one of the most valuable benefices in Cornwall, is endowed with the great tithes, subject to an annual payment of 20*l.* per annum to Exeter-College in Oxford. (Lysons, *Cornwall*, 225.)

[4] King Athelstan is said to have appointed Conan Bishop of S. German's in 936. According to an exemplification made of an inquisition in 1358, King Canute (1017-1035) gave to God and this church of St. German certain lands and tenements; this was the episcopal see; Brithwold was then its bishop; on his death, the see of Cornwall was united by Canute to that of Devonshire in the person of Livingus,

hye Altare of the same Priory on the ryght Hand ys a
Tumbe yn the Walle with an Image of a Bisshop, and over
the Tumbe a xi. Bisshops paynted with their Names and
Verses as Token of so many Bisshops biried theere, or that
ther had beene so many Bisshoppes of Cornwalle that had
theyr Seete theer. And at this Day the Bisshop of Exceter
hathe a Place, cauled Cudden Beke, joyning hard apon the
Sowth Est Side of the same Towne **Cuddenbeak.**

North Est of S. Germaynes vi. Myles apon the Ryver
of Tamar is a praty quik Market Town cawled Asshe,[5] set
from the Toppe of a Rokky Hille as by West to the Roote
of the same and very shore of Tamar Haven by Este. The
Tounes Men use boothe Marchandise and Fishing. [There
is] a Passage or Fery of a Quarter of a Myle over. There
is a Chapel of Ease in Asche.[6] The Paroche Chirch is
caullid S. Stephan's, about half a Mile of by South, the
Personage whereof is impropriate to Windesore College.[7] **Saltash.** **St. Stephens.**

---

who sat at Crediton; Leofric succeeded Livingus as bishop of Devon
and Cornwall; King Edward the Confessor translated the see from
Crediton to Exeter; afterwards Leofric founded at St. German's a
priory of canons regular in the room of secular canons; and the
patronage of the house was absolutely vested in the bishop of Exeter
for the time being. Of the ancient original cathedral church but little
vestige remains; but Bishop Walter Bronescombe consecrated the
conventual church of St. German's, erected perhaps on its site, in
1261. The nave of the church, 102 feet in length, was appropriated
to the use of the parishioners. A considerable part of the chancel
fell suddenly on a Friday, in 1592, shortly after the conclusion of the
public service. Not a trace of this most interesting portion of the
fabric is now visible, which was 55 feet long by 24 broad. The
eleven bishops may have been the bishops of Exeter from Leofric to
Walter Bronescombe.

St. German was born at Auxerre about the year 380, and was
consecrated Bishop of Auxerre in 418; he died at Ravenna in 418.
For the services rendered to religion during his two visits to England
and Wales, our ancestors cherished the most grateful veneration for
his memory. (Oliver, *Monasticon Exon.*, 1.)

5 There was a market attached to the castle of Trematon, and
probably held at Saltash, when the survey of Domesday was taken:
it is spoken of in that survey as a new market of the Earl's, which
had been prejudicial to the abbot's market at St. Germans. Saltash
was made a free borough in the reign of King John, or that of
Henry III., by Reginald de Valletort, who confirmed to the burgesses
divers privileges which they had enjoyed under his ancestors: these
privileges were confirmed by King Richard II. (Lysons, *Cornwall*, 291-2.)

6 Dedicated to St. Nicholas: the mayor nominates the minister.
(Lysons, *Cornwall*, 293.)

7 The church of St. Stephen's was given to Windsor College by
the Black Prince. (Lysons, *Cornwall*, 291.)

By S. Stephanes and in S. Stephanes Paroch ys a round
*Trematon Cas.* Castel of the Kinges cawled Tremeton (Tremertoun) as a
Man showld say the secund Forteres on Tamar.   It is a
great and auncient Castelle [set] apon a Rokky Hille, wherof
great Peaces yet stond and especially the Dungeon.   The
Ruines now serve for a Prison.   Great Libertees long to
*Valletort.* this Castelle.   The Valetortes, Men of great Possession,
wer Owners, and, as far as I can gather, Builders of this
Castel, and Owners and Lordes of the Toun of Aische.[1]

ii. Myles fro Asshe Northward ynto the Land is a smaul
*Cargreen.* Village cawled Caregrin, [and] Est of this is Bere Parke
*Bere.* and Hous in Devonshire dividid from Caregrin *tantum Tamara.*
I markid in sight, above Aschetoun a 2.   Miles or more the
principal Arme of Tamar Haven going up into the Land
*Calstock B.* about a 10.   Miles from that Place to Caulstoke Bridge,
witherto it almost ebbith and floweth.   And Shippes cum
*Morwellham.* up within a Mile of this Bridg to a Place caullid Morle-
*Morwell.* ham.   Morwel, the Abbat of Tavestok ['s] House [is] about a
Mile from Morleham.

*St. John's* [Below Lynher River] brekith a litle Creke out, caullid
*Lake.* John's or Antony ; and at the Mouth [of the Tamar] about
*Millbrook.* S. Nicolas brekith in a Creke goyng up to Milbrook 2. Miles
up in Land from the mayn Haven.   This Milbrok (Myl-
*Penlee Pt.* brooke) is a riche (symple) Fischar Toun.   Penle, a Fore
Land, lyith 3.   Miles lower from this Creeke into the Land,
*Rame Hd.* and the Promontorie of Ramehed a Myle lower.   Perse
*Mt. Edgcumbe.* Eggecombe[2] had a Manor by Ramehed, [and he] hath a

---

[1] The manor and honor of Trematon was held under Robert, Earl
of Moreton and Cornwall, in the reign of William Rufus, by Reginald
de Valletort, whose descendant, Roger de Valletort, the last heir male
of the family, gave it to Richard, Earl of Cornwall and King of the
Romans.   A survey of the Duchy of Cornwall, bearing date 1337,
describes a hall in Trematon-castle, with a kitchen and lodging-
chamber, as built by Edmund, Earl of Cornwall; and speaks of an
ancient chapel within the gate. (Lysons, *Cornwall*, 287-8.)  Carew,
in the reign of Elizabeth, says: "All the inner buildings are sunke
into ruine: onely there remaine the Ivie-tapissed wals of the Keepe,
and base Court, and a poore dwelling for the keeper of the Gayle."
(*Survey of Cornwall*, 111 *d.*)

[2] Sir Piers Edgcumbe mar. Johanna, the only dau. and heir of
James Dernford, widow of Charles Dinham, and thus obtained the
Manors of Rame and East Stonehouse, and other lands in Cornwall
and Devon.   He died 14 Aug., 1539.

goodly House in Cornewalle on Tamair at the Mouth of Plimmouth Haven.[1]

By the Ryver of Tamar from the Hedde North North Est yssuyng owt towarde the Sowthe, the Contery being Hilly, ys fertile of Corne and Gresse with sum Tynne Warkes wrought by Violens of Water. Hengiston beyng a Hy Hylle, and nere Tamar, yn the Est Part [of Cornewall], baryn of his self, yet is fertile by yelding of Tynne both be Water and Dry Warkes.[2]

Creekes from the Mouth of Plym and Tamar upon the Est side of the Haven [are]: The Mylle Bay; The Stone House Creke; Kaine Place Creke, wher is a Maner Place of Mr. Wise's; The Creek [Westonmill] having a Mille at the Hed, in lenght a 2. Miles; A 4. Mile upper, a Creke going up to Mr. Budoke's side, where is his Manor Place, and S. Budok Chirch, [and] ther dwellith by this Creke also Copston of Warley, a Man of xx. C. Marke of Lande, as it is saide; then is the uppermost, wher Tave Water cummith onto Tamar, and on the Est side of this Creek is Bukland, and on the West side is Bere, where the Lord Broke's House and Park was.

Plymmouth is the Est Port on the Sowth Se betwyxt Devonshyre. The Towne is about a 3. Miles from the Passage of Asche, [and] the *trajectus* self at Asche [is] half a Mile. The Ground betwixt the Passage and Plymmouth hath good Corn but litle Wood.

The Toun of Plymmouth is very large, and at this Tyme is devidid into 4. Wardes: The olde Towne Warde, Venarwarde, Lowewarde, [and] Vintrewarde alonge by the Gulf; and ther is a Capitaine yn eche of these Wardes, and undre eche Capitaine 3. Constables. This Town about King Henry the 2. tyme was a mene thing as an Inhabitation for Fischars, and after encreasid by a litle and a litle. The oldest Part of the Toun stoode by North and West (North and Est) sumwhat, and this Part is sore decayed, and now cum to the leste of the 4.

*Marginal notes:*

Hingston Down.

Millbay.
Stonehouse.
Keyham.
*Wise.*

*Budock.*
Budshead.
St. Budeaux.
*Copleston.*
Warleigh.

Buckland Monachorum.
Bere.
*Lord Brooke.*
Plymouth.

---

[1] Carew's statement that Mount Edgecumbe house was "builded and named" by Sir Piers Edgcumbe's son, Sir Richard, thus appears to be incorrect. (*Survey of Cornwall*, 99 d.)

[2] There is a local proverb, quoted by Carew, that
"Hengsten downe, well ywrought,
Is worth London towne, deare ybought."
(*Survey of Cornwall*, 115 d.)

The Name of Plymmouth Toun and the Privilege to
have a Mair was yn King Henry the 6. Dayes, the xvj.
Yer of his Reign, first grauntid by Act of Parlament.[1]    The
Prior of Plympton was afore chiefe Ruler in Plymmouth
and kept Courtes there.    The Toun was caullid afore by
the old name Sutton, and was devidid into Valetort, that
was in the North Part of the Toun, now the lest Parte of
it—this was longging to one Valetorte; the Midle and Hert
of the Town was cawllid Sutton Prior; the Est Part was
caullid Suttoun Rad, and in this Part was the White
Freres.[2]

In Sutton Prior standith the Paroch Chirch of S. Uthu,[3]
and the Grey Friars.[4]    One Painter, that of late dyed a
rich Marchaunt, made a goodly House toward the Haven,
wher Catarine, Princes Dowegar, took Water (lay at her
commynge out of Spayne).[5]    Ther is but one Paroch Chirche

Sutton
Valletort.

Valletort.

Sutton Prior.

Sutton Rauf.

Painter.

---

[1] The inhabitants petitioned the King and parliament to be incorporated as early as 1412.    For some time the prior and convent
appear to have opposed their views; but when the inhabitants
succeeded, in 1439, in obtaining the royal licence and an act of
parliament, which constituted them a corporation by the style of
the Mayor and Commonalty of the Borough of Plymouth, the prior
and convent addressed a petition to Bishop Lacy, representing that
it would be advantageous and commodious to convey to this municipal
body certain lands, tenements, franchises, fairs, markets, mills, rents,
and services, and praying his consent to dispose of the same.    (Oliver,
*Monasticon Exon.*, 130.)

[2] The convent of Carmelite or White Friars was established in
1314.    (Oliver, *Monasticon Exon.*, 152.)

[3] St. Andrew.

[4] The precise date of the foundation of the convent of Franciscan
or Grey Friars has not been ascertained, but in 1383 a licence was
granted by King Richard II. to alienate six acres of land in Plymouth to the Friars Minors in the same town, as a site for a certain
church, a belfry, and other buildings, and for the necessary habitation
of the same brethren anew to be made and constructed.    This (which
was perhaps only a new site of an older establishment) was near the
harbour of Sutton Pool on the north-western side; and the last remaining part of it was destroyed in 1813, when the present exchange
was erected in Woolster-street.    A part of the site was used for many
years as an inn called the Mitre Tavern.    (Oliver, *Monasticon Exon.*,
151.)

[5] "1501.    Here the Lady *Katherine*, daughter to the King or
Spaine, and wife to our Prince Arthur, tooke land, at her first
arriuall in England." (Carew, *Survey of Cornwall*, 114 d.)    This was
the unfortunate Catherine of Arragon, who was afterwards married
to Henry VIII., and, after being divorced from him, was styled
"Princess Dowager" until her death in 1536.

yn Plymmouthe, the Personage wherof was impropriate to
Plymton Priorie.[1]  One Thomas Yogge, a Marchant of       *Thomas Yogge.*
Plymmouth, paid of late yeres for making of the Steple of
Plymmouth Chirch, [but] the Toun paid for the Stuffe.
This Thomas Yogge made a fair House of More Stone in
the Toune toward the Haven, [and] a goodly House of
More Stone on the North side of the Chirch Yard of Plym-
mouth Paroche Chirche; [he also] build[ed] a fair Chapel
on the Northe side of Plymmouth Chirch.  Ther is an
Hospitale House on the North side of the Church.[2]  Ther
is a righte goodly Walke on an Hille without the Toun by
South, caullid the How, and a fair Chapel of S. Catarine[3]     The Hoe.
on it.

The Chirch and much of the Ground wheron Suttoun,
now caullid Plymmouth, was buildid was longging to one
of the Prebendes *titulo S. Petri & Pauli* of Plymtoun, a        Plympton
Collegiate Chirch, *alias Capella libera dni Regis*, before the   Priory.
Conquest.  Al such as hath by Continuance sins the tyme
of Henry the secund buildid Houses in Suttoun Prior, now
the greatest Part of Plymmouth, toke Licens of the Priorie
of Plymtoun as of their chief Lord.

The Mouth of the Gulph wherin the Shippes of Plymmouth lyith is waullid on eche side and chainid over in tyme
of Necessite.  On the South West side of this Mouth is a
Blok House; and on a rokky Hille hard by it is a stronge
Castel quadrate, having at eche Corner a great Round Tower,
[but] it semith to be no very old Peace of worke.  Hard
by this Castelle waul, Veysy, now Bp. of Excester, began      *Veysey.*
a peace of an high and stronge Waull.[4]

---

[1] The parish church of St. Andrew continued an appendage to
the priory nearly until the dissolution of the house. (Oliver, *Monasticon Exon.*, 131.)

[2] Licence was granted by Bishop Veysy in 1540 for service to
be performed thrice in the week in the chapel of the hospital near
the cemetery of the parish church of Plymouth. (Oliver, *Monasticon
Exon.*, 131.)

[3] This is mentioned in the episcopal registers in 1370, 1388, 1413,
and 1425. (Oliver, *Monasticon Exon.*, 131.) It is shown in the chart
of Plymouth Haven in the reign of Henry VIII., as reproduced in
Lysons' *Devon*.

[4] In 1520 Bishop Veysey granted an indulgence of forty days to
all true penitents assisting in the building of the walls and fortifications
of the town. (Oliver, *Monasticon Exon.*, 131.)

From Plymmouth by good enclosid Ground but Hilly to the Place wher I crossid over Plym Ryver at the Ebbe [was] about a 3. Miles.   There be 2. Bridges on Plym that be notably spoken of, Bykley and Plym.   I markid yn the Haven of Plym but 2. notable Crekes ; one on the West side of the Haven, entering into the Land about a Mile or more from the Haven Mouth, and another, bigger then it, on the

**Chelson.** Est side of the Haven, caullid Shilleston, about a 2. Miles from the Mouth of Plym Haven.   There is a goodly Rode for great Shippes betwixt the Haven Mouth and this Creeke.

After that I passid over Plym Ryver I rode about half **Tory Brook.** a Mile along by Torey Broke, whos Color is alway redde by the Sand that it rennith on and caryeth from the Tynne **Plympton** Workes with it ; and so to Plymtoun Marie, so caullid **St. Mary.** bycause the Chirch there is dedicate onto our Lady.   The Glory of this Towne stoode by the Priorie of Blake Chanons there buildid and richely endowid with Landes.[1]   The original Beginning of this Priorie was after this Fascion : **William** One William Warwist, Bisshop of Excester, displeasid with **Warelwast.** the Chanons or Prebendaries of a Fre Chapelle of the Fundation of the Saxon Kinges, because they wold not leve theyr Concubines, found meanes to dissolve their College, wherin was a Deane or Provost and 4. Prebendaries with other Ministers.   The Prebende of Plymton self was the Title of one, and the Prebend of S. Peter and Paule at Suttoun, now caullid Plymmouth, another.   Bisshop War- wist, to recompence the Prebendaries of Plymton, erectid a **Bosham in** College of as many as wer there at Bosenham in Southsax, **Sussex.** and annexid the Gift of them to his Successors, Bisshops of Excester.   Then he set up at Plymton a Priorie of Canons-Regular, and after was there buried in the Chapitre House.[2]

---

[1] This establishment, dedicated to the Blessed Mary and SS. Peter and Paul, of the order of St. Augustine, was founded in 1121 by William Warelwast, the nephew and chaplain of William the Conqueror, who had given to the See the church of Plympton many years before his advancement to the See of Exeter.   For this purpose a prebendal college of five members, namely, a dean and four prebendaries, supposed to have been founded there by King Edgar, was removed and transplanted to Bosham in Sussex.   (Oliver, *Monasticon Exon.*, 129.)

[2] His nephew, Robert Warelwast, the fifth Bishop of Exeter, was also buried there.   (Oliver, *Monasticon Exon.*, 129.)

Diverse Noble Men gave after Landes to this Priorie, emong whom was Walterus de Valle torta, Lord of Tremerton in Cornewal, and, as sum say, of Totenes, but yet I know no certentie of that. I know he was a Man of fair Possessions about Plymmouth, and he gave onto Plymtoun Priorie the Isle of S. Nicolas *cum cuniculis*, conteyning a 2. Acres of Ground, or more, and lying at the Mouthes of Tamar and Plym Ryvers. I hard say, That the Landes of Valletorte were for a Morther doone by one of them confiscate, and sins the great Part of them have remaynid yn the Kinge's Handes. There were buryed sum of the Courtneis and diverse other Gentilmen in the Chirch of the Priorie of Plymtoun.[1]

Plymtoun Mary stondith not apon Plym River, for it is distant almost half a Mile from it; but it stondith on Torey Brooke, by the Est Ripe of it, wherby the lower and first Buildinges of the Court of the Priorie be almost clene chokid with the Sandes that Torey bringgith from the Tynne Workes. One Prior Martine, the 3. or 4. Prior of Plymtoun, buildid the Substance of the Chirch that there a late stoode.[2] There is kept a Fair at Plymtoun Marie on S. John's Day at Midsomer.

Plymtoun Thomas is a Quarter of a Mile from Plymtoun Marie, so caullid of Thomas Beket; but now the Chirch there is of S. Mauricius, Knight and Martyr. In the side of this Toun is a fair large Castelle and Dungeon in it, whereof the Waulles yet stonde, but the Logginges within be decayed.[3]

Balduinus Redverse, Erle of Devonshire, was Lord of this Toun and Castelle; and after Isabella de Fortibus, the last of that Familie, was Lady of it. Many Gentilmen hold their Landes of this Castelle. This Isabella gave great Privileges to her Town of Plymton, wher yet is a pratie Market. The Courteneis, Erles of Devonshir, were syns Lordes of this Town.

From Plymtoun Thomas [I went] to Le Bridge of stone

*Walter de Valletort.*

Drake's Is.

*Courtenay.*

*Prior Martin.*

Plympton Earle.

*Baldwin de Redvers. Isabella de Fortibus.*

*Courtenay.*

Lee Mill Bridge.

[1] Many members of the Courtenay, Valletort, Strode, and other eminent families, selected its sacred precincts for the place of their interment. (Oliver, *Monasticon Exon.*, 129.)

[2] Martin became Prior in 1176. At present scarcely a vestige remains of any of the conventual buildings. (Oliver, *Monasticon Exon.*, 129, 131.)

[3] In Camden's time (1586) "the miserable remains of a castle."

Yealm R.
Yealmbridge.

of 3. Archis; this Bridge stondith on Yealme Water, and a 2. Miles lower on it is Yaulm Bridge, and a Mile lower it goith to the Se, a 4. Miles, as I esteme, by South Est from the Main Mouth of Plym Water.

Ivybridge.
Erme R.
Ermington Br.

Erme Mouth.

From Le Bridge to Ivy Bridge [is] a 3. Miles; the Ryver of Arme, or Armine, rennith under this Bridge, and a 2. Miles lower on it is Armington Bridge. This River rennith apon great Rokky Stones with no smaul Noise. The Mouth (Arme Haven), wher is no Haven, lyith ful of Flattes and periculus Rokkes, and no Ship cummith in Tempest hither, but in Desperation. Too of Philip, King of Castelle ['s] Shippes felle to Wrak in this Haven when he was dryven into England by Tempeste.

Modbury.

From Ivy Bridge to Modbury [is] a 2. Miles. The Ground is fertile of Corne and Pasture, and [there are] sum good Wooddes betwixt Plymtoun Thomas and Mod-burie. The Tounlette of Modbury is privilegid, and hath diverse Hamlettes longging onto it.

Rohan.
Okeston.
Champer-
nowne.

Sum say that the Ruans,[1] sum say that the Oxtons, were Lordes of Modbury. Campernulph[2] is now chief Lord there, and he told me that Oxton was Lord of it immediately afore the Campernulphes, but he contendid that the Campernulphes were Lordes of it afore the Oxtons.[3] Campernulphe of Modburie's Graundfather maried the sole Doughter and

---

[1] The family of Rohan or Rohant is apparently intended, which became merged by intermarriage with the Champernownes, but are not known to have been lords of Modbury. (Oliver, *Monasticon Exon.*, 297.)

[2] Sir Philip Champernowne, born about 1479, Sheriff of Devon 1527, died at Modbury 1545. (Vivian, *Visitations of Devon.*)

[3] Lysons says: "The manor of Modbury belonged to the Valle-torts, barons of Harberton. Roger Valletort conveyed it to Sir Alexander de Okeston, who had married Joan, widow of Ralph de Valletort, supposed to have been a concubine of Richard, Earl of Cornwall and King of the Romans. They had issue Sir John de Okeston, who died without issue, having, by the command of King Edward II., conveyed Modbury and other lands, formerly given to his father by Roger de Valletort, to Sir Richard Champernowne. This Sir Richard was son of Richard Champernowne, by Joan, daughter of the above mentioned Joan, whom Edmund, Earl of Cornwall, in a deed bearing date 12 Edward I., calls sister. Richard Champernowne, the father, was a younger son of Sir Henry Champernowne, of Clist Champernowne." (*Devon*, 342.) This Sir Henry presented to the living of Ilfracombe in 1272. (Vivian, *Visitations of Devon.*)

Heyre of Childerle of Devonshir by Excester, and had 80 *li.* Land by her.[1]

*Chidderleigh.*

There was another House of the Campernulphes more auncient, caullid Campernulphe of Bere.[2] The last of this House left a Doughter and Heire, caullid Blanch, and she was first maried onto Copestan of Devonshir, and after devorcid and maried onto the Lorde Brooke, Steward onto Henry the vij., and he had by her a 700. Markes of Land by Yere.

*Copleston.*
*Lord Brooke.*

There dwellith one Prideaux in Modburi, a Gentilman of an auncient Stoke and fair Landes, ontil be chaunce that one of his Parentes killid a Man, wherby one of the Courteneis, Erle of Devonshire, had Colum John and other Landes of the Prideaux. [There is a] Prideaux Ile in Modbury Chirch.

*Prideaux.*

*Courtenay.*
*Columbjohn.*

Hille, a Gentilman, [lives] in Modburi Paroche; this Name rose by a Lawier and Juge[3] that left onto his Heires a 300. Markes of Land. The Grand Father of Hille now lyving sold an 100 *li.* Land.

*Hill.*

Ther is one of the Fortecues dwelling in Modbury, whos Father had to wife the Mother of Syr Philip Chaumburne now lyving.[4]

*Fortescue.*
*Champer-*
*nowne.*

Ther was a House of Monks Aliens of the French Order

*Modbury*
*Priory.*

---

[1] William Champernowne, Sir Philip's grandfather, married Elizabeth, daughter and heir of John Chidderleigh, and died 1464. (Vivian, *Visitations of Devon.*)

[2] John Champernowne of Bere Ferrers, the last of this branch, died 1475. His daughter Blanche is stated by Vivian to have married Robert Willoughby, Lord Brooke, but no mention is made of a previous marriage to Copleston. (Vivian, *Visitations of Devon.*)

[3] Sir Robert Hill of Shilston was Justice of the Common Pleas, 16 Rich. II. His son and heir, Robert, married Margaret, daughter of Sir Richard Champernowne of Modbury. (Vivian, *Visitations of Devon.*)

[4] Wimpston, in this parish, was "the first seat of the clarous name of Fortescue in this kingdom." (Westcote, *View of Devon*, 394.) It was granted by King John to John Fortescue in 1209. (Lysons, *Devon*, 343.) Leland's statement as to the marriage does not agree with Vivian's *Visitations of Devon*, but it seems to be made on the authority of Sir Philip Champernowne himself. According to Vivian, Sir Philip's mother was Margaret, daughter of Sir Philip Courtenay of Molland, and Thomas Fortescue's father, John, married Isabell, daughter of Thomas Gibbes of Fenton. However, he may have married, secondly, Sir John Champernowne's widow, seeing that Sir John died in 1503, and John Fortescue did not die until 1519.

at Modbyri. The site of their Mansion is yet seene on the North side of the Chirche. The Founder was ther scant knowen, [but] I take it that Ruan or Oxton were Founders of it. This Priory with the Personage of Modbyri impropriate was given yn King Edward the 4. tyme to Eyeton College.[1]

Avon R.

From Modbyri to the Forde wher I passid over Awne Ryver [was] about a 4. or 5. Miles. This Water cummith

South Brent.

by Estbrenton, and a litle lower, even by the Toun, is a Bridge over Aune. Estbrenton is in the highway betwixt Plymmouth and Excestre, a vj. Miles from the Forde wher

Gara Br.
Sture.
Rolster.

I passid over Awne, and Garebridge on Aune is a 2. Miles lower. Mr. Stoure['s] House [is] a litle beyonde this Ford on an Hille side. From this Forde to Rostbridge (a Stone Bridge caullid Rostel) [is] a 2. Miles, wher I passid over a

Harbourne R.

Brooke caullid communely Harburne Water, but it is written, as I lerned, Hurbertoun. This Ryver cummith out of a Welle a 2. Miles by North Est above Rostbridge, and goith

Ashprington.
Corn worthy.

a 2. Miles lower to Bowbridge in the Valley betwixt Ascheprentoun and Corneworthy.

From Rostbridge to Totenes [is] a 2. Miles. Al the Ground betwixt Modbyri and Totenes [is] plentiful of good Gresse, Corn, and Woodde.

Totnes.

The Town of Totenes lyith along from the Toppe of an High Rokky Hille by West onto the Roote of it by Est. This Toun hath beene waullid, but the Waulles be now clene downe; a Man may see wher the Foundation was of them. Ther be yet 3. Gates by West, Est, and . . . The Castelle of Totenes stondith on the Hille North West of the Towne. The Castelle Waule and the stronge Dungeon be maintainid. The Logginges of the Castelle be clene in

---

[1] The priory was probably founded by a Valletort before the 13th century, but the register of Bishop Grandisson ascribes the honour of foundation to the Champernowne family, and the right of patronage continued in that family until the dispersion of the community. The establishment consisted of two monks and a prior, and depended on the great Benedictine house of Sancta Maria de Sancto Petro super Divam (St. Pierre sur Dive), in the diocese of Seez, in Normandy, the abbots of which exclusively nominated the priors of Modbury. It was dissolved by Henry VI. in 1442, and its revenues appropriated to his noble foundation of Eton College. A short time afterwards Edward IV. conveyed the property to his favourite abbey of Tavistock; but it was again restored to Eton College. (Oliver, *Monasticon Exon.*, 297-8.)

Ruine.[1]   Many Gentilmen hold their Landes by Gard and Service to this Castelle.

The Lordes Zouches were long Time Lordes of this Town and Castel, now Eggecombe by Gift upon the Attainder of Zouche.[2]

*Lord Zouch.*
*Edgcumbe.*

King John gave first Privilege of a Mairalte to Totenes,[3] [and] King Edward the First augmentid the Libertes.[4]

There is but one Paroch Chirch in Totenes, and that is set in the Midle of the Toun.   Ther is a greate Steple Tour, and the greatest Belles in al those Quarters.   There was a Priorie of Blak Monkes at the North Est side of this Paroch Chirch, [which was] impropriate to the Priorie of Totenes.[5] There is an Hospitale by the Chirch Yarde; [and] ther is a Lazar House on the South Part of the Toun endowid with sum Landes.[6]

*Totnes Priory.*

Totenes Bridge on Dart [is] of 7. Archis, [and] Litle Totenes [is] a flite shot byneth Totenes Bridge.   The Toune

---

[1] The outer walls of the castle were still standing in 1822. (Lysons, *Devon*, 533.)

[2] The honor or barony of Totnes, which had been part of Edward the Confessor's demesne, was given by William the Conqueror to Judhael, or Joel, who assumed the name of De Totneis. Having been banished the realm by William Rufus, that monarch gave his barony to Roger de Novant.   Notwithstanding this grant, it appears that, in the reign of King John, Henry Novant, and William de Braose, or Bruce, grandson of Joel de Totnes, held the barony in moieties.   Novant's moiety descended to the Valletorts.   Bruce's passed by marriage to Cantilupe, who eventually became possessed of the whole.   The heiress of Cantilupe brought it to the Lords Zouch, who possessed it for several generations.   On the attainder of John, Lord Zouch, in 1486, King Henry VII. gave it to Sir Richard Edgecumbe. (Lysons, *Devon*, 533.)

[3] "Totnes is said to have been governed by a mayor ever since the reign of King John. (See Camden and Browne Willis.)   That monarch granted the burgesses a charter of privileges in 1205, but it does not seem that they had a mayor before the reign of Henry VII., who granted them the power to elect a mayor annually, on St. Matthew's day." (Lysons, *Devon*, 532.)

[4] "The town has sent members to Parliament ever since the reign of Edward I., the right of election being vested in the corporation and freemen, between 60 and 70 in number." (Lysons, *Devon*, 532.)

[5] The priory of St. Mary, a cell of the great Benedictine abbey of SS. Sergius and Bacchus at Angers. (Oliver, *Monasticon Exon.*, 238.)

[6] In 1437 Bishop Lacy granted an indulgence to true penitents who should contribute to the support of the poor and the lepers or the hospital of St. Mary Magdalene at Totnes. (Oliver, *Monasticon Exon.*, 241.)

of Totenes is servid with Conducts of Water having 3. Castelles.

*Walter le Bon.* Delabont, Lord of Litle Totenes, erectid ther a Celle of Freres *ord. S. Trinitatis,* [but] Oldham, Bisshop of Excestre, suppressid this House, and gave the Landes to the Vicars of the Cathedral Chirch of Excestre.[1]

*Berry Pomeroy.* Byri Pomerey Town lyith hard by the Est Ende of Totenes Bridge, Byry Pomerey Chirch almost a Mile of, and Byry Pomerey Castelle aboute half a Mile from the Church.

*Dartington.* Dartington Park [is] half a Mile above Totenes Bridge, on the same Ripe of the Water that Totenes is. In this *Duke of* Park is a great Maner Place [that] longid to the Duke of *Exeter.* Excester; S. Liger, that maried the Duches of Excester, *St. Leger.* kept House in this Place.[2]

*Bidwell Brook.* A litle lower then this Parke cummith down on the same Ripe a Brooke from the West, caullid Gulle, and goith into Darte Ryver. The River of Darte by Tynne Workes carieth much Sand to Totenes Bridge, and chokith the Depth of the Ryver all downeward, and doth much Hurt to Dertmouth Haven. Derte Ryver cummith out of Dartemore, and the Hed of it is rekenid to be a 15. Miles above Totenes. *Dartmoor.* Dertmore is of a very great Compace, and is suche a Wilde Morisch and Forest Ground as Exmore is.

*Ashprington.* From Totenes to Aschprenton by Hilly but fruteful *Cornworthy.* Ground [is] a 2. Miles; thens to Corneworthy Village by like Ground a Mile, and here was a Priorie of Nunnes

---

[1] The chapel of the Holy Ghost and of St. Catharine at Warland, near Totnes, was begun to be erected 1270, on the land of Walter le Bon (no doubt the founder). Generally a priest of the Holy Trinity House of Hounslow was appointed to serve this chapel, but the collation to it was absolutely vested in the bishops of Exeter. Bishop Oldham, in 1508, appropriated this chapel to the vicars choral of Exeter cathedral. In 1822 some small remains were still to be seen in a cottage and stable at Warland. (Oliver, *Monasticon Exon.*, 240; Lysons, *Devon*, 534.)

[2] It was by King Richard II. given to John Holland, his half-brother, whom he created Earl of Huntington, and afterward Duke of Exeter. Henry Holland, last of that line, Duke of Exeter, who had married Ann, the sister of King Edward IV., taking part against the said king, fled, and was found drowned in the sea. The duke being dead without issue, the duchess remarried to Sir Thomas St. Leger, and held this land as her jointure. (Risdon, *Survey of Devon*, 161.)

lately suppressid.[1] From Corneworthy to Dertmouth by like Ground [is] a 4. Miles, [and] about half a Mile above Dertmouth Town is a Creke goyng out of the maine Streame of the Haven, caullid old Mylle Creke.

There is a Tounlet or I enterid into Dertmouth Toune, caullid Hardenesse, inhabitid most by Fischar Men and sum Marchauntes, having in it a Chapel of Clare,[2] and also the great Ruines of Hauley's Haul,[3] an exceding rich Marchant and a Noble Warriour. There is only a Bay fillid by fluddes with Salt Water driving at Ebbe the 2. Milles, that devidith Ardenes from Dertmouth Town; and over this Bay is a Stone Causey and 2. flatte Bridgges.

*Dartmouth.*

Ther be evident Tokens that of old Tyme ther hath beene much Building betwixt the Toun of Dertmouth now inhabitid and Stoke Fleminge, wherapon it must folow that Old Dertmouth stode that way, or els that Stoke Fleming was larger then it is now.

*Stoke Fleming.*

The Toune of Dertmouth lyith in lenght on a very Rokky Hille on the Haven side, about half a Mile from the very Mouth of it, and extendith in lenghth aboute a Quarter of a Mile. There be good Marchaunt Men in the Towne; and to this Haven long good Shippes. The Toune is servid with Conduct Water.

Ther is a fair Chirch in the Towne, but it is but a Membre of the Paroche Chirch of Tunstale, half a Mile

*Townstall.*

---

[1] The Augustinian priory of St. Mary.  Tanner, in his Notitia, says it was founded for seven religious women; but only five nuns had a voice at the election of Honora Vyvyan in 1461. (Oliver, *Monasticon Exon.*, 236.)

[2] The chapel of St. Clarus was licensed by Bishop Grandisson in 1331. It seems afterwards to have become the property of the Hawley family, perhaps in consideration of their having founded the chancel of the new church of the Trinity, commonly called St. Saviour's, which was dedicated in 1372. (Oliver, *Monasticon Exon.*, 170.) It was taken down in the reign of Charles II. (Lysons, *Devon*, 158.)

[3] This was probably the "Hawe" referred to by Risdon; Westcote spells it "How," but, as he makes it rhyme with "low," which is pronounced in the Devonshire as *law*, it is, no doubt, the same word, and in each case equivalent to *hall*. Hawley was so successful that the people had a proverb:—

"Blow the wind high, or blow the wind low,
  It bloweth good to Hawly's Hawe."

(Risdon, *Survey of Devon*, 169; Westcote, *View of Devon*, 425.)
See also Note 1 on p. 64.

*John Hawley.*

[off] on the top of an Hille.  John Hawley, a riche Marchant and Noble Warrior again[st] the French Men,[1] lyith burid afore the High Altare with his 2. Wives in Dertmouth Chirch.  Obiit aº Di. 1403.[2]  Copestan, now a Man of great

*John Copleston.*

Landes in Devonshire, maried the Heir Generale of Hawley, wherby his Landes were much augmentid.  Sum think that wher the Personage House of Tunstalle now is, was sumtyme an House or Celle of French Monkes.  The Personage of Tunstalle was impropriate to Torrebay Abbay.

*Guy de Brian.*

The Briens, emong whom Guy Brien was famose, were Lordes of Dertemouth Towne.

King John gave Privilege of Mairalte to Dertmouth.[3] Edward the 3. gave Licens to the Town of Dertmouth to purchase.  King Edward the 4. gave xx. *li.* fee to Dertmouth Towne,[4] Richard the 3. gave x. *li.* more, and Henry the 7. x. *li.*

*Sir George Carew.*
*Stoke Fleming.*
*St. Petrock's.*

A faire Bulwarke [was] made of late.  There be 2. Towers at the Haven Mouth and a Chaine to draw over; one of those Toures stondith by Sir George Carew['s] Castelle, caullid Stoke Fleming, at the Haven Mouth.  Ther was and is a Chapelle of S. Patrike, as I remember, yn the Castelle of Dartemouth, and it hath beene in tymes paste, as it apperith, sum litle Celle annexid to sum great Abbay.[5]

1 There is little doubt that Hawley was the merchant of Dartmouth who, in 1390, waged the navie of shippes of the ports of his owne charges, and tooke foure-and-thirty ships laden with wine to the summe of fifteene hundred tunns." (Stowe, *Annals*; Lysons, *Devon,* 154.)

2 This is the date of death of his second wife.  Hawley himself died 1408, and his first wife 1394.  The inscription is now imperfect, but is given in full in a foot-note to Westcote (*View of Devon*, 425.) The chancel was founded by Hawley.

3 Lysons says this seems to be a mistake: the earliest charter is apparently that of Edward III., who, in 1342, granted to the burgesses of Clifton, Dartmouth, and Hardnesse, the power of choosing a mayor, with other privileges, such as the holding pleas, &c. (*Devon*, 154.)

4 "King Edward IV., in 1481, covenanted with the men of Dartmouth to pay them 30*l.* per annum for ever, on condition of their building and maintaining a strong tower and bulwark of lime and stone, furnishing the same with artillery, and finding a chain of length and strength sufficient to secure the harbour." (Lysons, *Devon,* 156.)

5 "The church of St. Petrock, situated within the ruins of the old castle at Clifton, contains nothing remarkable.  It had been called the chapel of the Virgin Mary, before the foundation of a chantry, dedicated to St. Petrock, in the reign of Edward III." (Lysons, *Devon,* 158.)

The Mariners at Dertmouth counte the Haven of Plymmouth to be aboute a Kenning from Dartemouth.

Saultecumbe Haven, sumwhat barrid and having a Rok at the entering into it, is about a vij. Miles by West South West from Dertmouth; and aboute half a Mile withyn the Mouth of this Haven, longging to the Privileges of Dertmouth, is Saultcombe, a Fisshar Towne. The Est Point of Saltcombe Haven is a great Foreland into the Se, caullid the Sterte. Hilton Castelle, longing to Courteney of Poudreham, is about a Mile above Saltcomb on the same side of the Haven; and a 3. Miles upper at this Haven Hedde is Kingesbridg, sumtyme a praty Town.

Slaptoun, a praty College toward the Shore, is almost in the Midle way betwixt Dertmouth and Saltcombe Haven; Guy Brien was Founder of this College.[1] Ther is a very large Poole at Slapton a 2. Miles in lenghth. Ther is but a Barre of Sand betwixt the Se and this Poole; the fresch Water drenith into the Se thorough the Sandy Bank, [but] the Waite of the Fresch Water and Rage of the Se brekith sumtime this Sandy Bank. [There are] good Fisch in Slapton Poole.

I ferid over from Dartmouth Toun to Kinges Were, a praty Fisschar Towne again[st] Dertmouth, wherof Sir George Carew is Lorde. These Thinges I markid on the Est side of the Mouth of Dermouth Haven: First, a great Hilly Point caullid Doune, and a Chapelle on it, half a Mile farther into the Se then the West Poynt of the Haven; bytwixt Downesend and a Pointelet caullid Wereford is a litle Bay; Kingeswere Toun standith out as another Pointelet, and bytwixt it and Wereford is a praty litle Bay; a litle above Kinges Were Town goith a litle Crek up into the Land from the Maine Streame of the Haven, caullid Water Hed, a Place meete to make Shippes yn; about half a Mile above Water Hed goith into the Land a Creke, long in respect of the first, caullid the Nesse Creke; and a Mile above this is a greate Creke caullid Gaunstoun

*Salcombe.*

*Start Pt.*
*Ilton Cas.*
*Courtenay.*

*Kingsbridge.*
*Slapton.*

*Guy de Brian.*
*Slapton Ley.*

*Kingswear.*
*Sir George Carew.*

*Down End.*

*Waterhead.*

*Galmton.*

---

[1] Sir Guy de Brian, in 1373, founded in a chapel erected near the parish church, a collegiate chantry in honour of our Lady. As to the precise number of the clergy to be employed in the service of this college, the recorded documents are not altogether reconcileable. (Oliver, *Monasticon Exon.*, 322.) Lysons gives the number as a rector and five fellows, and four clerks. (*Devon*, 452.)

Creek, and Gaunston Village stondith at the Hed of it; this Creeke Hedde is heere about half a Mile from the Maine Se by the Cumpasing of it in Torrebay.

Paign*on.

From Kinges Were to Gaunton [is] a 3. Miles by Hilly Ground, [and] from Gaunton to Pentown almost 3. Miles. Here cummith downe a praty Brooke, and renning by the Shore Sandes goith into the Se in Torrebay.

Torquay.
*William,*
*Lord Briwere.*

*Peter*
*Fitzmatthew.*
*Dawney.*
*Fisacre.*

Berry Head.

Brixham.

Torrebay Village and Priorie [are] a Mile of. In this Abbay be 3. fair Gate Houses.[1] William Bruer the first made this House on his own Ground; [he] bought Torre Mohun therby and gave it to this Abbay.[2] Petrus filius Mathæi there buried gave land to it.[3] Dawney gave Northton to this Priory, [and] . . . . iseakre, a rich Merchant, gave much to [it.]

The West Point of Torrebay is caullid Byri; and more then within a Mile of this Point is a praty Towne of Fischar Men, caullid Brixham, and this Towne is a Membre of the Privilege of Dertmouth. I markid almost in the Midle of this Bay one House sette on the hard Shore; and a smaul Peere by it (in the Botom by Torre Priory) as a Socour for Fischar Botes. The Est Point of Torrebay ys caullid

Petit Tor.

Shag Rock.

Oar Stone.

Thatcher
Stone.

Peritorre (Petitorre), and to the sight it is not so much pointid into the Se as Byri Hed is; ther is by Peritorre a great Rokke caullid Isleston, as an Isle environid with the Se. Ther is another Rokky Isle, far bigger than Isleston, and is caullid Horestane; it lyith a Mile by South Est into the Se from Peritorre Point. There is also an Islet caullid Blak Rok; this lyith by the Shore about a Mile by South Est from Peritorre toward Teignmouth. I take this Bay of Torre by Estimation to be a x. Miles and more in

---

1 "Two of these have unfortunately disappeared. One of them fell from neglect about eighty years ago [i.e. about 1766], but another survives, which is probably coeval with the origin of the establishment, and still bids defiance to time. The roofless chapter-house, the prostrate masses of the central church tower, the refectory, and the stately grange, are still interesting." (Oliver, *Monasticon Exon.,* 169.)

2 It was a Norbertine or Premonstratensian Abbey founded in 1196 by William, Lord Briwere, and dedicated to the honour of the Holy Saviour, the Holy Trinity, and the Blessed Virgin. (Oliver, *Monasticon Exon.,* 169.)

3 Peter Fitzmatthew, Lord of Stokenham, was one of the original benefactors and the donor of valuable manor of Blackauton. (Oliver, *Monasticon Exon.,* 170; Lysons, *Devon,* 54.)

Cumpace, and Byri and Peritorre Pointes be distant a great Lege, that is, about a 4. Miles. Fisschar Men hath divers tymes taken up with theyr Nettes yn Torrebay Musons of Hartes, wherby Men juge that yn tymes paste it hath be[en] Forest Grounde.

The hole Ground bytwixt Torrebay and Exmouth booth sumwhat to the Shoore and especially inward is wel inclosid, fruteful of Corne and Grasse, and meatly welle woddid; and this Quarter is caullid the South hammes, being the frutefulest part of all Devonshire.

From Torrebay Priorie and Towne to Hacham [is] a 3. Miles. Hacham Lordship of olde Tyme longgid to one of the Archidekens,[1] of whom ther be dyverse fair Tumbes in the Chirch ther. This Lordship with other fair Landes cam to one of the Carews, and diverse of this Name be also buried in the same Chirch.

*Haccombe.*

*Archdeacon.*

*Carew.*

The very utter West Point of the Land at the Mouth of Teigne is caullid The Nesse, and is very hy redde clif Ground. The Est Point of this Haven is caullid the Poles. This is a low sandy Grounde other cast out by the Spring of Sand out of Teigne, or els throuen up from the Shores by rage of Wynd and Water; and this Sand occupieth now a great Quantite of Ground bytwene Teignmouth Towne, wher the Ground mountith, and Teignmouth Haven.

*The Ness.*

Ther be too Tounes at this Point of the Haven by Name of Teignemouth, one hard joining to the other. The Souther of them is Teignmouth Regis, wher is a Market[2] and a Chirch of S. Michael,[3] and a peace of an embatelid Waul again[st] the Shore; and this is taken for the Elder Town. And at the West side of this Town is a peace of the sanddy Ground afore spoken of, ther caullid the Dene, wheron hath

*Teignmouth.*
*East*
*Teignmouth.*

*The Den.*

---

[1] "At the time of making the Domesday Survey, the manor was held by Stephen de Haccombe under Baldwin the Sheriff. The heiress of Haccombe brought it to Sir John L'Ercedekne, or Archdeacon, whose son, Sir Warren, had two daughters co-heirs. The elder brought this estate to Sir Hugh Courtenay, and it passed with the elder of his daughters and co-heirs to Nicholas, Lord Carew." (Lysons, *Devon*, 250.)

[2] On Saturday, granted to the Dean and Chapter of Exeter, in 1253. (Lysons, *Devon*, 487.)

[3] "The church was originally a chapel to Dawlish: it is now esteemed a daughter-church; the perpetual curacy being in the gift of the vicar of that parish." (Lysons, *Devon*, 488.)

bene not many yeres syns diverse Howses and Wine Cellers. The Inhabitantes ther telle how their Toun hath bene defacid by the Danes, and of late Tyme by the Frenchmen.[1]  The other Toun, caullid Teignemouth Episcopi, standith a lytle by North on the same shore upper into the Haven.  Ther is a Chirch S. Jacobi.[2]

Teigne ebbith and flowith up a five Miles, not to, but as far as, Newton Busshelle.  First I markid a litle start above the Haven Mouth, on the West side of it, a Creeke caullid Stoken Teigne Hed, no great thing; ther is another Creeke called Come Teignehed, about half a Mile upper into the Haven.  The Hedde of Teigne-Mouth is a 20. Miles from Teignemouth that risith in Darte-More at a Place caullid Teigne Hed; Jagforde Bridge is half a Mile above the Towne, having a Market and 2. Faires, [and] is a 4. or 5. Miles from the Hed; Clifford Bridg of Stone [is] a 4. Miles lower; Brideford Bridg of Stone 4. Miles and more lower; Chiddeley Bridg of Stone a 5. Miles lower; Teigne Bridge a 3. Miles lower, in the Midle way betwixt Newton Busshel Market Toun and Kings Steinton.  Leman Water cummith a Mile byneth Newton into Teigne, [and] Aller Water goith into Teine almost at the same Place and Ripe wher Leman dothe.

From Teignemouth to Exmouth [is] about a 4. Miles, [and] from Exmouth to Exchester a vij. miles.

There lyith a great vaste plaine and baren Sandy feld at the West side and very point of Exmouth Haven; and a litle above this Sand goith in a Creke a Mile or therabout into the Land—sum caulle it Kenton Creke.  A 2. Miles upper in the Haven from this Creke is Kenton, a very pety thoroughfare; and a right goodly Chirch in it.  This Tounlet is within a very litle of the main Streme of the

*Margin notes:*
West Teignmouth.
Newton Bushell.
Stokein-teignhead.
Combein-teignhead.
Teign Head.
Chagford.
Clifford Br.
Bridford Br.
Chudleigh Br.
Teign Br.
Newton Bushell.
Kingsteignton.
Lemon R.
Aller R.
Kenton.

---

[1] " Both Camden and Risdon say that the Danes first landed in England at West Teignmouth in 787; but it appears to have been mistaken for Tynemouth, in Northumberland.  Teignmouth was burned by a French pirate in 1340." (Lysons, *Devon*, 489.)

[2] St. James the Less.  The present parish-church was erected, on the site of the old one, "under the powers of an act, passed in 1815, for enlarging and repairing the churches of East and West Teignmouth.  West Teignmouth is a daughter-church to Bishop's Teignton; and the minister, as perpetual curate, is appointed by the vicar of that parish.  Previously to 1816 the two adjoining parishes had been from time immemorial served by the same curate, who was appointed alternately by the vicars of Dawlish and Bishop's Teignton." (Lysons, *Devon*, 490-1.)

Haven.  Kenton Personage [is] impropriate to Saresbyri
Chirch.[1]

Powderham, late Sir William Courteneis Castelle, stondith
on the Haven shore, a litle above Kenton.  Sum say that *Sir William*
a Lady, being a Widow, buildid this Castelle; I think that *Courtenay.*
it was Isabella de Fortibus.[2]  It is strong, and hath a *Isabella*
Barbican or Bulwark to bete the Haven. *de Fortibus.*

Passing from Kenton I cam to  . . .  Village, a 2.
Miles of, seing a praty Lake on the lift Hond, and an Issue
out of it.  Thens to Exminstre, a praty Townlet, wher be
Ruines of a Maner Place embatelid in the Front; I trow *Marquis*
it longid to the Marquise of Excester. *of Exeter.*

On the Est side of Exmouth Haven [is] Exmouth, a
Fisschar Tounlet, a litle withyn the Haven Mouth.  Apsham,
a praty Tounlet on the Shore, [is] a 4. Miles upper in the
Haven; heere is the great Trade and Rode for Shippes that
usith this Haven, and especially for the Shippes and Marchant Menne's Goodes of Excester.  Men of Excester
contende to make the Haven to cum up to Excester self, [but]
at this Tyme Shippes cum not farther up but to Apsham.

The Town of Excester is a good Mile and more in
Cumpace, and is right strongly waullid and mainteinid.
Ther be diverse fair Towers in the Toun Waul bytwixt the
South and the West Gate; as the Waulles have be[en]
newly made, so have the old Towers decayed.  The Castelle
of Excester standith stately on a high Ground bytwixt the
Est Gate and the North.  Ther be 4. Gates in the Toune
by the names of Est, West, North, and South: the Est and
the West Gates be now the fairest and of one fascion of
Building, [but] the South Gate hath beene the strongest.

There be diverse fair Streates in Excester, but the High
Streate, that goith from the West to the Est Gate, is the
fairest; in this Streate be *castella, aquæductus, & domus civica.*

There be xv. Paroche Chirchis in the Towne.
The Cathedrale Chirch of S. Peter and Paule, the

---

[1] According to Lysons, "the rectory, manor, and great tithes
belong to the dean and chapter of *Windsor*, who are patrons of the
vicarage" (*Devon*, 300); but this must be a mistake for *Salisbury*,
to which Kenton has been a Prebend at least from the reign of
Henry II. (Oliver, *Ecclesiastical Antiquities*, i., 17.)
[2] Isabella de Fortibus, Countess of Albemarle and Devon, was
born 1236, and died 1293.  A full account of her is given by Mrs.
Rose-Troup in *Trans. Devon. Assoc.*, xxxvii., 206-45.

Cimiterie wherof, having 4. Gates, is environid with many fair Houses.

*John Ryse.*

The College House, wher the Cantuarie Prestes lyith, made of late tyme by John Rese, Dean of St. Burianes.

The Vicar's College.

The Carnarie Chapelle in the Cemitery, made by one John, Tresurer of the Cathedrale Chirch of Excester.

A Paroch Chirch in the Cimiterie.

There was a Priorie of S. Nicolas, a Celle to Bataille-Abbey, in the North side of the Toune.[1]

*John de Grandison.*

Joannes de Grandisono, Bisshop of Excester, made an Hospitale of S. John, and endowid it with Landes; this Hospital is hard by the Est Gate.[2]

There is another poore Hospitale in the Toun, wherin yet sik Men be kepte.

There was an House of Gray Freres bytwixt the North and West Gate neere the Towne Waulle, now a plain vacant Ground caullid Ferenhay.

*Friernhay.*

*Thomas Bytton.*

Bytten, Bisshop of Excester, remevid thens the Gray Freres, and buildid them an House a litle without the South Gate.[3]

---

[1] " It was formed out of some of the possessions given by William the Conqueror to his noble [Benedictine] Abbey of St. Martin, of Battle, in Sussex. Gunterus, a monk of Battle, appears to have been deputed simply to make arrangements for the infant institution, and, after a short residence here, was appointed Abbot of Thorney. Cono supplied his place as the first prior. Under the auspices of William Rufus, he was enabled to erect the conventual church of St. Nicholas as a cell to Battle Abbey." (Oliver, *Monasticon Exon.*, 113.)

[2] The hospital of SS. John the Baptist and John the Evangelist was founded about 1220, in the episcopacy of William Briwere, by two wealthy brothers, Gilbert and John Long, and with it was incorporated the hospital of St. Alexius, which had been founded in 1170, behind the priory of St. Nicholas, by William Prodom. The patronage was exchanged by the mayor and citizens, in 1244, for the Lepers hospital beyond the south gate. It was greatly befriended by the bishops of Exeter, and especially by Bishop Grandison, who converted it into an Augustine priory. (Oliver, *Monasticon Exon.*, 300-1.)

[3] The convent of Franciscans, or Grey Friars, was established before 1240. It was originally situated in an area behind St. Nicholas Priory, and between the north and west gates, and, in 1287, Edmund, Earl of Cornwall, granted the community a vacant spot of ground, afterwards called Friernhay, and later Bartholomew-yard. In 1291, under the patronage of Bishop Bytton, the friars removed to their new monastery beyond the south gate. The original conventual Church of Our Lady and St. Francis was standing nearly two centuries after the removal of the second. (Oliver, *Monasticon Exon.*, 330-1.)

There was an House of Blak Freres in the North side
of the Cemiterie of the Cathedrale Chirch, but withoute the
Close.[1] The Lord Russelle hath made hym a fair Place
of this House.[2]

*Lord Russell.*
Bedford
House.

There appere 2. fragmentes of Inscriptions of the
Romaines sette by chaunce of later tymes in the Town
Waulle renewid on the bak side of this House sumtyme
longging to the Blak Freres; one of them standith in a Tower
of the Waul, the other is in the Wall hard by the Towrre.

The Suburbe that lyith without the Est Gate of Excester
is the biggest of al the Suburbes of the Towne, and berith
the Name of S. Sithewelle,[3] where she was buried, and a
Chirch dedicate ther to her Name. The Suburbe without
the North Gate is caullid S. David downe, *alias* . . .
The Suburbe without the West Gate is caullid S. Thomas
Suburbe; in this Suburbe is a greate Stone Bridge of 14.
Arches ouer Ex River. The Suburbe without the South
Gate is caullid by the Name of S. Magdalene.

*Suburbs.*

St. Sidwell.

St. David's.
St. Thomas.

St. Leonard.

The Cathedrale Chirch of Excester remaynid after the
Tyme of Leofricus, the first Bisshop of Exeter, after one
Rate to the Tyme of Peter the first,[4] that began the
Cathedrale Chirch, now standing in Excester, and levied a
Subsidie of the Clargie of his Diecese to the setting forward
of it.

Cathedral.
*Leofric.*
*Peter Quivil.*

[1] The convent of Dominican or Black Friars was probably
founded by Bishop William Briwere, who died 1244. In 1259 Bishop
Bronescombe dedicated their conventual church, which became the
burying-place of several illustrious families. In 1831-2 Bedford Chapel
was erected nearly on its site. (Oliver, *Monasticon Exon.*, 334-6.)

[2] The dissolution of the house took place in 1538, and in the
following year the site, church, belfry, and cemetery, were granted
to John, first Lord Russell, son of James Russell, esq., by his wife
Alice (Wyse) of Sidenham, Devon. The site is now occupied by
Bedford Circus. (Oliver, *Monasticon Exon.*, 335-6.)

[3] Really Sativola, "Sithewelle" or Sidwell being merely a popular
nickname, because in all her representations she has for her emblems
a scythe and a well. She was the daughter of a Romanized Briton
of high dignity, named Perpius Aurelianus, after whose death his
widow, Sativola's step-mother, engaged one of her servants to
dispatch the maiden while she was intent on her devotions near a
well in what was afterwards called Sidwell's Mead. This occurred
about 510. (Chanter, *Devonian Year Book*, 1915, 96-7.)

[4] There was an intermediate Norman building, begun by William
Warelwast (1107-1136) and finished by Henry Marshall (1194-1206).
The towers still remain. Peter Quivil (1280-1291) designed the present
Decorated cathedral.

*John de*
*Grandison.*

Joannes de Grandisono, Bisshop of Excester, enlargid the West Part of the Chirch, making vij. Archis wher afore the Plot was made but of v. ; [and he] voltid the Body of the Chirch. This Joannes Grandisonus convertid the Landes

Ottery
St. Mary.

and Frutes of S. Marie Otery to a Collegiate Chirch ; sum think that ther was a Celle of French Monkes at Oterey, or an House of Religion yn France with Landes there, the wich Celle or Landes Graunson convertid to the use of the College now beyng in Otery.[1] [He] chaungid an hold Foundation of an Hospital of S. John's in Excester and melioratid it, putting crossid Brethern in it;[2] [and he] turnid an old Almose House of xij. poore Menne, and as many Women, to whom nomination was given *fratres Calendarum*, to the use of the Logging of the Vicares Chorales in the Cathedrale Chirch of Excester.[3] [He also] collectid the Legendes as they be now redde in Divine Services in the Diocese of Excester.

*Thomas*
*Brantyngham.*

Brentingham, Bisshop of Excester, finished this College [of Ottery St. Mary] in Building.

*Hugh Oldham.*

Hugh Oldham, Bisshop of Excester, gave and procurid a litle Celle of Freres Ordinis S. Trinitatis at Totenes.[4]

*Walter de*
*Stapeldon.*

Bisshop Stapleton of Excester voltid the Presbyterie.[5] [He] made also the Riche Fronte of Stone Worke at the High Altare, and the Riche Silver Table in the Midle of

*Edmund Lacey.*

it ;[6] yet sum say that Bisshop Lacye made this Sylver Table, but ther is no lykelyhod yn it.

---

[1] The manor of Ottery had been given by Edward the Confessor, in 1061, to the Dean and Chapter of St. Mary at Rouen, and Bishop Grandison purchased the manor and advowson from them in 1335. The parish church, which had been dedicated in 1260, was erected by the bishop into a collegiate church, for forty members, in 1337. (Oliver, *Monasticon Exon.*, 259-60.)

[2] See p. 70.

[3] See a paper on "The Kalendars and the Exeter Trade-Gilds before the Reformation," by Mrs. Rose-Troup, in *Trans. Devon. Assoc.*, xliv., 406-30.

[4] See p. 62.

[5] This is incorrect. The Fabric Roll assigns the *painting* of the choir vaulting to his first year, demonstrating that all but the painting was done in the time of his predecessor, Bishop Bitton (1292-1307). (Freeman, *Arch. History of Exeter Cath.*, 28.)

[6] Stapeldon's altar is commonly regarded as having been of silver; but this would not include the slab or *mensa*, for which the employment of stone was *de rigeur*. Such a phrase as '*tabula argentea*' would apply strictly to the front of the rectangular structure upon which the *mensa* was borne. (Freeman, *Arch. History of Exeter Cath.*, 98.)

Bisshop Neville, as I hard say, made the Chapitre House as it is now at Excester; syns I hard that Edmund Lacy began the Chapitre House, and Neville performid it.[1]

*George Neville*

## SEPULCHRA ECCL. EXON.

*In sacello S. Mariæ coram Altari sub plano marmore jacet Petrus Quivil:—*

Petra tegit Petrum, nihil officiat tibi tetrum.[2]

*Peter Quivil.*

*In boreali parte ejusdem Sacel. sub arcu:—*

Hic jacet Edmundus de Stafforde intumulatus,
Quondam profundus legum doctor reputatus.
Verbis facundus, comitum de stirpe creatus:
Felix & mundus pater hujus pontificatus.

*Edmund Stafford.*

*In Australi parte ejusdem sub arcu:—*

Gualterus Brounescombe Ep'us Exon.
Fundator collegii de Glasney apud Penrine.
Olim sincerus pater omni dignus amore
Primus Walterus magno jacet hîc in honore.
Edidit hic plura dignissima laude statuta,
Quæ tanquam jura servant hîc omnia tuta.
Atque hoc collegium quod Glaseney plebs vocat omnis,
Condidit egregium, pro voce data sibi somnis.
Quot loca construxit, pietatis quot bona fecit,
Quam sanctam duxit vitam, vox dicere quæ scit?
Laudibus immensis jubilet gens Exoniensis,
Et chorus & turbæ, quia natus in hac fuit urbe.
Plus si scire velis, festum statuit Gabrielis.
Gaudeat in cœlis igitur pater iste fidelis.[8]

*Walter Bronescombe.*

*In Presbyterio coram supremo altari:—*
Tho. Bytten Ep'us Exon.

*Thomas Bytton.*

---

[1] Bishop Lacy raised the Chapter House, Neville inserted the east window, and Bothe (1465-1478) erected the roof. (Freeman, *Arch. History of Exeter Cath.*, x., 89.)

[2] This gravestone was removed into the nave, probably in 1657, but was restored to its original position in 1820. (Britton, *Exeter Cath.*, 134.)

[3] Although Bishop Bronescombe erected St. Gabriel's Chapel as a place for his interment, this monument is apparently of a much later date. The fact that the inscription describes him as the *first* Walter who held this See, shows that it could not have been made until after the accession of a *second* Walter, viz. Stapeldon, in 1308. (Britton, *Exeter Cath.*, 133.)

William
Bruere.

Bruer Ep'us Exon fundator 4. dignit. Eccl. Exon.

This Inscription is given in a flatte Marble stone, under which Guliam Bruer, Bisshop of Exeter, is buried: "Hic jacet Gul. Bruer, Ep'us Exon. primus fundator quatuor dignitatum hujus Ecclesiæ."[1] The Graunt of King Edward the Confessor was that the Landes of viij. Monkes that were yn his Tyme yn the Abbay of Excester should be distributid emong 20 Prebendaries.

*In Australi parte Presbyterii:—*

James
Berkeley.

In Berkley natus jacet hic Jacobus tumulatus.

*In Boreali parte Presbyterii:—*

Walter de
Stapeldon.
Edmund Lacey.
Henry
Marshall.

Stapletun Ep'us Exon.
Lacey: whos tumbe Heines Dene of Excester defacid.[2]
Henricus Mareschal Ep'us Exon.

*In Australi Insula chori:—*

Hugh Oldham.
Sir Arthur
Chichester.

Oldham Ep'us Exon.
Chichester miles.

*In boreali Insula chori:—*

Sir John Speke.
Sir Richard
Stapeldon.

Speke in quodam Sacello.[3]
Stapletun Miles è regione sepulchri Stapletun Ep'i Exon.
    fratris ejus.[4]

*In Transepto Ecclesiæ ad Austrum:—*

John the
Chanter.

Joannes Ep'us Exon.

---

[1] He founded the office of Dean in 1225, appropriating to the deanery the churches of Braunton and Tawton, with their dependent chapels, Swimbridge and Landkey; and, in an extended sense of the term, he may be styled the founder of the offices of Precentor, Chancellor, and Treasurer, by the ample endowments which he annexed to them. (Britton, *Exeter Cath.*, 26-7.)

[2] "Under a flat arch, now forming part of the northern screen of the choir, is the tomb of Bishop Edmund Lacy, whose figure, in brass, was inlaid on the slab, as the indent yet shews." It was defaced by Simon Heynes, who became Dean in 1537, the reason attributed being that it had been a great resort of pilgrims. (Britton, *Exeter Cath.*, 137.)

[3] "At the east end of the north aile is the monumental chapel of Sir John Speke, Knt., which was founded in 1518. In the Parliamentary times a thoroughfare, which is still used, was made through this chapel, by which means much of the original work has been destroyed." (Britton, *Exeter Cath.*, 138.)

[4] "In the north aile, nearly opposite to the Bishop's monument, is that assigned to his brother, Sir Richard Stapeldon, Kt. This is a very singular memorial, but the attendant figures are so much broken as to be almost unintelligible." (Britton, *Exeter Cath.*, 135.)

*In Navi Ecclesiæ* :—

Hugo Courteney Comes Devoniæ & Margareta ejus uxor, filia & Heres [Humfredi de Bohun, Co. Hereford.] [1]

Brentingham Ep'us Exon. in boreali Navis Ecclesiæ è regione tumuli Hugonis Courteney Comitis Devoniæ. [2]

Joannes de Grandison extra portam occidentalem Navis Eccl. in Sacello. [3]

[The] Bridges on Ex [are]: Excester Bridge of xiiij. Archis; Cowley, a Mile and more upward, having a xij. Archis undre the Gut and Causey; Thorberton, about a 4. Miles upper; Tuverton Bridge, about a v. Miles upper. There brekith out a litle above [Cowley] Bridge an Arme out of Ex Ryver, and, after dryving certein Milles, returnith into Ex above Excester. From Cowley Bridge to Syriok Newton Bridg of 4. Archis over Cride Ryver [is] a 2. Miles *dim.*, and half a Mile farther is the Village or Tounlet of Syriak Newton. From Newton to Crideton [is] 2. Miles. The Ground betwixt Excester and Crideton [bears] exceding fair Corn, Gresse, and Wood.

Ther is a praty Market in Kirton. The Toun usith Clothing, and most therby lyvith. [4] The Place wher the old Cathedrale Chirch of Crideton stoode is now occupied with buildinges of Houses by the New Chirch Yarde side. The olde Chirch was dedicate to S. Gregory. The Chirch ther

*Hugh Courtenay.*

*Thomas Brantyngham.*

*John de Grandison.*

Exeter Br.
Cowley Br.
Thorverton Br.
Tiverton Br.

Creedy R.

Newton
St. Cyres.
Crediton.

---

[1] "In the nave, between the second and third columns from the transept, is the altar tomb of Hugh Courtenay, second Earl of Devon, and his Countess Margaret, daughter of Humphrey Bohun, Earl of Hereford and Essex, by Elizabeth, daughter of King Edward the First: the former died in 1377, and the latter in 1391." (Britton, *Exeter Cath.*, 136.)

[2] "On the opposite side of the nave was the monumental chapel of Bishop Brantyngham, which has been long ago destroyed." (Britton, *Exeter Cath.*, 136.)

[3] "He was interred within the small chapel of St. Radegundes, on the south side of the great western entrance; but his grave was profanely violated in the latter years of Queen Elizabeth, and his ashes 'scattered abroade, and the bones bestowed no man knoweth where.'" (Britton, *Exeter Cath.*, 38.)

[4] "Their market for kersies hath been very great, especially of the finer sort; (and before perpetuanos were wrought); for the aptness and diligent industry of the inhabitants (for making such cloth) did purchase it a supereminent name above all other towns, whereby grew this common proverb—as fine as Kirton spinning; (for we briefly call it Kirton)." (Westcote, *View of Devon*, 121.)

now stonding hath no maner or token of Antiquite.[1]    One Sir John Scylley, a Knight, and his Wife, sumtyme dwelling in that Paroche, be buried in the North Part of the Transept of this.[2]    The Bishop of Excester hath a Maner Place or Palace by the Chirch Yarde, and to this Maner Place there longith a Parke.[3]    Ther is a Deane, and he is as the Curate, but he is no Prebendarie of Course.[4]    Ther be xij. Good Prebendes in Kirton, besides certen Bursaries, Ministers and Choristes.[5]

[1] In 1511 Bishop Oldham reported the disastrous state of the fabric, and his successor, Bishop Veysey, in 1523 called upon the members of the college to contribute to its substantial repair. Probably their efficient exertions to restore it led Leland to make this statement, for, far from showing no token of antiquity, the building contains vestiges of various periods of architecture, including the Norman, which is clearly indicated in the central tower. Notwithstanding the extensive changes it underwent in the fifteenth century, the work may still be described as a church of Perpendicular character, founded on a basis of Norman and early English date. (Oliver, *Monasticon Exon.*, 77.)

[2] "A fair monument, supposed to be erected to this baron of Torrington, and owner of Rookford in Crediton parish, has lately [in 1846] been removed from the north transept to the extremity of the south aisle of the choir; but we doubt if it be as ancient, though in Scipio Squier's time [1607] the Sully arms ' were painted all over him '; it has certainly no insignia of the garter. A cenotaph to his memory may yet be seen in Ideslegh church." He died in 1387, at the age of 105, and had been engaged in the profession of arms during a period of 80 years, having been in the fight of Halidon Hill, at the siege of Berwick, at the battles of Cressy, Najara in Biscay, and Poictiers, and afterwards having fought in Spain. (Oliver, *Monasticon Exon.*, 76.)    Westcote (*View of Devon*, 124) refers to this monument to the worthy knight and his lady, but Lysons, in 1822, said there were then no traces of it. (*Devon*, 147.)

[3] "The manor and hundred of Crediton continued to belong to the bishops, and the palace probably to be their occasional residence, till the reign of Henry VIII., when Bishop Veysey surrendered them to the Crown.    In the same reign [1542] the Bishop, but with great reluctance, conveyed the park to Sir Thomas Dennis." (Lysons, *Devon*, 145; Oliver, *Monasticon Exon*, 77.)

[4] Leland is here incorrect, for the dean was a prebendary, as well as the vicar of the parishioners, but, owing to the laborious duty of attending to the spiritual concerns of such an extensive parish, he was for the most part exempted from assisting in the choir. (Oliver, *Monasticon Exon.*, 76.)

[5] The collegiate church of the Holy Cross was regarded as the first in rank among those in the diocese.    It consisted originally of eighteen canons or prebendaries, and eighteen vicars, which number having been reduced, was restored by Bishop Bronescombe in the thirteenth century.    Bishop Grandison appointed four choristers and four singing men, or lay vicars; three of the prebendaries, being

From Excester to Clist Bridg [is] a 3. Miles; under this Stone Bridge archid rennith a pratie Broke, caullid Clist, [and] this Broke goyng about half a Mile lower rennith by Clist, the Bisshop of Excester's goodly Manor Place.[6]   A 5. Miles farther I passid by a forde over a Riveret caullid Tale, that a Mile *dim.* lower above S. Mari Oterey Toun goith into Oterey Water.   Ther is a Bridge of Stone by the Ford of Tale, from [which] I rode about 2. Miles farther to Veniton Bridge, where Oterey Water is devided into 4. Armes by Pollicy to serve Grist and Tukking Milles. Apon 3. of these Streames I roode by fair Stone Bridges, [but] the First Arme of the 4. was the leste, and had no Bridge that I markid.   On the North side of the first Bridge was a Chapelle, now prophanid.

From Veniton Bridges to Honiton [is] a 2. Miles on the Est Ripe of Oter River.   Honiton is a fair long thorough Fare and Market Toun, longging to Courteney of Powdreham, beyng just xij. Miles from Excester by Est in the High Way to London.   A litle beyond Honiton I left London Way on the right Hond and rode North Est 3. Miles to Mohun's Oterey, sumtyme caullid Oterey Fleming.

Syr George Carew[7] hath a good Maner and Parke at Mohun's Otery.   [He] told me that this Lande was not the Landes of Mohun of . . . but of another Mohun, of whos Name ther were Barons.   He said that Mohun of Somersetshire, the Erle, bare in Gold a Crosse ingraile

*Clyst Honiton.*
*Clyst R.*

*Bishop's Court.*

*Tale R.*

*Taleford.*
*Fenny Bridges.*

*Honiton.*

*Courtenay.*

*Mohun's Ottery.*
*Sir George Carew.*
*Mohun.*

---

the principal dignitaries of the church, bore the titles of Precentor, Treasurer, and Dean.   The prebendaries restored by Bishop Bronescombe had no corps, but derived their income from other sources, and this is probably what Leland meant by referring to "twelve *good* prebends," i.e. prebends belonging to the foundation and separately named.   (Lysons, *Devon*, 148; Oliver, *Monasticon Exon.*, 75-6.)

6 The manor of Bishop's Clist was mortgaged to Bishop Bronescombe by Sir Ralph Sachville, when he went to France on the King's service.   The Bishop built a mansion on the manor, and laid out so much money upon it, that Sir Ralph could not repay it, so that in consequence the manor became attached to the See, and the mansion one of the episcopal palaces.   (Lysons, *Devon*, 236; Risdon, *Survey of Devon*, 62; Westcote, *View of Devon*, 196-8.)

7 Sir George Carew, eldest son of Sir William Carew and Jone, daughter of Sir William Courtenay of Powderham, was drowned in the *Mary Rose*, 1545.   The second son, Sir Philip, Knight of Malta, had been slain by the Turks before this date; and the third son, Sir Peter, died in Ireland, 1575.   And so this branch of the family became extinct.   (Vivian, *Visitations of Devon*.)

Sabelles, and that Mohun of Devonshir gave the Arme
with the pouderid Maunch.[1]  Much of the Land that this

*Fleming.*

Mohun had cam by an Heir General of one Fleming, that
was Lord of Stoke Fleminges Lordship and the Castelle at
Dertmouth.  Alanus Fleming was a notable Man on that
Stoke [stock].  Carew maried an Heir General of the
Stoke of Mohun of Devonshir.[2]  Carew['s] trew Name [is]

*Sir Nicholas
Carew.*

Montgomerik, and he is written thus in old Evidence:
Montgomerik Dns de Carew.[3]  Syr Nicolas Carew cam
out of this Stok.[4]  The very Auncient Armes of the Carews
be 3. Lions Sabelle in Gold.

Otter R.
Otterford.
Upottery.

Oterey risith flat North a 5. Miles above Mohun's Otery
at a Place caullid Oterford; thens it rennith a 4. Miles to
a Village caullid Upoter; thens a Mile to Mohun's Oterey.
Oterey goith from Mohun's Oterey to Honiton a 2. Miles;

[1] Both coats seem to have been borne by the same family at
different dates.  The earliest form was, " *Gules, a maunch Ermine* ";
but after Sir Reginald Mohun, the founder of Newenham Abbey,
had received a consecrated rose or flower of gold from Pope
Innocent IV., he assumed these bearings: " *Gules, a maunch Ermine,
the hand Argent, holding a fleur-de-lys Or.*"  These arms may be seen
in the spandril of the gateway arch of the dismantled seat of the
Carews at Mohun's Ottery, the arms of Carew occupying the other
spandril.  The later arms of Mohun, " *Or, a cross engrailed Sable,*"
was first adopted by Sir John de Mohun, great grandson of Sir
Reginald, and these arms were also used by the Abbots of that
monastery on their conventual seal as the arms of Mohun.  (Rogers,
"Sepulchral Effigies of North Devon " in *Trans. Exeter Dioc. Arch.
Soc.*, iii., second series, 258-64.)

[2] The last of the Flemings of Stoke Fleming " gave his lands to
the lord Reginald Mohun, in King Henry the third's reign, which
Reginald bestowed it on his younger son William, who had two
daughters, the one married to Sir John Carew, lord of Carew, in
Pembrokeshire;  the other to Meriot, who died without issue.
Eleanor had issue Sir Nicholas Carew, who died issueless, but before
his death conveyed his lands unto his brother John, whom his father
had by the daughter of Talbot; in memory whereof the house of
Carew hath ever borne the Mohun's arms, quarterly.  Albeit, they
are not descended from them, yet had they a large inheritance by
reason of that marriage." (Risdon, *Survey of Devon*, 170.)

[3] The earliest Carew, "Odo Carrio," to whom King Richard I.
gave Branton, Devon, was the son of William Fitzgerald and Maria
de Montgomery, daughter of Stephen, Constable of Cardigan,
ancestor of Montgomery of Ireland.  (Vivian, *Visitations of Devon.*)

[4] Sir Nicholas Carew, Baron Carew of Mullesford, married
Margaret, one of the four sisters and co-heirs of John, Lord
Dynham.  Both died in 1470, and were buried in the Chapel of
St. Nicholas, Westminster Abbey, "to whose memory an antient
plain tomb of grey marble is there still seen." (Prince, *Worthies of
Devon*, 161.)

thens to Veniton Bridge a 2. Miles: thens to S. Mary
Oterey. Oterey goith from S. Marie to Newton Bridge
about a Mile of; thens to Oter Mouth and the very Se a
v. Miles.

Oterton, a praty fischar Toun, standith on the Est side
of the Haven, about a Mile from Otermouth; and on the
West side of the Haven is Budelegh, right almost again[st]
Oterton, but it is sumwhat more from the shore than Oterton.
Lesse then an Hunderith Yeres sins Shippes usid this Haven,
but it is now clene barrid. Sum caulle this Haven Budeley
Haven, of Budeley Toun. Ther is a Fisshar Village lower
than Oterton, even at the very Est Sout Est¹ point of
Otermouth; this Village is caullid Salterne, and hath beene
in tymes past a thing of sum Estimation; and of this Village
the Haven of Otermouth was caullid Saltern Haven, or pera-
venture of a Crek cumming out of the mayn Haven into it.

From Mohun's Oterey to Colington [is] v. Miles by good
Corne, Pasture, and sum Wood. About a Mile or I cam
to Colington I saw from an Hille Shoute a right goodly
Maner Place, a Mile of on an Hille side, of the Lord
Marquise of Dorsete, and by it a goodly large Parke.²
The Toun self of Colington is no very notable Thing.
The Bisshop of Excester's Chauncelar is Vicar of this
Town and hath a fair House ther.³

Coley River rennith under the Rote of an Hille that this
Town stondith on, and passith by Colecombe Park, hard by
Colington, lately longging to the Marquise of Excester,⁴ and

---

¹ Should apparently be west-south-west.

² Shute, originally Schete, belonged to a family of that name,
and descended through the Pynes to the Bonvilles. William, Lord
Bonville, was beheaded after the battle of St. Albans, "leaving
behind him for heir Cicely, his grandson's daughter, a damsel of
tender years, who brought a large and rich inheritance to Thomas
Gray, Marquess of Dorset, half-brother, by the mother, to King
Edward V. (Westcote, *View of Devon*, 244.) The owner in Leland's
time was Henry Grey, 3rd Marquis of Dorset, father of the unfortunate Lady Jane Grey.

³ The dean and chapter of Exeter are patrons of this vicarage,
and appropriators of the great tithes. The church is in their
peculiar jurisdiction. (Lysons, *Devon*, 133.)

⁴ Colcombe Castle was a seat of the Earls of Devon. Henry
Courtenay's father had been deprived of the honours, but, on his
death in 1511, his son was allowed to succeed to the earldom, and
in 1525 he was created Marquis of Exeter. He was attainted and
beheaded in 1538.

thens going a Mile or more enterith betwixt Axbridge and Axmouth Towne into Ax Ryver.

Seaton.
Colyford.

From Colington to Seton [is] scant 2. Mile. I passid over Cole Water again at Coliford or I cam to Seton. Ther hath beene a very notable Haven at Seton, but now ther lyith betwen the 2. Pointes of the old Haven a mighty Rigge and Barre of pible Stones in the very Mouth of it, and the Ryver of Ax is dryven to the very Est Point of the Haven, caullid Whit Clif, and ther at a very smaul Gut goith into the Se; and her cum in small fisher Boates for socour. The Men of Seton began of late Dayes to stake and to make a mayne Waulle withyn the Haven, to have divertid the Course of Ax Ryver, and ther almost in the Midle of the old Haven, and ther to have trenchid thorough the Chisille, and to have let out Ax and receyvid in the mayn Se, but this Purpose cam not to effect; me thought that Nature most wrought to trench the Chisil, and ther to let in the Se.[1]

Haven Cliff.

The Town of Seton is now but a meane Thing, inhabited with Fischar Men, [but] it hath bene far larger when the Haven was good. The Abbate of Shirburne was Lord and Patrone of it.

*Abbot of Sherbourne.*

Wiscombe.
*Lord Bonville.*
*Marquis of Dorset.*

On the West Part over an Hille byyond Seton is Wiscombe, a fair Maner Place, sumtyme the Lord Bonville's, now longging to the Marquise of Dorsete.[2]

Beer.

Ther longgid [to Seaton] and doth yet a Chapelle of Stone, caullid Berewood, nere the Shore, scant half a Mile distant from the very Toune of Seton, and there is an Hamlet of Fischar Men. Ther was begon a fair Pere for Socour of Shippelettes at this Berewood, but ther cam such a Tempest a 3. Yeres sins as never in mynd of men had

---

[1] According to Risdon: "This place is memorable for the attempt of the inhabitants of *Colliton* to make a haven there, which they had solemnly named Colliton-Haven, and procured a collection under the great seal for the levying of money to effect the same; of which work there remaineth no monument, only the remembrance of such a place among strangers that know not where it stands, and is at this day a poor fishing village." (*Survey of Devon*, 31.)

[2] Anciently held by the family of Dalditch under the Abbey of St. Michael, in Normandy. The abbot of that house conveyed it to Sir Nicholas Bonville. (Lysons, *Devon*, 452.) Risdon says he made this his dwelling, and had here a large park for deer. (*Survey of Devon*, 33.)

before beene sene in that shore, and tare the Pere in Peaces.

I passid from Seton at Ebbe over the Salt Marsches and the Ryver of Ax to Axmouth, an old and bigge Fischar Toune on the Est side of the Haven. The Priory of Sion was Lord Patrone here; and heere I lernid that there is an Abbey in Normandy caullid Mountborow, and this Place shewith by Writinges that Axmouth, Sidmouth, and Oterton were Celles to it.[1]

Axmouth.

Ax risith a Mile Est from Bermistre, a Market Toun in Dorsetshir, and thens rennith South West a 4. Miles to Forde Abbay,[2] stonding in Devonshire on the farther Ripe of it; and hereabout is a limes[3] to Devonshir and Somersetshir.

Axe R.

Ford Abbey.

Ax then rennith to Axminstre, a pratie quik Market Toun a 3. Miles lower *ripa citeriori*; this Toun is in Devonshir. The Personage of Axmister, so I lernid, is impropriate to the Chirch of York.[4] The Chirch of Axmistre is famose by the Sepultures of many Noble Danes slain in King Æthelstane's Time at a Batel on Brunesdoun therby, and

Axminster.

---

[1] At the period of the Conquest Axmouth manor belonged to the Crown. It was subsequently granted to Richard de Redvers, who appropriated it and its church to the Benedictine abbey of St. Mary of Montbourg, in the diocese of Coutances in Normandy, but it is clear that no priory was ever erected on this manor. Otterton manor had been granted by William the Conqueror to the great Benedictine abbey of St. Michael in Periculo Maris, in the diocese of Avranches. In the reign of King John, if not before, it became a distinct priory for four monks; and that king is said to have granted to the abbey the manors of Sidmouth and Budleigh; but his supposed grant was probably a mere confirmation. Leland was, therefore, strangely misinformed when he states that Sidmouth and Otterton were cells to Montburgh Abbey; there was never any cell at all at Sidmouth. All these manors were seized by Henry V. as part of the possessions of foreign monasteries, and annexed to his noble foundation of Sion Abbey, Middlesex. (Oliver, *Monasticon Exon.*, 248, 320.)

[2] This was a Cistercian house, founded in 1137 by Adelicia, daughter of Baldwin, and sister and heiress of Richard de Bryonis, Baron of Okehampton. Richard had established a house in 1133 at Brightly, in Okehampton, but on his death the convent decided to abandon it and were induced by Adelicia to settle at Ford. (Oliver, *Monasticon Exon.*, 338.) Thorncombe parish, in which Ford Abbey is situated, was transferred to Dorset in 1844.

[3] Boundary.

[4] "The parsonage of Axminster, to which is attached the manor of Prestaller, was given by King Edward I. to the church of St. Peter at York." (Lysons, *Devon*, 24.)

by the Sepultures likewise sum Saxon Lordes slain in the same Feld.[1]

Ax thens rennith thorough Axmistre Bridge of Stone about a Quarter of a Mile lower than Axmistre Toun; sumwhat lower then this Bridge enterith Artey (Yartey) Ryver, being sumtyme a Raging Water, into the Ryver. Ther is a Stone Bridge on Artey about half a Mile from the Place wher it enterith into Ax; this Bridge of sum is caullid Kilmington Bridge, [from] a Village not very far it. About half a Mile lower then Axmistre Bridge is Newenham, sumtyme an Abbay of Bernardines, of the Foundation of Mohun, Erle of Somerset.[2]   Ax rennith a Mile *dim.* lower thorough Ax Bridg of 2. Archis of Stone; this Bridg servith not to pass over at High Tides, otherwise it doth. Thens Ax rennith half a Mile lower to Axmouth Town, and a Quarter of a Mile lower undre White Clif into the Ocean Se, ther caullid Ax Bay.

*Yarty R.*

*Kilmington.*

*Newenham Abbey.*

*Axe Br.*

*Seaton Bay.*

---

[1] The Saxon Chronicle says: "937.—In this year King Athelstan, and Edmund his brother, led a force to Brunanburgh, and there fought against Olaf; and Christ aiding, had victory: and they there slew five Kings and seven Jarls." Risdon develops this story as follows: " In King Athelstan's time there landed seven Danish princes in the mouth of the river, and marched up the valley unto a little hill, called Bremeldowne, where they incamped; from whence removing, they were met by King Athelstan's army, with whom were two dukes and the bishop of Sherbourne, when there was a bloody battle fought; which place is known by the name of Kingsfield to this day. There the Danes were driven to fly over the river, where to the number of six thousand were slain. This battle was not without much effusion of blood on the king's side; for there were slain the two dukes with the bishop, who were buried at Axminster. After this great victory, this place then being the king's demesne, he in thankful remembrance to God for the same, erected here a Minster, wherein seven priests should pray for the souls of those that were slain." (Risdon, *Survey of Devon*, 17.) To explain the number "seven," Lysons says: "King Athelstan gave the church of Axminster to seven priests, who were to pray for the souls of seven knights or earls, and many others, slain in battle with the Danes near this town." (*Devon*, 24.) But the seven earls of the Chronicle were, of course, themselves Danes, and could not have been the earls commemorated by Athelstan.

[2] This also was a Cistercian house, founded in 1247 by Reginald Mohun, the lord of Dunster, and his brother William. Reginald was buried here in 1258. "Scarcely one stone is left standing upon another, yet it is not difficult to trace out its site, with that of the chapter-house and cloisters." (Oliver, *Monasticon Exon.*, 357-8.)

# A SHORT SURVEY OF THE WESTERN COUNTIES    By a Lieutenant from Norwich 1635

A Relation of a short Suruey of the Westerne Counties, in which is breifely described the Citties, Corporations, Castles, and some other Remarkables in them. Obseru'd in a seuen Weekes Journey begun at Norwich, & thence into the West, on Thursday, August 4th, 1635, and ending att the same Place. By the same Lieutennant, that, with the Captaine and Ancient of the Military Company in Norwich, Made a Journey into the North the Yeere before. (Lansdowne MSS., No. 213/27.)

Axminster.
Ax Riuer.
Deuonshire.
Ottery Riuer.

City of Exeter.

From hence [Lyme] I made speed to Axminster, crossing there a pretty little Riuer, but before I entred into the Towne I entred a new Shire along to Hunnington ouer another Riuer, & from thence by some Seats of Knights, and Gentlemen w^{th} happy Guides, & faire wayes, from that Market Towne Hunnington, I ended my 5. weekes Trauell at a quiet Inne, the in the high, & cheifest Street there, of this fayre City, & had faire Quarter with my honest Countrywoman, who was the Gouernesse of that Family.

Before I entred this City, I met w^{th} 2 charitable workes in the Kings high way; the one was a fayre Hospitall[1] which was built by            , And the other, an vnusuall place wall'd in, for the burying place of poore Delinquents who vnfortunately spin out the thread of their Liues,

Axminster.
Honiton.

Exeter.

---

[1] Probably Livery Dole almshouses, founded in 1591 by Sir Robert Dennis.

Heavitree.

at that fearefull, spacious, & strong Tree; of w[ch] for the rarity thus much I transcrib'd.

5[to] Marcij 1557. This Place was blessed by the L[d] Bishop, giuen by M[r] John Peter then Mayo[r]. Inclos'd by the honest Matron Joan Tuckfeild, whose Soule Lord pardon.[1]

The Cathedrall St. Peter.

The first thing I view'd after my weary p'ceeding dayes Journey was the Cathedrall Church, the which was built, and finish'd, (some yeeres after the first foundation thereof lay'd), by a Saxon King: At her west entrance, I found a fayre Frontispice, which rep'sented to the eye, a liuely Prospect, viz[t] 3. Rowes of goodly great Statues, artificially cut in Freestone, (much like the Cathedrall at Wells), the highest whereof are the Prophets, Apostles, & Fathers, the other two of the Saxon & Roman Kinges. And on the top aboue them all, is K. Edward the Confessor, & Leofricus the 1. Bishop, receiuing his Congee desleere in an humble Posture on his Knee.

K. Athelstane.
Bishop Hall.
Dr. Peterson, Deane.
Mr. Cholmley, Subdeane.
Dr. Burnell, Church Chancellor.
Dr. Parry, B[ps] Chanc:
Dr. Hutchinson.
Dr. Killet.
Mr. Rob. Hall, Treasurer, Archdeacon of Cornwall.
Archdeacon Cotton.
Archdeacon Wilson.
Canons Resident.
20. Prebends.
4. Vicars.
16. Singing Men.
10. Singing Boyes.

Although the Cathedrall be not exceeding long, yet itt is very wide, fayre, & lofty, & hath standing on either side of her Crosse Isle 2. Towers, in one of them hangs a braue Ring of 8. Bells; In the other but one onely, but it is a goodly one, brother to Tom of Lincolne, sure one of the breed of Osney w[ch] (as they say) weighs aboue 10000. Weight, and is in Compasse 18. Foote.

1 "*Heavytree*, which (after some) took name of the execution of malefactors, where there is a plot of ground inclosed for their interment, and land also appropriated to buy them shrouds, by the relict of Tuckfield, of Exon, merchant, wherein she expressed her godly charity." (Risdon, *Survey of Devon*, 112.) The burying place at Ringswell was blest by Bishop Turbeville. Over the entrance gate, until the inclosure in 1827 was allowed to be desecrated and let for building, was legible the following inscription: "March 18 [?28], 1557. This place was bless'd by Lord James, Bishop, given by Mr. John Peter, then Mayor, inclosed by Mrs. Joan Tuckfield, late the wife of Mr. John Tuckfield, some time Mayor of Exeter." (Oliver, *Ecclesiastical Antiquities*, i., 47.)

For 2. things in her besides that great Bell,
she may compare w^th any of her Sisters in
England ; one is a stately, rich, high Seat
for the Bishop ; and the other is a delicate,
rich, & lofty Organ w^ch has more additions
then any other, as fayre Pipes of an extraordinary length, & of the bignesse of a
man's Thigh, which w^th their Vialls, &
other sweet Instruments, the tunable voyces,
and the rare Organist, togeather, makes a
melodious & heauenly Harmony, able to
rauish the Hearers Eares.[1]

**Monuments.**

The Monuments that are in this Church
are soe rich, and magnificent, as comes
little short of any other I had seene.

First in the South Ile of the Quire is a
faire, rich Monum^t of Alabaster & Marble,
whereon lyeth that good old Bishop Cotton,
in his Pontificall Robes, of pure white
Alabaster.

*William Cotton.*

Beyond the Quire on that side next the
wall, lyes 2. old warrio^rs in Marble ; the
one is Bohun Ea: of Hereford, in his Coat
of Maile, w^th his Sword & Target, in his
crosse legg'd Posture.[2]

*Humphrey de Bohun, Earl of Hereford and Essex.*

The other is one Chichester, an old
knight of y^e Rhodes in his Armo^r Cap a
pee : and in the same crosse-legg'd Posture.[3]

*Sir Arthur Chichester.*

A little further vp on the right hand,
lyes Bishop Adams, in a neat Chapell richly
gilt, w^th a faire & sumptuous Altar, now
much defac'd.

*Hugh Oldham.*

Right ouer on the other side, north

---

[1] This was before the famous organ erected by John Loosemoore.

[2] Humphrey de Bohun, Earl of Hereford and Essex, who was
slain at Burrow Bridge in 1322, and buried at York. This cenotaph
was most probably placed here by his daughter Margaret, wife of
Hugh Courtenay, second Earl of Devon. (Britton, *Exeter Cath.*,
135-6.)

[3] Traditionally said to be Sir Arthur Chichester, brother of Bishop
Robert Chichester (*d.* 1155). The Chichester arms were formerly
visible on the shield. (Britton, *Exeter Cath.*, 130.)

Monuments.

*Sir John Speke.*

*Sir John
Gilbert.*

*Valentine
Cary.*

*Walter
Bronescombe.*

*Sir John
Doderidge.*

*Lady
Doderidge.*

opposite vnto this, is another the like neat
Chappell lieth the Founder thereof, whose
name was Sir John Speake.[1]

On the South of the Lady Chappell lyeth
S^r John Gilbert in his Armo^r· w^th his Lady
by him, their Statues are Freestone.[2]

The Monum^t of the late Bishop Carey
of Alablast^r & Marble; & his Statue of
Alablaster.

Betweene that little Chappell, & the
Lady Chappell, is a neat & lofty Monum^t
w^th curious cutt stone whereon lyeth B^p
Blanscombe in Alablast^r· Hee built Glasney
Colledge in Cornwall: Hee was sent Am-
bassado^r to the Roman Empero^r. The
Empero^rs Armes; K. Edw. the Confessors,
& his owne, are fairely set out, & gilt.

Thereby is y^e E. of Arundells Coat, 300.
yeeres since.

At the vpper end of the Lady Chappell;
The Monument of that Learned, Religious,
wise, and worthy Judge Doddridge, very
rich, stately, & lofty of Alabaster, Marble,
& Touch, artificially cutt to the Life, in his
Judges Roabes.[3]

Neere him is a faire Monum^t for his
Lady, who was the Daughter of S^r [Amias]
Bamfeild.[4]

---

[1] Founded in 1518. (Britton, *Exeter Cath.*, 138.)

[2] Sir John Gilbert, elder brother of Sir Humphrey, *d.* 1596. His
wife was Elizabeth, daughter of Sir Richard Chudleigh of Ashton.

[3] Sir John Doderidge *d.* 1628.

[4] She was Dorothy, daughter of Sir Amias Bampfylde of Poltimore; *d.* 1614. These two monuments, which were constructed in
the cumbrous style of James the First's reign, were taken down
during the alterations to the Lady Chapel in 1822, and their respective
figures, with the pedestals, and some parts of the inscriptions, placed
under the recessed arches on the north side of the chapel. (Britton,
*Exeter Cath.*, 140.)

Monuments.

Adioyning vnto these lyes 2. old Abbots in Marble.[1]

By them is the Lady Smiths Hearse.[2]

Ouer ag^t B^p Blanscombe, is another faire, & neat Monum^t correspondent to that, in which lyeth B^p Stafford in Ala- *Edmund* baster; Hee was of y^e noble Family of the *Stafford.* Staffords, Dukes of Buckingham, and L^d Chancello^r.[3] Hee built y^e Castle at Plimouth.

In the wall thereby is M^rs Barrett's *Mrs. Eliz.* little neat Monument.[4] *Barrett.*

In the little Chappell, north of the Lady Chappell, is a faire Monum^t for S^r Gawin *Sir Gawen* Carey, & his Lady. *Carew.*

And by him vnder that Monum^t in Alabast^r lyeth, S^r Peter Carew in his *Sir Peter* Armo^r, elder Brother of the L^d Carew, *Carew.* Baron of Clopton; Hee was slaine by an Irish Knight.[5]

---

[1] Presumably the monuments of Bishops Bartholomew (*d.* 1184) and Simon de Apulia (*d.* 1223). They were apparently both removed from the north wall, and placed under the second arch in the south wall in 1822. The former is said to bear much similarity to the effigy of Abbot Laurentius, in the cloisters of Westminster Abbey. (Britton, *Exeter Cath.*, 131-3.)

[2] Presumably the first wife of Sir George Smith of Matford, and maternal grandmother of the famous George Monk, Duke of Albemarle.

[3] He was brother to Ralph, Earl of Stafford, and a kinsman of Richard II.

[4] On the east wall of this chapel is fixed a very clumsy monument of freestone, with the inscription: "To the memory of Mrs. Elizabeth Barrett, the wife of John Barrett, Gent., whose body is interred at the East end of Lady Chappell neere the high altar under a marbell stone." (Jenkins, *History of Exeter*, 306.)

[5] Against the north wall of St. Magdalene's Chapel is a large monument of Queen Elizabeth's time, which, in a recess of the basement division, contains the effigy of Sir Peter Carew, Knt., who was slain in Flanders; and in the upper part, under a canopy supported by piers and Corinthian columns, the effigies of Sir Gawen Carew and his Lady. (Britton, *Exeter Cath.*, 139.) Sir Peter was the eldest son of George Carew, Dean of Exeter and Archdeacon of Totnes, and died in 1581; his younger brother, Sir George, was made Lord Carew of Clopton in the third year of James I., and Earl of Totnes in the first year of Charles I. Sir Gawen was Sir Peter's uncle, and died in 1585, and "his lady" is presumably his third wife, Elizabeth, daughter of Sir John Norwiche. (Vivian, *Visitations of Devon.*)

*Monuments.*

*Walter de Stapeldon.*

*Sir Richard de Stapeldon.*

*Sir Peter Carew.*

*Edmund Lacey.*

*Henry Marshall.*

*William Parkhouse.*

*Hugh Courtenay.*

*Leofric.*

In the North Ile ag[t] the High Altar lieth in Alabaster, B[p] Stapleton, L[d] Treasurer to Ed: y[e] 2[d]. the custody of London was committed to him, in the King's Absence; Hee was there slaine by y[e] Mayo[r] & Citizens, and where Essex house now is, was obscurely bury'd, from whence hee was taken vp, and here interr'd.

Ouer ag[t] him lyeth his valiant Brother in his Armour, who in reuenge of his brothers death, killed the Mayo[r] in the Street, & being well mounted fled, but was stopt by a Cripple at the Gate, whereupon it had the name, & taken, and put to Death; His Horse halfe out of the Gate, and the Cripple holding fast his Bridle, are both artificially cut in Freestone.

On the wall is a neat Statue of S[r] Peter Carew, eldest son of Baron Carew of Clopton, kneeling.[1]

Also the Monum[ts] of Bishop Lacy, Bishop Marshall, and y[e] Anotomy of one Parkehouse, a Cannon.[2]

In the Church is a faire, & ancient Monum[t], whereon lyeth an Earle of Deuonshire, who was one of the Primier K[ts] of the Garter in Ed: y[e] 3[ds] time, in his Martiall weeds: and his Countesse by him who was of y[e] noble Family of Bohun.[3]

To end w[th] the Monum[ts], though it be the last, and plainest, yet must it not be omitted; Leofricus the first Bishop of the

---

[1] "Another memorial of the Carew family, formerly in the north aile of the choir, is now in the south tower: this is a mural cenotaph for Sir Peter Carew, Knt., who died in November, 1575, and lies buried at Waterford." (Britton, *Exeter Cath.*, 139.) He was a cousin of Lord Carew of Clopton, whose only son, also called Peter, died young, during his father's life. (Vivian, *Visitations of Devon.*)

[2] There was formerly in St. Andrew's Chapel an inscription that "*Willi Pkehous, philosophi ac medici*," a canon residentiary of this Church, was buried here in 1540. (Britton, *Exeter Cath.*, 139.)

[3] See note 1 on p. 75.

Church, who lyeth in a plaine Monum^t of Marble w^thout any Statue, at the South Doore, entring the Ile against the Quire, A° 1073.[1]

Aloft the Quire, right ag^t the South side of the High Altar, is a remarkable Place, w^ch is 3. Seats, wherein King Edw. the Confesso^r, & his Queen, on either hand of y^e Bishop did sit. It is yet rich, but nothing so glorious as it hath beene; their Statues being richly gilt, are quite defac'd, & pull'd downe.

There belongs to this Cathedrall a braue Cloister, all the Seeling aboue beeing adorn'd w^th curious & artificiall workes, one Quarter whereoff is conuerted into a faire Library.

Att the further end of the Library there is a Rarity, w^ch is a reall Anotomy of a Man, who (for his Delinquency) ended his Life at the heauy Tree: all his seuerall Bones, 248. his Teeth, 28. &c.: all fix'd, & plac'd in their proper places, w^ch was dissected by a skilfull Italian Doctor, with the approbation of the right reuerend and learned L^d Bishop of this Diocese, and with his leaue heere appointed to be kept.

Beside the Cloyster, there is a neat Chapter House, seel'd w^th Irish wood, & richly gilt; & close by it is a pretty Chappell, w^ch is christen'd by the name of the Holy Ghost, & is artificially caru'd about w^th Joyners worke.

Besides the Bishops Pallace, the Deans & Canons Houses, w^ch are in the large

---

[1] " In the South tower, against the eastern wall, is an ugly and cumbrous Monument, erected in 1568, at the instance of Hoker (when Chamberlain of this city), thus inscribed: " *Leofricus, the first Bysshoppe of Exeter, lyeth here.*" But this assertion is contrary to fact; for Leofric directed that his remains should be interred in his own chapel, and it is expressly declared, in an ancient manuscript account of this Church, preserved in the Bodleian Library, that he was buried in the crypt." (Britton, *Exeter Cath.*, 129.)

Close, there is a faire Colledge for the Vicars, w^th a great Hall, & w^thin this Court a Cup of good Ale, w^ch I liberally tasted off, w^th their honest Organist and some of the merry Vicars; where I will leaue them, & returne to the Citty againe, to obserue her Gou̅ment & Scytuation.

For her Gouernm^t, I found it order'd by a gentile & discreet Mayor, w^th a fayre Sword, a Mace, & a Cap of Maintenance with the assistance of 12. graue & rich Crimson Aldermen, and one Sheriff; they sitt in a goodly fayre Hall to distribute Justice, w^ch stands in the high Street. She hath 4. Captains to whom are equally quarter'd 600. trayn'd Soldiers, 150. in each Company. And for her Inhabitants, there is 20. hansome Churches, w^th the Cathedrall, wherein to pforme their Deuotions.

For her Scytuation it is sweet, cleane, & pleasant, being seated vpon the gentle ascent of a Hill, by a fayre Riuer, y^t comes running from the west part of her from her Hauen whither Ships comes vp, some 3. miles distance from the City. From thence their Goods & Marchandise are transported in the same Channell by Keeles & Lighters to their owne Doores. Ou̅ the said Riuer is a faire stone Bridge of 20. Arches, vnder w^ch the dainty Salmon Trouts come trolling, and sporting vp further into the Country, to spawne, w^ch watry creatures haue a forward thirsting in their moist trauell, as euidently appeares by their willing pgresse in their clyming, & iumping vp those stairy fallings, & water-falls of the Riuer, in many places, ag^t their passage seeming incredible, w^ch in this pleasant Riuer Ex may be pointed at w^th an Ecce; the head of w^ch Riuer springeth at solitary Exmore in Somersetshire, neere y^e Seuerne Sea.

The Riuer Ex.

The Buildings & Streets are faire, especially her high Street, from East to West Gate, by which stands that spacious goodly old Building belonging to a noble Lord : & in her is an ancient old Castle, which erewhile was the Pallace of the West Saxon Kings, now quite demolish'd, except only the walls, and Towers about the yard, in which stands an old Shire House where the Judges sit at the Assizes.

*Bedford House, The Castle.*

The City is inuiron'd about w$^{th}$ a Wall, about 2. Mile in Compasse, w$^{th}$ 5. Gates, & some watch Towers, and on y$^e$ out parts thereof she is guarded about w$^{th}$ pleasant walkes, and diuerse Bowling Grounds ; as one on the West by that sweet Streame ; another on the East ; and a pleasant one along by the deep valley on the North part, neere to the Citty South, on the banke of that sweet Riuer, stands a stately Building late y$^t$ good Judge's, I left so lately quietly resting in the Lady Chappell ; but it is time now to leaue this Citty, yet before I could part, I must taste a dish of sweet Salmon, & after it a Glasse of briske wine, w$^{th}$ my Landlord, & Landlady, my kind, and louing Country-woman, w$^{ch}$ was their curteous ffoy.[1]

*Mount Ratford.*

*Sir John Doderidge.*

I (after bidding farewell) then tooke Horse, and speeded on my Journey, but had no desire ouer Tamer, to y$^e$ horned-nock-hole Land's-end, nor her horned wayes to the rough, hard-bred, and brawny strong limb'd wrastling Inhabitants thereof. Nor to the north Riuers of Tow & Towridge.

Away therefore I troop'd for Taunton down ou rugged wayes, & through as rugged

---

[1] A farewell entertainment given to or by one who is about to set out on a journey. (*English Dialect Dict.*)

Bradninch.　Bradnidge.　a Mayo[r] Toone,[1] w[ch] is so poore, & ancient, as she hath quite lost all breeding, & good manners: for I could not passe her w[th]out a Volley of Female Gun-shot, which made me hasten away from her, as fast as I could

Wellington.　Willington, Somersetshire.　to a little better qualify'd Towne then the other, the which is in another Countie, and which is much better order'd (then this is, with their whole Corporation) onely by a

S[r] Francis Popham.　noble Knight, that hath his fayre Mansion there, & 3. mile short thereof on the top of a hill I bad Deuonshire Adieu.

## THE TRAVELS OF COSMO III., GRAND DUKE OF TUSCANY, THROUGH ENGLAND　By Count L. Magalotti 1669

Scilly Isles, St. Mary's.　The pilot, after consulting with the captain, resolved to sail to the island St. Mary, and to wait there, rather than at sea, for a change of weather, because less inconvenient to his highness. Turning the ship's head towards the west, they anchored in the harbour two hours after mid-day. The ship having hoisted the admiral's standard, was saluted by the fortress with seven guns, and was replied to with the same number, which it acknowledged again with three. The couriers immediately landed to prepare apartments; soon afterwards his highness disembarked, and was received by the lieutenant governor, who considered it his duty to accommodate him in the castle, and had ordered all the garrison under arms; whilst the guns in the meantime fired a numerous volley from the walls, to which the ship answered with fen discharges. His highness requested to lodge, according to his custom, in a private house; where having received

---

1 "Brodenedge, a mayor towne, though almost all the howses be clay, without any timber in the wall, except the doores, roofe, and windowes, which is the fashion of the country." (Symonds, *Diary of the Marches of the Royal Army*, 39.)

his commandant, he retired immediately, without going out any more that evening.

On the 30th [March] his highness walked up to the castle, accompanied by his commandant, and afterwards descended to make the tour of the fortifications. Both at his going in and coming out, the soldiery were paraded, and a salute was fired from all the guns; to which the ship answered with twenty-one rounds. On his returning home he entertained the commandant and captain at dinner. The day was spent in walking with these persons till late in the evening; and, returning home, he retired.

Nine leagues from the farthest westerly point of England, there is a space of sea, which, in a circuit of seventy miles, embraces a very great number of small islands and rocks, a great part of which are constantly covered with water, and are the cause of more shipwrecks than happen perhaps in all the other seas of Europe together. These islands, which, by modern geographers, are called the Sorlings, are, by the English, more commonly known by the name of Scilly; and under this denomination are generally comprehended the sunken ones, as well as the others; and amongst these last, which are about an hundred in number, as well the rocky and deserted ones as those which naturally produce grass, and those which the population has rendered in some degree fruitful. The last mentioned are seven in all: St. Mary's, which is the principal, St. Martin's, St. Agnes, Tresco, Bryer, Samson, and St. Hellena. On each of the two last, there is only a single family, which, besides an adequate number of cattle, cultivate as much land as is capable of affording them an abundant sustenance. Of the others, that of St. Mary is the principal, both on account of the capaciousness and security of its harbour, and the superior number of its inhabitants. Of these, all the islands together are estimated to contain about a thousand, who live separate in small towns, or rather assemblages of houses; in St. Mary's there are twelve or fourteen of them. Their habitations are low; but, in other respects, resemble the buildings of England, being made of excellent materials. The more common ones have a peculiar sort of covering by way of roof, having nothing but a simple mat spread over the rafters, drawn tight all round, and fixed firmly to the top of the walls. This, they say, is the sort of covering used very commonly in Bermuda, and it is necessary to renew it every year. The best houses are covered with slate; but these are few. The inhabitants are comfortable, and follow fishing; fish being here in great abundance, and much better than in the Channel: and they likewise attend to the cultivation of the land, which produces wheat and oats in exactly sufficient quantities for their support. Corn of late began to be scarce, in consequence of the increase of population produced by the marriages of the soldiers of the garrison with the islanders; but this has been remedied for some years past, by forbidding them to marry. In all the islands, no other trees are to be found but apple and cherry trees, which were planted a few years since by the present governor on his farm, and have thriven wonderfully. In digging the ground, there are found in many places a great number of very thick stumps of oak, which evidently belonged to trees of extraordinary magnitude. There is likewise a reasonable quantity of cattle; whence neither cheese nor butter are wanting; consequently of the necessaries, and even the comforts of life, few things are imported, as even beer is made here. The whole government is in the hands of the commandant of the fortress, *Godolphin.* who, at present, is Sir —— Godolphin, and as he has never been to take possession of it, it may be said that he is unknown here; hence the whole authority is vested in *Janowick.* Colonel Janowick, a gentleman of Cornwall, his lieutenant-governor.

The fortress stands on a hill, which shuts in the harbour to the east, and commands the whole water. On the highest part is a castle, founded by Queen Elizabeth in the year 1570, which consists of two small inclosures; that without having eight turrets, and that within four. At the foot of the hill, on the sea-shore, is a circular entrenchment, with embrasures in the most suitable situations, in which, and on the bastions of the fortress, are mounted 130 very beautiful iron culverins. The harbour is capable of containing five hundred ships with convenience, and is perfectly secure, in the first place, owing to the goodness of its bottom, and in the next place, from its being sheltered all round by the island and the neighbouring rocks. It appears open on the

south only, but yet is not less defended on this side than
on the others ; as a natural rock, which is always covered
with water, extends for three leagues in that direction. This
harbour may be entered and left with every possible wind,
having four large openings, to the north, south, west, and
east; the largest ships enter with safety, in any direction,
except that on the east it is necessary to wait for high water,
owing to the shallowness of the bottom : nevertheless it must
not be attempted when the sea is agitated, or the atmosphere
foggy, the channels which lead to it being very narrow and
winding. The temperature of the air is wholesome, clear
and serene, whence the mists do not continue more than
four hours.

In the time of the late war, the garrison consisted of six
hundred men ; at present, there are two hundred, the king
expending annually for the support of the fortress, officers,
and garrisons, about four thousand pounds sterling, including
the stipend of the governor, which is two thousand crowns,
and that of the chaplain, which is four hundred. Twenty
of the soldiers are employed to guard the castle of Bryer, **Bryer Cas.**
which is situated at the mouth of the harbour of Grimyby. **Grimsby Har.**
This is likewise very secure and spacious, but more difficult
to enter, and consequently to sail out of, than that of St.
Mary's ; for which reason, in order to get in with safety,
many ships fire a gun as a signal, on which a boat or
shallop is sent off by the governor with experienced persons,
who conduct them into port. For this service a crown is
paid, besides the anchorage, which is three shillings, the
perquisite of the governor of the fortress, to whom belong
even the wrecks which remain on these rocks, in case none
of the crew escape ; but from this custom ships of war
belonging to the king are exempt. The inhabitants of this
island are reckoned very zealous observers of the genuine
Anglican religion, and the most loyal subjects which the
king has in all the kingdom. This was very clearly shewn
in the late revolution ; they having been the last to surrender to the new government, after a long and obstinate
defence, and after having afforded a faithful and secure
retreat in the island of St. Mary's to the late king, who,
after he had been defeated in the battle of Worcester, took
refuge here, to wait for a conjuncture more favourable to

his interests, although, at last, after the delay of a month, he resolved to go over to France.

On the 31st, the wind having changed to the N.W., the captain sent very early in the morning to notify his departure to his highness, who came on board before nine o'clock, after having received the homage of the governor, and been accompanied by him to the boat. When he left the shore, the fortress fired a royal salute, which was answered, as soon as his highness got on board, with twenty-five guns ; the castle saluted again as he quitted the harbour, and the frigate replied with the same number as before. As soon as they had cleared the rocks, they made sail, and, in about two hours, towards mid-day, they were abreast of the cape of Land's End ; and having soon after entered the Channel, and passed Falmouth, we found ourselves, at sunset, only one league from the point of Dedman, which signifies " the dead man." It was then night, and the wind still continuing favourable, and finding ourselves close to land, in order that we might not overshoot the point of Plymouth in the night, we began to tack backwards and forwards ; and continued in this manner, till four o'clock of the morning of the 1st of April, when the wind got round to the north, being thus directly in the teeth of those who attempted to enter the harbour ; yet, thanks to the goodness of the ship, and the great exertions and industry of the pilot, they so gained upon the wind in five or six tacks, that they succeeded in coming to an anchor before two o'clock in the afternoon. About nine o'clock the next morning we rejoined our comrade, which had parted company the very first evening that we sailed from Corunna. Having steered more directly for the cape of Brittany, in two days and a half she made the Sorlings, and four days afterwards anchored at Plymouth, where, receiving no intelligence of us for four days, she sailed back to the Sorlings in quest of us ; but discovering us the preceding evening, as we passed Falmouth, where she was lying at anchor, she happily came up with us in the morning. When within gun shot, she saluted with a discharge of seven guns, to which we answered with five. The captain then coming on board, presented to his highness letters from Colonel Gascoyne, written two days before at Plymouth ; but a few hours afterwards, when the

*Land's End.*

*Dodman Pt.*

*Gascoyne.*

frigate began to enter the harbour, he came himself to make
his obeisance to his highness, bringing with him Major
Andrews, deputy to Sir Charles Cotterel, the master of the
ceremonies, and introducer of ambassadors at court.[1]  He
was commissioned by the king to offer his services, and
accompany his highness on his journey, and to see that
every necessary accommodation was provided for his lodgings.
Being therefore introduced into the state cabin, he paid his
respects to his highness, and then went back on deck, where
he had not stood long, before the Signors Antonio Antinori
and Lorenzo del Rosso appeared in another boat.  Having
anchored in the middle of the bay of Plymouth, the frigate
saluted the fortress with eleven guns, and, receiving eleven
guns in reply, acknowledged them with three, which, however, did not remain unanswered ; the castle also saluted the
frigate with seven guns, and she returned the salute with
five.

His highness then landing, the frigate saluted with all
the ordnance, both in the upper and lower tiers, making
altogether, twenty-one rounds.  To this salute succeeded
that of the castle, and to that succeeded the fortress and
the forts which guard the entrance of the two banks ; altogether, sixty discharges.  On disembarking, the mayor and
aldermen, in their habits of ceremony, came to receive and
compliment his highness, which, as it had not been notified
to him, he could not avoid.  A few paces further on, stood
the military governor expecting him, who paid his respects
to him in the name of his majesty, and then accompanied
him to his lodging, with all the military officers, walking
between a double line of soldiers of the garrison, under
arms, with colours flying, trumpets sounding, and drums
beating, besides the festive shouts and acclamations of a
very numerous population, who, for want of room in the
public streets, had filled the roofs of the houses and the
shrouds and rigging of the ships which were at anchor in
the dock.  A lodging was prepared for his highness in the
house of Mr. Jenings, one of the principal merchants, and,
at present, alderman of the town.  The governor then

*Andrews.*
*Cotterell.*

*Antinori.*
*Del Rosso.*

*Jenings.*

---

[1] Sir Charles Cotterell (1615-1687 ?) was master of the ceremonies
1641-9, and again 1660-86.  (*Dict. Nat. Biography.*)

arrived, and having been introduced into his highness's apartment, soon after retired. With the same view of making their obeisance, there arrived from their country seats, Sir Richard Edgecomb[1] and Mr. Prideaux,[2] both gentlemen of consideration in the county, who were immediately introduced by Signor Gascoyne; and, when they had gone, his highness retired to rest.

*Edgcumbe.*
*Prideaux.*

On the 2nd, the two captains and the officers of the frigate came to pay their respects to his highness, and to thank him for the liberal presents they had received from him. Captain Hart had received the sum of one thousand crowns; Captain Fooly, one hundred pounds sterling; the lieutenant of the frigate the same; and the pilot, besides his share of two hundred pistoles given to be divided amongst the soldiers and sailors, a gold medal, with his highness's portrait. After these had departed, the governor arrived, who introduced all his captains, ensigns, and other chief officers of the garrison, to congratulate his highness; and, after these, he was congratulated by Sir William Stroude,[3] one of the gentry of the province. After dinner, his highness, attended by the governor, embarked to see the two rivers which disembogue themselves into this harbour; but the weather being very snowy, he was obliged to return before he had well put off from the shore. Soon afterwards, he walked on foot to the city, to view two churches; and, on his return home, he stopped at a shop where marbles are sold, such as are found in the province; and at the house of an ingenious mechanic, a maker of watches and other automatical machines.

*Hart.*
*Fooly.*

*Strode*

On the 3rd, the captains came to take leave of his highness, and, with them, two young gentlemen volunteers, who were presented by Signor Castiglione, in the name of his highness, with two rich gold collars. Afterwards, Mr. Stroude arrived, and shewed his highness different specimens

*Castiglione.*

---

[1] Sir Richard Edgcumbe of Mount Edgcumbe (1640-1688), K.B. before the Coronation of Charles II. (Vivian, *Visitations of Cornwall*.)

[2] Presumably Peter Prideaux (1626-1705), who succeeded his father in the baronetcy in 1682. He was M.P. for Liskeard 1661, and mar. Elizabeth, sister of John Grenville, Earl of Bath. (Vivian, *Visitations of Devon*.)

[3] Sir William Strode of Newnham, knighted 5 Dec., 1660. (Vivian, *Visitations of Devon*.)

of the mines of lead, tin, and loadstone, lately discovered by him in that neighbourhood. His highness made him stay and dine with him, in company with the governor, that is, the lieutenant of my Lord John Greenvile, Earl of Bath, first gentleman of the chamber to the king.[1] The following day he was taken to see the fortress, where, both on his entrance and departure, he was saluted by all the guns, and by three discharges of musketry from the soldiery, who, happening to be on parade at the time his highness arrived at the governor's quarters, drew up in squadrons under his windows. In the saloon, was the governor's wife[2] and four other ladies, with whom his highness partook of a collation prepared for him; after which, he went with them to see the house and private armory of the governor. Having made the tour of the fortifications and bastions, as far as the weather permitted (and a very heavy snow beginning to fall) he returned home.

*Grenville, Earl of Bath.*

At seven o'clock of the same day, his highness, accompanied by the governor, went into a boat, and by the assistance of the tide, was carried to Saltash, a small town on the right bank of the river Tamar, where formerly flourished the same commerce which is now transferred to Plymouth. It was his intention to have gone higher up, in order to see the new tin-mines lately discovered by Sir W. Stroude; but having arrived at the last mentioned place very late, in consequence of the wind being against him, he resolved to return, after having made a short perambulation through the lower parts of the city. On his return, passing under the castle of St. Frances, he was saluted by it with discharges of artillery, and the same compliment was paid by the entrenchments which guard the mouth of the eastern river, which his highness, having reached after a long walk, returned back to dinner. He detained the governor to dinner, and at the bottom of the table, below the gentlemen

*Saltash.*

[1] He was the eldest surviving son of Sir Bevil Grenville, who was killed at Lansdowne 1643. He was born 1628, created Earl of Bath at the Restoration, and on 13 May, 1661, he was appointed Governor of the Town and Castle of Plymouth and of St. Nicholas Island, a post which he held till the year 1695. (Granville, *History of the Granville Family*, 352.) His lieutenant was Sir —— Skelton. (See p. 101.)

[2] Jane, daughter of Sir Peter Wych, Knt., Comptroller of the Household to Charles I. (Vivian, *Visitations of Cornwall.*)

of his suite, he caused the master of the house to be seated. To-day he did not go out, and conversed a long time with the governor, who took him to see the plan of a new fortification. After him, Sir Richard Edgecumbe and Mr. Prideaux came to pay their respects and wish him a good journey, and thus the day ended; his departure for Exeter being determined upon for the day following.

Plymouth (descriptive).

Plymouth, in the last century, was a poor village, inhabited by fishermen. It is now so increased in buildings and population, that it may be reckoned among the best cities of England, having between twelve and fifteen thousand inhabitants. This great advantage it derives from the capaciousness and convenience of a large bay, which, extending itself inland between two promontories, not only admits ships to a tranquil and secure sheltering place, but conveys them with the tide, which is here very powerful, into two other bays still farther inland, being the spacious channels of two rivers, which empty themselves into the sea, one to the west and the other to the east of the farthest point of the larger bay. The first, which is the Tamar, is navigable for six miles by the largest men of war which the king possesses, and for ten, by merchant ships of all kinds, and as its windings form frequent bays, surrounded by mountains, it affords them perfectly secure places of retreat. Vessels could formerly get three or four miles up the other river, but as the Channel is narrower, and the cutting down of the roads for the purpose of reducing the land to a state of cultivation, has loosened the earth from the neighbouring mountains, this, coming down with the rain, has so filled up the bottom that little more than a mile is practicable for the larger frigates. On the sea-side, towards the east, and near the coast, is a small isolated mountain, called St. Michael's, capable of defending, to a certain extent, the first entrance of the port. There are other fortifications at the mouths of the rivers; on the Tamar, is an ancient castle, called St. Francis; on the highest part of a small island, and on the Plym, an entrenchment of earth, well supplied with artillery; a similar one defends the mouth of the dock, towards the city; and others are disposed on a rock which protects, in front, the whole length of the bay. All these are, nevertheless, commanded

by the new citadel, which the king built to be a check
upon the inhabitants, who shewed themselves on a former
occasion, prone to sedition;[1] and that spirit being now
fostered by the influx of wealth, which a flourishing commerce produces, renders them objects of reasonable suspicion.
This citadel is placed on the top of a mountain, which forms
the bottom of the bay from without, and serves as a defence
to the port, against the sea; hence it commands equally the
sea and the town, and batters or defends, as occasion may
require, all the before-mentioned fortifications. The building
is all of stone, and is furnished with breast-work. The plan
is totally irregular, having three demi-bastions, and four
entire ones, of different proportions. In the interior of it,
it is said, that the king wishes to build a private habitation
for himself. The governor of it, is my Lord John Granville,
Earl of Bath; and Sir —— Skelton is his lieutenant. Five
companies, of about seventy men each, officers and soldiers,
are on duty there; one of these belongs to the duke's
regiment.[2] The men are very handsome, and in excellent
order; four companies wearing red jackets, lined with yellow,
and that of the duke, yellow, with red lining. In the citadel
and the forts, are, altogether, one hundred and thirty pieces
of cannon, the greater part of iron; Cromwell having carried
off all the brass ones from the different fortresses, in order
to equip the vessels of his fleet. The city cannot be seen
from the sea, and is almost shut up by a gorge of the
mountains, on the lowest skirt of which it is situated. Its
extent is not very considerable. The buildings are antique,
according to the English fashion; lofty and narrow, with
pointed roofs, and the fronts may be seen through, owing
to the magnitude of the glass windows in each of the different
stories. They are occupied from top to bottom. There are
two churches of gothic architecture. In spirituals, Plymouth
is subject to the Bishop of Exeter; in temporals, it has the
ordinary government, composed of the mayor, the head of

---

[1] The foundation stone was laid by the Earl of Bath in 1666, but
the citadel was apparently not yet completed, for over the main
gateway is inscribed the date "1670," as well as the Earl's arms.
(Granville, *History of the Granville Family*, 353-4.)

[2] Duke of Albemarle's. The Duke and Lord Bath were first
cousins, their mothers being daughters of Sir George Smith of
Exeter. (Vivian, *Visitations of Devon; Visitations of Cornwall*.)

the council, and thirty-six inferior magistrates, called aldermen, who are chosen every year in the month of May ; but of these only twenty-four give their attendance: their dress is a gown, reaching to the ground, made of black cloth, richly ornamented with stripes of velvet, also black, and having square collars lined with skin of the same colour. The life of the city is navigation. The inhabitants export lead and tin in greater quantities than any other article, and with these they go to the Canaries, and to the Western Islands. To Barbadoes, in the new world, and in every part of Europe, they act as carriers, conveying merchandize from place to place, at an immense profit to themselves. Hence it is that, in Plymouth, only women and boys are to be seen ; the greater part of the men living at sea ; and hence also, the town is exceedingly well supplied ; all the necessaries of life being found there, and every thing exempt from duty, except wine, which, as it is not produced in this island, is necessarily imported from foreign countries ; and not only is there great plenty of meat, cloth, and linen, but of many other articles that administer to luxury and to pleasure ; and silversmiths, watchmakers, jewellers, and other artists of this description, are not wanting. In the neighbourhood are very rich veins of marble of different colours, some of which are black veined with white, and take a most beautiful polish. At a little distance some mines of tin have been opened on the estate of Sir ——

*Berkley.* Berkley, which yield eighty per cent., besides a considerable quantity of gold and silver ; not far from these they have discovered another of load-stone, which, although very far from rich, shows that the earth has a great disposition to the production of minerals. The sea produces oysters in great abundance, and of excellent quality, and the rivers a great quantity of salmon. Besides the tax of two shillings, which the inhabitants and neighbourhood pay annually, and which is called road right, the king derives very considerable advantage from the customs of this port ; every ship which anchors here being obliged to pay five per cent. on the merchandize they discharge; half of which, however, is returned, whenever it is re-shipped for other parts. They likewise pay four-pence per ton for the lights which burn in the light-houses at night.

# THE TRAVELS OF COSMO III

On the 5th of the same month, Sir Jonathan Spark[1] *Spark.*
came to pay his respects to the serene prince, accompanied
by his son. This gentleman is an inhabitant of Plymouth,
in the neighbourhood of which he possesses an estate of a
thousand pounds a year; consequently he is considered the
principal person of the place. The governor then came to
take leave, and afterwards Sir Richard Edgecumbe and Mr.
Prideaux came in, to wish his highness a good journey.
About three they dined, and towards five, took their
departure; his highness being attended by the governor
on horseback, who, when they had got two miles from
Plymouth, appeared at the coach-door, to take leave once
more. He had wished to have paraded the military, as
was done on his highness's arrival, but the latter courteously
declined it. When they had proceeded about a mile after
the governor's departure, there came galloping up to the
coach Sir Copleston Bampfylde,[2] with his wife and sister. *Bampfylde*
They happened to be hunting in that neighbourhood, and
wished not to lose the opportunity of performing an act of
respect to his highness. The serene prince stopped the
carriage and received their compliments, but did not alight
to salute them, not knowing till afterwards, who the ladies
were. They passed through the small village of Halbom- *Horrabridge.*
bridge, consisting of a few houses thatched with straw;
and, after travelling some distance, arrived at Okehampton, *Okehampton*
to sleep. On alighting, his highness was received by the
mayor and aldermen; and put up at the Angel Inn. The
whole of the country was hilly, with some rather abrupt
mountains; some parts were desert, and others tolerably
fertile, cultivated with wheat and oats; the fields being
surrounded with hedges and dry walls. Okehampton is a
place of little account, situated on the small river Hocan; *Okement R.*
the houses are built of earth and stone, and thatched with

---

[1] Presumably Jonathan Sparke, who was bap. 29 Dec., 1639, at
St. Andrew, Plymouth. (Vivian, *Visitations of Devon.*)

[2] Sir Copleston Bampfylde, Bart., was born at Poltimore 1636,
and died at Warleigh, in the parish of Tamerton, an ancient seat
of the Copleston family, and at this time the residence of Colonel
Hugh Bampfylde, Sir Copleston's son and heir. Sir Copleston
married twice, viz., first, Margaret, dau. of Francis Bulkeley, of
Burgate, Hants, who was living 1657, and second, Jane, dau. of
Sir Courtenay Pole, of Shute. (Prince, *Worthies of Devon;* Vivian,
*Visitations of Devon.*)

straw; and its whole consequence is derived from the abundance of cheese produced in the adjacent country, which is famous for cows; and this is sold in considerable quantities to the dealers who come hither every week in great numbers.

On the 6th, after dinner, they departed, and arrived in the evening at Exeter, going by the direct road till they passed Crediton, commonly called Kerton, a village with a considerable population, all of whom are occupied in the wool manufactory.[1] The country was uneven, but more fertile and better inhabited than that passed over the preceding day; everywhere were seen fields surrounded with rows of trees, meadows of the most beautiful verdure, gentlemen's seats, and small collections of houses. The materials of which these are constructed are mud, mixed up with short straw and chips of slate, and they are thickly thatched with straw. Two miles from the city, after they had passed the bridge of Isca, called by the English Ex, several of the principal gentlemen of the city came to meet and pay their respects to his highness, who, descending from his carriage, answered with his usual courtesy. When he reached the city, the people of which assembled in such numbers as to fill the suburbs and all the streets through which his highness passed, he alighted at the inn called the New Inn, where several gentlemen shortly arrived from the neighbouring places to pay their compliments to him. Soon after, the mayor, aldermen, and bailiffs, unexpectedly arrived in their magisterial habits of ceremony, with the insignia of justice and mace-bearers before them: they found his highness upstairs in the saloon, who, after having received them graciously, and desired the mayor to be covered, heard, and replied to, his congratulations. He requested his highness to give him a public entertainment at his own house, which invitation his highness refused, on the plea of his being incog., a plea he made use of elsewhere; and, above all, on account of the haste in which he was, from his impatience to be in London and kiss the hands of his majesty the king. After they were gone, Sir

Crediton (Kerton).

Cowley B. Exeter.

---

[1] See note 4 on p. 75. "Crediton, vulgo called Kirton, a great lowsy town, a corporate towne governed by a bayliffe." (Symonds, *Diary of the Marches of the Royal Army.*)

Arthur Ackland[1] came in, a young man of seventeen years *Acland.*
of age, who, by the death of his father, is come into
possession of a fortune of two thousand pounds per annum.
Also Messrs. John and Dennis Rolle, sons of Sir John Rolle,[2] *Rolle.*
one of the two lieutenants-general of the county under the
general.  This gentleman is one of the richest in the country,
having an estate of six thousand pounds sterling per annum,
besides a considerable property in ready money; which will
enable him to give a reasonable fortune to his younger sons.
With him the day ended.

On the 7th, his highness went to the cathedral church *Cathedral.*
at the hour of prayer, about nine o'clock, and stood a
considerable time in conversation with Signor Castiglini
and Sergeant-Major Andrews in the body of the church,
observing with much curiosity the place set apart for the
offices of religion, which are performed according to the
Anglican Liturgy, by the clergy, assisted by the bishop,
who is, at present, Doctor Antony Sparrow, lately elected to *Sparrow.*
this see;[3] which was vacated by the translation of Dr.
Seth Ward to that of Salisbury.  The bishop was seated *Ward.*
in a marble tabernacle, on the Epistle-side, on a seat
covered with red cloth, dressed in the habit which was
used by the Catholic bishops of the kingdom before the
apostacy; namely, a surplice over a black vest, and a mantle
of the same colour; on his head he wore a small cap, similar
to that of the Roman pontiffs, without any other ornament;
and before him, on the edge of the tabernacle, over which
was extended a large canopy of red cloth, was placed a
cushion, and on that the book; and under the tabernacle,
on a level with the floor of the church, in an enclosure of
wood, stood the wife of the bishop, and his children, no less
than nine in number.  In the prebendal stalls, sat, according

---

[1] Sir Arthur Acland, 4th Bart., was the only son of Sir John
Acland, 3rd Bart. (*d.* 1655), and his wife Margaret, daughter of
Dennis Rolle of Stevenstone.  He died in 1672, during his minority,
and was succeeded in the baronetcy by his uncle, Sir Hugh Acland.
(Vivian, *Visitations of Devon.*)

[2] Sir John Rolle inherited the Rolle property on the death of his
distant cousin, Henry Rolle of Beam, who died in 1647.  He married,
in 1648, Florence, eldest daughter of Dennis Rolle of Stevenstone.
(Vivian, *Visitations of Devon.*)

1667.

to their rank, the dignitaries and canons, in their canonical habits, i.e. a surplice, and a mantle of black silk, differing in shape from that of the bishop, as being narrower both before and behind. These, in conjunction with other regular choristers, sang the psalms in the English language, in a chant similar to the Gregorian, making their pauses to the sound of the organ, which has been erected lately on the wall separating the choir from the rest of the church, and is of a most exquisite tone.[1] In reciting the prayers ordained by their ritual, they all fell on their knees, the choir making alternate responses; and after a chapter from scripture, and from one of the epistles of St. Paul, had been read, a minister went to the altar in his surplice, and turning round to the people, read distinctly, standing, the Commandments of the Decalogue; and at each commandment, the choir answered in their own language, with a musical cadence, "Lord, have mercy upon us." When this was over, a hymn was first given out by a singer under the pulpit, and then sung by the whole choir; and this being ended, the preacher, in his surplice, immediately began his sermon, leaning on a cushion placed in the middle of the pulpit, which is opposite to the bishop's seat, who is obliged to attend at the prescribed times, both at morning prayers and at vespers, and at all the other offices. Departing hence, his highness went to see the ancient castle, and then making a tour round the walls of the city on the outside, he returned home to dinner, entertaining at table, besides the usual gentlemen, Colonel *Gascoyne.* Gascoyne, the two brothers Rolle, Mr. Ford,[2] one of the *Rolle.* two lieutenants of the county, lately appointed secretary to *Ford.* Lord Robert, for the purpose of accompanying him to *Kirkham.* Ireland, and Major Andrews. After dinner Mr. Kirkam,[3] who is the only Catholic gentleman in the county, came to pay his respects to his highness, and soon afterwards, Sir John Rolle, who came from his house in the country, on purpose to pay his obeisance. After their departure, his highness went to Sir John Rolle's house, to visit his wife, who received him in a room where were assembled, along

---

[1] This was the organ erected by John Loosemoore in 1664, not the one described by the Norwich Lieutenant in 1635. (See p. 85.)

[2] Sir Henry Ford of Nutwell, *bap.* 1617, *d.* 1684.

Sir William Kirkham, or Francis, his son.

with her, her three daughters;[1] Miss Earl, sister of a rich gentleman of the county, who, they said, was to be the wife of the eldest son of Sir John above-mentioned;[2] and three sisters of Mr. Kirkam, who were unmarried, and Catholics, cousins on the mother's side to Sir John Rolle. His highness conversed standing, and on taking leave, returned directly home, and passed the evening without any other occurrence worth mentioning.

*Earl.*

Exeter, the capital of the county of Devonshire, is a small city, situated on the river Isca, about ten miles from the sea. The river there empties itself into a large bay, up which the largest vessels, even those of three hundred tons burden, can pass safely as far as Topsham, a village three miles from Exeter; whence merchandize is conveyed in smaller boats quite up to the city. The advantage of this commerce is very great; about thirty thousand persons being continually employed in the county, in making baize and different sorts of light cloth. It is sold to all parts, being sent to the West Indies, Spain, France, and Italy; but the greater part goes into the Levant. The very best cloth is also made, both for home consumption and for exportation; but the trade in this is not considerable, in comparison with the other. There is not a cottage in all the county, nor in that of Somerset, where white lace is not made in great quantities; so that not only the whole kingdom is supplied with it, but it is exported in very great abundance. The population of the city is from twenty to twenty-five thousand souls; amongst which, according to the custom of the kingdom, there is no nobility except such as come from time to time from their country houses, which are their constant residence, to look after their affairs.

Exeter (descriptive). Exe R.

Topsham.

The cathedral church of St. Peter is a very considerable edifice; the architecture is Gothic; but it deserves praise from its size, and from having its exterior faced with stone. The façade is ornamented with different figures in stone, both in high and low relief, representing Saints both

---

[1] Vivian only mentions two daughters, Margaret and Florence, the latter of whom was married, in 1681, to Sir Bourchier Wrey, Bart. (*Visitations of Devon.*)

[2] John Rolle married, in 1677, Lady Christiana, daughter of Robert Bruce, Earl of Aylesbury. (Vivian, *Visitations of Devon.*)

of the Old and New Testament. Many of these have been
injured and broken in the time of Cromwell. . . . The
church is long, and divided in the inside into three open
naves. The arches are low, and rest upon round pillars ;
over these are galleries which run almost round the whole
church ; it is lighted in every direction by large windows,
in the glass of which are reflected the figures of saints, as
also, round the body of the church, the tombs, and the
marble monuments of the ancient Catholic bishops, whose
statues have been defaced by the scorn and derision of
the Independents. It is the residence, as has been already
said, of the bishop ; whose revenue, formerly of five thousand pounds sterling, was reduced, after the alienations made
by Cromwell, to five hundred. At present, some estates
having lapsed to it, it has again risen to eight hundred ;
and there are hopes that it will daily be augmented by
lapses of a similar kind. There are said to be twelve
canons, besides four ministers, whose business it is to
preach. The music of this church is reckoned amongst
the best in the kingdom, owing to the good stipends which
the chapter is enabled to give, in consequence of its
excellent revenues, which are entirely distinct from those
of the bishop. To the chapter, which might with greater
propriety be called, the opera of the church, belongs everything relating to worship and to the church service. There
are twenty other parishes ; but no other church or public
building can be compared to the cathedral. At the bottom
of the body of the church, where the altar stands, are
written on two large tables the ten commandments ; at
the sides of which are painted Moses and Aaron : over
these tables is the cipher of the name of JESUS. On the
altar table is laid a covering of red velvet, which, extending
itself on each side, falls in front down to the ground ; and over
this is spread a table cloth. On one side of the table, is a
large cushion of velvet of the same colour ; and this sup-
ports a silver basin and chalice. There are likewise two
vessels for preserving the wine which they make use of at
the Lord's Supper, and two candlesticks of brass. On the
Gospel-side, stands the ancient seat of the bishop, but the
present one is in a large marble tabernacle, surmounted by
a very high lantern ; the ornaments of which being taken

from the Passion of Christ our Lord, shew it to have been formerly (as was the custom in ancient times) the Pix of the most Holy Sacrament. Now the seat of the bishop is there, in which he assists at the service, and curtains of taffeta are stretched from pillar to pillar; this throne is placed on the Epistle-side, at the head of the choir, which is in the body of the church, in the middle aisle.

The other public building of the city is the Old Castle, which is a square enclosure, surrounded by walls with ancient towers, dismantled indeed both of guns and troops, there being in the city no other soldiers than the militia before described, commanded by the lieutenants, who are created by the king, and who in this county are eight in number. In the castle are two buildings, where, at stated times, are held the courts of justice; the one on the right, being appropriated to civil, the other to criminal causes. The city is entirely surrounded by walls with towers, built by king Athelstan, son of Edward I., in the year 924. These extend as far as the river, over which is a bridge of stone with ten arches, which leads to a large suburb on the other side. The city is intersected almost in the middle by a very large and straight street, full of very rich shops, which is its best and most considerable part. In the square of the cathedral is a most beautiful summer walk, under the shade of trees, into several rows of which it is distributed, like those which are customary in Holland. The head of the county is the sheriff; he is usually one of the principal gentry of the county, is changed every year, and is chosen by the king. The militia is dependant upon the lieutenants, who also are chosen by the king, but under orders of the general. For settling the civil and criminal causes of the county, four times a-year, that is, every three months, the assize, or assembly of judicature, meets, at which two judges of the parliament are present, who come from London on purpose, together with certain other deputies of the county, to see that the laws of the kingdom are rigorously observed. The especial civil government of the city is administered according to the general usage of the kingdom, by the mayor, assisted by the aldermen and bailiffs; the former of whom are five, and the latter thirteen. The aldermen, as well as the mayor, wear a very noble dress, being a large gown of red cloth with a cape lined with black skin, plaited very full above the waist, which is rather high, and entirely lined with yellow skin, with stripes of black velvet, which in front, that is, on each side of the opening, falls down almost to the ground. The bailiffs likewise wear gowns of black cloth, richly laced with velvet of the same colour. When the magistracy goes out on any occasion of ceremony, a page goes before, in a robe of black cloth, with a mace in his hand; he is followed by eight other inferior officers in a similar dress, but much longer; afterwards come four mace-bearers in cloth gowns that reach to the ground, with a silver collar round their necks, from which hangs a medal, carrying small silver maces in their hands, which rest on their right shoulders. Then comes the sword-bearer, as they call him; he always walks in boots, in a robe of black velvet, reaching to the ground; a large sword in his hand, the insignia of justice, and a red hat on his head, embroidered with gold, which is never taken off except to the king himself, because it was the cap of Henry VIII., who, in passing through Exeter, made a present of it for this particular service. The mayor comes last, on the right hand of the oldest of the aldermen; the other four come behind, two and two.

On the morning of the 8th, his highness sent Platt to present his compliments to the mayor. Towards noon, Mr. Kirkam and the Messrs. Rolle came to wish him a good journey; after which, having dined, he got into his coach, and departed for Axminster, where he arrived at an early hour. The road was through an uneven country, divided into fields under the plough, and spacious meadows for feeding cows, in which this district abounds. At first we suffered a good deal of inconvenience, because they had to travel a road full of water, and muddy, though not deep. We passed through Honiton, a small but populous village, situated in a valley, and having ascended a hill, from which we could see the sea, we arrived at Axminster, where we found the master of the horse of Henry Howard,[1] brother

*Honiton.*

*Axminster.*
*Howard.*

---

[1] Henry Howard (1628-1684) was the second son of Henry Frederick Howard, 3rd Earl of Arundel. He was created Baron Howard of Castle Rising, and sent as envoy to Morocco, 1669; and he succeeded his brother as Duke of Norfolk, 1677. (*Dict. Nat. Biography.*)

of the Duke of Norfolk, and of my Lord Philip, grand
almoner to the queen, who delivered to Colonel Gascoyne
a letter from his master, in which he excused himself for
not coming in person to pay his respects to his highness,
in consequence of his approaching departure on his embassy
to Fez; and informed him that he had sent his carriage to
Salisbury, to be at the service of his highness. The master
of the horse was admitted to an audience by the serene
prince, and departed that same evening for London. His
highness then went out to walk, and passed the evening in
seeing some ancient medals, which had been dug up in this
neighbourhood, and were brought for his inspection by the
minister of the church.

Axminster is a collection of two hundred houses, many
of which are made of mud, and thatched with straw. It
contains nothing considerable, except the parish church,
which has a tower, in which are bells so well tuned, that
their sound is exceedingly harmonious and agreeable. The
trade of the inhabitants consists in the manufactory of
woollen cloth.[1]

# THROUGH ENGLAND ON A SIDE SADDLE  By CELIA FIENNES  1695

I entered into Devonshire five miles off from Wellington,
just on a high ridge of hills which discovers a vast prospect
on each side full of enclosures and lesser hills, which is the
description of most part of the West. You could see large
tracts of grounds full of enclosures, good grass, and corn,
beset with quicksets and hedgerows, and these lesser hills
which are scarce perceivable on the ridge of the uppermost, yet the least of them have a steep ascent and descent
to pass them.

Culimton is a good little market town, and [has a] market
cross and another set on stone pillars. Here was a large
meeting of near four or five hundred people; they have a very    Cullompton.

---

[1] According to Westcote, it was in 1630 famous for the fine flax
thread there spun. (*View of Devon*, 61, 246.)

good minister, but a young man. I was glad to see so many, though they were but of the meaner sort, for indeed it is the poor [that] receive the gospel, and there are in most of the market towns in the West very good meetings. This little place was one continued long street, but few houses that struck out of the street.

From thence ten miles to Exeter, up hills and down as before, till one attains those uppermost ridges of all which discover the whole valley; then you sometimes go a mile or two on a down till the brow of the hill begins in a descent on the other side. This city appears to view two miles distant from one of those heights, and also the River Ex, which runs to Topshum, where the ships come up to the bar; this is seven miles by water, from which they are attempting to make navigable to the town, which will be of mighty advantage to have ships come up close to the town to take in their serges, which now they are forced to send to Topshum on horses by land, which is about four miles by land. They had just agreed with a man that was to accomplish this work, for which they were to give 5 or 6,000£, who had made a beginning on it.[1]

Exeter is a town very well built, the streets are well pitched, spacious noble streets, and a vast trade is carried on. As Norwitch is for " coapes, callamanco, and damaske," so this is for serges. There is an incredible quantity of them made and sold in the town.[2] Their market day is Friday, which supplies with all things like a fair almost;

Topsham.

Exeter.

---

[1] About 1675 the Chamber commenced the extension of the canal to the Topsham Sluice, called in later documents after its keeper, Trenchard's Sluice. On 16 July, 1698, they " Resolved that the old work for the bringing up of ships be forthwith widened and deepened from the Key to Trenchard's Sluices." Also " This day (12 Sept.) certain articles made between the Chamber and Mr. Wm. Baly, for widening and digging the new canal or river, making a stone wear, and digging the broad from the key thereunto, passed the common seal." The agreement was for £9,000, but Bayly, having proceeded so far as to render the canal impassable, ran away with the money. An Act of Parliament could not be got, but by 1728 the canal had been made passable, though only for small vessels. (Oliver, *Exeter*, 257-8; Freeman, *Exeter*, 214.)

[2] " The late made stuff of serges, or perpetuanos, is now (1630) in great use and request with us, wherewith the market at Exeter is abundantly furnished of all sorts and prices; fine, coarse, broad, narrow; the number will hardly be credited." (Westcote, *View of Devon*, 60.)

the markets for meat, fowl, fish, garden things, and the dairy produce take up three whole streets besides the large market house set on stone pillars, which runs a great length, on which they lay their packs of serges. Just by it is another walk within pillars, which is for the yarn. The whole town and country is employed for at least twenty miles round in spinning, weaving, dressing and scouring, fulling, and drying of the serges. It turns the most money in a week of any thing in England. One week with another there is £10,000 paid in ready money, sometimes £15,000. The weavers bring in their serges, and must have their money, which they employ to provide them yarn to go to work again. There is also a square court with pent-houses round, where the malters are with malt and oatmeal, but the serge is the chief manufacture. There is a prodigious quantity of their serges they never bring into the market, but are in hired rooms which are noted for it, for it would be impossible to have it all together. The carriers I met going with it, as thick, all entering into town with their loaded horses; they bring them all just from the loom, and so they are put into the fulling-mills, but first they will clean and scour their rooms with them, which, by the way, gives no pleasing perfume to a room, the oil and grease, and I should think it would rather foul a room than cleanse it, because of the oils, but I perceive it is otherwise esteemed by them, which will send to their acquaintances that are tuckers the days the serges come in for a roll to clean their house—this I was an eye-witness of. Then they lay them in soak in urine, then they soap them and so put them into the fulling-mills, and so work them in the mills dry till they are thick enough; then they turn water into them, and so scour them. The mill does draw out and gather in the serges. It is a pretty diversion to see it—a sort of huge notched timbers like great teeth. One would think it should injure the serges, but it does not. The mills draw in with such a great violence that, if one stands near it and it catch a bit of your garments, it would be ready to draw in the person even in a trice. When they are thus scoured, they dry them in racks strained out, which are as thick set one by another as will permit the dresses to pass between, and huge large fields occupied this way almost all round the town, which is to the river side; then, when dry, they pick out all knots, then fold them with a paper between every fold, and so set them on an iron plate and screw down the press on them, which has another iron plate on the top, under which is a furnace of fire of coals—this is the hot press. Then they fold them exceeding exact, and then press them in a cold press. Some they dye, but the most are sent up for London white.

I saw the several vats they were a-dyeing in of black, yellow, blue, and green, which two last colours are dipped in the same vat,—that which makes it differ is what they were dipped in before, which makes them either green or blue. They hang the serges on a great beam or great pole on the top of the vat, and so keep turning it from one to another—as one turns it off into the vat, the other rolls it out of it; so they do it backwards and forwards till it is tinged deep enough of the colour. Their furnace that keeps their dye-pans boiling is all under that room made of coal fires. There was in a room by itself a vat for the scarlet, that being a very changeable dye, no waste must be allowed in that; indeed, I think they make as fine a colour as their "bowdies" are in London. These rollers I spake of, two men do continually roll on and off the pieces of serge till dipped enough. The length of these pieces is or should hold out 26 yards.

This city does exceedingly resemble London, for besides these buildings I mentioned for the several markets, there is an Exchange full of shops like our Exchanges are, only it is but one walk along as was the Exchange at Salisbury House in the Strand; there is also a very large space railed in by the Cathedral with walks round it, which is called the Exchange for Merchants, that constantly meet twice a day, just as they do in London. There are seventeen churches in the city, and four in the suburbs. There is some remains of the Castle walls; they make use of the rooms which are inside for the Assizes; there are the two bars, besides being large rooms with seats and places convenient and jury room. Here is a large walk at the entrance between rows of pillars. There is, besides this, just at the market-place a Guildhall, the entrance of which is a large place set on stone pillars, beyond which are the rooms for

Guildhall.

the session or any town affairs to be adjusted. Behind this building there is a vast cistern, which holds upwards of 600 hogsheads of water, which supplies by pipes the whole city; this cistern is replenished from the river, which is on purpose turned into a little channel by itself to turn a mill, and fills the engine that casts the water into the trunks which convey it to this cistern.[1] The water engine is like those at Islington and Darby, as I have seen, and is what now they make use of in divers places either to supply them with water or to drain a marsh or overplus of water.

The river X is a fine stream; they have made several    Exe R.
bays or weirs above the bridge, which cast the water into many channels for the convenience of turning all their mills, by which means they have composed a little island, for at the end it again returns into its own united channel. These weirs make great falls in the water, it comes with great violence; here they catch the salmon as they leap, with spears. The first of these bays is a very great one; there is one below the bridge which must be taken away when the navigation is complete, for they will need all their water to fill it to a depth to carry the ships, for just by the bridge is the quay designed, or that which now is already[2] they will enlarge to that place. Just by this quay is the custom house,[2] an open space below with rows of pillars, which they lay in goods just as they are unladen out of the ships in case of wet. Just by are several little rooms for land waiters, &c., then you ascend up a handsome pair of stairs into a large room full of desks and little partitions for the writers and accountants—it was full of books and files of paper. By it are two other rooms, which are used in the

[1] 1694.—The utility of having the water from the river Exe conveyed to the houses of this city being taken into consideration by the chamber, an act of Parliament was procured, and an engine for that purpose erected (at the head of the new leat) on a very ingenious model; which, notwithstanding the elevated situation of the city, plentifully supplies (by the help of wooden pipes) such inhabitants who, on payment of an annual rent, are desirous of being furnished therewith. (Jenkins, *Exeter*, 193.)

[2] 1675.—The quay and adjoining island were levelled and encompassed with a strong wall, alongside which ships may lie with great conveniency, either to discharge or take in their cargoes. A new custom-house was built on the quay, with convenient offices and cellars for storing goods. (Jenkins, *Exeter*, 179. See also note 1 on p. 112.)

same way when there is a great deal of business. There are several good conduits to supply the city with water besides that cistern; there is also a very fine market cross.

**Cathedral.**

The Cathedral at Exeter is preserved in its outside adornments beyond most I have seen, there remaining more of the fine carved work in stone, the figures and niches full and in proportion, though, indeed, I cannot say it has that great curiosity in work and variety as the great Church at Wells. It is a lofty building in the inside, the largest pair of organs I have ever seen, with fine carving of wood, which runs up a great height and made a magnificent appearance. The choir is very neat, but the Bishop's seat or throne was exceeding and very high, and the carving very fine and took up a great compass full of all variety of figures, something like the work over the Archbishop's throne in St. Paul's, London, but this was larger if not so curious. There were several good monuments and effigies of Bishops; there was one of a judge and his lady that was very curious, their garments embroidered all marble and gilt and painted.[1] There was a very large good library, in which was a press that had an anatomy of a woman.[2] The tower is 167 steps up, on which I had a view of the whole town, which is generally well built. I saw the Bishop's palace and garden. There is a long walk as well as broad, enclosed with rows of lofty trees which make it shady and very pleasant, which went along by the ditch and bank on which the town wall stands.

There are five gates to the town; there is also another long walk within shady trees on the other side of the town, which leads to the grounds where the drying frames are set up for the serges.

**Chudleigh.**

From thence I passed the bridge across the River Ex to Chedly, which was nine miles, mostly lanes and a continual going up hill and down, some of them pretty steep hills; and all these lesser hills, as I have observed, rise higher and higher till it advances you upon the high ridge which discovers to view the great valleys below full of those lesser hills and enclosures with quickset hedges and trees and rich land, but the roads are not to be seen, being

---

[1] Sir John Doddridge and his wife (see p. 86.)    [2] See p. 89.

all along in lanes covered over with the shelter of the hedges and trees. Then when I was on the top hill, I went three or four miles on an open down which brought me to the edge of another such a ridge, which was by some steps to be descended as it was gained by the lesser hills one below another till I came to the bottom, and then I had about two or three miles along on a plain or common, which for the most part are a little moorish by reason of their receiving the water that drains from the several great hills on either side, and so then I am to rise up another such a range of hills, and as near as I could compute in my riding it was six or seven miles between one high ridge of hills to that over against it, whereas were there a bridge over from one top to the other it could not be two miles distant; but this does give them the advantage of several acres of land by reason of the many hills, which, if drawn out on plains, as in some other parts, would appear much vaster tracts of land. On these hills, as I said, one can discern little besides enclosures, hedges, and trees; rarely can see houses unless you are just descending to them; they always are placed in holes, as it were, and you have a precipice to go down to come at them. The lanes are full of stones and dirt, for the most part because they are so close, the sun and wind cannot come at them, so that in many places you travel on causeys which are uneven also for want of a continued repair.

From Chedly to Ashburton is 11 miles more, in all 20 miles from Exeter, the roads being much the same as before. This Ashburton is a poor little town—bad was the best inn. It is a market town, and here are a great many dissenters and those of the most considerable persons of the town; there was a presbyterian, an anabaptist, and a quakers' meeting.

Thence I went for Plymouth, 24 long miles, and here the roads contract and the lanes are exceeding narrow and so covered up you can see little about; an army might be marching undiscovered by anybody, for when you are on those heights that show a vast country about, you cannot see one road. The ways now become so difficult that one could scarcely pass by each other, even the single horses, and so dirty in many places, and just a track for one

Ashburton.

horse's feet, and the banks on either side so near, [that]
were they not well secured and mended with stones stuck
close like a dry wall everywhere when they discover the
banks to break and moulder down, [they] would be
in danger of swallowing up the way quite; for the
quicksets and trees that grow on these banks (which are
some of them natural rocks and quarries, others mended
with such stone or slate stuck edgeways to secure them)
loosen the mould, and so make it moulder down sometimes.   I passed through several little places and over some
stone bridges.   The waters are pretty broad, so there are four
or five arches [in] most bridges, all stone.   The running of
the waters is with a huge rushing by reason of the stones
which lie in the water, some of them great rocks, which
give some interruption to the current, which finding another
way, either by its sides or mounting over part of it, causes
the frothing of the water and the noise—the rivers being
full of stones, bigger or less.

About four or five miles from Ashburton I came to a little
place called Dean, and at the end of it ascended a very
steep hill, all rock almost; and so it was like so many steps

**Dean Clapper
Hill.** up.   This is called Dean Clapperhill; it was an untoward
place, but not so formidable to me as the people of the
place where I lay described it, having gone much worse
hills in the North.   All along the road where the lanes are
a little broader you ride by rows of trees on each side, set
and kept exactly even and cut, the tops being for shade
and beauty, and they in exact form as if a grove to some
house.   At first I thought it was near some houses till the
frequency and length proved the contrary, for there are very
few, if any, houses near the road, unless the little villages
you pass through.   This country being almost full of stone,
the streets and roads, too, have a natural sort of paving or
pitching, though uneven.   All their carriages are here on
the backs of horses, with sort of hooks like yokes stand
upon each side of a good height, which are the receptacles
of their goods, either wood, furze, or lime, or coal, or corn,
or hay, or straw, or what else they convey from place to
place, and I cannot see how two such horses can pass
each other, or indeed in some places how any horse can
pass by each other, and yet these are the roads that are

all hereabouts. Some little corners may jut out that one may a little get out of the way of each other, but this is but seldom.

Two miles from Plymouth we come to the river Plym, just by a little town all built of stone, and the tiling is all flat, which with the lime it is cemented with makes it look like snow, and in the sun shining on the slate it glisters.

*Plympton.*

Here I came in sight on the right hand of a very large house built all with this sort of stone, which is a sort of marble. Even all quarries are, and some fine marble. This house looked very finely in a thicket of trees like a grove, and was on the side of a hill and led just down to the head of the river Plym, which is filled with the tide from the sea, and here I crossed it on a stone bridge. So I rode two miles most by the river, which increases and is a fine broad stream, and at the town, which is its mouth, it falls into the sea. The sea here runs into several creeks, one place it runs up to the Dock and Milbrook, another arm of the sea goes up to Saltash and Port Eliot.

*Saltram (?)*

Plymouth is two parishes, called the Old Town and the New; the houses all built of this marble and the slate at the top looks like lead and glisters in the sun. There are no great houses in the town; the streets are good and clean, [and] there is a great many, though some are but narrow; they are mostly inhabited with seamen and those which have affairs on the sea, for here up to the town there is a depth of water for ships of the first rate to ride. It is a great sea and dangerous by reason of the several points of land, between which the sea runs up a great way, and there are several little islands also, all which bear the several tides hard one against the other. There are two quays: the one is a broad space which leads you up into the broad street, and is used in manner of an Exchange for the merchants' meeting,[1] for in this street also is a fine stone cross and also a long market house set on stone pillars. There are several good conduits to convey the water to the town, which conveyance the famous Sir Francis Drake (which did encompass the world in Queen Elizabeth's days and landed

*Plymouth.*

---

[1] 1672.—The Exchange or Walk on the New Quay built. (Jewitt, *Plymouth*, 230.)

safe at Plymouth) gave to the town.[1] There are two churches in the town,[2] but nothing fine. I was in the best, and saw only King Charles the First's picture at length at prayer, just as it is cut on the frontispiece of the "jnenicum."[3] This picture was drawn and given the church when he was in his troubles, for some piece of service shown him.[4] The altar stands in the chancel or railed place, but it stands table-wise the length and not up against the wall. The font was of marble, and, indeed, so are all the buildings here, for their stone is all a sort of marble, some coarser, some finer. There are four large meetings for the dissenters in the town, taking in the quakers and anabaptists.

**Devonport.**   The mouth of the river just at the town is a very good harbour for ships; the dockyards are about two miles from the town—by boat you go to it the nearest way—it is one of the best in England. A great many good ships built there, and the great depth of water which comes up to it though it runs for two miles between the land, which also shelters the ships. There is a great deal of buildings on the Dock, a very good house for the masters and several lesser ones, and house for their cordage and making ropes and all sorts of things required in building or refitting ships. It looks like a little town. The buildings are so many, and all of marble with fine slate on the roofs, and at a little distance it makes all the houses show as if they were covered with snow and glisters in the sun, which adds to their beauty.

---

1 1589.—The town agreed with Sir Francis Drake to bring in the water of the River Meve, and gave him £200 in hand, and £600 for which he is to compound with the owners of the land over which it runneth. In December, 1590, Sir Francis Drake began on the rivulet, and brought it into the town 25 miles, the 24th of April following, and before Michaelmas he built six mills, two at Widey and four at the town, also divers conduits. (Jewitt, *Plymouth*, 123-5.)

2 St. Andrew's or Old Church, and Charles' or New Church.

3 This is the famous "Eikon Basilike," a "portraiture of his Sacred Majesty in his sufferings."

4 1681.—Mr. James Yonge was chosen churchwarden this year of Saint Andrew's parish, who rebuilt the gallery, painted it, set up the King's, Town's, and Bishop's arms thereon, as also the picture of King Charles the Martyr, with pertinent inscription. (Jewitt, *Plymouth*, 235.) Charles' Church was also named after King Charles I.

The fine and only thing in Plymouth town is the Citadel or Castle,[1] which stands very high above the town, the walls and battlements round it with all their works and platforms are in very good repair and look nobly, all marble, full of towers with stone balls on the top and gilt on the top; the entrance being by an ascent up a hill looks very noble over two drawbridges and gates, which are marble as is the whole, well carved, the gate with armoury and statues all gilt, and on the top seven gold balls.    The buildings within are very neat, a large apartment for the Governor, with others that are less for the several officers.    There is a long building also, which is the arsenal for the arms and ammunition, and just by it a round building well secured, which was for the powder round the works in the platform for the guns, which are well mounted and very well kept.  Walking round I had the view of all the town, and also part of the main ocean, in which are some islands.    There is St. Nicholas Island with a fort in it; there it was Harry Martin, one of the King's judges, was banished during life.  There you can just discover a lighthouse which is building on a mere rock in the middle of the sea;[2] this is seven leagues off; it will be of great advantage for the guide of the ships that pass that way.

From the platform I could see the Dock, and also just against it I saw Mount Edgecomb, a seat of Sir Richard Edgecome's; it stands on the side of a hill all bedecked with woods, which are divided into several rows of trees in walks, the house being all of this white marble.    It is built round a court, so the four sides are alike; at the corners of it are towers, which, with the lantern or cupola in the middle, look well.    The house is not very lofty, nor the windows high, but it looked like a very uniform neat building and pretty large.    There is a long walk from one part of the front down to the waterside, which is on a descent guarded with shady rows of trees.    There is a fine terrace

*Citadel.*

*Drake's Is.*
*Henry Martin.*
*Eddystone.*

*Mount Edgcumbe.*

---

[1] The Citadel was begun in 1665 and completed in 1670.    In the latter year it was inspected by King Charles II., with the Dukes of York and Monmouth.    (Jewitt, *Plymouth*, 226, 228.)

[2] This was the first Eddystone Lighthouse begun by Mr. Henry Winstanley in 1696 and finished in 1700.    It was destroyed by the great storm of 1703, and its ingenious architect, who was superintending some repairs, perished in its ruins.

walled in.  At the waterside are open gates in the middle
and a summer house at each end, from whence a wall is
drawn round the house and gardens and a large park, the
wall of which I rode by a good while; so that altogether
and its situation makes it esteemed by me the finest seat
I have seen and might be more rightly named Mount
Pleasant.

Cremyll
Ferry

From Plymouth I went one mile to Cribly Ferry, which
is a very hazardous passage by reason of three tides meeting.
Had I known the danger before, I should not have been very
willing to have gone it, not but this is the constant way all
people go, and saved several miles' riding.  I was at least
an hour going over; it was about a mile, but indeed in
some places, notwithstanding there were five men rowed
and I set my own men to row also, I do believe we made
not a step of way for almost a quarter of an hour, but,
blessed be God, I came safely over; but those ferry boats
are so wet and then the sea and wind are always cold to
be upon, that I never fail to catch cold in a ferry boat, as
I did this day, having two more ferries to cross, though
not so bad or half so long as this.

Millbrook.

Thence to Milbrooke two miles and went all along by
the water, and had the full view of the dockyards.  Here I
entered into Cornwall, and so passed over many very steep,
stony hills, though here I had some two or three miles of
exceeding good way on the downs, and then I came to the
steep precipices—great rocky hills.  Ever and anon I came
down to the sea and rode by its side on the sand, then
mounted up again on the hills, which carried me mostly in
sight of the South Sea.  Sometimes I was in lanes full of
rows of trees, and then I came down a very steep, stony

Looe.

hill to Lonn, 13 mile, and here I crossed a little arm of the
sea on a bridge of 14 arches.  This is a pretty big seaport,
a great many little houses all of stone, and steep hill much
worse and three times as long as Dean Clapper hill, and so
I continued up and down hill.  Here, indeed, I met with
more enclosed ground, and so had more lanes and a deeper
clay road, which by the rain the night before had made it
very dirty and full of water in many places; in the road
there are many holes and sloughs wherever there is clay
ground, and when by rains they are filled with water, it is

difficult to shun danger. Here my horse was quite down in one of these holes full of water, but by the good hand of God's providence which has always been with me ever a present help in time of need, for giving him a good strap he flounced up again, though he had gotten quite down his head and all, yet did retrieve his feet and got clear off the place with me on his back.

So I came to Hoile, eight mile more; they are very long miles the farther west, but you have the pleasure of riding as if in a grove in most places—the regular rows of trees on each side the road as if it were an entrance into some gentleman's ground to his house. I ferried over again across an arm of the sea; here it was not broad but exceeding deep. This is the South Sea, which runs into many little creeks for several miles into the land, which is all the rivers they have. I observed this to be exceeding salt, and as green as ever I saw the sea when I have been a league or two out from the land, which shows it must be very deep and great tides. This Hoile is a narrow, stony town, the streets very close, and as I descended a great steep into the town, so I ascended one up a stony long hill far worse and full of shelves and rocks and three times as long as Dean Clapper hill, which I name because, when I was there, they would have frighted me with its terribleness as the most inaccessible place as ever was and none like it, and my opinion is that it was but one or two steps, to other places forty steps, and them with more hazard than this of Dean Clapper.

Well, to pass on, I went over some little heath ground but mostly lanes, and those stony and dirty, three miles and half to Parr; here I ferried over again, not but when the tide is out you may ford it. Thence I went over the heath to St. Austins, which is a little market town where I lay, but their houses are like barns up to the top of the house. Here was a pretty good dining room and chamber within it, and very neat country women. My landlady brought me one of the West-country tarts; this was the first I met with, though I had asked for them in many places in Somerset and Devonshire. It is an apple pie with a custard all on the top. It is the most acceptable entertainment that could be made me. They scald their cream and milk in

Hall, opposite Fowey (?)

Par.

St. Austell.

most parts of those countries, and so it is a sort of clouted cream as we call it, with a little sugar, and so put on the top of the apple pie. I was much pleased with my supper, though not with the custom of the country, which is a universal smoking, men, women, and children have all their pipes of tobacco in their mouths and so sit round the fire smoking, which was not delightful to me when I went down to talk with my landlady for information of any matter and customs among them. I must say they are as comely sort of women as I have seen anywhere, though in ordinary dress—good black eyes and crafty enough and very neat.

Half a mile from thence they blow their tin, which I went to see. They take the ore and pound it in a stamping mill which resembles the paper mills, and when it is as fine as the finest sand—some of which I saw and took—this they fling into a furnace and with it coal to make the fire. So it burns together and makes a violent heat and fierce flame ; the metal by the fire being separated from the coal and its own dross, being very heavy falls down to a trench made to receive it at the furnace hole below. This liquid metal I saw them shovel up with an iron shovel, and so pour it into moulds, in which it cools, and so they take it thence in sort of wedges, or pigs I think they call them. It is a fine metal in its first melting—looks like silver ; I had a piece poured out and made cold for to take with me. The ore as it is just dug looks like the thunderstones, a greenish hue full of pendust—this seems to contain its full description—the shining part is white.

I went a mile farther on the hills, and so came where they were digging in the tin mines. There were at least 20 mines all in sight, which employ a great many people at work almost night and day, but constantly all and every day, including the Lord's Day, which they are forced to prevent their mines being overflowed with water. More than 1,000 men are taken up about them ; few mines but had then almost 20 men and boys attending it, either down in the mines digging and carrying the ore to the little bucket which conveys it up, or else others are draining the water and looking to the engines that are draining it, and those above are attending the drawing up the ore in a sort of windlass as it is to a well. Two men keep turning, bringing up one and letting down another. They are much like the leather buckets they use in London to put out fire, which hang up in churches and great men's halls. They have a great labour and great expense to drain the mines of the water with mills that horses turn, and now they have the mills or water engines that are turned by the water which is conveyed on frames of timber and trunks to hold the water, which falls down on the wheels as an overshot mill, and these are the sort that turns the water into the several towns I have seen about London, Darby, and Exeter, and many places more. They do five times more good than the mills they use to turn with horses, but then they are much more chargeable. Those mines do require a great deal of timber to support them and to make all those engines and mills, which makes fuel very scarce here. They burn mostly turves, which is an unpleasant smell; it makes one smell as if smoked like bacon. This ore, as said, is made fine powder in a stamping mill which is like the paper mills, only these are pounded dry and no water let into them as it is to the rags, to work them into a paste. The mills are all turned with a little stream or channel of water you may step over; indeed they have no other mills but such in all the country. I saw not a windmill all over Cornwall or Devonshire, though they have wind and hills enough, and it may be it is too bleak for them. In the tin mines there is stone dug out and a sort of spar something like what I have seen in the lead mines at Darbyshire, but it seemed more solid and hard; it shines and looks like mother of pearl. They also dig out stones as clear as crystal, which are called Cornish diamonds. I saw one as big as my two fists, very clear and like some pieces of crystal my father brought from the Alps in Italy. I got one of those pieces of their Cornish diamonds as long as half my finger, which had three or four flat sides with edges; the top was sharp and so hard as it would cut a letter on glass.

Thence I went to ———, six miles good way, and passed by 100 mines, some on which they were at work, others that were lost by the waters overwhelming them. I crossed the water on a long stone bridge, and so through dirty, stony lanes three miles, and then I came into a broad coach road, which I have not seen since I left Exeter; so I went

*Boscawen.*
Tregothnan.

three miles more to Mr. Boscawen's—Trygothy—a relation of mine. His house stands on a high hill in the middle of a park with several rows of trees, with woods beyond it. The house is built all of white stone like the rough coarse marble, and covered with slate. They use much lime in their cement, which makes both walls and cover look very white. There is a court walled round with open iron gates and bars. The entrance is up a few stone steps into a large high hall and so to a passage that leads foreright up a good staircase. On the right side is a large common parlour for constant eating in, from whence goes a little room for smoking that has a back way into the kitchen, and on the left hand is a great parlour and drawing-room—wainscotted all very well, but plain. The great parlour is cedar; out of it is the drawing-room, which is hung with pictures of the family, that goes into the garden, which has gravel walks round and across, but the squares are full of gooseberry and shrub trees and looks more like a kitchen garden, as Lady Mary Boscawen told me, out of which is another garden and orchard, which is something like a grove—green walks with rows of fruit trees. It is capable of being a fine place with some charge; the rooms above are new-modelled, three rooms wainscotted and hung as the new way is, and the beds made up well, one red damask, another green, another wrought some of the Lady's own work and well made up, which is her room with a dressing-room by it. There is a dressing-room and a room for a servant just by the best chamber. There are two other good rooms unaltered, with old hangings to the bottom on wrought work of the first Lady's, Lady Marget's[1] work, that was my cousin german; within that room was a servant's room and back stairs, and there was just such another apartment on the other side. Between all from the stairs a broad passage leads to a balcony over the entrance, which looked very pleasantly over the park, but in the cupola on the leads I could see a vast way, at least 20 miles round; for this house stands

---

[1] Hugh Boscawen, bap. 21 Aug., 1625, bur. 10 June, 1701, at St. Michael Penkivel. He married Margaret, daughter and co-heir of Theophilus Clinton, Esq., of Lincoln. She was bur. 1 Nov., 1688, as "Lady Margaret," and was undoubtedly the "Lady Marget" referred to in the text. "Lady Mary Boscawen" was presumably a second wife, but is not mentioned in Vivian's *Visitations of Cornwall*.

very high to the land side eastward, and the south was
the Great Ocean which runs into Falmouth, that is the
best harbour for ships in that road.

Six miles from this place westward was to Truro, and    Truro.
the north to the hills full of copper mines.  Here I was very
civilly entertained.  From thence I returned back, intending
not to go to the Land's End, which was 30 miles farther,
for fear of the rains that fell in the night, which made me
doubt what travelling I should have; so to St. Columb I    St. Columb.
went, a pretty long 12 miles.  Here I met with many rows
of elm trees, which I have not found in any country except
Wiltshire ; these were mostly so, though there were also
ashes and oaks.  The hedges were hazel, thorn, and holly,
but to see so many good rows of trees on the road is surprising and looks like the entrance to some gentleman's
house, and I cannot tell but some of them were so, though
a mile off from the house.

The next day, finding it fair weather on the change of
the moon, I altered my resolution and so went for the
Land's End by Redruth, 18 miles, mostly over heath and    Redruth.
downs, which were very bleak and full of mines.  Here I
came by the copper mines, which have the same order in
the digging and draining, though here it seems drier and I
believe not quite so annoyed with water.  The ore is something as the tin, only this looks blackish, or rather a purple
colour, and the glistering part is yellow as the other was
white.  They do not melt it here, but ship it off to Bristol
by the North Sea, which I rode in sight of, and is not
above two or three miles from hence, which supplies them
with coals for their fuel at easier rates than the other side,
Plymouth and the South Sea, because since the war they
could not double the point at the Land's End, being so
near France the pirates or privateers met them.  Indeed,
at St. Ives they do melt a little, but nothing that is con-    St. Ives.
siderable—that is 10 miles from Redruth, which is a little
market town.  Here they carry all their things on horses'
backs, so that of a market day, which was Friday, you see
a great number of horses little of size, which they call
Cornish "canelys."  They are well made and strong and will
trip along as light on the stony road without injury to
themselves, whereas my horses went so heavy that they

wore their shoes immediately thin and off, but here I met with a very good smith that shoe'd the horses as well as they do in London, and that is not common in the country.

**Penzance.**

**Hayle.**

From Redruth I went to Pensands, 15 miles, and passed by the ruins of a great fortification or castle on a high hill about three miles from Redruth, and passed to Hailes, and so went by the seaside a great way, it being spring tide it was a full sea. Just over against it there was a church which was almost sunk into the sands, being a very sandy place. So I went up pretty high hills and over some heath or common, on which a great storm of hail and rain met me and drove fiercely on me, but the wind soon dried my dust coat. Here I came by a very good grove of trees, which I thought was by some gentleman's house, but found it some farmer's.

The people here are very ill guides and know very little from home, only to some market town they frequent, but will be very solicitous to know where you go and how far, and from whence you came and where is your abode. Then I

**St. Michael's Mount.**

came in sight of the hill in Cornwall called the Mount; it is a rock in the sea which at the flowing tide is an island, but at low water one can go over the sands almost just to it. It is but a little market town, which is about 2 miles from Panzants, and you may walk or ride to it on the sands when the tide is out. It is a fine rock and very high—several little houses for fishermen in the sides of it just by the water. At the top is a pretty good house where the Governor lives sometimes—Sir —— Hook his name is; there is a tower on the top, on which is a flag. There is a chair or throne on the top, from whence they can discover a great way at sea, and here they put up lights to direct ships.

Pensands lies just as a shore to the main South Ocean, which comes from the Lizard, and being on the side of a hill with a high hill all round the side to the landward, it looks so snug and warm, and truly it needs shelter, having the sea on the other side and little or no fuel—turf and furze and fern. They have little or no wood and no coal, which differences it from Darbyshire—otherwise this and to the Land's End is stone and barren as Darbyshire. I was surprised to find my supper boiling on a fire always supplied with a bush of furze, and that to be the only fuel to dress a joint of meat and broth, and told them they could not roast me anything, but they have a little wood for such occasions, but it is scarce and dear, which is a strange thing that the ships should not supply them. They told me it must all be brought round the Land's End, and since the war they could not have it. This town is two parishes; one church in the town, and a little chapel and another church belonging to the other parish, which is a mile distance. There is also a good meeting-place.

There is a good quay and a good harbour for the ships to ride, by means of the point of land which runs into the sea in a neck or compass which shelters it from the main and answers the Lizard Point, which you see very plain—a point of land looks like a double hill, one above the other, that runs a good way into the sea. The Land's End is 10 miles farther, pretty steep and narrow lanes, but it is not sheltered with trees or hedgerows, this being rather desert and like the Peak country in Darbyshire, dry stone walls, and the hills full of stones, but it is in most places better land and yields good corn, wheat, barley, and oats, and some rye. About two miles from the Land's End I came in sight of the main ocean on both sides, the south and north sea, and so rode in its view till I saw them joined at the point, and saw the island of Sily, which is 7 leagues off the Land's End. They tell me that in a clear day, those in the island can discern the people in the main as they go up the hill to church, and they can describe their clothes. This church and little parish, which is called Churchtown, is about a mile from the point. The houses are but poor cottages, like barns to look on, much like those in Scotland, but to do my own country the right, the inside of their little cottages are clean and plastered and such as you might comfortably eat and drink in, and for curiosity sake I drank there and I met with very good bottled ale.

The Land's End terminates in a point or peak of great rocks which runs a good way into the sea. I clambered over them as far as safety permitted me. There were abundance of rocks, and shoals of stones stand up in the sea a mile off, some here and there, some quite to the shore, which they name by several names of Knights and Ladies rolled up in mantles from some old tradition or fiction.

Lizard Point.

Land's End.

Scilly I.

Sennen (?).

The poets advance description of the amours of some great
persons; but these many rocks and stones, which look
like the Needles in the Isle of Wight, make it hazardous
for ships to double the point, especially in stormy weather.
Here at the Land's End they are but a little way off
Havre.
France; two days' sail at farthest convey them to Hauve
de Grace in France, but the peace being but newly entered
into with the French, I was not willing to venture, at
least by myself, into a foreign kingdom, and being then at
the end of the land, my horse's legs could not carry me
through the deep, and so returned again to Pensands, ten
miles more, and so came in view of both the seas and saw
the Lizard Point and Pensands and the Mount in Cornwall,
which looked very fine in the broad day, the sun shining
on the rock in the sea.

Hayle.

Then I continued my return from Pensands to Hailing,
and now the tide was down and so much land appeared
which lay under water before, and I might have forded
quite across; many that know the country do, but I took
the safer way round by the bridge. Here is abundance
of very good fish, though they are so ill supplied at
Pensands because they carry it all up the country east and
southward. This is an arm of the North Sea, which runs in
a great way into the land; it is a large bay when the sea
comes in, and, upon the next hill I ascended from it, I
could discover it more plain to be a deep water and the
supply of the main ocean. Just by here lay some ships,
and I perceived as I went, there being a storm, it seemed
very tempestuous and is a hazardous place in the high
Redruth.
tides; so I came to Redruth.

I perceive they are very bleak in these countries,
especially to this North Ocean, and the winds so troublesome they are forced to spin straw and so to make a caul
or network to lay over their thatch on their ricks and
outhouses, with weights of stones around to defend the
thatch from being blown away by the great winds, not but
they have a better way of thatching their houses with reeds,
and so close that when it is well done, will last twenty
years, but what I mention of braces or bands of straw is
on their ricks, which only is to hold a year. These places,
as in some other parts, indeed all over Cornwall and

Devonshire, they have their carriages on horses' backs, this being the time of harvest, though later in the year than usual, being the middle of September, but I had the advantage of seeing their harvest bringing in, which is on a horse's back with sort of crooks of wood like yokes on either side—two or three on a side stand up, in which they stow the corn and so tie it with cords, but they cannot so equally poise it but the going of the horse is like to cast it down sometimes on the one side and sometimes on the other, for they load them from the neck to the tail and pretty high, and are forced to support it with their hands, so to a horse they have two people, and the women lead and support them as well as the men, and go through thick and thin—sometimes I have met with half a score horses thus loaded—they are indeed but little horses, their "canelles"[1] as they call them, and so may not be able to draw a cart; otherwise I am sure three or four horses might draw three times as much as four horses carry, and where it is open ground and roads broad, which in some places here it was, I wondered at their labour in this kind, for the men and women toiled like their horses, but the common observation of custom being as a second nature, people are very hardly convinced or brought off from, though never so inconvenient.

From Redruth I went to Truro, 8 miles, which is a pretty little town and seaport, and formerly was esteemed the best town in Cornwall; now is the second, next Lanstone. It is just by the copper and tin mines, and lies down in a bottom, pretty steep ascent as most of the towns in these countries, that you would be afraid of tumbling with nose and head foremost. The town is built of stone—a good pretty church built all stone and carved on the outside; it stands in the middle of the town, and just by there is a market house on stone pillars and hall on the top; there is also a pretty good quay. This was formerly a great trading town and flourished in all things, but now as there is in all places their rise and period, so this, which is become a ruinated disregarded place. Here is a very good meeting,

Truro.

Launceston.

---

[1] Goonhillies or gunnellies, so named after Goonhilly Downs. (*New English Dict.*)   See also p. 127.

but I was hindered by the rain the Lord's Day, else
should have come to hearing, and so was forced to stay
where I could hear but one sermon at the church, but by
it saw the fashion of the country, being obliged to go a
mile to the parish church over some grounds which are
divided by such stiles and bridges uncommon, and I never
saw any such before; they are several stones fixed across,
and so are like a grate or large steps over a ditch that is
full of mud or water, and over this just in the middle is a
great stone fixed sideways, which is the stile to be clambered
over. These I find are the fences and guards of their
grounds one from another, and indeed they are very troublesome and dangerous for strangers and children. I heard a
pretty good sermon, but that which was my greatest pleasure
was the good landlady I had—she was but an ordinary
plain woman, but she was understanding in the best things
as most—the experience of real religion and her quiet sub-
mission and self-resignation to the will of God in all things,
and especially in the placing her in a remoteness to the
best advantages of hearing, and being in such a public
employment which she desired and aimed at the discharging so as to adorn the Gospel of her Lord and Saviour,
and the care of her children.

Tregothnan.    From Truro, which is 9 miles from Falmouth and 4
miles from Trygolny, which was the place I was at before
with my relation, that would have engaged my stay with
them a few days or weeks, to have given me the diversion
of the country, and to have heard the Cornish nightingales
as they call them, the Cornish chough—a sort of jackdaw,
if I mistake not, a little black bird which makes them a
visit about Michaelmas and gives them the diversion of the
notes, which is a rough sort of music not unlike the bird I
take them for, so I believe they by way of jest put on the
Cornish gentlemen by calling them nightingales; but the
season of the year inclined to rain, and the days declining,
I was afraid to delay my return, and these parts not
abounding with much accommodation for horses, theirs
being a hard sort of cattle and live much on grass or furzes,
of which they have the most, and it will make them very
fat, being little hardy horses, and as they jest on themselves
do not love the taste of oats and hay, because they never

permit them to know the taste of it.   But my horses could not live so, especially on journeys, of which I had given them a pretty exercise, and their new oats and hay suited not their stomach.   I could get no beans for them till I came back to St. Columbe again, which from Truro by St. Mitchel was 12 miles, mostly lanes and long miles.   As I observed before, I saw no windmills all these countries over: they have only the mills which are over-shot, and a little rivulet of water you may step over turns them, which are the mills for grinding their corn and their ore or what else.

St. Columb.
Mitchell.

From St. Columbe I went to Waybridge 6 long miles. Thence to Comblefford, over steep hills 9 miles more; some of this way was over commons of black moorish ground full of sloughs.   The lanes are defended with banks wherein are stones, some great rocks, others slaty stones, such as they use for tiling.   Comblefford was a little market town, but it was very indifferent accommodations, but the rains that night and next morning made me take up there till about 10 o'clock in the morning; it then made a show of clearing up and made me willing to seek a better lodging.

Wadebridge.

Camelford.

Two miles from this place is a large standing water called Dosenmere Pool in a black moorish ground, and is fed by no rivers except the little rivulets from some high hills, yet seems always full without diminution and flows with the wind and is stored with good fish, and people living near it take the pleasure in a boat to go about it. There is also good wild-fowl about it; it seems to be such a water as the mere at Whitlesome in Huntingtonshire by Stilton; it is fresh water and what supply it has must be the rivulets that must come from the South Sea, being that wayward towards Plymouth.   As I travelled I came in sight of a great mountain esteemed the second highest hill in England, supposing they account Black Combe in Cumberland the first, but really I have seen so many great and high hills I cannot attribute preeminence to either of these, though this did look very great and tall, but I think it is better said the highest hill in each county.

Dosmare Pool.

Brown Willy(?)

I travelled four pretty long miles much in lanes, and then came into a common where I crossed the great roads which on the right hand leads a way to Plymouth and the

Barnstaple.

Delabole.

Hartland
Point.
*Earl of Bath.*
Stowe.
Lundy I.

Launceston.

South Sea, the left hand to Bastable and the North Sea, which conveys the stone or rather marble which they take from hence at Bole, remarkable quarries for a black stone, exceeding hard and glossy like marble, very durable for pavements. This they send to all parts in time of peace, and London takes off much of it.

Here I rode over a common or down four miles long in sight of the North Sea, and saw Hartly Point, which is the Earl of Bath's, just by his fine house called Stow, his fine stables of horses and gardens. There I discerned the Pcint very plain, and just by I saw the Isle of Lundy, which formerly belonged to my grandfather, William, Lord Viscount Say and Seale, which does abound with fish and rabbits and all sorts of fowls—one bird that lives partly in the water and partly out, and so may be called an amphibious creature ; it is true that one foot is like a turkey, the other a goose's foot ; it lays its egg in a place the sun shines on and sets it so exactly upright on the small end that there it remains till taken up, and all the art and skill of persons cannot set it up so again to abide.

Here I met with some showers which by fits or storms held me—to Lanston, 4 miles more ; these 12 miles from Cambleford were not little ones, and what with the wet and dirty lanes in many places I made it a tedious journey. I could see none of the town till just as I was, as you may say, ready to tumble into it, there being a vast steep to descend to, when the town seemed in a bottom, yet I was forced to ascend a pretty good hill into the place. Lanston is the chief town in Cornwall where the assizes are kept. I should have remarked at the Land's End that Pensands was the last corporation in England, so this is one of the last great towns, though no city, for Cornwall is in the diocese of Devonshire, which is Exeter. There is a great ascent up into the Castle, which looks very great, and in good repair the walls and towers round it. It is true there is but a part of it remains, the round tower or fort being still standing and makes a good appearance. The town is encompassed with walls and gates. It is pretty large, though you cannot discover the whole town, being up and down in so many hills. The streets themselves are very steep unless it be at the market-place, where is a long and handsome space set on stone pillars with the town hall on the top, which has a large lantern or cupola in the middle, where hangs a bell for a clock, with a dial to the street. There are in this place two or three good houses built after the London form by some lawyers, else the whole town is old houses of timber work.

At a little distance from the town, on a high hill I looked back and had the full prospect of the whole town, which was of pretty large extent. A mile beyond I crossed on a stone bridge over a river and entered into Devonshire again, and passed through mostly lanes which were stony and dirty by reason of the rains that fell the night before, and this day, which was the wettest day I had in all my summer's travels, hitherto having had no more than a shower in a day, and that not above three times in all, except when I came to Exeter. As I came down from Taunton there was small rain most of the afternoon, but this day was much worse, so that by that time I came through lanes and some commons to Oakingham, which was 15 miles, I was very wet. This was a little market town, and I met with a very good inn and accommodation, very good chamber and bed, and came in by 5 of the clock, so had good time to take off my wet clothes and be all dried and warm to eat my supper, and rested very well without sustaining the least damage by the wet. I should have remarked that these roads were much up and down hill through enclosed lands and woods in the same manner the other part of Cornwall and Devonshire was, gaining by degrees the upper grounds by one hill to another, and so descending them in like manner. These rains fully convinced me of the need of so many great stone bridges, whose arches were so high that I have wondered at it, because the waters seemed shallow streams, but they were so swelled by one night and day's rain that they came up pretty near the arches, and ran in most places with such rapidity and looked so thick and troubled as if they would clear all before them. This causes great floods, and the lower grounds are overwhelmed for a season after such rains, so that had I not put on and gotten beyond Lanston that day there would have been no moving for me till the floods, which hourly increased, were run off.

Okehampton.

Crockernwell.

Next day I went to Cochen Well, 10 miles, mostly good open way except a hill or two which were steep and stony; though this was the longer way and about, yet by reason of the former rains it was the safest, for the lower way was run over by the waters which are land floods from the swelling brooks, which are up in a few hours and are sunk in the same time again—the ways were somewhat dirty.

Exeter.

Thence to Exeter, 10 miles more, but this was the basest way you can go, and made much worse by these rains, but its narrow lanes full of stones and loose ground, clay, and now exceeding slippery by the rains. A quarter of a mile on this side of the town I stood on a high bank from whence the prospect of the city of Exeter was very pleasant; I could see it to great advantage, the Cathedral and other churches' spires with the whole town, which in general is well built, with the good bridge over the Ex, which is a fine river, on whose banks are several rows of trees all below the town. The walks all about it augment the beauty of the city. From whence I went to Topsham,

Topsham.

3 miles, which is a little market place and a very good quay; hither they convey on horses their serges, and so load their ships which come to this place, all for London.

Starcross.

Thence I saw Starre Cross, where the great ships ride, and there they build some ships. This was up the river, 5 or 6 miles up the river, but the tide being out could not go, and it was ten miles by land and their miles are so long here, I could not go it, seeing almost as well the ships that lay there as if at the place.

Exeter.
Goswill.
Sir E. Harrison.
Honiton.

Thence I returned to Exeter, 3 miles, where I had been very kindly entertained by Mr Goswill and his wife, which was one my brother, Sir Edmond Harrison, did employ in buying serges. From Exeter I went to Honiton, 15 miles, all fine gravel way, the best road I have met with all in the west. Here it is they make the fine bone lace in imitation of the Antwerp and Flanders lace, and indeed I think it's as fine; it only will not wash so fine, which must be the fault in the thread. Honiton is a pretty large place, a good market-house, near it a good church with a round tower and spire which was very high and a little peculiar in its form, somewhat like a pigeon-house roof. Here is a very large meeting of dissenters.

Thence I went to Axminster, seven miles more, but not so good way, being much in lanes stony and dirty and pretty much up and down hills, like the other parts of those countries. Beyond Axminster, where I passed over the river Ax on a pretty large bridge, I came to Somerset-shire again.

*Axminster.*

# ITINERARIUM CURIOSUM
## By Dr. William Stukeley  1724

Beyond Chard to Honiton is a very bad road of stones and sand, over brooks, spring-heads, and barren downs. From the hill-tops about Stockland I first had sight of the southern ocean; a most solemn view, a boundless extent of water thrown into a mighty horizontal curve. Beyond Honiton the scene of travelling mended apace, and the fine Devonshire prospects entertained the eye in a manner new and beautiful; for here the hills are very long and broad, the valleys between proportional, so that the vastly-extended concavity presented an immense landscape of pastures and hedge-rows distinct, like a map of an actual survey, and not beyond ken: these are full of springs, brooks, and villages, copses and gentlemen's seats; and when you have passed over one hill, you see the like repeated before you, with Nature's usual diversity. They told me of a great cairn, or heap of stones, on Black Down, called Lapper-stones; probably a sepulchral monument.

*Honiton.*

*Black Down.*

Exeter is the famous *Isca Dumnoniorum* of the Romans, the last station this way in Antoninus his Itinerary; *Pen Cair* of the Britons, the capital. It is a large and populous city, built upon a pleasant eminence on the eastern bank of the river Ex, or *Isca* when latinized. I suppose the original word signifies no more than waters, like the French *eaux*, a collection of them, or several rivers, or branches of rivers, running parallel; and that whether it be wrote *Ax*, *Ex*, *Ix*, *Ox*, or *Ux*; of which many instances all over England. This river is navigable up to the city, but the tide comes not quite so high. The walls take in a very great compass,

*Exeter.*

being a parallelogram of 3,000 Roman feet long, 2,000 broad, having a gate on every side. It lies oblique to the cardinal points of the compass, and objects its main declivity to the south-west. What adds to its wholesomeness and cleanliness is that the ground is higher in a ridge along the middle of its length, declining on both sides; further, on the south-west and north-west sides it is precipicious, so that, with the river, the walls, the declivity of ground and ditch without side, it was a place of very great strength, and well chosen for a frontier against the ancient *Corinavii*. It was built with a good omen, and has been ever in a flourishing condition. The walls are in pretty good repair, having many lunettes and towers, and make a walk round the city, with the advantage and pleasure of seeing the fine country on the opposite hills, full of wood, rich ground, orchards, villages, and gentlemen's houses. The beauty of the place consists mainly of one long street, running the length of the parallelogram, called Highstreet, broad and straight; the houses are of a very old, but good model, spacious, commodious, and not inelegant; this street is full of shops well furnished, and all sorts of trades look brisk. The people are industrious and courteous: the fair sex are truly so, as well as numerous; their complexions, and generally their hair likewise, fair; they are genteel, disengaged, of easy carriage and good mien. At Mr. Cole's the goldsmith[1] I saw an old ground-plot of this city in Queen Elizabeth's time: there has been since a vast increase of buildings within and without the city; the situation renders it of necessity clean, dry, and airy. The soil hither from Honiton was rather sandy than stony, whence it must needs be very healthful; and it is of a convenient distance from the sea. They drive a great trade here for woollen manufacture in cloths, serges, stuffs, etc. All along the water-side innumerable tenters or racks for stretching them. Here is a good face of learning too; many booksellers' shops: I saw a printed catalogue of an auction of books to be sold there. I saw the coloss head of the empress Julia Domna dug up near Bath, in Dr. Musgrave's garden, which his father calls

*High St.*

*Cole.*

*Musgrave.*

---

[1] Joseph Cole was one of the wardens of the Exeter Goldsmiths' Guild in 1712. (Chanter, *Trans. Devon. Assoc.*, xliv., 465.)

*Andromache*: the head-dress is like that of her times, and her bust at Wilton; nor is the manner and carving despicable: the graver has not done it justice. It is the noblest relique of British antiquity of this sort that we know: it is twenty-one inches from the top of the attire to the chin, and belonged to a statue of twelve foot proportion, set upon some temple or palace originally. In the same place is the inscription of Camillus published by him: I saw his library, a very good collection of books, coins and other antiquarian *supellex*; likewise a treatise, ready for publication, of the original gout, which he wrote thirty years ago, before his other two. The doctor had made this distemper his particular view through his long practice; and this country remarkably abound with patients of that sort, which he attributes in a great measure to the custom of marling the lands with lime, and the great use of poor, sweet cider, especially among the meaner people.[1]

In the northern angle of the city, and highest ground, is Rugemont castle, once the royal residence of the West-Saxon kings, then of the earls of Cornwall: it is of a squarish figure, not very large, environed with a high wall and deep ditch; there is a rampire of earth within, equal in height to the top of the wall at present, and makes a terrace-walk overlooking the city and country. In the morning, the air being perfectly serene, and the sun shining, I observed from this place all the country southward, between the sea and Exeter, covered with a very thick fog: the west side of the city and country beyond it very clear. In this place is the assize-house and a chapel. In the wall of this castle is a narrow cavity quite round, perhaps for conveyance of a sound from turret to turret.[2] Dr. Holland supposes this to have been a Roman work originally; and it is not unlikely that it was their *prætorium*,

*Rougemont Castle.*

---

[1] Dr. William Musgrave (1655?-1721), physician and antiquary; fellow of New College, Oxford, 1677-92; B.C.L., 1682; M.D., 1689; F.R.S., 1684; secretary of the Royal Society, 1685; F.R.C.P., 1692; practised at Exeter; published three treatises on arthritis, 1703, 1707, 1776, and four volumes of "Antiquitates Britanno-Belgicæ," 1719-20. (*Dict. Nat. Biography.*)

[2] More likely the cavity was formed by the decay of the balks of timber used for bonding the wall.

or garrison.    Beyond this ditch is a pleasant walk of trees, and a little intrenched hill, called Danes castle.

Cathedral.

The cathedral is a good pile of building : two old towers stand on the north and south transept of the most ancient part.    The organ is remarkably large ; the diapason pipes fifteen inches diameter, and set against the pillars of the church.    The west front of the church is full of old statues. Many religious foundations in the city are converted into streets and houses, full of numerous families and thriving inhabitants, instead of lazy monks and nuns.    King Edward I. in the Saxon times founded the monastery of Exeter, anno 868 ; Athelstan enlarged it for the Benedictines in 932 ; Edward Confessor translated those monks to Westminster,

*Leofric.*

and made this an episcopal see.    Leofricus, a Briton, was the first bishop, and founder of the cathedral : he was chaplain to King Edward the Confessor, anno 1046 ; he gave his lands at Bampton in Oxfordshire to this church ; he has a monu-

*Wm. Warelwast. Bruere.*

ment in the southern transept.[1]    Warewast, the third bishop, began to build the choir, 13 Henry I.    Bishop Brewer created the dean and prebends in the time of Henry III.

*Quivil.*

Bishop Quivel built the body of the church to the west end, 13 Edward I. ; he instituted the sub-dean and singing men.    Bishop Grandison lengthened the cathedral by two

*Grandison.*

arches, and is buried in a little chapel in the west end ; bishop

*Lacey. Neville. Courtenay.*

Lacy began the chapter-house, and bishop Nevil finished it ; bishop Courtney built the north tower, or rather repaired it, and gave that large bell called *Peter* ; the dean and chapter built the cloisters.    St. Mary's Chapel, at the end of the choir, is now turned into a library : this, I suppose, is what bishop Leofric built.    The bishop's throne in the choir is a lofty Gothic work.    Here are many monuments of bishops in the cathedral.

The present deanery, they say, was a nunnery.    The monastery of St. Andrew at Cowic was founded by Thomas Courtney, earl of Devon[2] ; a cell to Bec abbey in Normandy ;

---

[1] Erected in 1568 at the instance of Hoker.    (See note 1 on p. 89.)

[2] The Benedictine Priory of St. Andrew's, Cowick, was colonized from the abbey of Bec in Normandy in the reign of Henry II. or earlier, and it is stated to have received its first endowment from William, the son of Baldwin the sheriff.    However, the Courtenays were considered as the founders and patrons of the priory.    (Oliver, *Monasticon Exon.*, 153-4.)

it was dissolved in the time of Edward III.[1]  Roger
Holland, I suppose duke of Exeter, lived in it in the time
of Edward VI.[2]  St. Nicholas' priory was a cell to Battle
abbey[3]; St. John's was of Augustine friars[4]; Polesloe, a
mile off, dedicate to St. Catherine, a nunnery of the Benedictine order[5]; Marsh was a cell to Plympton[6]; Cleve was
a monastery of Black canons[7]; St. James' priory, of Cluniac
monks[8]; Grey friars, without South-gate, were Franciscans[9]; Gold-hays, without West-gate, Black friars[10]; the
Bear inn was the abbot of Tavistock's house; the Black-
lion too was a religious house[11]; Lathbier another,[12] near
Larkbear.

---

[1] The convent was surrendered in 1451, when King Henry VI.
assigned its revenues to his noble foundation at Eton.  Thirteen years
later, King Edward IV. withdrew this donation from Eton College,
and assigned it to his favoured abbey of Tavistock, in whose possession
it continued until the general suppression of religious houses.  (Oliver,
*Monasticon Exon.*, 154.)

[2] There was no Holland, Duke of Exeter, having the Christian
name of Roger, and the dukedom became extinct in the reign of
Edward IV.  Risdon says: "In the reign of King *Henry* the sixth
Roger Holland had his dwelling *at the foot of the hill*, whence it
took its name below the hill, but at this day is called *Bow Hill*."
(*Survey of Devon*, 117.)

[3] See note 1 on p. 70.  For a general description of the conventual houses of Exeter and the neighbourhood, see an article by
Miss Kate M. Clarke in *Devon Notes and Queries*, iii., 129-151.

[4] See note 2 on p. 70.

[5] This priory was founded by Lord William Briwere in the time
of Henry II.  (Oliver, *Monasticon Exon.*, 162.)

[6] The ancient cell or priory of St. Mary de Marises, commonly
called Marsh Barton, in the parish of Alphington.  It is mentioned
in a letter to Robert de Warelwast, Bishop of Exeter between
1155 and 1160.  Hardly a vestige of this cell has been allowed to
remain.  (Oliver, *Monasticon Exon.*, 133-4.)

[7] Cleeve Abbey is in Somerset, and was of the Cistercian Order.

[8] Dependent on the abbey of St. Martin-in-the-Fields, near Paris,
and founded by Baldwin de Redvers, Earl of Devon, before 1143.
(Oliver, *Monasticon Exon.*, 191.)

[9] See note 3 on p. 70.

[10] The convent of Dominican or Black Friars was situated on the
site of the present Bedford Circus.  (See note 1 on p. 71.)

[11] We believe the prior of Plympton's town residence or inn was
what is now called by the name of the Black Lion Inn.  (Oliver,
*Monasticon Exon.*, 131.)

[12] In St. Leonard's, the smallest parish in Devonshire (it contains
but 150 acres), is an ancient dwelling called Lerkebeare, or Larke-
beare, strangely thought to have been a monastic or religious
establishment.  On 18 July, 1416, Bishop Stafford granted a licence
to Nicholas Bowden, to have divine service performed during a
twelvemonth in his house of Lerkebeare in the parish of St. Leonard.
(Oliver, *Ecclesiastical Antiquities*, i., 165.)

the new river below Radford mount. Thus had these holy
locusts well-nigh devoured the land.

In Corry lane, over-against St. Paul's church, is a little
old house called King Athelstan's, said to have been his
palace, built of large square stones, and circular arches
over the doors. It seems indeed to have been originally a
Roman building, though other later works have been added
to the doors and windows; over the door in the street is
a very small niche crowded into the wall, as if it had been
converted into a religious house; in the yard a winding
stone staircase is added. One arch of South-gate seems to
be Roman. No doubt the walls of the city are upon the
Roman foundation for the most part, and great numbers of
antiquities have been found here. In digging behind the
guild hall in Pancras lane, they found a great Roman pavement of little white square stones eight foot deep. A pot
of Roman coin of two pecks was dug up, two years ago,
near St. Martin's church: I saw some of them in Dr·
Musgrave's possession, of Gordian, Balbinus, Philippus,
Julia Mæsa, Geta, Gallienus, and the like. Mr. Loudham,
surgeon in this city, has many of them among his curious
collection of antiquities, manuscripts, etc. Mr. Reynolds the
schoolmaster is a great collector and preserver of such
learned remains. St. Mary Arches church, and St. Stephen's
Bow, by their names seem to have been built out of Roman
temples.

The bridge over the *Isca* is of great length, and has
houses on both sides and both ends; a considerable void
space in the middle: there is a church upon it with a tower
steeple. In the Guild-hall are the pictures of general Monk,
and the princess Henrietta Maria, born at Bedford House,
a palace in this city, during the civil wars. The composition of the stone of this country is entirely made of little
black pebbles, incrusted in a sandy matter of a red colour
and mouldering nature.

Leaving Exeter, my farthest western longtitude at present,
I steered my course back again along the sea-side, enwrapped
in contemplation with the poet,

Undæ quæ vestris pulsatis littora lymphis,
Littora quæ dulces auras diffunditis agris !    VIRG.

Nor could I think myself alone, when so much new

entertainment was presented to me every minute.   Much rock-
samphire grows upon these cliffs.   The Roman road seems
to have crossed the Otter at Hertford.   At Woodbury is
a camp.   I passed by Sidmouth, and came to Seaton, a little
village upon the mouth of the river Ax.   This Mr. Camden
conjectures to have been the Roman *Moridunum*, and with
reason.[1]   It has been a great haven and excellent port, of
which they still keep up the memory; the river runs in a
large valley, having high ground on each side; the shore is
rocky, high and steep, consisting of the ends of hills which
here run north and south; the ground at bottom under the
rocks is marly; the waves wash it down perpetually, under-
mining the strata of stone, which from time to time fall
down in great parcels.   At present this haven mouth, which
is a good half mile over, is filled up with beach, as they call
it; that is, coggles, gravel, sand, shells, and such matter as
is thrown up by the roll of the ocean: so that the river
water has but a very narrow passage on the east side under
the cliff.   The beach was covered over with *papaver luteum
corniculatum*,[2] now in blossom: the people in the isle of Portland call it *squat maw*, i.e. bruise herb, and use it in that
case, no doubt, with good success, where both intentions
are answered, of dissolving the coagulated blood, and easing
pain.   On the west side, near Seaton, upon a little eminence
is a modern ruined square *pharos* built of brick; they
remember it sixteen foot high; and two guns lie there.
They say there were formerly many great foundations of
houses visible nearer the sea than the present town, but
now swallowed up; and in all likelihood there stood the
Roman city.   More inward toward the land, beyond the
great bank of beach, is a marsh which the sea has made,
landing itself up when its free flux is hindered; this is full
of salt-pans, into which they take the sea-water at high
tides.   When they dig these places they find innumerable
keels and pieces of vessels, with nails, pitch, anchors, etc.,
six or eight feet deep, because it was formerly part of

Harpford.
Woodbury.
Sidmouth.
Seaton.

---

[1] The 'reason,' as is so often the case, is based on false etymology.
Both Camden and Stukeley supposed the name to mean "a town on
the hill *by the sea*," whereas it more probably means "the *great* hill
fort."   The site is much more likely to have been Hembury Fort, near
Honiton. (P. O. Hutchinson, *Trans. Devon. Assoc.*, xiv, 516-24.)

[2] The yellow horned poppy, *Glaucium luteum*.

the haven; anchors have been found as high as Axminster and beyond it, though now there is no navigation at all: so great a change has Time produced in the face of Nature, upon these confines of the two great elements always opposing each other.

Sic volvenda ætas commutat tempora rerum.    LUCR. V.

Honey Ditches.

Half a mile off, upon higher ground, on the western side is a castle in a pasture, but formerly tilled, called Honey Ditches[1]: it is moated about, and perhaps walled; for they dig up much square stone there. The place is an oblong square, containing about three acres: I guess it to have been the garrison of the port. Just by the present haven-mouth is a great and long pier or wall, jutting out into the sea, made of great rocks piled together to the breadth of six yards. They told me it was built many years

Courd.

ago by one Courd, once a poor sailor, who, being somewhere in the Mediterranean, was told by a certain Greek, that much treasure was hid upon Hogsdon hill near here, and that this memorial was transmitted to him by his ancestors; Courd, upon his return digging there luckily found the golden mine, which enriched him prodigiously, so that at his own expense he built this wall, with an intent to restore the harbour.[2] The people hereabouts firmly believe the story, and many have dug in the place with like hopes; and as an argument of its truth, they say some of his family are still remaining, that live upon their estate got by him.

Colyford.

A mile higher on the same western side of the river is Cullyford, where was the ancient road from London to Exeter passing over at Axbridge, which is now a stony ford, with two bridges that traverse the valley and the river, once a haven. Here have been many inns and houses, and a considerable town. They talk of great stone vaults

---

[1] See a paper by P. O. Hutchinson in *Trans. Devon. Assoc.*, xvii, 277-80.

[2] This must, I think, refer to the natural pebble-ridge at the mouth of the Axe, for Leland says the attempt "to make a mayne Waulle . . . com not to effect" (p. 80), and Risdon says "of this work there remaineth no monument, only the remembrance of such a place among strangers that know not where it stands" (*Survey of Devon*, 31). Further, Lysons at a subsequent date says "There is now no pier at Seaton, but coal and culme are landed by the aid of boats" (*Devon*, 435.)

being found; so that it probably arose from the destruction of *Moridunum*, as Culliton adjacent, from it.  Further, it was a corporation, and they now keep up their claim by an annual choice of a mayor, who has a mace too, but I suppose not of great elegance.

I suppose the Foss road went on the east side of Chard, and so by Axminster and Culliton, to Seaton or *Moridunum*, where properly it begins ; whence if we measure its noble length to the sea-coast in Lincolnshire, at Grimsby or Salt-fleet, where I imagine it ends, it amounts to 250 Roman miles in a straight line from north-east to south-west.  Your lordship (Lord Pembroke) presented me with an oyster, found a little northward of Axminster, where the very fish appears petrified with its cartilaginous concretion to the shell, all in their proper colours. Colyton.

# A TOUR THROUGH GREAT BRITAIN
## By a Gentleman (Daniel Defoe)  1724

From Chard we proceeded into Devonshire, and arrived at Honiton.  This is a large and beautiful market-town, very populous and well built, and it is so very remarkably paved with small pebbles that on either side the way a little channel is left shouldered up on the sides of it, so that it holds a small stream of fine clear running water, with a little square dipping-place left at every door; so that every family in the town has a clear, clean running river (as it may be called) just at their own door, and this so much finer, so much pleasanter, and agreeable to look on, than · that at Salisbury (which they boast so much of), that, in my opinion, there is no comparison. Honiton.

Here we see the first of the great serge manufacture of Devonshire—a trade too great to be described in miniature, as it must be if I undertake it here, and which takes up this whole county, which is the largest and most populous in England, Yorkshire excepted (which ought to be esteemed three, and is, indeed, divided as such into the East, West, and North Riding).  But Devonshire, one entire county, is so full of great towns, and those towns so full of people,

In my travel through Dorsetshire I ought to have
we come to Devonshire we find almost all the great towns,
are some large populous towns that do not choose, but then
there are so many that do, that the county seems to have
However, as I say above, there are several great towns

Honiton is one of those, and may pass not only for a
pleasant good town, as before, but stands in the best and
if they please to observe the prospect for half a mile till
their coming down the hill and to the entrance into Honiton,
the view of the country is the most beautiful landscape in the
any one place in England. It is observable that the market
of this town was kept originally on the Sunday, till it was

From Honiton the country is exceedingly pleasant still,
and on the road they have a beautiful prospect almost all
the way to Exeter (which is twelve miles). On the left-
hand of this road lies that part of the country which they
call the South Hams,[2] and which is famous for the best

[1] Lysons was unable to find any grant of the market on record:
it was held by prescription on Saturday for corn, &c. (*Devon*, 280.)
Sir William Pole says the market at East Budleigh was anciently
held on Sunday.

[2] This is incorrect. The South Hams is the district bounded by
the rivers Tamar and Teign, Dartmoor, and the Channel. It was
"famous for that noble rough cyder, which is generally preferred to
the soft, sickly Hereford redstreak; and so near wine in taste, that
it has tempted some vintners and coopers in London, as well as in
other cities and towns, to mix it with their port wines." (Luckombe,
*England's Gazetteer*, 1751.)

cider in that part of England ; also the town of St. Mary-
Oterey, commonly called St. Mary Autree.    They tell us
the name is derived from the river Ottery, and that from
the multitude of otters found always in that river, which
however, to me, seems fabulous.    Nor does there appear to
be any such great number of otters in that water, or in
the county about, more than is usual in other counties or
in other parts of the county about them.    They tell us
they send twenty thousand hogsheads of cider hence every
year to London, and (which is still worse) that it is most
of it bought there by the merchants to mix with their wines
—which, if true, is not much to the reputation of the
London vintners.    But that by the by.

From hence we came to Exeter, a city famous for two
things which we seldom find united in the same town—viz.,
that it is full of gentry and good company, and yet full of
trade and manufactures also.    The serge market held here
every week is very well worth a stranger's seeing, and next
to the Brigg market at Leeds, in Yorkshire, is the greatest
in England.    The people assured me that at this market
is generally sold from sixty to seventy to eighty, and sometimes a hundred, thousand pounds value in serges in a week.
I think it is kept on Mondays.[1]

They have the river Esk here, a very considerable river,
and principal in the whole county ; and within three miles,
or thereabouts, it receives ships of any ordinary burthen,
the port there being called Topsham.    But now by the
application, and at the expense of the citizens the channel
of the river is so widened, deepened, and cleansed from the
shoal, which would otherwise interrupt the navigation, that
the ships come now quite up to the city, and there with ease
both deliver and take in their lading.[2]

This city derives a very great correspondence with
Holland, as also directly to Portugal, Spain, and Italy—
shipping off vast quantities of their woollen manufactures
especially to Holland, the Dutch giving very large

Ottery
St. Mary.

Exeter.

Exe R.

Topsham.

---

[1] In Lysons' time (1822) it was held on Friday, in the parish of
St. Mary Major : it had been held in Cromwell's time in the cloisters,
but was removed in 1660 to St. John's Hospital, and thence to South-
gate Street. (*Devon*, 194.)

[2] See note 1 on p. 112.

commissions here for the buying of serges, perpetuans, and such goods[1]; which are made not only in and about Exeter, but at Crediton, Honiton, Culliton, St. Mary-Autry, Newton Bushell, Ashburton, and especially at Tiverton, Cullumbton, Bampton, and all the north-east part of the county—which part of the county is, as it may be said, fully employed, the people made rich, and the poor that are properly so called, well subsisted and employed by it.

Exeter is a large, rich, beautiful, populous, and was once a very strong city; but as to the last, as the castle, the walls, and all the old works are demolished, so, were they standing, the way of imaginary sieges and attacks of towns is such now, and so altered from what it was in those days, that Exeter in the utmost strength it could ever boast would not now hold out five days open trenches—nay, would hardly put an army to the trouble of opening trenches against it at all. This city was famous in the late civil unnatural war for its loyalty to the King, and for being a sanctuary to the Queen, where her Majesty resided for some time, and here she was delivered of a daughter, being the Princess Henrietta Maria, of whom our histories give a particular account, so I need say no more of it here.

The cathedral church of this city is an ancient beauty, or, as it may be said, it is beautiful for its antiquity; but it has been so fully and often described that it would look like a mere copying from others to mention it. There is a good library kept in it, in which are some manuscripts, and particularly an old missal or mass book, the leaves of vellum, and famous for its most exquisite writing.

**Totnes.**
About twenty-two miles from Exeter we go to Totness, on the River Dart. This is a very good town, of some trade; but has more gentlemen in it than tradesmen of note. They have a very fine stone bridge here over the river, which, being within seven or eight miles of the sea, is very large; and the tide flows ten or twelve feet at the bridge. Here we had the diversion of seeing them catch fish with the assistance of a dog. The case is this:—On the south side of the river, and on a slip, or narrow cut or channel made on purpose for a mill, there stands a corn-mill; the

---

[1] See note 2 on p. 112.

mill-tail, or floor for the water below the wheels, is wharfed up on either side with stone above high-water mark, and for above twenty or thirty feet in length below it on that part of the river towards the sea; at the end of this wharfing is a grating of wood, the cross-bars of which stand bearing inward, sharp at the end, and pointing inward towards one another, as the wires of a mouse-trap.

When the tide flows up, the fish can with ease go in between the points of these cross-bars, but the mill being shut down they can go no farther upwards; and when the water ebbs again, they are left behind, not being able to pass the points of the grating, as above, outwards; which, like a mouse-trap, keeps them in, so that they are left at the bottom with about a foot or a foot and a half of water. We were carried hither at low water, where we saw about fifty or sixty small salmon, about seventeen to twenty inches long, which the country people call salmon-peal; and to catch these the person who went with us, who was our landlord at a great inn next the bridge, put in a net on a hoop at the end of a pole, the pole going cross the hoop (which we call in this country a shove-net). The net being fixed at one end of the place, they put in a dog (who was taught his trade beforehand) at the other end of the place, and he drives all the fish into the net; so that, only holding the net still in its place, the men took up two or three and thirty salmon-peal at the first time.

Of these we had six for our dinner, for which they asked a shilling (viz., twopence a-piece); and for such fish, not at all bigger, and not so fresh, I have seen 6s. 6d. each given at a London fish-market, whither they are sometimes brought from Chichester by land carriage. This excessive plenty of so good fish (and other provisions being likewise very cheap in proportion) makes the town of Totness a very good place to live in; especially for such as have large families and but small estates. And many such are said to come into those parts on purpose for saving money, and to live in proportion to their income.

From hence we went still south about seven miles (all in view of this river) to Dartmouth, a town of note, seated **Dartmouth.** at the mouth of the River Dart, and where it enters into the sea at a very narrow but safe entrance. The opening into Dartmouth Harbour is not broad, but the channel deep enough for the biggest ship in the Royal Navy. The sides of the entrance are high-mounded with rocks, without which, just at the first narrowing of the passage, stands a good strong fort without a platform of guns, which commands the port.

The narrow entrance is not much above half a mile, when it opens and makes a basin or harbour able to receive 500 sail of ships of any size, and where they may ride with the greatest safety, even as in a mill-pond or wet dock. I had the curiosity here, with the assistance of a merchant of the town, to go out to the mouth of the haven in a boat to see the entrance, and castle or fort that commands it; and coming back with the tide of flood, I observed some small fish to skip and play upon the surface of the water, upon which I asked my friend what fish they were. Immediately one of the rowers or seamen starts up in the boat, and, throwing his arms abroad as if he had been bewitched, cries out as loud as he could bawl, "A school! a school!" The word was taken to the shore as hastily as it would have been on land if he had cried "Fire!" And by that time we reached the quays the town was all in a kind of an uproar.

The matter was that a great shoal—or, as they call it, a "school"—of pilchards, came swimming, with the tide of flood, directly out of the sea into the harbour. My friend whose boat we were in, told me this was a surprise which he would have been very glad of if he could but have had a day or two's warning, for he might have taken 200 tun of them. And the like was the case of other merchants in town, for, in short, nobody was ready for them, except a small fishing-boat or two—one of which went out into the middle of the harbour, and at two or three hauls took about forty thousand of them. We sent our servant to the quay to buy some, who for a halfpenny brought us seventeen, and, if he would have taken them, might have had as many more for the same money.[1] With these we went to dinner; the cook at the inn broiled them for us, which is their way of dressing

---

[1] At Bridport, "such was the plenty of fish that year that the mackerel, the finest and largest I ever saw, were sold at the seaside a hundred for a penny."

them, with pepper and salt, which cost us about a farthing, so that two of us and a servant dined—and at a tavern, too —for three farthings, dressing and all. And this is the reason of telling the tale. What drink—wine or beer—we had I do not remember; but whatever it was, that we paid for by itself. But for our food we really dined for three farthings, and very well, too. Our friend treated us the next day with a dish of large lobsters, and I being curious to know the value of such things, and having freedom enough with him to inquire, I found that for 6d. or 8d. they bought as good lobsters there as would have cost in London 3s. to 3s. 6d. each.

In observing the coming in of those pilchards, as above, we found that out at sea, in the offing, beyond the mouth of the harbour, there was a whole army of porpoises, which, as they told us, pursued the pilchards, and, it is probable, drove them into the harbour, as above. The school, it seems, drove up the river a great way, even as high as Totness Bridge, as we heard afterwards; so that the country people who had boats and nets catched as many as they knew what to do with, and perhaps lived upon pilchards for several days. But as to the merchants and trade, their coming was so sudden that it was no advantage to them.

Round the west side of this basin or harbour, in a kind of a semicircle, lies the town of Dartmouth, a very large and populous town, though but meanly built, and standing on the side of a steep hill; yet the quay is large, and the street before it spacious. Here are some very flourishing merchants, who trade very prosperously, and to the most considerable trading ports of Spain, Portugal, Italy, and the Plantations; but especially they are great traders to New-foundland, and from thence to Spain and Italy, with fish; and they drive a good trade also in their own fishery of pilchards, which is hereabouts carried on with the greatest number of vessels of any port in the west, except Falmonth.

A little to the southward of this town, and to the east of the port, is Torbay, of which I know nothing proper to my observation, more than that it is a very good road for ships, though sometimes (especially with a southerly or south-east wind) ships have been obliged to quit the bay and put out to sea, or run into Dartmouth for shelter.

Torbay.

I suppose I need not mention that they had from the hilly part of this town, and especially from the hills opposite to it, the noble prospect, and at that time particularly delightful, of the Prince of Orange's fleet when he came to that coast, and as they entered into Torbay to land—the Prince and his army being in a fleet of about 600 sail of transport ships, besides 50 sail of men-of-war of the line, all which, with a fair wind and fine weather, came to an anchor there at once.

This town, as most of the towns in Devonshire, are, is full of Dissenters, and a very large meeting-house they have here.[1]   How they act here with respect to the great dispute about the doctrine of the Trinity, which has caused such a breach among those people at Exeter and other parts of the county, I cannot give any account of.    This town sends two members to Parliament.[2]

From hence we went to Plympton, a poor and thinly-inhabited town, though blessed with the like privilege of sending members to the Parliament, of which I have little more to say but that from thence the road lies to Plymouth, distance about six miles.

Plymouth.

Plymouth is indeed a town of consideration, and of great importance to the public.   The situation of it between two very large inlets of the sea, and in the bottom of a large bay, which is very remarkable for the advantage of navigation.   The Sound or Bay is compassed on every side with hills, and the shore generally steep and rocky, though the anchorage is good, and it is pretty safe riding.   In the entrance to this bay lies a large and most dangerous rock, which at high water is covered, but at low tide lies bare, where many a good ship has been lost, even in the view of safety, and many a ship's crew drowned in the night, before help could be had for them.

Eddystone.

Upon this rock (which was called the Eddystone, from

<hr>

[1] There is an old Presbyterian meeting-house at Dartmouth ; the congregation was originally established by the celebrated nonconformist divine, John Flavel (1630?-1691), author of some popular Calvinistic works which have gone through several editions. (Lysons, *Devon*, 158.)

[2] The borough sent representatives to one of the parliaments of Edward I., and regularly sent two members from 1341 to 1832, and then one until 1868, when it was disfranchised.

its situation) the famous Mr. Winstanley[1] undertook to    *Winstanley.*
build a lighthouse for the direction of sailors, and with great
art and expedition finished it; which work—considering its
height, the magnitude of its building, and the little hold
there was by which it was possible to fasten it to the rock—
stood to admiration, and bore out many a bitter storm.
Mr. Winstanley often visited and frequently strengthened
the building by new works, and was so confident of its
firmness and stability that he usually said he only desired
to be in it when a storm should happen; for many people
had told him it would certainly fall if it came to blow a
little harder than ordinary.

But he happened at last to be in it once too often—
namely, when that dreadful tempest blew, November 27,
1703. This tempest began on the Wednesday before and
blew with such violence, and shook the lighthouse so much,
that, as they told me there, Mr. Winstanley would fain
have been on shore, and made signals for help: but no
boats durst go off to him; and to finish the tragedy, on the
Friday, November 26, when the tempest was so redoubled
that it became a terror to the whole nation, the first sight
there seaward that the people of Plymouth were presented
with in the morning after the storm was the bare Eddystone,
the lighthouse being gone; in which Mr. Winstanley and
all that were with him perished, and were never seen or
heard of since. But that which was a worse loss still was
that, a few days after, a merchant's ship called the *Winchelsea*,
homeward bound from Virginia, not knowing that the Eddystone lighthouse was down, for want of the light that should
have been seen, ran foul of the rock itself, and was lost
with all her lading and most of her men. But there is now
another lighthouse built on the same rock.[2]

As I say, Plymouth lies in the bottom of the Sound, in the
centre between the two waters, so there lies against it, in
the same position, an island, which they call St. Nicholas,    *Drake's I.*

---

[1] Mr. Henry Winstanley, of Littlebury, in Essex, a celebrated
mechanic. The work was first undertaken in 1696, but it had scarcely
been completed three years when it was destroyed. (Lysons, *Devon,*
407.) See also p. 121.

[2] The new lighthouse was begun by Mr. John Rudyerd in 1706,
and after resisting the fury of the waves for 46 years, was destroyed
by fire in 1755. (Lysons, *Devon,* 4078.)

*Lambert.*

Catwater.

Hamoaze.

Devonport.

on which there is a castle which commands the entrance in to Hamoaze, and indeed that also into Catwater in some degree. In this island the famous General Lambert, one of Cromwell's great agents or officers in the rebellion, was imprisoned for life, and lived many years there.[1]

On the shore over against this island is the citadel of Plymouth, a small but regular fortification, inaccessible by sea, but not exceeding strong by land, except that they say the works are of a stone hard as marble, and would not soon yield to the batteries of an enemy; but that is a language our modern engineers now laugh at.

The town stands above this, upon the same rock, and lies sloping on the side of it, towards the east—the inlet of the sea which is called Catwater, and which is a harbour capable of receiving any number of ships and of any size, washing the eastern shore of the town, where they have a kind of natural mole or haven, with a quay and other conveniences for bringing in vessels for loading and unloading; nor is the trade carried on here inconsiderable in itself, or the number of merchants small.

The other inlet of the sea, as I term it, is on the other side of the town, and is called Hamoaze, being the mouth of the River Tamar, a considerable river which parts the two counties of Devon and Cornwall. Here (the war with France making it necessary that the ships of war should have a retreat nearer hand than at Portsmouth) the late King William ordered a wet dock—with yards, dry docks, launches, and conveniencies of all kinds for building and repairing of ships—to be built; and with these followed necessarily the building of storehouses and warehouses for the rigging, sails, naval and military stores, etc., of such ships as may be appointed to be laid up there, as now several are; with very handsome houses for the commissioners, clerks, and officers of all kinds usual in the King's yards, to dwell in. It is, in short, now become as complete an arsenal or yard for building and fitting men-of-war as any the Government are masters of, and perhaps much more convenient than some of them, though not so large.

[1] "1683.—Lambert, that old rebel, dyed this winter on Plymouth Island, where he had been a prisoner 15 years and more." (Jewitt, *Plymouth*, 237.)

The building of these things, with the addition of rope-walks and mast-yards, etc., as it brought abundance of trades-people and workmen to the place, so they began by little and little to build houses on the lands adjacent, till at length there appeared a very handsome street, spacious and large, and as well inhabited ; and so many houses are since added that it is become a considerable town, and must of consequence in time draw abundance of people from Plymouth itself.[1]

However, the town of Plymouth is, and will always be, a very considerable town, while that excellent harbour makes it such a general port for the receiving all the fleets of merchants' ships from the southward (as from Spain, Italy, the West Indies, etc.), who generally make it the first port to put in at for refreshment or safety, from either weather or enemies.

The town is populous and wealthy, having, as above, several considerable merchants aud abundance of wealthy shopkeepers whose trade depends upon supplying to sea-faring people that upon so many occasions put into that port. As for gentlemen—I mean those that are such by family and birth and way of living—it cannot be expected to find many such in a town merely depending on trade, shipping, and seafaring business : yet I found here some men of value (persons of liberal education, general knowledge, and excellent behaviour), whose society obliges me to say that a gentleman might find very agreeable company in Plymouth.

From Plymouth we pass the Tamar over a ferry to Saltash—a little, poor, shattered town, the first we set foot on in the county of Cornwall. The Tamar here is very wide, and the ferry-boats bad ; so that I thought myself well escaped when I got safe on shore in Cornwall.   *Saltash.*

Saltash seems to be the ruins of a larger place ; and we saw many houses, as it were, falling down, and I doubt not but the mice and rats have abandoned many more, as they say they will when they are likely to fall.   Yet this town is governed by a mayor and aldermen, has many privileges, sends members to Parliament, takes toll of all vessels that

---

[1] It was originally called Plymouth Dock, and did not receive its present name Devonport until 1824.   It was incorporated as a municipality in 1837.

pass the river, and has the sole oyster-fishing in the whole river, which is considerable.

This town has a kind of jurisdiction upon the River Tamar down to the mouth of the port, so that they claim anchorage of all small ships that enter the river; their coroner sits upon all dead bodies that are found drowned in the river and the like, but they make not much profit of them.   There is a good market here, and that is the best thing to be said of the town; it is also very much increased since the number of the inhabitants are increased at the new town, as I mentioned as near the dock at the mouth of the Hamoaze, for those people choose rather to go to Salt-ash to market by water than to walk to Plymouth by land for their provisions.   Because, first, as they go in the town boat, the same boat brings home what they buy, so that it is much less trouble; second, because provisions are bought much cheaper at Saltash than at Plymouth.   This, I say, is like to be a very great advantage to the town of Saltash, and may in time put a new face of wealth upon the place.

They talk of some merchants beginning to trade here, and they have some ships that use the Newfoundland fishery; but I could not hear of anything considerable they do in it. There is no other considerable town up the Tamar till we come to Launceston, the county town, which I shall take in my return; so I turned west, keeping the south shore of the county to the Land's End.

From Saltash I went to Liskeard, about seven miles. This a fashionable town, well built; has people of fashion in it, and a very great market; it also sends two members to Parliament, and is one of the five towns called Stannary Towns—that is to say, where the blocks of tin are brought to the coinage; of which, by itself, this coinage of tin is an article very much to the advantage of the towns where it it settled, though the money paid goes another way.

This town of Liskeard was once eminent, had a good castle, and a large house, where the ancient Dukes of Cornwall kept their court in those days; also it enjoyed several privileges, especially by the favour of the Black Prince, who as Prince of Wales and Duke of Cornwall resided here. And in return they say this town and the country round it raised a great body of stout young fellows, who entered into his service and followed his fortunes in his wars in France, as also in Spain. But these buildings are so decayed that there are now scarce any of the ruins of the castle or of the prince's court remaining.

The only public edifices they have now to show are the guild or town hall, on which there is a turret with a fine clock ; a very good free school, well provided ; a very fine conduit in the market-place ; an ancient large church ; and, which is something rare for the county of Cornwall, a large, new-built meeting-house for the Dissenters, which I name because they assured me there was but three more, and those very inconsiderable, in all the county of Cornwall ; whereas in Devonshire, which is the next county, there are reckoned about seventy, some of which are exceeding large and fine.

This town is also remarkable for a very great trade in all manufactures of leather, such as boots, shoes, gloves, purses, breeches, etc. ; and some spinning of late years is set up here, encouraged by the woollen manufacturers of Devonshire.

Between these two towns of Saltash and Liskeard is St. Germans, now a village, decayed, and without any market, but the largest parish in the whole county—in the bounds of which is contained, as they report, seventeen villages, and the town of Saltash among them ; for Saltash has no parish church, it seems, of itself, but as a chapel-of-ease to St. Germans. In the neighbourhood of these towns are many pleasant seats of the Cornish gentry, who are indeed very numerous, though their estates may not be so large as is usual in England ; yet neither are they despicable in that part ; and in particular this may be said of them—that as they generally live cheap, and are more at home than in other counties, so they live more like gentlemen, and keep more within bounds of their estates than the English generally do, take them all together.

Add to this that they are the most sociable, generous, and to one another the kindest, neighbours that are to be found ; and as they generally live, as we may say, together (for they are almost always at one another's houses), so they generally intermarry among themselves, the gentlemen seldom going out of the county for a wife, or the ladies for

St. Germans.

a husband; from whence they say that proverb upon them was raised, viz., " That all the Cornish gentlemen are cousins."

On the hills north of Liskeard, and in the way between Liskeard and Launceston, there are many tin-mines. And, as they told us, some of the richest veins of that metal are found there that are in the whole county—the metal, when cast at the blowing-houses into blocks, being, as above, carried to Liskeard to be coined.

From Liskeard, in our course west, we are necessarily carried to the sea-coast, because of the River Fowey or Fowath, which empties itself into the sea at a very large mouth. And hereby this river rising in the middle of the breadth of the county and running south, and the River Camel rising not far from it and running north, with a like large channel, the land from Bodmin to the western part of the county is almost made an island and in a manner cut off from the eastern part—the peninsula, or neck of land between, being not above twelve miles over.

**Fowey.**    On this south side we came to Foy or Fowey, an ancient town, and formerly very large—nay, not large only, but powerful and potent; for the Foyens, as they were then called, were able to fit out large fleets, not only for merchants' ships, but even of men-of-war; aud with these not only fought with, but several times vanquished and routed, the squadron of the Cinque Ports men, who in those days were thought very powerful.

Mr. Camden observes that the town of Foy quarters some part of the arms of every one of those Cinque Ports with their own, intimating that they had at several times trampled over them all. Certain it is they did often beat them, and took their ships, and brought them as good prizes into their haven of Foy; and carried it so high that they fitted out their fleets against the French, and took several of their men-of-war when they were at war with England, and enriched their town by the spoil of their enemies.

Edward IV. favoured them much; and because the French threatened them to come up their river with a powerful navy to burn their town, he caused two forts to be built at the public charge for security of the town aud river, which forts—at least, some show of them—remain there still. But the same King Edward was some time after

so disgusted at the townsmen for officiously falling upon
the French, after a truce was made and proclaimed, that he
effectually disarmed them, took away their whole fleet, ships,
tackle, apparel, and furniture; and since that time we do
not read of any of their naval exploits, nor that they ever
recovered or attempted to recover their strength at sea.
However, Foy at this time is a very fair town; it lies
extended on the east side of the river for above a mile, the
buildings fair. And there are a great many flourishing
merchants in it, who have a great share in the fishing trade,
especially for pilchards, of which they take a great quantity
hereabouts. In this town is also a coinage for the tin, of
which a great quantity is dug up in the country north and
west of the town.

The River Fowey, which is very broad and deep here,
was formerly navigable by ships of good burthen as high
as Lostwithiel—an ancient and once a flourishing but now
a decayed town; and as to trade and navigation, quite
destitute; which is occasioned by the river being filled up
with sands, which, some say, the tides drive up in stormy
weather from the sea; others say it is by sands washed
from the lead-mines in the hills; the last of which, by the
way, I take to be a mistake, the sand from the hills being
not of quantity sufficient to fill up the channel of a navigable
river, and, if it had, might easily have been stopped by the
townspeople from falling into the river. But that the sea
has choked up the river is not only probable, but true;
and there are other rivers which suffer in the like manner
in this same country.

*Lostwithiel.*

This town of Lostwithiel retains, however, several advantages which support its figure—as first, that it is one of
the Coinage Towns, as I call them: or Stannary Towns,
as others call them; (2) the common gaol for the whole
Stannary is here, as are also the County Courts for the
whole county of Cornwall.

Behind Foy and nearer to the coast, at the mouth of a
small river which some call Lowe, though without any
authority, there stand two towns opposite to one another,
bearing the name of the River Looe—that is to say, distinguished by the addition of East Looe and West Looe.
These are both good trading towns, and especially fishing

*East Looe.*
*West Looe.*

towns; and, which is very particular, are separated only by the creek or river, and yet each of them sends members to Parliament. These towns are joined together by a very beautiful and stately stone bridge having fifteen arches. East Looe was the ancienter corporation of the two, and for some ages ago the greater and more considerable town; but now they tell us West Looe is the richest, and has the most ships belonging to it. Were they put together, they would make a very handsome seaport town. They have a great fishing trade here, as well for supply of the country as for merchandise, and the towns are not despisable. But as to sending four members to the British Parliament (which is as many as the City of London chooses), that, I confess, seems a little scandalous; but to whom, is none of my business to inquire.

Passing from hence, and ferrying over Foy River or the River Foweth (call it as you please), we come into a large country without many towns in it of note, but very well furnished with gentlemen's seats, and a little higher up with tin-works.

The sea making several deep bays here, they who travel by land are obliged to go higher into the country to pass above the water, especially at Trewardreth Bay, which lies very broad, above ten miles within the country, which passing at Trewardreth (a town of no great note, though the bay takes its name from it), the next inlet of the sea is the famous firth or inlet called Falmouth Haven. It is certainly next to Milford Haven in South Wales, the fairest and best road for shipping that is in the whole isle of Britain, whether be considered the depth of water for above twenty miles within land; the safety of riding, sheltered from all kinds of winds or storms; the good anchorage; and the many creeks, all navigable, where ships may run in and be safe; so that the like is nowhere to be found.

There are six or seven very considerable places upon this haven aud the rivers from it—viz., Grampound, Tregony, Truro, Penryn, Falmouth, St. Mawes, and Pendennis. The three first of these send members to Parliament. The town of Falmouth, as big as all the three, and richer than ten of them, sends none; which imports no more than this —that Falmouth itself is not of so great antiquity as to its

**Tywardreath.**

**Falmouth.**

rising as those other towns are; and yet the whole haven takes its name from Falmouth, too, unless, as some think, the town took its name from the haven, which, however, they give no authority to suggest.

St. Mawes and Pendennis are two fortifications placed at the points or entrance of this haven, opposite to one another, though not with a communication or view; they are very strong—the first principally by sea, having a good platform of guns pointing athwart the Channel, and planted on a level with the water. But Pendennis Castle is strong by land as well as by water, is regularly fortified, has good out-works, and generally a strong garrison. St. Mawes, otherwise called St. Mary's, has a town annexed to the castle, and is a borough sending members to the Parliament. Pendennis is a mere fortress, though there are some habitations in it, too, and some at a small distance near the seaside, but not of any great consideration.

St. Mawes.

Pendennis Castle.

The town of Falmouth is by much the richest and best trading town in this county, though not so ancient as its neighbour town of Truro; and indeed is in some things obliged to acknowledge the seigniority—namely that in the corporation of Truro the person whom they choose to be their Mayor of Truro is also Mayor of Falmouth of course. How the jurisdiction is managed is an account too long for this place. The Truro-men also receive several duties collected in Falmouth, particularly wharfage for the merchandises landed or shipped off; but let these advantages be what they will, the town of Falmouth has gotten the trade—at least, the best part of it—from the other, which is chiefly owing to the situation. For that Falmouth lying upon the sea, but within the entrance, ships of the greatest burthen come up to the very quays, and the whole Royal Navy might ride safely in the road; whereas the town of Truro lying far within, and at the mouth of two fresh rivers, is not navigable for vessels of above 150 tons or thereabouts.

Some have suggested that the original of Falmouth was the having so large a quay, and so good a depth of water at it. The merchants of Truro formerly used it for the place of lading and unlading their ships, as the merchants of Exeter did at Topsham; and this is the more probable in that, as above, the wharfage of those landing-places is still the property of the corporation of Truro.

But let this be as it will, the trade is now in a manner wholly gone to Falmouth, the trade at Truro being now chiefly (if not only) for the shipping off of block tin and copper ore, the latter being lately found in large quantities in some of the mountains between Truro and St. Michael's, and which is improved since the several mills are erected at Bristol and other parts for the manufactures of battery ware, as it is called (brass), or which is made out of English copper, most of it dug in these parts—the ore itself also being found very rich and good.

Falmouth is well built, has abundance of shipping belonging to it, is full of rich merchants, and has a flourishing and increasing trade. I say "increasing," because by the late setting up the English packets between this port and Lisbon, there is a new commerce between Portugal and this town carried on to a very great value. It is true, part of this trade was founded in a clandestine commerce carried on by the said packets at Lisbon, where, being the King's ships, and claiming the privilege of not being searched or visited by the Custom House officers, they found means to carry off great quantities of British manufactures, which they sold on board to the Portuguese merchants, and they conveyed them on shore, as it is supposed, without paying custom. But the Government there getting intelligence of it, and complaint being made in England also, where it was found to be very prejudicial to the fair merchant, that trade has been effectually stopped. But the Falmouth merchants, having by this means gotten a taste of the Portuguese trade, have maintained it ever since in ships of their own. These packets bring over such vast quantities of gold in specie, either in *moidores* (which is the Portugal coin) or in bars of gold, that I am very credibly informed the carrier from Falmouth brought by land from thence to London at one time, in the month of January, 1722, or near it, eighty thousand *moidores* in gold, which came from Lisbon in the packet-boats for account of the merchants at London, and that it was attended with a guard of twelve horsemen well armed, for which the said carrier had half per cent. for his hazard.[1]

This is a specimen of the Portugal trade, and how considerable it is in itself, as well as how advantageous to England; but as that is not to the present case, I proceed. The Custom House for all the towns in this port, and the head collector, is established at this town, where the duties (including the other ports) is very considerable. Here is also a very great fishing for pilchards; and the merchants for Falmouth have the chief stroke in that gainful trade.

Truro is, however, a very considerable town, too. It **Truro.** stands up the water north and by east from Falmouth, in the utmost extended branch of the Avon, in the middle between the conflux of two rivers, which, though not of any long course, have a very good appearance for a port, and make a large wharf between them in the front of the town. And the water here makes a good port for small ships, though it be at the influx, but not for ships of burthen. This is the particular town where the Lord-Warden of the Stannaries always holds his famous Parliament of miners, and for stamping of tin. The town is well built, but shows that it has been much fuller, both of houses and inhabitants than it is now; nor will it probably ever rise while the town of Falmouth stands where it does, and while the trade is settled in it as it is. There are at least three churches in it, but no Dissenters' meeting-house that I could hear of.

Tregony is upon the same water north-east from **Tregony.** Falmouth—distance about fifteen miles from it—but is a town of very little trade; nor, indeed, have any of the towns so far within the shore, notwithstanding the benefit of the water, any considerable trade but what is carried on under the merchants of Falmouth or Truro. The chief thing that is to be said of this town is that it sends members to Parliament, as does also Grampound, a market town and **Grampound.** borough, about four miles farther up the water. This place, indeed, has a claim to antiquity, and is an appendix to the Duchy of Cornwall, of which it holds at a fee farm rent and pays to the Prince of Wales as duke £10 11s. 1d.

---

[1] The value of the moidore was fixed in 1714 at 27s. 6d. (See *Devon and Cornwall Notes and Queries*, viii., 22.)

per annum. It has no parish church, but only a chapel-
of-ease to an adjacent parish.

**Penryn.**

Penryn is up the same branch of the Avon as Falmouth,
but stands four miles higher towards the west; yet ships
come to it of as great a size as can come to Truro itself.
It is a very pleasant, agreeable town, and for that reason
has many merchants in it, who would perhaps otherwise
live at Falmouth. The chief commerce of these towns, as
to their sea-affairs, is the pilchards and Newfoundland fishing,
which is very profitable to them all. It had formerly a
conventual church, with a chantry and a religious house
(a cell to Kirton); but they are all demolished, and scarce the
ruins of them distinguishable enough to know one part from
another.[1]

**Helston.**
**Caber R.**

Quitting Falmouth Haven from Penryn West, we came
to Helston, about seven miles, and stands upon the little
River Cober, which, however, admits the sea so into its bosom
as to make a tolerable good harbour for ships a little below
the town. It is the fifth town allowed for the coining tin, and
several of the ships called tin-ships are laden here. This
town is large and populous, and has four spacious streets,
a handsome church, and a good trade. This town also sends
members to Parliament.

**Marazion.**

Beyond this is a market-town, though of no resort for
trade, called Market Jew. It lies, indeed, on the seaside, but
has no harbour or safe road for shipping.

**Helford.**

At Helford is a small but good harbour between Falmouth
and this port, where many times the tin-ships go in to
load for London; also here are a good number of fishing
vessels for the pilchard trade, and abundance of skilful
fishermen. It was from this town that in the great storm
which happened November 27, 1703, a ship laden with tin was
blown out to sea and driven to the Isle of Wight in seven
hours, having on board only one man and two boys.

**Penzance.**

Penzance is the farthest town of any note west, being
254 miles from London and within about ten miles of the

---

[1] The collegiate church of Glasney was founded by Bishop
Bronescombe in 1267, but it was not a cell to Kirton or Crediton
church, to which Bronescombe was also a benefactor. (Oliver,
*Monasticon Exon.*, 48, 75.)

promontory called the Land's End ; so that this promontory is from London 264 miles, or thereabouts. This town of Penzance is a place of good business, well built and populous, has a good trade, and a great many ships belonging to it, notwithstanding it is so remote. Here are also a great many good families of gentlemen, though in this utmost angle of the nation ; and, which is yet more strange, the veins of lead, tin, and copper ore are said to be seen even to the utmost extent of land at low-water mark, and in the very sea—so rich, so valuable, a treasure is contained in these parts of Great Britain, though they are supposed to be so poor, because so very remote from London, which is the centre of our wealth.

Between this town and St. Burien, a town midway be- tween it and the Land's End, stands a circle of great stones, not unlike those at Stonehenge, in Wiltshire, with one bigger than the rest in the middle. They stand about twelve feet asunder, but have no inscription ; neither does tradition offer to leave any part of their history upon record, as whether it was a trophy or a monument of burial, or an altar for worship, or what else ; so that all that can be learned of them is that here they are. The parish where they stand is called Boscawone, from whence the ancient and honorable family of Boscawen derive their names.

Near Penzance, but open to the sea, is that gulf they call Mount's Bay ; named so far from a high hill standing in the water, which they call St. Michael's Mount : the seamen call it only the Cornish Mount. It has been fortified, though the situation of it makes it so difficult of access that, like the Bass in Scotland, there needs no fortification ; like the Bass too, it was once made a prison for prisoners of State, but now it is wholly neglected. There is a very good road here for shipping, which makes the town of Penzance be a place of good resort.

A little up in the county towards the north-west is Godolchan, which though a hill, rather than a town, gives name to the noble and ancient family of Godolphin ; and nearer on the northern coast is Royalton, which since the late Sydney Godolphin, Esq., a younger brother of the family, was created Earl of Godolphin, gave title of Lord to his eldest son, who was called Lord Royalton during the life of his father.[1] This place also is infinitely rich in tin-mines.

I am now at my journey's end. I must now return *sur mes pas*, as the French call it; though not literally so, for I shall not come back the same way I went. But as I have coasted the south shore to the Land's End, I shall come back by the north coast, and my observations in my return will furnish very well materials for another letter.

\*    \*    \*    \*    \*    \*

My last letter ended the account of my travels, where nature ended her account, when she meeted out the Island, and where she fixed the utmost western bounds of Britain; and, being resolved to see the very extremity of it, I set my foot into the sea, as it were, beyond the farthest inch of dry land west, as I had done before near the town of Dover, at the foot of the rocks of the South Foreland in Kent, which, I think, is the farthest point east in a line; and as I had done, also, at Leostoff in Suffolk, which is another promontory on the eastern coast, and is reckoned the farthest land eastward of the Island in general.

I now turned about to the east, and as, when I went west, I kept to the southern coast, of this long county of Cornwall, and of Devonshire also, so in going east, I shall keep the north shore on board. The first place of any note we came to, is St. Ives, a pretty good town, and grown rich by the fishing-trade; it is situated on the west side of a deep bay, called St. Ives Bay, from the name of the town. This bay is opposite, on the land side, to Mount's Bay, which I spoke of in my last, in my account of Penzance.

It is a very pleasant view we have at Maddern Hills, and the plain by them, in the way from Land's End to St. Ives, where, at one sight, there is a prospect of the ocean at the Land's End west; of the British Channel at Mount's Bay south; and the Bristol Channel, or Severn Sea, north; at St. Ives, the land between the two bays being not above four or five miles over, is so situated, that upon

St. Ives.

---

[1] Sidney Godolphin, third son of Sir Francis Godolphin and brother of Sir William Godolphin, Bart., was bap. 15 June, 1664, created Baron Godolphin of Rialton, 1684, and Viscount Rialton and Earl of Godolphin, 1706, died 15 Sept., 1712, and bur. 8 Oct., 1712, in Westminster Abbey. (Vivian, *Visitations of Cornwall.*)

the hill, neither of the two seas are above three miles off, and very plain to be seen; and also, in a clear day, the islands of Scilly, though above thirty miles off.

From this town and port of St. Ives, we have no town of any note on the coast; no, not a market town, except Redruth, which is of no consideration, 'till we come to Padstow Haven, which is near thirty miles. The country is, indeed, both fruitful and pleasant, and several houses of gentlemen are seen as we pass; the sands, also, are very pleasant to the eye, and to travel upon. Among the gentlemen's houses is Lanhidrock, the seat of the Earls of Radnor, who are Barons of Truro, and were so, long before they obtained the title of Radnor; also a good house belonging to the ancient family of Trefusis.

In viewing these things, we observed the hills fruitful of tin, copper, and lead, all the way on our right hand, the product of which is carried all to the other shore; so that we shall have little to say of it here. The chief business on this shore is the herring fishery; the herrings, about October, come driving up the Severn Sea, and from the coast of Ireland, in prodigious shoals, and beat all upon this coast as high as Biddeford, and Barnstable, in Devonshire, and are caught in great quantities by the fishermen, chiefly on account of the merchants of Falmouth, Foy, and Plymouth, and other ports on the south.

Padstow is a large town, and stands on a very good harbour for such shipping as use that coast, that is to say, for the Irish trade.

The passage from this town to Ireland is called by writers to be no more than twenty-four hours, but not justly: It is true that Padstow being the first, and best, if not the only haven on this shore, the trade from Ireland settled here of course, and a great many ships in this harbour are employed in the commerce; but to say, they make the voyage in four-and-twenty hours, is to say, It has been so, or, on extraordinary gales of fair wind, it may be done; but not one in twenty-four ships makes its voyage in twenty-four hours; and, I believe, it may be said they are oftener five or six days in the passage.

A little way within the land south-west from Padstow, lies St. Columb, eminent for nothing but its being the ancient

*Redruth.*

*Lanhydrock.*
*Earl of Radnor.*

*Trefusis.*

*Padstow.*

*St. Columb.*

*Arundell*
*of Trerice.*

*Prideaux.*

Bodmin.

Tintagel.

*King Arthur.*

The Hurlers.

estate of the famous Arundel of Trerice, of late years made noble by King Charles II. being still famous in the present Lord Arundel of Trerice;[1] also between them, is a very ancient seat of a family of the name of Prideaux, who, in Queen Elizabeth's time, built a very noble seat there, which remains to this day, though time makes the architect of it look a little out of fashion.[2]

Higher within the land, lies the town of Bodmyn, once one of the coining towns for tin, but lost it to Lestwithyel: however, this town enjoys several privileges, some of which are also tokens of its antiquity.

The coinage towns were, in Queen Elizabeth's time, four; namely, Leskard, Lestwithyel, Truro, Helston. Since that, in King James's time, was added Penzance.

Tintagel Castle lies upon this coast a little farther, a mark of great antiquity, and every writer has mentioned it; but as antiquity is not my work, I leave the ruins of Tintagel to those that search into antiquity; little or nothing, that I could hear, is to be seen at it; and as for the story of King Arthur being both born and killed there, 'tis a piece of tradition, only on oral history, and not any authority to be produced for it.

We have nothing more of note in this county, that I could see or hear of, but a set of monumental stones, found standing not far from Bodmyn, called The Hurlers, of which the country, nor all the writers of the country, can give us no good account; so I must leave them as I found them.

The game called the Hurlers is a thing the Cornish men value themselves much upon. I confess I see nothing in it, but that it is a rude violent play among the boors or country people; brutish and furious, and a sort of an evidence that they were once a kind of barbarians. It seems to me something to resemble the old way of play,

---

[1] Richard Arundell was created Baron Arundell of Trerice 1664, and died 1687. John, second Baron, died 1697; John, third Baron, died 1706; and John, fourth Baron, died 1768, when the title became extinct. (Vivian, *Visitations of Cornwall.*)

[2] Place House, Padstow. The first of that name at Padstow seems to have been Humphry Prideaux, born about 1573, who marri d Honour, dau. of Edmund Fortescue of Fallopit. (Vivian, *Visitations of Cornwall.*)

as it was then called, with Whirle-Bats, with which Hercules slew the giant, when he undertook to clean the Augean stable.[1]

The wrestling in Cornwall is, indeed, a much more manly and generous exercise, and that closure, which they call the Cornish hug, has made them eminent in the wrestling rings all over England, as the Norfolk and Suffolk men are for their dexterity at the hand and foot, and throwing up the heels of their adversary without taking hold of him.

I came out of Cornwall by passing the river Tamar at Launceston, the last, or rather the first, town in the county, *Launceston.* the town showing little else but marks of its antiquity; for great part of it is so old, as it may, in a manner, pass for an old, ragged, decayed place, in general. It stands at a distance, almost two miles, from the river, over which there is a very good bridge; the town is eminent, however, for being, as we call it, the County Town, where the assizes are always kept.

In the time when Richard, Earl of Cornwall, had the *Earl of* absolute government of this county, and was, we might say, *Cornwall.* King of the country, it was a frontier town, walled about, and well fortified, and had, also, a strong castle to defend it; but these are seen now only in their old clothes, and lie all in ruins and heaps of rubbish.

It is a principal gain to the people of this town, that they let lodgings to the gentlemen who attend here in the time of the assizes and other public meetings; as particularly, that of electing Knights of the Shire, and at the County Sessions, which are held here; for which purposes the town's people have their rooms better furnished than in other places in this country, though their houses are but low; nor do they fail to make a good price to their lodgers, for the conveniences they afford them.

The town sends two members to parliament, and so does Newport, a little village adjoining, and which, indeed, is but *Newport.* a part of Launceston itself; so that the town may be said, almost, to choose four members of parliament.

There is a fine image or figure of Mary Magdalen upon the tower of the church, which the Catholics fail not to pay

---

[1] Hurling was played with a ball only, no bats or cudgels of any kind being employed. (Carew, *Survey of Cornwall,* 73d-75d.)

their reverences to, as they pass by. There is no tin, or copper, or lead, found hereabouts, as I could find, nor any manufacture in the place; there are a pretty many attorneys here, who manage business for the rest of their fraternity at the assizes. As to trade, it has not much to boast of, and yet there are people enough in it to excuse those who call it a populous place. There is a long nook of the county runs north from this place, which is called the Hundred of Stratton, and in which there is one market town and no more, the name of which is Stratton; but has nothing in it, or about it, worth our making any remarks.

Passing the River Tamar, about two miles from Launceston, we enter the great county of Devon, and as we enter Devonshire in the most wild and barren part of the county, and where formerly tin mines were found, (though now they are either quite exhausted, or not to be found without more charge than the purchase, if found, would be worth), so we must expect it a little to resemble its neighbour country for a while.

The River Tamar here is so full of fresh salmon, and those so exceeding fat and good, that they are esteemed in both counties above the fish of the same kind found in other places; and the quantity is so great, as supplies the country in abundance, which is occasioned by the mouth of the river being so very large, and the water so deep for two leagues before it opens into Plymouth Sound, so that the fish have a secure retreat in the salt water for their harbour and shelter, and from thence they shoot up into the fresh water in such vast numbers to cast their spawn, that the country people cannot take too many.

As we are just entered Devonshire, as I said above, it seems at first sight a wild, barren, poor country; but we ride but a few miles 'till we find an alteration in several things: (1) more people; (2) larger towns; (3) the people all busy and in full employ upon their manufactures.

At the uppermost and extreme part of the county, north-west, there runs a huge promontory, a mountainlike proboscis, into the sea, beyond all the land on either side, whether of Devonshire or of Cornwall. This they would fain have called Hercules's Promontory, and Mr. Camden in his writing, and his map-maker also, calls it *Herculis*

**Stratton.**

**Tamar R.**

**Hartland.**

*Promontorium*; but the honest sailors, and, after them, the
plain country people, call it, in downright modern English,
Hartland Point or Harty Point, from the town of Hartland,
which stands just within the shore and is on the very
utmost edge of the county of Devon. It is a good market
town, though so remote, and of good resort too, the people
coming to it out of Cornwall, as well as out of Devonshire ;
and particularly the fisher boats of Barnstable, Biddiford,
and other towns on the coast, lying often under the lee,
as they call it, of these rocks, for shelter from the south-west
or south-east winds, the seamen go on shore here and
supply themselves with provisions ; nor is the town un-
concerned in that gainful fishing trade, which is carried on
for the herrings on this coast, many seamen and fishing
vessels belonging to the town.[1]

From this point or promontory, the land, falling away
for some miles, makes a gulf or bay, which, reaching to
the headland or point of Barnstable river or haven, is called
from thence, Barnstable Bay.  Into this bay, or at the
[east] end of this bay, the Rivers Taw and Tower empty   Taw R.
themselves at one mouth, that is to say, in one channel ;   Torridge R.
and it is very particular, that as two rivers join in one
channel, so here are two great trading towns in one port,
a thing which as it is not usual, so I cannot say 'tis any
advantage to either of them ; for it naturally follows that
they rival one another, and lessen both ; whereas, had they
been joined together in one town, or were it possible to
join them, they would make the most considerable town,
or city rather, in all this part of England.

These are the towns of Barnstable and Biddiford, or,   Barnstaple
as some write it, Bediford.  The first of these is the most   and Bideford.
ancient, the last the most flourishing.  The harbour or river
is in its entrance the same to both, and when they part,
the Tower turning to the right, or south-west, and the Taw
to the south-east, yet they seem to be both so safe, so
easy in the channel, so equally good with respect to shipping,
as equidistant from the sea, and so equally advantageous,
that neither town complains of the bounty of the sea to

---

[1] This description is so inaccurate that it is obvious Defoe never
visited the place.

them, or their situation by land; and yet of late years the town of Biddiford has flourished and the town of Barnstable rather declined.

**Bideford.**
Biddiford is a pleasant, clean, well-built town. The more ancient street, which lies next the river, is very pleasant, where is the bridge, a very noble quay, and the custom-house. This part also is very well built and populous, and fronts the river for above three-quarters of a mile; but, besides this, there is a new spacious street[1] which runs north and south, or rather north-west and south-east, a great length, broad as the High Street of Excester, well-built, and, which is more than all, well inhabited with considerable and wealthy merchants, who trade to most parts of the trading world.

Here, as is to be seen in almost all the market towns of Devonshire, is a very large, well-built, and well-finished meeting-house, and, by the multitude of people which I saw come out of it, and the appearance of them, I thought all the town had gone thither, and began to enquire for the church; but, when I came to the church, I found that also, large, spacious, and well filled too, and that with people of the best fashion. The person who officiates at the meeting-house in this town, I happened to have some conversation with, and found him to be not only a learned man, and master of good reading, but a most acceptable gentlemanly person, and one who, contrary to our received opinion of those people, had not only good learning and good sense, but abundance of good manners and good humour—nothing sour, cynical, or morose in him, and, in a word, a very valuable man; and, as such a character always recommends a man to men of sense and good breeding, so I found this gentleman was very well received in the place, even by those whom he differed from in matters of religion, and those differences did not, as is usual, make any breach in their conversing with him. His name, as
**Bartlet.**
I remember, was Bartlet.[2] But this is a digression—I wish I could say the like of all the rest of his brethen.

---

[1] Bridgeland Street.

[2] William Bartlet, minister from 1700 to 1719, son and grandson of two former ministers of that name; his grandfather held the rectory during the Commonwealth, and was ejected in 1662.

The trade of this town being very much in fish, as it is also of all the towns on this coast, I observed here that several ships were employed to go to Liverpool and up the River Mersey to Warrington, to fetch the rock salt which is found in that county, which rock salt they bring to Biddiford and Barnstable, and here they dissolve it into brine in the sea water, joining the strength of two bodies into one, and then boil it up again into a new salt, as the Dutch do by the French and Portugese salt. This is justly called salt upon salt, and with this they cure their herrings; and as this is a trade which can be but of a few years standing, because the rock itself has not been discovered in England much above twenty years, so the difference in curing the fish has been such, and it has so recommended their herrings in foreign markets, that the demand for them has considerably increased, and consequently the trade.[1]

There is indeed a very fine stone bridge over the river here, but the passage over it is so narrow, and they are so chary of it, that few carriages go over it; but as the water ebbs quite out of the river every low water, the carts and waggons go over the sand with great ease and safety. The arches of the bridge are beautiful and stately, but, as for saying one of them is so big that a ship of 60 tons may sail under it, etc., as a late author asserts,[2] I leave that where I find it, for the people of Biddiford to laugh at. If it had been said the hull of such a ship might pass under the bridge, it might have been let go; but as he says, it may *sail* under it, which must suppose some or one of its masts standing too, this puts it past all possibility of belief, at least to those who judge of such things by rules of mechanism, or by what is to be seen in other parts of the world, no such thing being practicable either at London Bridge, Rochester Bridge, or even at York, where the largest arch in England is supposed to be.

Biddiford was anciently the inheritance of the family of

---

[1] In 1755, a writer in the *Gent's Mag.* (xxv., 446) laments that the "herring fishery has failed for some years, and so has the manufacturing rock salt into what was called salt upon salt."

[2] Bishop Gibson's additions to his translation of Camden's *Britannia*, first published in 1695. "It is so high, that a ship of 50 or 60 tunn may sail under it."

*Earl of Bath.*

*Barnstaple.*

Granville, or Greenfield, as formerly called, and the Earl of Bath, who is the heir and chief of the family, is now Baron of Biddiford, Viscount Lansdowne, and Earl of Bath.[1]

As Biddiford has a fine bridge over the Tower or Towridge, so Barnstable has a very noble bridge over the Taw, and though not longer, is counted larger and stronger than the other. These two rival towns are really very considerable; both of them have a large share in the trade to Ireland, and in the herring fishery, and in a trade to the British colonies in America; if Biddiford cures more fish, Barnstable imports more wine and other merchandises; they are both established ports for landing wool from Ireland—of which by itself.

If Biddiford has a greater number of merchants, Barnstable has a greater commerce within land, by its great market for Irish wool and yarn, etc., with the serge-makers of Tiverton and Excester, who come up hither to buy. So that, in a word, Barnstable, though it has lost ground to Biddiford, yet, take it in all its trade completely is full as considerable as Biddiford; only, that perhaps it was formerly superior to it, and the other has risen up to be a match to it.

Barnstable is a large, spacious, well-built town, more populous than Biddiford, but not better built, and stands lower; insomuch, that at high water in spring tides, it is, as it were, surrounded with water. The bridge here was built by the generous gift of one Stamford, a citizen and merchant of London,[2] who, it seems, was not a native of this place, but by trading here to his gain, had kindness enough for the town to offer such a benefaction to them as they enjoy the benefit to this day.

The bridge at Biddiford, as above, was likewise a gift; but was, as they say, done by collections among the clergy, by grant of indulgences and like church management: but be it

---

[1] Sir John Grenville was created Earl of Bath, Viscount Lansdowne, and Baron Granville of Kilkhampton and Bideford. Charles, his son and heir, was killed by the accidental discharge of a pistol when preparing to attend his father's funeral, and they were both buried the same day, 22 Sept. 1701, at Kilkhampton. William Henry, the third Earl, died of the small-pox in 1711, when the title became extinct. (Vivian, *Visitations of Cornwall.*)

[2] See note 7 on p 3.

how it will, both the towns are infinitely obliged to the benefactors.

Behind Biddiford, that is as we come from Launceston, are several good towns, though I observed that the country was wild and barren ; as Tavistock, belonging to the house of Bedford, and giving the title of marquis, to the eldest son of that illustrious ducal family ;  the town of Torrington, on the same river Towridge that Biddiford stands on ; the title of Earl of Torrington was first given to the late General Monk, Duke of Albemarle,[1] in honour, and for a reward of his loyalty, in restoring King Charles II., and the line being extinct in his son, it was given by King William III. to Admiral Herbert,[2] who came over with him and was immediately made Admiral of the British fleet, to defend the possession of the crown in the person of that prince ; and since that to Sir George Bing,[3] one of our present admirals, and one who asserted the authority and power of the British navy against the Spaniards, at the late sea-fight near Cape Passaro in Sicily : so that the town of Torrington seems to be appropriated to the honour of the defenders of the British sovereignty at sea.

Another town in this part of the country is Okehampton, vulgarly Okington, a good market town, which gave title of Baron to the Lord Mohun, and sends two members to the Parliament.  It is a manufacturing town, as all the towns this way now are, and pretty rich ; and having said this, I have said all, unless it be that in the records of antiquity it appears to have been much more considerable than it is now, having 92 knights' fees belonging to it.  But as I studiously avoid meddling with antiquity in these accounts, studying to give you the present state of the countries and towns through which I travel, rather than what they have been, so I say no more of those things than needs must.

*Tavistock.*
*Duke of Bedford.*
*Torrington.*

*Monk, Earl of Torrington.*

*Herbert, Earl of Torrington.*

*Byng, Viscount Torrington.*

*Okehampton.*

*Mohun, Baron Okehampton.*

---

[1] George Monk was created Baron Monk, Earl of Torrington, and Duke of Albemarle, in July, 1660.  His son, Christopher, died in Jamaica in 1688.

[2] Arthur Herbert was created Earl of Torrington in 1689, after an indecisive action with the French in Bantry Bay.

[3] George Byng was created Baronet in 1715, and Viscount Torrington in 1721.  He served under Admiral Herbert in 1689, and held command in the Mediterranean, 1718-20, destroying the Spanish fleet off Cape Passaro on 31 July, 1718.

Ilfracombe.

A little above Barnstable, north-east upon the coast, stands a good market and port town, called Ilfarcomb, a town of good trade, populous and rich, all which is owing to its having a very good harbour and road for ships, and where ships from Ireland often put in, when, in bad weather, they cannot, without the extremest hazard, run into the mouth of the Taw, which they call Barnstable Water; and this is one reason which causes the merchants at Barnstable to do much of their business at this port of Ilfarcomb.

*Hubba.*

Kenwith Castle.

Antiquity tells us long stories of the Danes landing on this coast; of Hubba, the Danish King, being slain here, that is at Kennith Castle, between this place and the mouth of the Taw and Torridge, and that the place was called Hubbastow ever after, from the burying of this prince there; all this may be true, for aught we know, but I could neither find nor hear of this Castle of Kennith, or burial place, Hubbastow, or anything of the ruins or remains of them in the country; so I shall trouble you no farther about them.[1]

The sea coast in this county runs a little farther east by north, but I found there was nothing of moment to be seen there, except fishing towns, and small creeks, on which

Combe Martin.

are two small market towns, viz. Combe Martin and Porlock, 'till we came to Minehead.

Exe R.

Leaving the coast, we came, in our going southward, to the great River Exe, or Isca, which rises in the hills on this north side of the county, and that so far as, like the Tamar, it begins within four or five miles of the Severn Sea; the country it rises in is called Exmoor. Camden calls it a filthy, barren ground,[2] and, indeed, so it is; but as soon as the Exe comes off from the moors and hilly country, and descends into the lower grounds, we found the alteration; for then we saw Devonshire in its other countenance, viz. cultivated, populous, and fruitful; and continuing so 'till we came to

Tiverton.

Tiverton, a town which I mentioned before, but did not fully describe.

Next to Excester, this is the greatest manufacturing town in the county, and, of all the inland towns, is next to it in

[1] The present " Kenwith Castle," in Northam parish, was then called Henniborough. The identification was originally made by Mr. R. S. Vidal, F.S.A., of Cornborough, in 1810, and is now generally accepted by antiquaries.

[2] "A dreary barren tract," according to Gibson's translation.

wealth and in numbers of people. It stands on the River
Exe, and has over it a very fine bridge, with another over
the little River Lowman, which, immediately after, falls into          *Lowman R.*
the Exe just below the town. Antiquity says, before those
bridges were built, there were two fords here, one through
each river, and that the town was from thence called
Twy-ford-ton, that is, the town upon the two fords,
and so by abbreviating the sounds Twy-for-ton, then
Tiverton; but that I leave to the learned searchers into
ancient things.

But the beauty of Tiverton is the Free-School, at the east
entrance into the town, a noble building, but a much nobler
foundation. It was erected by one Peter Blundel, a clothier,          *Peter Blundell.*
and a lover of learning, who used the saying of William of
Wickham to the King when he founded the Royal School
at Winchester, viz. that if he was not himself a scholar,
he would be the occasion of making more scholars than any
scholar in England. He has endowed it with so liberal a
maintenance that, as I was informed, the schoolmaster has,
at least, sixty pounds per annum, besides a very good house
to live in, and the advantage of scholars not on the foundation, and the usher in proportion; and to this he added
two fellowships and two scholarships, which he gave the
maintenance for to Sydney College in Cambridge, and
one fellowship and two scholarships to Baliol College in
Oxford, all which are appointed for the scholars bred up
in this school; and the present reverend master was a
scholar upon the foundation in the same school.

As this is a manufacturing country, as above, we found
the people here all fully employed, and very few, if any,
out of work, except such as need not be unemployed, but were
so from mere sloth and idleness, of which some will be
found everywhere.

From this town there is little belonging to Devonshire
but what has been spoken of, except what lies in the road
to Taunton, which we took next, where we meet with the
River Colamb, a river rising also in the utmost limits of          *Culm R.*
the shire towards Somersetshire, and giving name to so many
towns on its banks, as leaves no room to doubt of its own          *Culm Davy.*
name being right, such as Colamb David's, Ufcolambe,          *Uffculme.*
Columstock, and Columbton; the last is a market town, and          *Culmstock.*
          *Cullompton.*

they are all full of manufacturers, depending much on the master manufacturers of Tiverton.

The county of Devon has been rich in mines of tin and lead, though they seem at present wrought out; and they had their stannary towns and coinage, as well as in Cornwall; nay, so numerous were the miners or tinners, as they are called in this county, that they were, on occasion of a national muster, or defence, regimented by themselves, and were, in short, a separate militia from the trained bands or militia of the county; but now we see the tin works in Devonshire is quite laid aside, not one tin mine being at work in the whole county. There are, indeed, some copper-works undertaken on the north side, as we were told (but I do not find that they are yet brought to perfection); and about Ilfarcomb, Combe Mertin, also at Delverton, in the north part of the county, they have been at work to see if they can recover some silver mines which, in the time of King Edward III., were so large that they employed three hundred miners, besides other workmen, and brought that Prince great sums of money for the carrying on his wars against France:[1] what progress they are now like to make in it, I cannot yet learn.

**Ilfracombe.**
**Combe Martin.**
**Dulverton.**

# TRAVELS THROUGH ENGLAND
## By Dr. Richard Pococke 1750

**Axminster.**

Sept. 20. From Lyme I went four miles almost directly north to Axminster on the river Ax in Devonshire, the bounds between the two counties being a little to the west of Lyme. This place is in the high road from London to Exeter. In the church they show two tombs, which they say are of two Saxon kings; and they have a tradition in the country that a battle was fought in Kingsmead near Mestern, in which one of them they say was killed. The

---

[1] In the reign of Edward I., 337 were brought out of Derbyshire to work the silver mines at Combe Martin. They are said to have been at that time very productive, and to have furnished money for the wars, in the reign of Edward III. They were again worked with success in the reign of Queen Elizabeth, by Sir Beavis Bulmer. (Lysons, *Devon*, 136.)

account we have is, that they are the Saxon princes slain by the Danes, in the battle of Brunaburg; and King Athelstan in remembrance of the victory built a minster here for seven priests to pray for the souls of the slain.[1] One of the tombs is on the north side of the quire with long robes, the head is off, but there are some remains of what looks like a coul. This, I was told some antiquaries said, was a bishop. The other was in the north isle, and both under niches; it has a coul over the head, and something in both hands which might be a crucifix, it looks very much like the statue of a woman. Digging lately at the west end of the church they found bones fill'd with lead, but no lead on the outside of the bones. I saw one of them. There is a chapel to the north of the church which is very old, and is now used as a school, and the south door of the church is very ancient; and what is particular, across the inside of the arch are eleven reeds cut in stone about two inches diameter. The capitals in the church are four angels holding shields of arms and their wings meeting the corners.

*King Athelstan.*

Going to Honiton I went over a hill of gravelly soil and came to a small stream which falls into the Ax, and crossed two more hills of clay and came to Honiton on the Autre; the east side of this town was burnt down four years agoe.[2] We went on in the afternoon and came to Venne bridges, over some rivlets that fall into the Autre, which rise so high that the roads are sometimes impassible for a few hours. Here King Edward the VI's army under S[r] John Russel and Lord Grey defeated the Cornish and Devonshire rebels.[3] Coming to Fair mile I saw the seat of S[r] Wm. Young,[4] and going up the hill saw the town of Autre, and had a glorious view from the top of it of the hills to the east of Autre fringed at top as in a strait

Honiton.

Otter R.

Fenny Bridges.

*Lord Russell.*
*Lord Grey.*
Fairmile.
*Sir Wm. Yonge.*
Ottery St.
Mary.

---

[1] See note 1 on p. 82.

[2] In 1747. (Lysons, *Devon*, 281.)

[3] The battle was fought by Lord Russell (afterwards Earl of Bedford) some days before Lord Grey arrived. (Froude, *History of England*, iv, 429-30; Rose-Troup, *Western Rebellion of 1549*, 252-61.)

[4] The "Great House" at Colyton. Sir William Yonge, 4th baronet, was M.P. for Honiton, 1715-54, and Tiverton, 1754; and died 1755.

line with the heathy ground, and then into the vale in which the Ex runs, and several rivlets that fall into it, and of the city of Exeter. When we came to the bottom of this hill I found it a red sandy soil all the way to Exeter.

**Exe R.** The river Ex rises near the north coast of Devonshire, having no considerable town upon it but Tiverton, Exeter, and Topsham; Dulverton, Bampton, and Samford are on rivlets that fall into it; two large streams joyn it from the north-east, Columbton having a town on it of the same name, and Bradninch; and from the north-west the river Credy, on which stands Crediton.

**Exeter.** The situation of Exeter is very delightful, being on a rising ground to the north of the river, which here runs to the east, and makes several little islands by the town. At the north-east corner of the town is the castle call'd Rougmont, which is ruinous, but there is a very old door case to the principal building within it. From the walls of the castle there is a pleasant prospect of the city and of the low hills round it. The city is computed to be about a mile and a half in circumference, the walls for the most part are built on the brow of the rising ground, except to the east, where there is but a little ascent and very gradual. The long High Street runs from the east gate to the walls something to the north of the west gate; six streets are mentioned as coming into it on each side, but they are only lanes. It is surprising to see how the great street is filled on a market day with people, and

**Cathedral.** great plenty of all sorts of provisions. The cathedral is a grand building; they say St. Maries chapel was built

**King Athelstan.** by King Athelstan, but it must have been rebuilt, for it is a modern fabrick in comparison of that time. It is probable one cf the towers after the Italian way was built at a distance from it, and that then they built the body of the church to it, so as that this tower and the other built like it on the other side make a sort of cross isle. The church seems to have been much raised since it was first built, the lower part of the body being old and the upper part of a much more modern architecture, if I rightly recollect, probably raised when the isles were added to it, as they were certainly on each side of the quire after the choir was built. There are some curious old paintings in the skreen under the organ, which is esteemed the largest in England.

The Bishop's throne is a Gothick work carv'd in wood, rising like a pyramid almost to the top of the walls, and is very fine. They have in the church the monument of Bishop Stapleton, founder of Exeter College in Oxford, of Hugh Oldham, Bishop and second founder of C.C.C., Oxford; he is buryed under the wall, being, they say, excommunicated by the Pope,[1] but appealed from the sentence, 'tis to be supposed to a general council, there having been a dispute between him and the mitred abbot of Tavistock; and the Pope gave it in favour of the abbot, and excommunicated him because he would not submit to the sentence. To the south of the church is a cloyster, adjoyning to it a very good chapter house, built as it is said by Edward Lacy the 22d bishop. The old church dedicated to St. Mary and St. Peter by King Athelstan, and rebuilt by King Canute for the Benedictine Monks, who were moved to Westminster by Edward the Confessor, and then the See of the Bishop was removed from Crediton to this conventual church, to which See St. Germains had been not long before united. The habitations of the Bishop, Dean, Dignitaries and Prebends are inclosed with the close wall on every side except to the east, where they are bounded by the town wall, and the whole enclosure is called the Close. But some of their predecessors have been less generous than the present dignitaries, who have laid out more in improving their houses than the others got by setting off their lands and houses, at the very entrance of their own, some of which are converted into shops.

There is a tradition that the brown free-stone of which the cathedral is built was brought from France, which is undoubtedly an error. The stone most used for building is a red crumbling free-stone with pebbles in it, dug out of a quarry of Hevitree a mile from the town; they have a harder sort of the same kind from Exmore thirty miles distant. To the east of the town they have a large

*Walter de Stapeldon. Hugh Oldham.*

*Edmund Lacey. King Athelstan.*

Heavitree.
Exmoor.

---

[1] As to his place of sepulture he built the tomb, etc., before the quarell with the Abbot, and therefore this story of his being buried out of the church because excommunicated is a vulgar error.—(*Note by Dr. Pococke.*)

workhouse, and an hospital for sick and maimed containing about 130 beds, set on foot by Dean Clark.[1]  Without the south-gate on the spot of the Priory of Grey Franciscans is a great manufacture of narrow cloths and shalloons, extending all down to the river, and the cloths when they are hung up make a very beautiful appearance; this place is called the Friars.   There is a beautiful walk called Northern-hay, on the north side of the castle and town, over the hanging ground.   Josephus Iscanius,[2] a celebrated poet, was of this place.   This town has suffered in several wars; was besieged by Perkin Warbeck;[3] and by the rebels of Cornwall and Devonshire against Edward VI.[4]   It held out for K. Charles 1st as long as they possibly could, and the Princess Henrietta, afterwards Dutchess of Orleans, was born here.[5]

On Sep. 21st. in the afternoon, I went from Exeter, on the west side of the river, and saw Topsham on the east side, which is a considerable trading town, as the shipping come up to it.   I passed by Powderham Castle on the river Ken; this is the seat of the very ancient family of the name of Courtney of the blood royal of France.   I went on to Star Cross, and crossed over the river to Exmouth, situated near the place where the Ex empties itself into the sea, and is chiefly inhabited by fishermen and publicans, it being a place to which the people of Exeter much resort for diversion and bathing in the sea, and the situation is so pleasant, having beautiful litle hills to the east finely improved, and a view of the fine country on the other side, that some persons of condition have come to live at the place, which they are improving by a gravel walk to the river, that is to be planted, and they are going to make a bowling green.   Sr John Colliton has a garden full of curious plants chiefly from

Marginal notes: *Dr. Alured Clarke.* *Friernhay.* *Northernhay.* *Josephus Iscanus.* *Perkin Warbeck.* *Princess Henrietta.* Topsham. Powderham Castle. Kenn R. *Courtenay.* Starcross. Exmouth. *Sir John Colliton.*

---

[1] The hospital was founded by the zealous exertions of Dr. Alured Clarke, then dean of Exeter, in 1741.  (Lysons, *Devon*, 232.)

[2] Joseph of Exeter, Latin poet, accompanied Archbishop Baldwin to Palestine, 1188; his principal poem, 'De Bello Trojano,' long current under names of Dares Phrygius and Cornelius Nepos, first published as his own at Frankfort, 1620, and edited by Jusserand, 1877. (*Dict. Nat. Biography.*)

[3] In 1497.

[4] In 1549.

[5] June 16th, 1644.

America, where he has a son settled. He has the magnolia or lawrel-leav'd tulip in blossom, and also the Carolina sword blade aloe ; he has also the trumpet tree, the Carolina raspberry tree, the anemony tree, and Carolina kidney bean tree, the artichoke or orange myrtle, the flowers of which are in clusters and of a reddish cast, a beautiful turn cap'd Carolina martagon, which is red and white, the motle-leav'd tulip tree, which seems to be only the occidental plane-tree, the serpentine euphorbium, the coat of which resembles the scales of a serpent, but it is very much raised.

Directly east of Topsham is Clyst St. Maries, where the Parliament forces[1] barricaded themselves up by laying trees across the way and planting their ordinance; but when they heard Lord Russel was at Woodbery they endeavoured to surprize him ; but he routed them, pursued them to this place, and then to the heath, and entirely defeated them.[2] *Clyst St. Mary.* *Woodbury.* *Lord Russell.*

Sept. 22.  I went over again to Star Cross, and ascended up to Malmhead, the seat of the late Mr. Ball, and now of Mr. Apreece, but is upon sale ;[3] it is a fine situation on the side of a hill, with beautiful plantations of most sorts of firr and the cedar of Lebanon, with walks through it ; the most beautiful part is a terrace up the sides of the hill behind the house, and a winding walk round the hill. Above the wood on the heigth of the hill is an obelisk,[4] which is a land mark ; it is built of free-stone and the pedestal is thirty feet square, and I suppose may be towards 80 feet high, but it is built on a good model.  I went over the heath to Tinmouth, which country is mostly a sort of gravel, abounding in a large flinty stone, but towards the sea shoar it is a red sandy stone.  Tinmouth, East and West, are under the hills, and appear very beautiful from the other side, the land round 'em being improved in orchards.  The Tower *Mamhead.* *Thomas Balle.* *T. H. Apreece.* *Teignmouth.*

[1] It is not clear why the author calls the enemy "the Parliament forces." They were local rebels. (See p. 179.)

[2] Aug. 3rd, 1549. (Rose-Troup, *Western Rebellion of 1549*, 262-277.)

[3] Thomas Balle, the last of the family, died in 1749: soon after which Mamhead was sold by his heir, Thomas Hussey Apreece, to Joseph Gascoyne Nightingale, whose sister brought it to her husband, Wilmot Vaughan, the first Earl of Lisburne. (Lysons, *Devon*, 327-8.)

[4] The obelisk of Portland stone, on Mamhead point, about 100 feet high, was built by Thomas Balle, about the year 1742. (Lysons, *Devon*, 328.)

of West Teingmouth church is very old, with only pike holes in it, and was probably first built as a tower of defence.[1] They have a slight platform to defend the harbour, with a rampart of earth round it:[2] the Danes who were sent to make discoveries landed hereabouts in the year 800 and took the town;[3] it was burnt by the French in the late wars.[4]

*Torquay.*

We ascended the hills, and approached towards Torbay, which has its name from the parish of Tor, where there is an abbey.  Through this parish we rid between the marble hills to a part of the bay, which we cross'd.  These hills are the first beginning of the marble country; but I observed that in the bottom of the bay it was a free-stone and sand,

*Brixham.*

*Paignton.*

*William III.*

*Mr. Yarde.*
Churston-
Ferrers.
? Galmton
Common.

and on the other side likewise, at Brixham, the hills are marble.  We lay at Paignton, a poor town of farmers at the bottom of the bay.  King William landed about two miles and a-half to the west [? south] of Paignton, and about half a mile to the east [? north] of Mr. Yards, of Cheshunt, as I conjecture, in a little bay I observ'd in that situation.[5] He went with his army about half a mile to Gayton Common, and sent for carriages and horses which did not come as soon as they expected; but the King and army came that night to Paignton, where they lay,[6] and went on the next

---

[1] Although the church was rebuilt about 1823, the old tower remains as it was. (Lake, *Trans. Devon Assoc.*, vi., 384.)

[2] The battery was built in accordance with a petition presented in 1744, by the principal inhabitants of East and West Teignmouth and Shaldon, to Sir William Courtenay, stating that the French had plundered and burnt the place in 1690, and that they then threatened a second visit. (Lysons, *Devon*, 490.)

[3] Both Camden and Risdon say that the Danes first landed in England at West Teignmouth, in 787; but it appears to have been mistaken for Tynemouth, in Northumberland, which is certainly the Tinemutha of the Saxon Chronicle. (*Lysons, Devon*, 489.)

[4] In 1690.  (See Note 2 above.)

[5] This seems to refer to Elbury Cove, but there does not appear to be any evidence in support of this "conjecture."  "The actual spot on which the Prince landed was where the fish market now stands [at Brixham], and the stone on which the Prince first placed his foot was long preserved there, and pointed out with pride and veneration." (Windeatt, *Trans. Devon. Assoc.*, xii., 212).

[6] It is not definitely known where the Prince lodged that night, but "Mr. Peter Varwell, of Exeter, the representative of an old Brixham family, says that it has always been handed down in his family as a positive fact that one of his ancestors assisted the Prince to land, and gave him his first night's lodging in his humble abode in Middle Street." (Windeatt, *Trans. Devon. Assoc.*, xii., 212.)

day towards Exeter. I was informed that the person who came first to meet him at his landing had a chain given to him, and the Right Honourable Arthur Herbert, who was the admiral that brought over King William, and afterwards the Queen, was made Earl of Torrington and Baron Herbert of Torbay.[1] It is also said that Vespasian landed here, when he came against Arviragus, King of Britain. And in time of war the fleet of England has often laid in this bay. To the south [? north] of Tor is the parish of St. Maries, the church of which is said to be the oldest in Devonshire, but has no appearance of great antiquity.

*Baron Herbert of Torbay.*

*Vespasian.*

St. Mary-church.

Sept. 23. From Paignton I went over Gayton Common, and crossed the river Dort to Ditsham, a village with a litle street in it, and a large ancient church new modelled, where I first saw one of those carved stone pulpits, of which sort there are many in this country; in the niches of it are also relievos of saints with ornaments of vines between them.

Dittisham.

The minister's house is a very pleasant hermitage, commanding a view of the river, which is narrow there, and forms a bason below, and a much larger above; the glebe rises up the hills to the south and west, and there is the third part of a mannor[2] annexed to it, left by one co-heiress of three; and the rector holds a court of renewing his leases, in which they swear fealty to the lord; it consists of thirty-two tenements, to each of which there is a house and about half an acre of land on three lives, and there is a piece of land of [blank] acres of the same tenure.

Sept. 24. I went up the river to Totness, which is a neat town, situated on the side of the hill, and there are remains of an old castle with an high mount within it, on which there was a circular building;[3] it commands a fine view, and from it I saw the obelisk of Malmhead: this town is a great thorow fare from Exeter to Plymouth, tho' not the post road; it abounds in good shops to supply the country, and has a cheap and plentiful market. The people are polite and generous.

Totnes.

---

[1] Arthur Herbert was created Earl of Torrington in 1689, after indecisive action with the French in Bantry Bay.

[2] The manor of Dittisham Wales. (Lysons, *Devon*, 164.)

[3] See H. Michell Whitley, "Totnes Castle and Walled Town." (*Trans. Devon Assoc.*, xlviii., 189-198.)

**Brixham.**

Sept. 25. From Ditsham I crossed the water towards Torbay to Brixham, to see a well which ebbs and flows, as some say, nine times in an hour; but the springs being low we could not discern it, but it does ebb and flow when the springs are high. There is a key below the village, and a great fishing trade is carried on from it, for they supply all the country as far as Bristol. This side of the bay is lime stone, which is carried from this place along the shoar to the east; the country to the west side near as far as Plymouth is of a slaty stone.

**Dartmouth.**

From Brixham I went to Dartmouth, a town made up of three boroughs, Hardness to the north, Clifton to the south, and Dartmouth in the middle: this town consists of one street by the water and of several houses built up the sides of the hills in an extraordinary manner. There is a beautiful Gothick skreen in the church. They have a pretty good trade to Newfoundland, Spain, and Portugal. Mr.

*Smith.*

Smith, vicar of this place, was the person that wrote Dr. Pococke's[1] Life before his works, down to the Restoration.

*Newcomen.*
*Savery.*

Mr. Newcomen, an ironmonger here, with Captain Savory, invented the fire engine[2]: his son and daughter found out the beautiful sea-plants here on the rocks and on the shoar after storms; they are exquisitely fine and in great variety, I think not inferior to those brought from the East Indies, and are very ornamental with glass and frames; they dip 'em frequently in fresh water, to take off the salt which would otherwise give; and are at great pains in spreading and separating the branches.

**Modbury.**

From Dartmouth we went over a hilly country, and crossing the river Aume came to Modbury, a town built on the side of two hills, on each side of a valley, and has a great trade in serges. Near this is Wimpston, the seat of the Fortescues, of which family there have been

**Wimpston.**
*Fortescue.*

---

[1] Edward Pococke, orientalist, born 1604, died 1691. "His learning was the admiration of Europe." (*Dict. Nat. Biography.*)

[2] See Rhys Jenkins, "Savery, Newcomen, and the Early History of the Steam-engine." (*Trans. Devon Assoc.*, xlv, 343-367; xlvi, 455-477.)

[3] The manor was granted by King John to John Fortescue in 1209, and appears to have been the first residence of that ancient and noble family in the county. It was alienated about 1600. (Lysons, *Devon*, 343.)

many great and eminent lawyers, and particularly the person who writ *De Laudibus Legum Angliæ*, Chancellor of England temp. H. 6.[1]

Sept. 26. We went on westward, and crossed the river Arm, afterwards the Alm or Yalm, on which is Yampton, the place of residence of Ethelwold, a Saxon King.[2] We went on to Plimpton, a small town on a rivlet which falls into the river Plim, on the north side of the town, and to the west of the church are remains of a castle about 140 yards long from east to west, and eighty from north to south, defended by a ditch between 30 and 40 feet deep, which was full of water, having another fossee round it, and at the west end is a round mount about 100 feet high, with the ruins of a circular building on it, about 24 yards diameter, and the walls are ten feet thick.[3] There is also a well endowed free school here with an handsome spatious school house,[4] and Mr. Treby has a good house and gardens adjoyning the town. Half a mile to the west of it is Plimpton St. Mary, where there was a college of secular canons, displaced by a bishop, because they would not part with their wives or concubines.[5] We came to the bay near the mouth of the Plim, to the west of which is Saltrum, a beautiful improvement of Mr. Parker's,[6] and had a very pleasant ride to Plymouth.

*(marginal notes:)* Erme R. Yealm R. Yealmpton. *Ethelwold.* Plympton. Plym R. *Treby.* Saltram. *Parker.*

---

[1] Sir John Fortescue, author of "De Laudibus Legum Angliæ," was Lord Chief-Justice of the King's Bench, 1442, but not Lord-Chancellor.

[2] Here, according to tradition, the Saxon King, Ethelwold, had his palace, whose lieutenant, Lipsius, was also here interred. (Risdon, *Survey of Devon*, 193.)

[3] Camden describes the remains as "the miserable remains of a castle," and in 1822 there were scarcely any remains of the buildings, but the earth works showed it to have been a place of great strength. (Lysons, *Devon*, 410.)

[4] The grammar-school was founded and endowed, in 1658, by Sergeant Maynard, as one of the trustees of the estates left by Mr. Elize Hele, to charitable uses. (Lysons, *Devon*, 410.)

[5] A prebendal college consisting of five members, namely, a dean and four prebendaries, supposed to have been founded there by King Edgar, was removed and transplanted to Boseham in Sussex by Bishop William Warelwast in 1121, and in its place was founded the large Augustinian priory of SS. Peter and Paul. (Oliver, *Monasticon Exon.*, 129.)

[6] Saltram was purchased in 1712 by George Parker, and his son built the mansion, his grandson was in 1774 created Baron Boringdon, and his great-grandson was in 1815 created Viscount Boringdon of North Molton, and Earl of Morley. (Lysons, *Devon*, 412.)

Plymouth.

Plymouth is situated near the mouth of the river Plym, and on a head of land to the south of it is the fort, between which and the town are the bake houses of the navy. In the bay is the Island of St. Nicholas, where there is a battery and a barrack for invalids, who are quarter'd there and in this fort. General Lambert was exiled for life in this island,[1] and King Charles 2, the Duke of York, and many of the Court, going out in a yatch from Portsmouth for pleasure, were drove into Plymouth, and were received at Mount Edgcomb. They went to St. Nicolas Island and conversed with Lambert, and not bringing him away with them was a very unpopular thing, entirely thrown by the people on the Duke of York. Lambert died there about the time of the Revolution.[2]

*Gen. Lambert.*

Devonport.

The dock is near two miles from Plymouth on the river Tamer. It is finely situated, and there are five docks for building, cut out of the rock, and lined with Portland stone. One of them is a dock for three ships, and within another is a wet dock, and there are communications from one to the other by bridges over the entrances to them. Beyond the dock is the gun wharf, which is a large platform cut out of the rock, which is between twenty and thirty feet higher than the platform; on the upper part of this and of the dock are very convenient habitations for the officers.

Mount Edgcumbe.
*Lord Edgcumbe.*

Catwater.
Oreston.

I had the pleasure to be shown Mount Edgcomb by the lord[3] of it and his sons. It is by far the finest situation I ever saw, exceeding every thing in the beauty of the near prospects; Catwater Bay appearing like a lake encompassed with a town (Orson being upon it), is one of the most beautiful landscapes that can be conceived. Then the town of Plymouth, the Fort and the Isle St. Nicolas, the village of Stoke up in the country, Crimble Passage, the glorious view of the dock and the town adjoyning to it, of Saltash, a borough up the River Tame, of the King's brew houses

Stoke.
Cremyll
Passage.
Saltash.

---

[1] 1667.—Thomas Stutt, Mayor. "Just upon the election of this man, Lambert, that arch rebell, brought prisoner to this Island, Saint Nicholas." (Jewitt, *History of Plymouth*, 228.)

[2] 1683.—"Lambert, that old rebel, dyed this winter on Plymouth Island, where he had been a prisoner 15 years and more." (Jewitt, *History of Plymouth*, 237.)

[3] Richard Edgcumbe, created Baron Edgcumbe in 1742, died 1758. (Vivian, *Visitations of Cornwall.*)

on a bay under Mount Edgcomb, and of Milbrook at the
end of it, of Start Point to the east, Ediston Lighthouse
to the south, and Dodman and Lizard Points to the west,
all which, together with the grand view of the ocean, make
it the finest situation for prospects, which appear very beautiful in a moveable camera obscura, made in a centry box,
which shuts up. To add to all this L^d Edgcomb has improved
this place by making a fine lawn before the house, and to
the east of it, below which is a fine grown old wood, an
avenue in the front, and fish ponds and wood down the
hill to the west and north, a park improvement behind the
house all up the hill, which makes away toward Ramhead,
and is part of the west side of the Bay of Plymouth; and,
what is very curious, the side of the hill planted down not
only on the east to the water, but also to the south, in the
face of the very main ocean, where firs, pines, arbutus,
laurustine, and cypress, thrive exceedingly, and there is a
terrace on the side of the hill through this wood. The house
is built with turrets like a castle, having a high saloon in
the middle.

Sept. 27. We went westward five miles from this place
to Orost Hole, where we dined with L^d Edgcomb, who was
going to Lestwithiel, and went on to St. Germain, which
stands on a river, into which the tyde comes and makes a
large basin before Mr. Elliot's house, and improvement, from
which the village rises up the side of the hill; and above
the house is the ancient Priory Church of St. Germains,
where in the Saxon times was a bishop's see built, where
St. Germain, Bishop of Auxerre, resided for some time, who
was sent to oppose the Pelagian Heresie. In memory of
him King Athelstan built a fair church, and removed the
see of Cornwall to this place from Bodmin, where they
had been infested by the Danes. For all the country having
been under the see of Dorchester, in Oxfordshire, the see
was afterwards removed to Winchester, and King Athelstan
took two bishopricks out of it, Cornwall, the see of which
was fixed at Bodmyn, and Devonshire, fix'd at Taunton;[1]
the latter was removed to Kirton or Crediton. Cornwall

Millbrook.

Eddystone
Lighthouse.

Rame Head.

Crafthole.
Lostwithiel.
St. Germans.
Port Eliot.
*Eliot.*

*St. Germain.*

*King
Athelstan.*

---

[1] This is probably intended to refer to Bishop's Tawton, a
manor belonging to the bishopric, but there is no evidence that the
see was ever fixed at that site.

was afterwàrds united to that, and, anno 1050, the see was removed to Exeter. The church door and a window in that end is very old, and the two square towers may be old, on one of which an octagon building is erected. After the see was removed it was turned into a priory of Canons Regular. From St. Germain we went by a very uneven road to Duloe, which formerly consisted of a rectory and vicaridge, now consolidated. In the parish church is buryed Sr. John Coleshill, who was a Knight banneret of the time of King Edward the 3d.

Sept. 28. In the afternoon we set out for Fowey, and passed by Trelawn, the estate of the late Bishop of Winchester, Sᵣ Jonathan Trelawney, and now of his son, Sᵣ John Trelawney.[1] It is an old building with a chapel to it and fine woods near it. Opposite to Fowey is the seat of Mr. Keke, who has a fine terrace walk over the cliff on the river. Fowey is a very good harbour, and the town is pleasantly situated on the west side of the river.

Sept. 29. We crossed Par Bay to Par, a small key and harbour near St. Blazey. Here we first saw a stream work of tin, that is, of tin stone and tin grains wash'd down to the bottom from the lodes or veins. They find it at different depths, in what they call loose ground. When they come to what they call the fast ground they give over digging; this is the solid earth, suppos'd never to have been moved. We went up higher and saw where they had dug for what they call shodes, which is digging in the side of the hills to see if they can find any tin stones, call'd shode stones, which are like pebbles; and when they find them they dig above them again, according to the direction they find them in, and so at last they generally find the lode: and we saw along the top of the hill the works which had been made upon the lodes.

We came to a little tinning town called St. Austle, partly built of more stone or grey granite, and partly of a free stone, which they find on a river about three miles to the south-south-west. We went up the hill, and struck

*Duloe.*

*Sir John Coleshill.*

*Fowey.*
*Trelawne.*
*Sir Jonathan Trelawny.*
*Sir John Trelawny.*
*Mr. Keke.*

*Par Sands.*
*Par.*
*St. Blazey.*

*St. Austell.*

---

[1] Sir Jonathan Trelawny, Bart., was bishop successively of Bristol, Exeter, and Winchester. When Bishop of Bristol, he was one of the seven bishops committed to the Tower. He died in 1721, and his son, Sir John Trelawny, Bart., died without issue in 1754.

out of the way, to the south, to other tin works called
Pool-gooth, where they have a fire engine, and on the other _Polgooth._
side of the vale are L⁴ Edgcomb's works.   We went on
to Grampound, a very poor town situated on the side of _Grampound._
a litle river which rises out of the hills about St. Roach; _Roche._
below Grampound, Tregony stands on it.   Grampound was _Tregoney._
formerly famous for a manufacture of gloves.   There are
tin stream works on the east side of the river.   From
St. Blazey to Grampound, which is a tin country, we found
the soil very indifferent and covered with heath ; but from
Grampound to Truro it is a very good country, and there
is no sign of tin.   We came to Probus, a village pleasantly _Probus._
situated on a river.   There is a fine tower to the church,
beautifully adorned with Gothick ornaments.   We came to
Truro, a small trading town, in which there are many _Truro._
good houses ; and many wealthy people live here, who have
got considerable fortunes by the tin trade, and also several
merchants and shop keepers who supply the country, the
town being pretty much in the centre of the tin and copper
mines ; there is also a great trade in supplying the tin works
with timber and the fire engines with coal.   The church is
a most elegant building of about Henry the 8th's time,
with some old painted glass in it and curious sculpture
on the south and east fronts, and the letter which King
Charles the First writ to the people of Cornwall on their
loyalty towards him is put up in the church.   There is
a handsome tomb of the Roberts in the church, the ancestors _Roberts._
of Lord Radnor, and the tomb of one Fitz Hibben, _alias_ _Fitz Hibben._
Phibben, who, being made a slave by the Turks, he and
about ten more overcame sixty Turks on board a ship,
three or four of his companions being killed, and went
with the ship into Spain.   He was offered a ship of war
by the King of Spain if he would become a Catholick, but
he refused it.   This happened about the beginning of the
last century.

Oct. 1.   On the 1st of October I set forward from Truro
to the west, enter'd on a wild heathy country, and came
in three miles to Casewater, a country of tin and copper. _Chacewater._
I had the curiosity to see the nature of the tin works.
They call a work a balle.   [_Then follows a detailed description._]
A succession of men are always in the mine, except on

Sundays. They work eight hours, from six to two, and from two to ten, and from ten to six, and are out of the mine sixteen hours. When they come up, they call it coming to the grass. When the ore is brought up, women and children are employed in breaking it, and separating the country[1] from the ore, and the tin from the copper. No copper is smelted here, but is bought for smelting houses at Bristol and other parts. The men are paid so much a tun for what they deliver separated from the country. In the mines in general the lord has a fifteenth, and the owner, called the bounder, has a tenth.

**Redruth.**

From this place we went three miles to Red Ruth, a small tin town, where they have a great market of provisions once a week, and a great sale of shoes brought from all parts round for near thirty miles; and there are at the market generally 4 or 5000 people. The foot of

**Carnbrea.**

Carne Bray hill comes to the rivlet, it is the beginning of a ridge of hills; this end of it is very curious, the top and sides abounding in a large masse of grey granite, many of which lye one on another. The castle is very curious: 'tis a very small building on three or four of these stones; at one end there are five of them one over another, in other parts two or three, and lying loose in such a manner that one sees between them under the foundation of the castle. To the west of it is what they call the altar, which is a large flat granite stone; in it are seven litle basins, most of which, if not all, have communication one with another; they are so shapeless that I thought it might be the softer parts of the stone worn away. But Mr. Borlace and others are of opinion that it is a work of art, and served in some religious worship.

Farther west is a pile of great stones lying one on another from three to five, and three or four in length. Two or three years ago they found some coins on this hill, some Roman and some British; but, what are most curious, are of a pale gold, with the reverse of a horse or person sitting and some other figures ill done; but the heads of some of them on the other side are very good and resemble the head of Jupiter, which I think, without doubt, are

---

[1] The stone or earth on each side of the lode.

Phœnician or some coin of the ancients. Twenty or thirty years ago a man digging for stone observed a cavity, and opening it, sent down a boy, who found a litle cell, with a nich at one end, and a book in it, which was carried to the minister of Red Ruth, no body knew what language it was; but the book was taken away in leaves by those who came to see it. From this hill we had a view of both seas and of St. Michael's Mount. We came to some stamping mills, which is the first process the ore goes through after it is brought from the mines, which is performed by water mills that work the stamping irons, and pound the ore very small. [*Then follows a detailed description of the manner of dressing tin or preparing it for smelting.*]

We passed by Trechiedy, a very grand new house, offices and improvements of Mr. Basset's,[1] but in a sad situation. We passed by a smelting house at Angarick, and then had to the north that great bank of sand on which a village called Philack is situated. This sand is good manure and great quantities of it are taken from this place, and the hill is constantly encreasing from the sea, where the small river Hele empties itself; we came opposite to Lelant, and turned to the south along the strand, which is made by a sort of bay from the sea. We passed by Hele, a small port with warehouses, and so we arrived at a poor village called St. Erth. There were some thoughts by a private person of proposing a scheme of cutting a communication from this river to the south sea, but the mouth of this river would be always choaked with sand, and the ground is so high to the south that it would be a work of great expence and would answer no end, as they are so near the western point of England, except in time of war, when ships might pass from one channel to another without danger of privateers, which frequently snap them up in their passage between Scilly Islands and the Land's End or Cape Cornwal.

Oct. 2. From S[t.] Erth I went on Oct. 2[d.] across the river to Trelarth, a smelting house for tin, and then northward to Lelant; the sand is gaining upon the ground here, insomuch that several people have lost the profitable soil,

*Marginal notes:* Tehidy. Angarrack. Phillack. Hayle R. Lelant. Hayle. St. Erth. Lelant.

---

[1] Francis Basset, died 1769.

St. Ives.

and they say it blows from the bar of the river.   In the way to S$^{t.}$ Ives I saw a tin work, and I observed a black granite here, and a sort of a black stone like the touchstone, of which kind the rocks are about S$^{t.}$ Ives.

S$^{t.}$ Ives is situated on the side of a hill over the bay, to the north-west of Hele river; there is a head sets out to the east, on which there is a chapel built, and a platform of seven guns on the east side;[1] they have a considerable trade here of pilchards, which they barrel and send to Spain and Portugal.   We went from this place over very disagreeable heaths called Downs towards Morva; about the middle of the downs we came to the foot of a hill, where I observed a small oblong enclosure about 15 feet by 10, made by the granite stones set up an end; from this, I observed stones set up an end in a winding form, and, if I mistake not, extending from the four corners, which I thought might relate to the ancient serpent worship.   About a hundred yards to the west, and nearer the foot of the hill, I observed a circle made by stones laid flat and fill'd up with stone.   We ascended the hill and came to a circle

Nine Maidens.

call'd the Nine Maidens, it is about 23 yards in diameter. It consists of twenty stones from two feet to three broad, and from four feet to seven high, and three yards apart, except that there is an opening to the west eight yards wide. About 100 near north there is another stone.   .   .   It may be supposed these were call'd the Nine Maidens from so many of them being higher than the rest.   We descended

Morvah.
Madron.
St. Buryan.

St. Just.

to the north-west to Morva, observing old works along the hills, and saw Madern and S$^{t.}$ Burien, to the south and south-west, where the tin works begin and continue, for four or five miles all through the parish of S$^{t.}$ Just.   I here observed that they put up poles on their works, which is to show that they are working in those places, for anciently the Dukes of Cornwall gave leave to all people to work for ore, provided they marked out their bounds, and these are called bounders; if they met, they were to give over and put a bound mark at the place: they had a property as long as they work'd, which was signifyed by putting up the poles, but in length of time the bounders came to make

[1] See p. 23.

this priviledge a perpetual chattel, which they can now dispose of as they please and remains their property, tho' they do not work; but they have no property in the surface.

We saw Cape Cornwall, the south-west point of England, to the north of which is a litle bay, that is a fishing cove.

Oct. 3. I went from S⁺ Just to Sennam, and a mile further to the Land's end, the most western point of England, where the granite rocks extend into the sea, and I went on them as far as it is safe to go; beyond them are some rocks called the Long Ships; a litle to the north I went down the sea cliff, and saw a vein of tin which they are working. They find here a great variety of shells. We came by a litle port at the north-west corner of the bay call'd Newlin, where Guavous Lake is esteemed the securest part of the bay: about a mile further is Pensance. This is a town of some trade in pilchards, which they send to Spain; and they have a good mole and a platform for guns near it. A mile up the hill to the north-west is Castle Horneck, which commands a fine view of the bay and particularly of the Mount, which from this place looks like a rich piece of Gothick carved work.

Oct. 4. I went to see S⁺ Michael's Mount, commonly called the Cornish Mount in this country, and in Cornish Caricause in Cous, that is, a hoary rock in a wood; for tho' it is now an island in the bay when the tide is in, yet they say that the sea has gained, that there was formerly a wood on the spot, and that they sometimes discover trees under the sands. A ridge of rocks extend from it about a quarter of a mile to the beach, by which they can go to it when the tide is not high. The foot of it is near a measured mile in circumference. It consists of grey granite, the stones of which on the west side lye in a beautiful disorder; on the east side there is so much earth that there is a hanging garden on part of it. They found a tin vein in the rock, which was worked some time ago, and a very rich ore was dug out of it. Mr. Borlace[1] showed me a celt or copper instrument of war, which, if I mistake not, he said was found here; and it is said that they found

_Cape Cornwall._

_Sennen._
_Land's End._

_Longships._

_Newlyn._
_Gwavas Lake._
_Penzance._

_Castle Horneck._

_St. Michael's Mount._

_Wm. Borlase._

---

[1] William Borlase, the antiquary, who held the living of Ludgvan.

spear-heads, battle axes, and swords of copper all wrapt up in linnen, when they were digging for tin.  William, Earl of Cornwall,[1] in the time of Henry the first, built a cell here for two or three monks, and probably the chapel.  It is said that the monks pretending that S[t.] Michael had appeared to them was the occasion of giving it the name of S[t.] Michael's Mount.  The chapel is lately repaired by the late S[r] John S[t.] Aubyn, and there are some convenient compartments made by him out of the old buildings, as he took great delight in this place, where he usually spent his summers.  They say the whole mount is consecrated ground, and the people of Market Jew have a burial place at the foot of the hill.  John Earl of Oxford, after Henry 6th was defeated in Barnet field, whose part he had taken, fortifyed himself here against Edward IV, and defended it bravely till his men gave way on the assault[2]; and Duke of Hamilton was in this fortress when the Parliament forces took it, and the lines they drew are still to be seen towards Ludgvon.  At the north foot of the mount is a safe mole for shipping, and several warehouses and publick houses are built on the south side of it.  Opposite to the mount is Market Jew, said to be derived from Market Jupiter, because the market is on a Thursday; it is a small fishing town and no harbour, the chief trade is in fish and deals. We went on towards Helston and saw many tin works in the way; and at a distance to the north-east Godolphin, the ancient seat of the noble family of that name, who have been there ever since the Conquest.  At these tin works the river Hele rises, within two miles of the south sea, and consequently this is the place that must have been cut across for a communication.  We came to Helston, a borough town situated on a hill and the side of it, a small river running by it, which empties it self into Loo pool, a large lake made by a neck of land between it and the sea; below this there are large timber yards, and they have shops in the town to supply the neighbouring country.

The margin notes: *William, Earl of Cornwall.* *St. Aubyn.* *John, Earl of Oxford.* *Duke of Hamilton.* *Ludgvan.* *Marazion.* *Helston.* *Godolphin.* *Hayle R.* *Helston.* *Looe Pool.*

---

[1] Son of Robert, Earl of Moreton.  (*Cf.* Leland's account, p. 28.)

[2] He " arrived heere by shipping, disguised himselfe, with some of his followers, in Pilgrims habits, therethrough got entrance, mastred the garrison, and seyzed the place." (Carew, *Survey of Cornwall*, 155.)

Oct. 5.  We went nine miles to the south near as far as Lizard Point, to see the Soapy rock, which is in a little opening in the cliff, where a rivlet runs over a vein of soapy rock into the sea, the lode or vein running along the bottom of the valley; it is about four feet wide, most of it is mixed with red, like the terra lemnia, and the stone or walls on each side are of the same colour, and they find some of it hard and unfit for use even in the vein; there are white patches in it, which is mostly valued for making porcelane, and they get five pounds a ton for it, for the manufacture of porcelane, now carrying on at Bristol, there being much trouble in separating the white from the red; but they have received instructions lately not to be so exact in separating it, probably on their not being able to afford it at that price. There is a narrow vein of green earth near it, and about twenty yards west a small vein of white, which seemed to me not to be of so soapy a nature.  It feels like soap, and being so dear it must be much better than pipe clay; there is a vein of something of the like nature at the Lizard Point.  We went to the south-east towards Helford, and coming on the downs of heath I observed about a dozen barrows near the dry tree, which forms something of a circle; these are mentioned by the name of Erth and are called heaps of large stones, as they may be, but are now covered over with heath. We came to Helford, a sort of narrow bay from the sea into which several rivlets fall.  It is a very fine harbour, and they have a key and about a dozen houses only, being frequented chiefly for the export of corn.  I crossed the ferry, and passing by some coarse lead mines, after travelling half a mile farther came to Falmouth.

Falmouth is situated on the water and up the side of the hills, in a fine harbour into which several small rivers fall, the principal of which, being the Vale or Fale, gives name to the town.  The harbour is reckoned the best in England, next after Plymouth, and a great number of ships might anchor in it.  King William settled packet boats from this place to Spain, which, when we were in war with that kingdom, were removed to Lisbon; and there are four packet boats that go to that port.  The post comes once a week with the packets for Lisbon and Spain, for there are now two packet boats that go to the Groyne.  Every passenger that goes to Lisbon

*Lizard Point.*

*Helford R.*

*Falmouth.*

*Fal R.*

*Lisbon.*

*Corunna.*

pays four pounds to the Post Office; and the common price to the captain for accomodations is four or five moidores. This has occasioned a counterband commerce between this place and those ports, which of late has been much interrupted by the searches of the custom house officers; for it is not permitted that these boats should trade. Their chief commerce here is an export of salt pilchards, which they catch in great abundance with the Dungarvan net, which encloses 'em. They have also a great export of tin and corn and an import of timber, iron, and coals for the tin works. There are two fortresses at the entrance of the harbour; that

Pendennis Castle.

to the west is on an high peninsula, and is called Pendennis Castle; it was built about the time of Henry VIII. and is very strong. I saw the lines which the Parliament army made, who took it by intercepting their provisions. Mr.

Carteret. Killigrew.

Carteret, of the Isle of Jerzey, sent them frequent supplies. Below this castle is the seat of the Killigrews; the famous jester was of the family.[1] On the other side is the fort of St.

St. Mawes.

Maws, built by Henry VIII.; the hamlet is a borough. This fort is now entirely neglected. The harbour is supposed to be what Ptolemy calls Cenionis Ostium.

Penryn.

About two miles from Falmouth, on the same opening, stands Penryn, at the mouth of a small rivlet, pleasantly situated on the side of a hill over the creek; it is a borough, and has a good share in the same kind of trade as Falmouth.

Truro.

We went through this town on the 14th in the evening to Truro, over the moors, on which there are some tin works, and pass'd by a smelting house within a mile of Truro. [*Then follows a description of the process of smelting tin.*] They cast [the tin] in a granite mould, on which is the device of the smelting house and the initial letters of the person's name who 'coyns it. They stamp on it afterward the initial letters of the person who owns the tin, and the number of the blocks run that quarter; it is then carried to the mint towns. They are Lestwithiel, Truro, Helston, Leskard, and by connivance Pensance. Here they take off a piece at the corner and try it, and put the mint mark on it. At Truro they commonly coin about 3170, at Pensance about 1700, at

---

[1] Presumably Thomas Killigrew the elder (1612-1683), dramatist, who was "well known as a wit." (*Dict. Nat. Biography.*)

Helston about 600, and at the other towns they coin none, or very litle.

Oct. 15 [*sic*]. I went to St. Agnes Hill, where within these few years the richest tin-works have been discovered. [*Here follows a description of the kind of tin produced and the processes of treatment.*] The mines of St. Agnes are so rich that Mr. Donithorn, to whom they belong, pointed to me out of which he said he got the value of twelve thousand pounds in six months ; and the ore is worth four pence a pound before it is sent to the smelting house. From St. Agnes we went eight miles to Modishole or Mitchell, commonly called Mutchel, a poor village which is a borough, the roadway being across disagreeable heaths.

*St. Agnes Beacon.*

*Donithorn.*

*Mitchell.*

Oct. 9. We went to the south-west about five miles, and came to Gosmore, out of which the river Fale rises, a large morass, in which there are great stream works for tin, but there are no lodes found near it. Here are remains of some works called the Fats, which probably had their names from the fat or rich veins. On the north side of it is Castle Downs or Danes, a high, broad hill, on the top of which is an encampment, said to be made by the Danes when they landed here. It consists of three fosses, and is 164 yards in diameter within the trenches. To the south-east of the morass is Hensborough, looked on as the highest ground in Cornwall, but I should think that some of the eastern hills were higher. There are some signs of shoading on this hill. The foot of it stretches along the south side of the morass, on which stands St. Denis. To the north of the hill and east of the morass is a great curiosity, Rock rock, of dark grey granite. It rises up, I suppose, near sixty feet, in some parts perpendicular ; in others great masses of granite which have tumbled from it forming a very rough descent from it. On the top is a building said to be an hermitage, which, tho' small, occupies the whole top of the rock.[1] It is ascended by a ladder where it is perpendicular ; and I have been informed that even some ladies of masculine courage have gone into it. Near it is the village of Rock, and a good church belonging to it.

*Goss Moor.*

*Castle Downs.*

*St. Dennis.*
*Roche Rocks.*

*Roche.*

---

[1] The remains of a little chapel in the Decorated style, dedicated to St. Michael, and said to have been once tenanted by a hermit, and more recently by a solitary leper. (Murray's *Handbook of Devon and Cornwall*, 5th ed., 197.)

From this place we went north-west along by Castle Downs

again, and came to St. Columb, a small town situated on a
height in a fine uneven country; and two miles further near

west came to Nanswidden, the seat of Mr. Hoblyn,[1] who has
built a fine house of a stone found near the sea of a greenish
cast, the coin stones are of moor stone or granite, and the
cornish of Bath stone. He has a fine library in it, which
contains a very curious collection of books. He is improving
the natural situation in a very good taste. There is a stream
here which comes from Gosmoor, and they had formerly
stream works here. Their white lime is made of the Plymouth
stone; but this gentleman has found a stone near the sea
which makes a good building brown lime.

Oct. 10. From Nanswithen I went on October the 10th

through S[t.] Columb, and going in the road to Wadbridge,
about three miles, we came on the heath to what they call the

Nine Sisters, which are nine stones from four to six feet high,
of a sort of a stone which appears to me to be a blew marble
with veins of white in it, that may be a spar. The eastern
stone has been thrown down, and is twelve feet long. On
the rising grounds near are some barrows, and in a field near
it are many large stones, some of which I thought after I left
the place had been disposed in some order by art. From

thence we crossed the moor and descended near St. Issey to
a litle stream which falls into a creek made by the tide which

comes up the river Camel, and so came to Padstow.

Near the shoar some miles to the south-west is Lanhern,
the ancient seat of the Arundels, created barons by the title
of Lord Arundel of Wardour in Wiltshire,[2] and farther west
towards St. Agnes I was informed a church and parsonage-
house was buried in the sand, and that they built a church
only four hundred yards distant from the old church; if I

mistake not it is Perran-in-zabulot, near which is St. Cuthbert,
where by the seaside is an allum water, esteemed very good
for washing and healing any outward sores, especially such
as are of a scorbutick nature.

Padstow is situated in a little hollow of a hill, which is

---

[1] Robert Hoblyn of Nanswhyden, M.P. for Bristol, died without
issue in 1756.

[2] Sir Thomas Arundell was created Baron Arundell of Wardour
in 1605.

at the mouth of the river Camel, that rises almost directly
to the east near Camelford, where Leland saies King Arthur
the British hero was slain, and there is a tradition confirmed
by Marianus that a great battle was fought here between
the Saxons and the Britains about the year 820; near that
place is Nun's Pool, call'd Allernon, which they have a
notion is good to cure madness, by dipping the person in
it, and a litle farther on the coast is Tintagel, where they
say King Arthur was born.    At Padstow is a pretty good
mole, but there is a large bar, at the west end of which is
a very narrow entrance to the harbour.    They have a trade
to Ireland in corn, and to Bristol for many goods, and  to
Wales for coal; and they have a trade in the fine light
slates of Denbole, which are brought to it from Port Isaac.
At the upper end of the town the Prideaux's have a seat,
which was left by a distant relation to the son of Dean
Prideaux, whose son now enjoys it;[1] it is a very fine
situation and well improved.

From Padstow I went to the south-east, and had a fine
view of Padstow and of the country to the east from the
high grounds, and came in five miles to Wadbridge, which
is over the Camel.    We went four miles mostly near the
river and through a well timber'd country to Pencarrow,
the seat of the Molesworths, baronets.    The present Sr John
married a daughter of Sr Nicholas Morrice's, and Sr William
his son left Sr John's second son an estate of above 3000 l.
a year, being the dock of Plymouth, leaving near the same
to Sr John St. Aubin, a nephew by another sister;[2] and
the house and furniture at Werrington, and an estate of
1500 l. a year entailed, to Mr. Morrice, a descendant from
their common ancestor Secretary Morrice.[3]    I went to a
heighth over the park to see an ancient camp.    To the south

Camel R.
Camelford.

Altarnun.

Tintagel.
Padstow.

Port Isaac.
Prideaux
Place.
*Dean Prideaux.*

Wadebridge.

Pencarrow.
*Molesworth.*
*Morice.*

Devonport.
*St. Aubyn.*
Werrington.

[1] Edmund Prideaux, son of Humphrey Prideaux, D.D., Dean of
Norwich, died in 1745, and his son Humphrey died in 1793.  (Vivian,
*Visitations of Cornwall.*)

[2] Sir John Molesworth of Pencarrow, 4th bart., mar. Barbara,
dau. of Sir Nicholas Morice of Werrington, bart., and died 1766.
Sir John St Aubyn, 3rd Bart., mar. Catherine, another dau. of Sir
Nicholas Morice, and died 1744.  (Vivian, *Visitations of Cornwall.*)

[3] Sir William Morice, Secretary of State at the Restoration, died
1676.  His great grandson, Sir William Morice, dying without issue
in 1749, the title became extinct.  Werrington was afterwards purchased by the Duke of Northumberland.

is a circular entrenchment 64 yards in diameter within the fossees, which are double, the outer fossee being about 10 ft. deep and the inner 15; to the north of the entrance and 27 yards from it is a semi-circular entrenchment, and another to the north of that, 44 yards from its entrance, then an oblong square joyns on to that 160 yards long from south to north, and there seemed to have been another of great extent, which probably enclosed the whole.

From this place we went three miles to Bodmyn, situated on the sides of two hills, on each side of a rivlet, which falls a litle below it into the Camel; it is a long town but seems to be very poor.    In 905, King Edward the Elder founded a bishop's see here, but being disturbed by the Danes it was removed to St. Germain.    In 926, King Athelstan founded an Abbey of Benedictines here, destroyed by the Danes in 981, the lands of which were granted by the Conqueror to Robert, Earl of Moreton and Cornwall; but in 1110 Algar Duke of Cornwall rebuilt the abbey, and put black canons into it, and the church is now converted into a court-house; the east window of which appears to have been a fine piece of work, but of a later date.    The parish church they say belonged to a priory; it has a very ancient door case at the west end, and was probably the door case of the cathedral, tho' the cathedral it is said was entirely demolished by ye Danes, and then ye see was translated to St. Germans.    On the hill to the north of the town is an old tower and the foundations of a small church, which they say was the old parish church.[1]

Perkin Warbeck gathered his forces here before he went to Exeter, and in King Edward VI. time the Cornish and Devonshire people rendezvoused here against the King.

Oct. 11.    We went near Lord Radnor's seat, and came to a beautiful narrow valley, the hills on each side of which are covered with wood; in the middle of it runs the river Fowey; and on a litle hill in this vale adjoyning to the hills to the north is the Castle of Restormil, which is a circular building, encompassed with the fossee about twenty feet deep: there are seven apartments in it formed like wise a circle within, each of them being about 18 feet deep.

---

[1] Cf. Leland's account of Bodmin, pp. 16-18.    Algarus is described as "a nobleman," but he was certainly not "Duke of Cornwall."

From the room opposite to the gate way is an entrance to an oblong square room about eighteen feet by twenty-three, built as a tower without the circle, which seems to have been the grand room. This was the castle of the Earls and Dukes of Cornwall, and was probably built about the time of the Conquest. Uzella of Ptolemy is thought to have been about this place.

From thence I went about a mile to the litle town of Lestwithiel, on the same river, situated in the bottom and on the side of the steep hill. Here the Earls of Cornwall seem to have had another house, and probably their chief offices and domesticks, Restormil not seeming large enough to receive the attendants of such great princes. There are remains of the ancient house, part of it is converted into a jayl, and another part into a coinage house for the tin. The spire-steeple of this church is a curious old building, there are not above 2 or 3 more in Cornwall. I went a mile to Lanlivery to see some large granite stones in a field to the south-west of the church; one of them measured about 30 feet by 20 and fifteen feet high.

I return'd to Listwithiel and went on through Boconnock Park, and came to an old circular encampment on a hill called Castle Cart; there is a double fossee round it, and it is about nine-two yards in diameter within the trenches. I came to Duloe again, where I was shown in a field five large stones which seemed to have made part of a small enclosure, that probably might have been some ancient burial place.

Oct. 12. I went on to Leskard, pleasantly situated on the side of two hills and a hollow ground between them; on the east side of the town was a castle, of which there are now hardly any remains. From this place I went three miles to Redgate inn, and came to a heath at the foot of Ring-Cheese, where there are great tin works. In a field near it is what they call the other half-stone, one is in the form of half of a seat cut in stone, it is in a litle pit; the other is a granite stone about nine feet high, two feet thick one way and eighteen inches the other, and at the top there is cut a sort of a groove; both of them seem to be only parts of two stones which made a cross; and by some accident might seperate and be carried away for other uses; as I was informed, one of them was to

*(margin notes:)* Lostwithiel. Lanlivery. Boconnoc. Duloe. Liskeard. Redgate.

make a gate post; it is probable they formed a cross, and it is said an inscription was found on one of them importing that Donert or Dungarth gave that land for the benefit of his soul, which it seems was given to the Religious when Doniert King of Cornwall was drowned in 872; the words are " Doniert Rogavit Pro Anima."[1]

Hurlers.

Going on towards Ring-Cheese we passed by a stone about eight feet high with a cross on it. We soon after came to the stones which they call hurlers. There are, first, four stones which seem with some others to have made a small circle; a litle farther is a circle of thirteen stones mostly four or five yards apart, but by the distances in four places there seem to have been four more, and to the south there is a large opening of twenty-three yards, and in another place of forty yards, if I mistake not, towards the north. Further northward is another of twelve stones, mostly at about the same distances, there are two wide openings of about twenty yards towards the south with only two stones between them; and by the other spaces between some of the stones there seem to be eight wanting, one of the stones larger than the rest is six feet high, six broad at bottom, and two feet thick. I went

Cheesewring.

to the top of the hill called Ring-Cheese; at the bottom of it is a stone-cutter's grott cover'd with one stone thirty-five long, nine broad, and three thick. On the top of the hill we saw those stones over one another like cheeses, which give name to the hill. The most remarkable heap consists of five stones one over another; and five much larger over them, which have been left so, without doubt, by the washing away of the earth from them. On many of those I saw such holes as we observed in Carn-bray.

Hingston Down.

Oct. 13. I ascended the famous hill, or rather mountain, called Hengston, formerly called Hengist Hill, where antiently there were great works; and they have begun to work again in some parts of it. About 831 the Cornish Britains who joyned with the Danes under Hengist to drive out the Saxons were here forced to a battle by King Egbert,

[1] Ornamental cross-base standing in a field at Redgate named ' Pennant,' close to " The Other Half-Stone." In 1849 it was taken out of a pit in which it had lain for some years, and was again set up. Filling the front in five lines is the inscription, DONI ERTRO GAVIT PROAN IMA (*Victoria History of Cornwall*, i., 419.)

and defeated and cut to pieces by him; from which time it is
suppost the hill has had the name of Hengist Hill, from Hengist,
their first leader into Britain. There are two summits to this
hill; the western, called Kits Hill, the eastern, called Calstock,
where we saw some tin works. Under Kits Hill, on Hengston,
Callington is pleasantly situated, a borough town. From this
place we came towards the part of the hill call'd Calstock,
where we saw some tin mines, which are now working, and
great marks of old ones. We descended down the hill to the
Tamer, to Newbridge, below which is Calstock, where they
have a manufacture of coarse earthen ware, and particularly
of earthen ware ovens, and they were attempting some things
of a finer sort with a yellow clay brought from St. Stephen's,
near Saltash, from Hollowmore Bay, near St. Germans, and
also from Kelly. I was informed that they were endeavouring
to set up such a manufacture as they have in Staffordshire, at
Bovey Tracey, near the river Tynge, in Devonshire, where
they have plenty of good pipe clay, and have found a coal that
will serve for that purpose; towards the top it has an offensive
smell, but not below, and appears like a black wood; the
clay also over it will burn, and smells like amber; it is in
layers or strata, inclining to the south. Below Calstock is
Culteel, where the branch of the family of the Edgcombs
formerly lived from which Lord Edgcomb is descended, the
house from which they have their first origin and name being
in the parish of Milton, five miles north of Tavistock, where
one Mr. Edgcomb now lives, of which family was the late
Rector of Exeter College in Oxford. Mount Edgcomb came
into the family by a marriage.[1]

I crossed over the Tamer into Devonshire, and in about
two miles came to Tavistock, situated in a bottom between
hills, on the river Teave, that runs through the town; below
it the river Walkham falls into the Tavy, and above it the
Lamber, on which Lamerton stands, and above that the rivlet
called Burne. Oragavius, Duke of Devonshire and Cornwall,
had his palace here, and his son Ordulf built the abbey, and a
nich in the old wall of the church remaining in a court of a
house built on the site of the church is supposed to be his

Kit Hill.
Calstock Hill.
Callington.

Tamar R.
Newbridge.
Calstock.

Bovey Tracey.
Teign R.

Cotehele.
*Edgcumbe.*

Milton Abbot.

Tavistock.
Tavy R.
Walkham R.
Lamerton.
*Ordgar.*
*Ordulph.*

---

[1] Sir Piers Edgcumbe, Kent., who died 1539, mar. Joanna, dau.
and heiress of James Dernford of Stonehouse and Rame, widow of
Charles Dinham.

tomb; he is said to have been a very active man, of a gigan-
tick stature, and they show in the parish church a thigh bone
twenty-one inches long, which they say was Ordulf's bone.
There was a school in this abbey for the Saxon language, and
the fabrick continued till of late; there was also a press here,
and it is said that a Saxon grammar was printed here about
the beginning of the last century.[1]   It was the last abbot but
*Hugh Oldham.*  one who had the contest with Hugh Oldham, Bishop of
Exeter; and the last abbot was mitred and made a baron in
Parliament about three months before the Dissolution.   The
*Duke of*  several mannors belonging to it are now mostly in the Duke
*Bedford.*  of Bedford; Werrington, late Sʳ William Morrice's, was the
Werrington.  park of the abbey.
*Morice.*
Lamerton.       From Tavistock I went two miles to Lamerton, where, in
the church, are some remains of good paintings in the
windows; the east window was given by the last Abbot of
Tavistock, who was mitred, in which he is represented in a
posture of devotion.   There is also a remarkable monument
*Tremayne.*  in it of the Tremaynes, which was renewed about forty years
agoe, with the statues of the family in the base; about three
feet high, and particularly the twins, who, being alike in
lineaments, always sympathized in hunger, thirst, sleep, and
pain, and were both killed in Queen Elizabeth's reign, in 1563,
at the battle of Newport.[2]

Launceston.       Oct. 15.   I went nine miles to Launceston, in Cornwall,
situated on the side of a hill over a rivlet, which falls into
the Tamer about two miles lower.   The church here is a
great curiosity, being built of granite, and all the outside
adorn'd with reliefs of coats of arms, and between every
coat is one letter, so as in the whole it makes up the Ave
Maria; over the door is St. George and the Dragon, and
St. Roch giving his garment to a poor man.   The church
is dedicated to St. Mary Magdalene, and at the east end
she is represented in a prostrate posture; in a grotto on
each sille are litle figures as playing on all sorts of musical

[1] Only two books printed here are now in existence, viz., a
translation of Boetius (1525) and the Stannary Laws (1534).   There
is no record of the Saxon grammar, called the *Long Grammar*, having
been seen.   (Worth, *Hist. of Printing in Devon, Trans. Devon. Assoc.*,
xi., 499.)

[2] See account in Risdon's *Survey of Devon*, 216-7.   Newport is
Newhaven, now better known as Havre.

instruments. This is very singular, and resembles the
Egyptian way of adorning the outside of their temples with
hierogliphicks. On the south side of the town is the castle,
in an irregular oblong square figure; the strongest part of
it is a great heigth, which seems to have been made steeper
by art, on which there is a round building, the walls of
which are ten feet thick, and at the distance of seven feet
another circular building within of the same thickness, and
I believe about thirty feet in diameter within; there is a
staircase up through the wall to the top, and it seems to
have consisted of two stories.

From Launceston we crossed the water to Newport, a
litle village which is a borough, and ascended up to Werrington, late Sᴿ William Morrice's park. It is a very fine
rising ground on each side of the river Atre, and beautifully
improved in wood and lawn; to the left, on a heigth, is a
building to represent a ruinous castle, and lower in the park
Sᴿ William began a temple of the sun, which appears in a
wood: to the right there is a very fine terrace, winding
round the hill, and above it, opposite to the house, a
triumphal arch, on the model of that on Sidon Hill, at
Highcleer. Descending we came to a hermitage, like that
at Richmond, and beyond it is a model of what is called
the Tomb of the Horatii, near Albano. Returning down
towards the river there is a large alcove trellis seat, and
above the river forms a beautiful serpentine river. From
the river we went up to the house; the old part is a roomy,
convenient building, before which and adjoyning to it
Sᴿ William built three rooms, with a large gallery leading
to them; in the front is a bow window with the door in it;
over this is an attick story; 'tis built rather in the style of
a lodge; it is of brick, with the door case and the middle
window of each side and at each end of Portland stone,
with a balustrade; and it seems to be built as to be enlarged
at pleasure by building round a court. In the old house
are some good pictures, as the views of Caniletti, two
pieces of Salvador Rosa, Lucretia of Guido, Henry VIII.
and one of his queens, very good, but rather better colouring and more life than Holben's usually are, two or three
small pieces of Poussin, and his capital piece of a land
storm, which cost 500*l*. To the west is a small building

Newport.
Werrington.
*Morice.*
Ottery R.

in a wood; and farther on the hill is the church built by
Sʳ William Morris,[1] with a Gothick tower and a turret on
each side of it: the church is Gothick without, and in niches
round are some old statues of the apostles, which were given
him from some ancient building; it is Roman architecture
within and the porch on one side and a vault on the other,
with a seat over each, one for the family the other for the
servants, form a cross.    This park is to be looked on as
one of the most beautiful in England, and part of it is in
Cornwall and part in Devon shire, the river being the bounds
between the two counties.    And now having finished Cornwall, I shall give some account of the dutchy, and of the
customs of it.    The Conqueror gave it as an earldom to

*Robert, Earl of Moreton.* Robert de Moreton, his half brother by his mother, with
793 mannors, and not long after it was settled in the next
heir to the Crown, and erected into a dutchy.    The lands
are of three kinds: the old dutchy lands, leased out at a
certain rent, and renewable every seven years, paying only
6*d.* fine; the new dutchy, leased out at a certain rent, but
renewed with a fine at will, and then other lands, leased
out for a term of years at pleasure.    The auditor holds a
sessions for renewing.    The Duke, the Prince of Wales,
has a lord warden, an auditor receiver, and other officers.
The lord warden holds the Stannary Courts and the Con-
vocation, the members of which are chosen by Launceston,
Lestwithiel, Truro, and Helston, each sending six convocators,
who choose a speaker; they can adjourn as to time, but
not from the place they are called to.    Their business [is]
to make laws in relation to the tin mines and tinners; and
the Duke has a prison at Lestwithiel, where they are confined
for debt.    The Prince of Wales has such a court also for
Devon shire, where 'tis call'd a Parliament, and those which
are chosen by the four towns of Tavistock, Ashburton,
Chegford, and Plimpton, are called Parliament men, six for
each: they meet on Dartmore mountain, at a place called
**Crockern Tor.** Crockern Tor, in the parish of Wydecomb, where there is
a stone table and single stones round for the members to
sit on, from which place they adjourn to do business.    They
both met in Queen Anne's time.    The Duke's lands bring

---

[1] The church was rebuilt in 1742. (Lysons, *Devon*, 552).

in about twelve thousand pounds a year, and the tin mines 4,000 *l.*, but the prince does not receive above 10,000 *l.* in the whole.

In Cornwall and Devon shire they have few wheel carriages by reason of the steep hills, but every thing is carried either on hooks on each side of the horses, which are long or short according to the nature of the burthen; they have drags for drawing up the side of steep fields, and what wheel carriages they have are drawn by oxen and horses which they use for ploughing. They have a particular way of dressing their land in Devon shire and Cornwall, which must be very useful in uneven countrys, which is taking the earth round the field for about ten feet broad, and laying it in a heap with lime; they also plough the field slightly, and mix up the top part with sand, and lay it in heaps, and spread both over the fields; the best of the soyl in the steep grounds washing down to the lower parts of the field makes it a very good manure. About Penzance, in the rocks, are jays with red bills and legs, called a Cornish jay, and by Pliny Pyrrho corax.[1] They make great use here of Cloume ovens, which are earthen ware of several sizes, like an oven, and being heated they stop 'em up and cover 'em over with embers to keep in the heat; and in the very western parts they have pot-ovens, a round piece of iron which is heated, on which the bread is put, and then it is cover'd over with a pot, on which they heap the embers to keep in the heat. In Devon shire and Cornwall they keep up the old institution of rural deans; they are appointed at the visitation, generally a new incumbent; they are obliged to go round to all the churches within the deanery, and direct proper repairs to be made, and a certificate to be returned to them in such a time that the repairs are accordingly finished; and if they do not, the rural dean returns 'em to the Bishop's Court, and process issues out against them. They have a custom in many parts for the clerk to read the first lesson, and so that office is frequently very ill executed. The churches in both these counties are large fabricks, with fine square towers built to most of them. In the western parts of Cornwall they keep

---

[1] Generally called "Cornish Chough," *Pyrrhocorax graculus*, Linn.

their parish feasts with great prophaneness and debauchery. The people of Cornwall are very hospitable and exceeding civil to strangers, and the common people are much polished and ready to do all kind offices, which I observed more especially among the tinners. But they cannot be defended in falling in so violent a manner not only on wrecks but on ships that are drove in with all the people, and might be saved, but the common people come and plunder, even to the breaking up the vessels.

**Lyd R.**

Oct. 18. I went by Brentor to see a fall of a rivlet into the Lyd; and, coming down to the Lyd, saw the remains of a hermit's cell, adjoyning to a chapel in a most retired place between the hills, covered with wood; it belonged to the Abbey of Tavistock. Going above a mile up the river I observed the marks of tin stream works, and came to the cascade which falls down a rock so near perpendicular that 150 feet in the inclined plain make the fall of 110 feet perpendicular. The stream may be about three feet broad, and the rock setts out a litle, about 30 feet from the top, and more than that about 20 feet lower. In other places it glides smoothly down the rock, and below this it may be four feet in breadth, and it rushes down through the rocks to this fall 95 feet and 70 in perpendicular heigth. From this we went up the hill, crossed the stream above, and came to the bridge

**Lydford.**

over the Lyd at Lyd ford, the single arch of which I guessed might be about 10 feet wide where it makes a semicircle built on the rock, but stretching out two or three feet farther to the south. It is over the Lyd, which I suppose is 100 feet below it, the rock being uneven on each side, and the river working down under the bridge in beautiful cascades. About a mile higher up the rocks are so close that the river seems to fall down out of a hole of the rock. There is a square castle here on a low mount; it may be about 60 feet square, and probably had a large precinct which was destroyed not long after the Conquest. Lydford is now only a poor village, but was formerly a considerable place, as it appears from the Conqueror's Survey book that it could be taxed only when London and Exeter was taxed and in the same manner; and the custody of this castle was given to men of the greatest quality. They formerly sent members to Parliament, and it

**Dartmoor.**

is said that all Dertmore is in this parish.

I went to the north-east round the end of Dartmore, and
in eight miles came to Okehampton, situated between the Ock
and a small river to the east, which joyns it so that it falls into
the Tawridge, that runs by Biddiford and empties it self into
the river below Barnstaple near the sea.    Okehampton is a
small town at the foot of Dartmore, being supported by the
thorough fare into Cornwall from Exeter and other parts, and
by a manufacture of white serges, which are dyed at Exeter.
There is an indifferent chapel in the town, the parish church
being a mile off.   Half a mile to the west of the town are
the remains of an old castle, the square tower still standing
on a mount.   It is mentioned in Domesday book as held of
the king by Viscount Baldwin, and it afterwards came to
the Courtenays, Earls of Devonshire.   The river Dart rises
near this place, which falls into the sea at Dartmouth, after
having run through all Dartmore.   This chain of hills is
twenty miles long and fourteen broad, many rivers rising
out of them.   There are many villages all round the foot of it,
which feed their cattle there in summer, not less than 100,000
sheep, and it supplies them with excellent turf.   The people
about this moor are as civilised as in other parts (tho' vulgarly
reputed otherwise).   There is a great variety of what they
call morestone or granite on it.   It was made a forest in
King John's time,[1] and tin works were then carried up on to
Dartmore, but have not been worked for many years; those
who have been over the hills say they were only stream
works.   There is the black game on those hills, call'd the
black grous and the heath-poult.   The cock is black with
white feathers in the tail, as large as a hen; the hen, something less, is of the colour of the woodcock, and they are in
such plenty that they sell for eighteen pence a piece; the first
is mostly black, but there are good spots in it that might be
cultivated [sic].   The parish of Wythicomb comes further of
any place on the hills.   There are two places, Belliford and
Hartland,[2] about four miles from Chegford, where there are
two or three houses of herdsmen.

Oct. 19.   I went five miles to the river Tau, which runs to

*Okehampton.*

*Earls of Devon*

*Widecombe.*
*Bellever.*
*Hartland.*
*Chagford.*

*Taw R.*

[1] The whole county of Devon, except Dartmoor and Exmoor,
were disafforested by John, Earl of Mortein, afterwards King John,
in Richard I'st time, he being lord of Devon and Cornwall by the
gift of his brother Richard.—(*Note by Dr. Pococke.*)

[2] Bellever and Hartland are both near Postbridge.

Barnstable, and, having crossed it, I found another sort of face of the country, the red soil with the red sandstone, and all the country full of rising grounds, and small hills beautifully improved.   Three miles further I came to a poor little town, called Bowe, where they have a manufacture of serge. Seven miles further is Crediton, a long town, the west end of which is almost all new built, it having been burnt about six years ago.   There is a manufacture in the town of serges and narrow clothes.   This was a bishop's see, which was removed from Tawton[1] to this place, Devonshire being the Diocese, which with Cornwall and the diocese of Wells containing Somersetshire, was the bishoprick of Sherborn from about the year 900.   There were but two or three Bishops of Taunton before the see was removed to this place, and in 1050 it was removed to Exeter.   A collegiate church was founded here.   The present church is a large building; in it is the tomb of S$^r$ William Peryan, L$^d$ Chief Baron of the Exchequer, who dyed in 1605,[2] and the monuments of the Tuckfields of Teadbourne, who have a house and park near, and were formerly buryed in this church;[3]  and in the cross isle is a very old monument of a man and a woman, the latter having on her head the square coif.   A meadow to the east of this church they call the Palace Meadow, where it is supposed the bishop's house was; and further east is a mead called My Lord's Meadow, which is a long meadow on the river, they say four miles round;  this, they supposed, belonged to the bishop.   At the west end of the town are the remains of the chapel of St. Laurence; that is, all but the south side, and they have built tenements in it; they say it was burnt when the town suffer'd by fire.[4]

---

[1] The see was never at [Bishop's] Tawton, and there were no " Bishops of Taunton."

[2] Sir William Peryam was born at Exeter, 1534, and died at Little Fulford, near Crediton, 9 Oct., 1604 (*Dict. Nat. Biography.*)  The monument has his effigies, in his judge's robes. (Lysons, *Devon*, 147.)

[3] A monument of John Tuckfield, who died in 1630, with his effigies in a ruff between two medallions.   Also memorials to Mary, wife of John Tuckfield, co-heiress of Pyncombe, 1675; and Walter Tuckfield, 1676.   Tedbourne, or Venny Tedbourne, was the original residence of the Tuckfield family, who settled at Crediton as woollen-manufacturers, and are said to have been the first clothiers who established a foreign trade. (Lysons, *Devon*, 146-7).

[4] The chapel of St. Laurence's Hospital very frequently occurs in the episcopal registers, and was usually served by a member of

In the large meadow the Devon shire rebells assembled and fortifyed them selves in Edward VI. time, and went from it and laid siege to Exeter. I went nine miles mostly over hills to the river Ex at Brickley Bridge. Those hills command a fine view, more especially to the north and north-west, and from them I saw the hills that run to the sea beyond the river Ex about Minehead.

Bickleigh Br.

From Crediton to Tiverton I observed a slate stone among the red soil which probably is a stratum in the hills between the Creedy and the Ex. From this bridge I went on the west side of the river three miles to Tiverton; the hills on each side of the Ex, on which there is an agreeable mixture of wood and fields, affording a very pleasant prospect. Tiverton is situated between two rivers, the Ex and the Leman, the principal part of the town being on a heigth over the former; and a rivlet is brought through the town, and is divided so as to run through every street. This parish is divided into three portions, given to three persons, and [blank] College puts in a fourth, and these in their turns weekly take care of the church and chapel of St. George.[5] The church is a handsome fabrick with a small

Tiverton.

Creedy R.

Lowman R.

---

the Trinity convent at Houndeslow. It is mentioned in a deed of Bishop Bruere, dated at Crediton, Dec. 3, 1242. Adjoining it was a reclusorium for an anchorite, expressly provided by the said bishop. (Oliver, *Monasticon Exon.*, 78.) The fire occurred on Sunday, Aug. 14, 1743, when 460 houses were burnt down, and sixteen persons perished in the flames. The damage, at a low estimation, was computed at 40,000 *l*. (Lysons, *Devon*, 144.)

[5] The parish is divided into four districts, called Pitt Quarter, Tidcombe Quarter, Clare Quarter, and Prior's Quarter. The rectory is similarly divided into four portions, and Prior's portion was separated by Baldwin de Ripariis, the first Earl of Devon of that name, and given to the priory of St. James, in the suburbs of Exeter, to which it became appropriated. This priory being a cell to the foreign monastery of Clugny, was seized into the hands of the Crown, and was by King Henry VI. given to King's College, Cambridge. The College appoints a curate to perform a fourth part of the service of the church of Tiverton. The remainder of the parish is said to have been divided into three portions by Hugh Courtenay, Earl of Devon, about 1335, but it must have been at a much earlier period, for there is abundant evidence that the Courtenay family presented to the three portions or prebends as early as the middle of the preceding century. The chapel of St. George was begun in 1714 and finished in 1730; it was made a perpetual cure, with a salary of 60*l*. per annum, to be paid in portions of 15*l*. each to the portionists of Tidcombe, Pitt, and Clare, and to the curate of Prior's portion, each of whom officiates monthly on the Sunday after he has officiated at the old church of St. Peter's. (Lysons, *Devon*, 506, 514-5.)

library adjoyning; and Mr. John Greenoway in 1517 built a fine chapel on the south side of the church, in which he is buryed.   He also built and founded an hospital and chapel for six poor men, which is an handsome building, embellished with Gothick ornaments and small statues.   The chapel is an handsome building with galleries of the Ionick order. The castle is finely situated over the river, and there are great remains of it.   There was a chapel in it, which, I suppose, is that in which Edward Courtney, Earl of Devonshire, and his wife were buryed.   On the monument was this remarkable inscription :

> Ho, ho, who lies here?
> 'Tis I, the Earl of Devonshire,
> With Kate my wife, to me full dear.
> We lived together fifty-five year.
> That we spent we had.
> That we left we lost.
> That we gave we have.[1]

This castle now belongs to S[r] John Carew.[2]

There is a free school here for reading and writing, in which 100 boys are taught gratis.   But the greatest bene- faction in this town was that of Mr. Peter Blundell, clothier, who built a free school and endowed eight scholarships at Baliol College in Oxford and as many at Sidney College in Cambridge.   It is a handsome building of free stone consisting of one room, divided only by a passage into the upper and lower school, and behind it an apartment for the master and usher.

They have a small manufacture here of serges, shalloons, and druggets, which with the thorough fare is the chief support of the town.   This town has frequently suffered by fire.

Oct. 20.   I went on eastward, the road being exceeding good, in a sandy soil, and I saw Columbton on the river Columb, which falls into the Ex.   It was the demesne of the King of the West Saxons, and Alfred left it to his youngest son Ethelward.   Coming towards the borders of this country

---

[1] There has been much controversy as to the identity of this Earl, and, in any case, the name of his wife is given incorrectly.   However, it seems most likely that the inscription was intended to apply to Edward Courtenay, who was created Earl of Devon in 1465, and died in 1509 at the age of 82, and to his wife *Elizabeth*, dau. of Sir Philip Courtenay of Molland.   (Vivian, *Visitations of Devon*.)

[2] Sir John Carew of Haccombe, 5th bart.

I saw West Leigh and the quarries of lime stone in the hills near it, which is a blewish stone with white veins in it, and is the only limestone in all this country. To the east of it is Hulcombe, where there is an old castle. All the prospects here are very delightful of a rich, well inhabited country, and fine hills to the south-east. Passing over a common we came at the bottom of the valley into Somerset shire. All the country to the south from Totness to Plymouth is called Southam, which is so famous for cyder, but by the introduction of the Herefordshire redstreak of late years they make far better cyder near Exeter. They let the apples fall, and put them in heaps in the orchard to rot and ferment, and then grind and press them out. They have an apple called the bitter-sweet, which gives a fine flavour to the cyder; the menagement afterwards is drawing off frequently.

*Westleigh.*

*Holcombe Rogus.*

*South Hams.*

# A TOUR TO THE WEST OF ENGLAND
## By the Rev. S. Shaw 1788

From Wellington we journeyed on the next stage to Columpton. About halfway near the bleak hill of Maidendown, we pass the division of the two counties and enter Devon north east. The soil is various, the hills in these parts naturally barren, and the lower grounds fruitful, but the whole much improved by manure. The air is mild and healthful in the latter but very sharp on the former, which we now felt; and arrived at Columpton well prepared to enjoy a comfortable breakfast. This is a larger and better market town than the last, and displays more of the woollen manufacture.

*Cullompton.*

From hence to Exeter we passed much hilly ground and through a very picturesque village of moss-clad houses, called Bradninch. Next saw on our right, Sir Thomas Ackland's at Columb-John, a very neat white mansion, beautifully situated under a wood-crowned knowl, surrounded with a park of deer, and a fine vale in front, graced with the pleasing objects of a lofty village tower, and distant hills. From the summit of Stockhill, two miles from Exeter, you have a glorious circular prospect, the ground gradually falling every way from this centre into a deep and beautiful vale, enriched with

*Bradninch.*
*Columb-John.*

*Stoke Hill.*

various seats, villages, and the fair city; the vast circumference rising again to a noble range of verdant mountains,
heaped and intersected in most variegated order; while on
their distant tops the sea-mark towers distinguish its frontier
country, and the river Ex opening towards the south winds
broadly to the channel.   The common traffic and business of
this country is mostly done by horses with panniers and
crooks; the former are well known every where, but the latter
are peculiar to the west, and are simply constructed, with four
bent heavy sticks in the shape of panniers, but the ends
awkwardly projecting above the rider's head; with these they
carry large loads of hay or garden vegetables.   The country
people ride in a prodigious large boot of wood and leather
hung instead of stirrup to the horse's side and half open,
which they call gambades.

The city of Exeter and capital of this county is situated
on a gradual descent on the east side the river Ex, whence it
derives its name.   On the highest part of the hill on which
this city is built, and on the north-east extremity, stands the
remains of Rougemont Castle, so called from the redness of
the soil.   The ruin represented in Mr. Gross's view, 1768,
which is the entrance into the castle yard, was part of the
exterior walls or out-works; these enclose a considerable
space, in shape somewhat like a rhombus, with its angles
rounded off; they were defended by four towers, two on
the west, and two on the east side.   Its terrace and walls
afford a delightful prospect of the city and surrounding
country.

The streets and buildings in general wear the venerable
aspect of antiquity.   The principal street and thoroughfare
is very long and spacious, and to the west very much
improved by an elegant bridge of three large arches over
the river, and numerous small ones continued up the street
to bring it to a level, which has been finished about 10
or 12 years, and cost near £20,000.[1]

---

[1] An Act of Parliament for building a new bridge higher up the
river than the old one, passed in 1769.   The first stone of the new
bridge was laid Oct. 4, 1770, and the work was in great forwardness
when it was destroyed by a flood in 1775; the work commenced
again by laying the first stone of another structure, July 8, 1776.
The last arch was turned in 1777, and in 1778, the new bridge having
been opened, the old bridge was pulled down. (Lysons, *Devon*, 198.)

In the east part stands the cathedral, originally a monastery, founded by King Athelstan for Benedictine Monks, and made an Episcopal See by Edward the Confessor, the building was carried on by Leofric, and various have been the after additions for almost 400 years, and yet the uniformity is so congruous as to appear like the workmanship of one architect. But we cannot speak of the external appearance in any other light than as heavy and unpleasant, particularly when viewed within the precincts; a very different idea is given within, in every respect magnificent and pleasing. The whole length, including the library beyond the altar, is about 390 feet, breadth 70, and transept 135. The whole was lately new repaired and varnished with most suitable combination of colours, very unlike that tawdry mixture which so much defiles the dignity of Wells. The body of this church is used for public preaching and early prayers, and filled with pews, a throne for the Bishop, &c., in a manner I never saw before. The west window is adorned with modern painted glass, representing seven of the Apostles, St. Paul, Luke, Matthew, Peter, Mark, John and Andrew, with the arms of those nobility and gentry of the diocese, at whose joint expence it was executed with much taste and ingenuity, by Mr. Picket, of York.[1] The screen displays much fancy and magnificence of antiquity, representing from the creation to the ascension in curious colours. The choir is particularly light and beautiful, the east window contains good old painting; the altar piece finely devised and ornamented with a perspective view of the inside of the church, painted in the reign of James I., and the throne of most curious workmanship, the carvings of the canopy are 60 feet high.

Another principal building, situate at a small distance east of this city, is the Devon and Exeter Hospital, for the benefit of the decayed, sick and indigent, one of the most laudable charities ever encouraged, which reflects great credit on its first founder, Dr. Alured Clark, dean of this church, 1740[2];

*King Athelstan. Edward the Confessor. Leofric.*

*Wm. Peckitt.*

*Alured Clarke.*

[1] This was in 1766, but Peckitt's work failed to satisfy the modern artistic sense, so in 1904 the window was restored and fresh glass inserted as a memorial to Archbishop Temple, who had been Bishop of Exeter 1869-1885.

[2] Dr. Alured Clarke (1696-1742) became dean of Exeter in 1741. (*Dict. Nat. Biography.*)

and though supported by a very bountiful subscription, yet I was told that the numbers of poor manufacturers with which it is crowded, render it necessary to raise an immediate supply by further contribution. This woollen business, though not so flourishing as formerly, employs an abundance of hands, and is chiefly wrought in the surrounding villages and brought here to be dyed, &c., which we saw in passing over the bridge amongst the suburbs, consisting of dye-houses and drying frames, spread in crowds on the banks of the river.

Haldon.

Sir Rob. Palk.

From hence we ascend the immense hill of Halldown, near seven miles in length and three broad; about half way up we have a pleasing view of Halldown house, the elegant seat of Sir Robert Palke, Bart., built after the manner of Buckingham house,[1] and well surrounded with plantations. Though in itself a barren flinty common, this vast summit displays one of the noblest prospects in this kingdom. To the south a most glorious expanse of sea, with the river Ex winding from the City into it, begirt with numerous villages, seats, &c., the other three points affording at the same time some of the boldest and most beautiful inland scenes imaginable. The evening closed in too fast to give us all its charms in perfection, such as the adjacent new tower-like summer-house might yield upon a favourite day. We now descended with haste to our place of rest, the small old market-town of Chudleigh, which gives name to a very ancient family, and title of baron to the Cliffords, Sir Thomas, Lord High Treasurer of England, being created by Charles II., whose seat, called Ugbrook, is close adjacent.

Chudleigh.
Lord Clifford.

Ugbrooke.

Early next morning we proceeded to Ashburton; about half a mile on this road hang the rude heads of a large black marble rock, which commands a wild view of the hills, woods, and vales beneath; this curious stratum, found in large bodies in this part of the country, we saw here converted by fire into very useful lime for dressing and improving the land, a great part of which is arable and pasture, as well as abounds in cyder fruits, this year so uncommonly plentiful. In these marble quarries they get large blocks, and send them to

---

[1] The house was built by Sir George Chudleigh, 4th Bart., d. 1738. After some intermediate sales it was purchased by Sir Robert Palk, Bart. (Lysons, Devon, 296; Vivian, Visitations of Devon.)

Plymouth, London, &c. which for hardness and variety of veins are little inferior to foreign productions. Passing over some rugged moors we saw on our left the seat of Mr. Templar.[1] Ashburton is a neat market-town of one principal street, built chiefly of the white slate found in these parts. It has a large handsome church, built cathedral wise with a tower 90 feet high and a leaden spire. Claims also the privileges of a very ancient borough by prescription under the government of a portreeve, chosen annually at the lord's court. The choice of the two members is by the voice of all house inhabitants, who are returned by that officer. It is likewise one of the four stannary towns for the county, and gives title to a new-made law Lord (Dunning) now deceased, an original inhabitant, if not a native.[2] After breakfast we left this place for Plymouth. Arrived at Ivy bridge, we dined at a most excellent inn, and afterwards proceeded without much observation till we approached the vicinity of Plymouth, in which are several good seats; particularly one at Saltram, belonging to Lord Borringdon,[3] whose situation and hanging woods by the side of this arm of the sea might be deemed worthy much attention, was there not so great a rival (Mount Edgecumb) just opposite.

Plymouth is situated between two very large inlets, made by the union of the Plym and Tamar with the channel, which forms a most noble bay, or sound, for ships of the greatest burden. The inlet of this sea, which extends many miles up the country north, to the river Tamar, is called Hamouze, and parts Devon from Cornwall. The other which receives the Plym, is called Catwater, an harbour capable of containing any number of vessels, which is appropriated chiefly for trade, to Virginia, the Sugar Islands, and the Streights. In the reign of Edward III. we find this place considerable; afterwards it much decayed, and dwindled into a small fishing town; about two centuries ago the convenience of the haven gave rise to its increase, and now we see it a most flourishing

*Side notes:* Stover. *Mr. Templer.* Ashburton. *Dunning.* Ivybridge. Saltram. *Ld. Boringdon.* Plymouth. Hamoaze. Catwater.

---

[1] Stover Lodge, in the parish of Teigngrace, was built about 1781. (Lysons, *Devon*, 486.)

[2] John Dunning, born at Ashburton 1731, solicitor-general 1768-70, created Baron Ashburton 1782, and died 1783.

[3] John Parker was created Baron Boringdon 1774, and died at Saltram 1788.

and able port, protected by a strong fort, built by Charles II., consisting of five regular bastions, &c. The docks for building and repairing war ships, begun by King William III., in 1691, are now brought to the highest perfection, which we shall describe anon in the order we saw them. Our first business was to view the streets and buildings of the old town, which engrossed but little of our time, being vile and almost dangerously narrow; it has however two handsome churches, St Andrew, and Charles-church, so called from its being dedicated to the memory of Charles I. This being a borough town under the government of a mayor, &c., the streets about the town hall we saw now crowded with people about to choose a new one, as is usual at this season of the year.

**Mount Edgcumbe.** We went next to visit Mount Edgecumbe, the delightful seat of the noble Lord of the same name, situate on the opposite side of the Ham-ouze. The way from hence is **Stonehouse.** through Stonehouse, a populous place, to Dock, which **Devonport.** surprised us with a very large display of spacious streets, intersecting each other at right angles, very different from the place we had just left; as the inhabitants here are chiefly mechanics, &c., belonging to the docks, the houses are slightly built, either of plaster, or slate stone, abundantly got hereabouts, and will not bear a minute inspection, but have a good effect at a distance. Leaving our carriage we walked to the passage, and crossed without any difficulty about three quarters of a mile to the other side of the water, which thus divides the two counties. A ring at the bell just beyond procures a necessary attendant, who shows and explains the whole of this terrestrial paradise. A gradual ascent up the lawn leads to the house, an ancient gothic structure with three fronts; the east looking full upon the Sound.

The internal improvements, that were now making, prohibited our inspection; take therefore Carew's account (published 1605), which is lively and accurate. We proceeded along what was the green terrace, but has been lately gravelled and had a fine view of the harbour, the old town of Salthouse, on the opposite hill Mr. Harrison's seat, Stonehouse, Dock, **Drake's Is.** and Plymouth, &c., in the Sound, Nicholas Island, fatal sometimes to unwary ships. Last December twelve months, three, heavy laden with iron, split upon the rocks and were lost.

The bold termination on the eastern shore, is called Withey Hedge. From hence we continue through bowers of various foliages, oaks, chestnuts, limes, plantains, variegated sycamores green and white, &c., to an alcove opposite the gate into the deer park, which affords a similar sweet view. The first object after entering the park, is a moss house; from this we next come to an open bench looking full upon the Merchants harbour of Catwater. Lord Borrington's pleasant place at Saltram has a charming effect here, bosomed in its own woods and backed by Devon hills. South east in the sound at a small distance from the shore, rises a high crag called Mews-stone; to this little island about 14 years ago a man was transported for seven years, where he quietly remained his due time without setting foot on other land. Leaving this habitation to his daughter he went to Loo Island, about thirty miles further in Cornwall. She still remains here, a widow with three children, her husband being lately drowned. We now were hid awhile in sweet foliage till we came upon the large terrace beyond the park. Here the watery expanse burst full upon the view, and from the vast arch we pass under, with a glass I could plainly see Eddystone light-house, four leagues from hence, and three from any land. The present useful work was rebuilt under the direction of Mr. John Smeaton, F.R.S., and allowed to be the completest in Europe.[1]

From hence we descend through serpentine bowers of bays, myrtles, arbutuses, laurestinuses, &c. to Lady Damer's garden, (so called), at the end of which is a large stone alcove with a complimentary inscription. Ascending again by similar zigzags to the terrace, the opening here presents a fine view of Corson Bay and the two little ports, Kingston and Corsan, the haunts of smugglers; the former stands in Devon, the latter in Cornwall, only separated by a small creek.[2] Here was the scene of much confusion in the late war, when the French fleet was daily seen to float about

*Marginal notes:* Mew Stone. Looe Is. Eddystone. Cawsand Bay. Kingsand. Cawsand.

[1] This, the third, lighthouse was begun in 1757, and finished in 1759. The outside and basement were of granite, and the interior of Portland stone; and the height of the main column was 70 feet. It has been re-constructed on Plymouth Hoe.

[2] At this time the parish of Maker, in which Mount Edgcumbe (formerly called West Stonehouse) is situated, was partly in Devon and partly in Cornwall. In 1844, the Devonshire part, namely the tithing of Vaultersholme, was annexed to Cornwall.

this bay, meditating destruction to the docks at Plymouth. Our guide gave us a genuine piece of intelligence, which he had lately received from two officers, who were in the French service at the time, and showed him the two places thought of for landing their men, one on this side Kingston, the other on the hill beyond; but their designs were inefficient, and happily prevented.     Winding beautifully round we came next to a gothic alcove, built from the materials of an old chapel, the inside of which gives a picturesque view of nothing but the sea, the fore-ground an hollow verdant slope to the margin of the water.     In our walk from hence we saw very fine cork-trees, live-oaks, &c.; the variety of heath and other blossoms hanging around gave all the luxuriant tints of a real garden.

We now entered the deer park again, and crossed where our defensive regiments are encamped.     On the summit of the hill stands a lofty parish church, belonging to Corsan, Kingston, and Milbrook; from the tower are placed various signals, and the circular prospect is here immense.     Descending now the common walk to the house, we came to the white alcove on the dry walks, (so called), which fronts full north, and gives a beautiful perspective up the harbour, St. John's Lake, St. Germans and Milbrook, with an intermixture of Devon and Cornwall.     Passing towards the front grounds again, we saw many very noble trees, oaks of near twenty different sorts, fine flourishing chesnuts, and cedars of Libanus.     In a part called the wilderness, is placed a flat stone two feet square, with so much nicety as to catch a glimpse of seven different towers; viz., Anton, Dockyard, the new chapel at Dock, Stoke, Plymouth old and new churches, and Plymstock.     Near the water stands a neat Doric alcove, with an inscription from Thomson.     A little beyond is a battery of 22 guns, for the purpose of salutes, &c.     Lastly we saw the orangery, an excellent building, 100 feet by 30, where the fruit ripens in almost equal perfection with that abroad.

We now took leave of these enchanting scenes, and made a comfortable repast at the passage house, called Cremil, which pays the rent of £400 per ann. to Lord Edgecumbe, besides the expense of seven men, boats, &c. We afterwards returned across, to inspect the nature and

**Maker.**

**Cremyll.**

extent of the docks, which are inexpressibly surprising and magnificent. To obtain a sight of them is difficult, requiring a form of your names and abodes, with the addition of some resident person of Plymouth, to be sent to the Governor or Commissioner. Such caution is necessarily used, that any remarks with pen or pencil are forbid; therefore a full and accurate description must not here be expected. Besides the several dry and wet docks heretofore established, they are still adding to the numbers. One in particular, of the first-rate dimensions, cut out of the solid rock, and beautifully lined and faced with Portland stone, may challenge the universe to show its equal. A most extensive wet dock for masts is now finishing; the immense range of buildings for stores, and warehouses for sails, and rigging, &c., and dwellings for the Commissioner, Clerks, and all other necessary officers, are well worth the notice of strangers. Within themselves too are the immense forges for making anchors, and all other iron work, belonging to ships of the largest size. The whole contains a space of 70 acres. Amongst the numerous men of war which now lay in harbour, were the *Royal Cerberus*, of 100 guns, and several others newly launched; also was refitting the ———, taken from the Spaniards in the last war, and when finished to be honoured with the name of *Gibraltar*. We now retired to our inn at Plymouth.

Having visited the most striking features of this place, our next object was to extend about 40 miles into Cornwall, where we might obtain a sufficient knowledge of its valuable mines. By tradition we learn that there was formerly a tract of land called the lioness, extending towards the Scilly Islands, now either sunk into, or swallowed up by the sea. The middle part of the county is for the most part mountainous and rough, but the valleys are fertile enough of themselves, and they incredibly enrich them with a fat sea-sand, and other sea-manure, called ore-weed.

Liskeard from hence is the best and easiest road to St. Austle and Truro, where the mines principally centre; but in order to enjoy as much of the sea and noble prospects as possible, we crossed the passage again at Dock, and leaving Mount-Edgecumbe on our left, passed on the sands under the cliff to Milbrook, where we saw the King's

Crafthole.

brewery, and ascended the hills through steep rough roads to Craftshole, a small dirty village; here coming upon the vast expanse of sea the views and breezes were delightful, and with a glass we plainly saw Edystone light-house with the waves dashing against the rock beneath. The farmers were busy manuring with this sand peculiar to these parts, which they draw mostly on heavy carts with six bullocks, coaxing them along by an unpleasant monotony of language; a custom that seems more efficacious than the violent persuasion of blows and whips.

Looe.

Our object was now to obtain on any terms a passage to Loo, without losing sight of this noble sea. Saddle horses would render the difficulty of this route a pleasure, but with any carriage it is deemed impracticable. The descent is near a mile, by a narrow zig-zag just sufficient to admit the wheels; and the least mishap at any of these turns must inevitably have plunged both into the abyss below. We happily accomplished our design with safety, and a few huts we soon after passed, poured forth their little tribes to gaze at us with astonishment. Our vehicle was to them a rary-show of the first kind, as those of the sea, which they had always before their eyes, would be to the most remote inlander.

Whitesand Bay.

East Looe.
Looe R.
West Looe.

*Buller.*

Looe Is.
*Sir Hen. Trelawney.*

*Finn.*

The alternate bays and promontories now afforded us much enjoyment after our fatigue, and the next mile to the bay of White-sand, was quite a luxury. The road from hence was so narrow, besides other difficulties to encounter, that we deviated a little to the right, which soon brought us to East Loo, a small ill-built town on the river Loo, separated only by this water from another still smaller, called after the same manner, West Loo. They are both corporate boroughs, sending two members to parliament under the influence of Mr. Buller, uncle or brother to the Judge, but formerly belonging to the Courtney family. The scene here is truly picturesque, the river winding betwixt two immense woody hills, not unlike some parts of the Wye. Opposite the mouth of this river stands the small island of the same name, belonging to Sir Henry Trelawney, whose seat is not far from hence; this at a trifling acknowledgment is inhabited by an old man, mentioned at Mews-rock, Plymouth, whose name is Finn, and here by his own industrious cultivation of wheat and other grain, he reaps a comfortable subsistence. At the proper season of the year, various sea-fowl resort to these rocks for the purpose of incubation. After dinner we crossed the bridge of 13 arches; and passed through West Loo in our way to Lostwithiel.

As we entered the welcome Lostwithiel and our Hotel *Lostwithiel.* (so the inns in this country are mostly called) the voice of mirth and gladness loudly met our ear; we were no strangers to the occasion, having lately seen the same at Plymouth, viz. a choice of Mayor for this corporate town, succeeded by a grand dinner and night of general festivity. The members are elected by the votes of the capital burgesses, and the interest rests at present with Lord Edgecumbe, who was now here. *Lord Edgecumbe.*

In the morning we proceeded to St. Austle, eager to satisfy our curiosity with mineral observations. The road was smooth but hilly, the country at first heathy and bad. Descending to St. Blazey, we had a small specimen of a *St. Blazey.* wash tin mine, &c. which was now finished and filled up. A little further on our right, we passed a fine old place belonging to Mr. Carlion, called Tregreen, situate on a *Carlion.* pleasant airy eminence, richly planted, and commanding *Tregreen.* much prospect towards the sea. Again we were surrounded with a bleak heath, thinly bespotted with huts and common mines. From hence we arrived at St. Austle, a pleasant *St. Austell.* little town on the west-side of a hill, and about two miles from the south shore. Its streets and buildings are superior to what we had lately seen, and mostly of the moor stone of the country, mixed with spar and ore, which works soft and easy, but hardens by an exposure to the air and weather. This happy spot is blessed by a peculiar flavour, with all the comforts and riches of life, without feeling the inconveniences and troublesome broils of a borough. And from being the capital of those inestimable mines so peculiar to this county, may justly be called the Peru of Great Britain. The smelting houses belonging to Messrs. Fox and Co. are *Fox and Co.* excessively curious, particularly the blowing-house for making what is called grain tin, there being only two other of these blowing houses for grain tin, and those within a mile of this, in the known world. The grain tin is produced from the strongest heat of charcoal, whereas the other is smelted, and separated from its alloy by common sea coal.

The five coinage towns, or stannary courts, are Leskeard, Lostwithiel, Truro, Helston, and Penzance; where, lest the Dukes of Cornwall should be defrauded of the tax or tribute, it is ordered that all the tin be carried to one of these towns to be weighed, coined, and pay the impost. These courts are held before the lord warden and his substitutes, in virtue of a privilege granted to the workers in tin mines, to sue and be sued only in their own courts, that they may not be drawn from their business, which is highly profitable to the public, by attending their law-suits in other courts. St. Austell, though not mentioned by Camden or other writers as a stannary town, we find now more replete with business of this kind than the rest; a court is held here every six weeks for the purpose of settling disputes which chiefly arise about boundaries. Before this law was settled, the whole was a scene of confusion, blood-shed, and slaughter, between the proprietors of lands and the miners; now the boundarer and proprietor have an equal share, and the miners quietly earn their profits under this influence and protection.

All ranks in this county are very sociable, generous, and kind to each other;[1] being bounded on all sides, except Devon, by the sea, emigrations and intermixtures are less frequent than in other parts of the kingdom; so that they usually marry amongst themselves; whence comes the proverb, "that all Cornish gentlemen are cousins." I was greatly pleased to see the respect and veneration which the lower class in this town have for the gentlemen around them, from whose assistance and protection they seem to derive a great share of happiness than I ever heard expressed in any other place.

Pilchards are a small fish, caught in vast abundance on these shores which are exported from Movagizy, Pensance, &c. to France, Spain, and Italy; sometimes 8, or 900 hogsheads in a season. A very fine oil is produced from these fish, which they pile up in great heaps as long and broad as the house made for the purpose will permit, and breast-high; then with proper boards, weights, &c. they press the oil out into a gutter, which communicates with a vessel fixed in the ground at one end of the house.

---

[1] Lady Fanshawe, in her *Memoirs*, says : "The gentlemen of this county are generally loyal to the Crown and hospitable to their neighbours, but they are of a crafty and censorious nature, as most are so far from London."

Besides the various sorts of stones, spars, granites, &c., with which this county abounds, a curious stone called the warming-stone hath here frequently been found, which is of such a nature, that when once heated it will continue warm eight or ten hours. The swimming stone, which has also been found in these parts, consists of rectilinear lamina, as thin as paper, intersecting each other, in all directions, and having unequal cavities between them; this structure renders the stone so cellular as to swim in water. The asbestos, or amiantus, of several kinds have also been discovered here; this stone is so fibrous that linen has been made of it, which fire could not consume, but this art has been long lost.

Of Lostwithiel nothing scarce remains but a small town in the valley, situate on the river Fowey. This was, and is at present called the county town, though now Launceston is really so, yet the common gaol for the whole stannary is here, and also the sheriff's court for the county. The Fowey was formerly navigable to this town, which enabled the inhabitants to carry on a considerable trade, but this through neglect has long been on the decline. But like the rest of these rivers, it abounds in fish; in the months of May and June they take here a black trout, some of which are near three feet in length. About the end of August another sort appears, called the bartholomew trout. This is generally about 18 inches long, of a fine red colour and in much higher esteem than the other. Salmons also are taken here plentifully. At the town of Fowey, about six miles below, the river forms an extensive harbour.

*Lostwithiel.*
*Fowey R.*

*Fowey.*

On returning eastward again towards Leskard, we deviated about a mile to view the ruins of Raistormal Castle; the ancient residence of the Dukes of Cornwall, situate on a large eminence behind Mr. Gregor's pleasant house, whose grounds and plantations amidst a variety of natural inequalities of wood, hill and vale afford a charming scene.

*Restormel Cas.*

*Gregor.*

We ascended to inspect the ruins, a circular pile of strong walls, about 30 feet diameter within, 40 high, hung very picturesquely with ivy, &c. The materials are a most durable composition of hard cement and uneven shells of Elvin stone, so nicely fabricated as to appear at a small distance like one well wrought stone, or poured as a fluid into frames.

The entrance is by a projecting portal to the west, which displays the remains of six rooms, and a small chapel: on one side of which are the visible traces of a vase for holy water, and under this a small bath, to the east was a large altar piece; our guide said he had often found relics of painted glass; and on the outside, in the surrounding foss he showed us where he had dug up two perfect skeletons lying arm in arm. At a small distance from hence is a considerable burying place, where bones have been often found. Descending to the house again, we crossed the river, and moved eastward through a grove of laurels and young oaks, which soon brought us to the turnpike road, on a wild extensive waste; no pleasing object to attract the eye, but a lofty pyramid on our right, belonging to Lord Camelford, at Boconnock; while on our left the northern hills reared their barren heads like Scotia's crags. Approaching Leskard we ascended a vast hill, through a wood called Lady Park, the property of Lord Elliot.

*Lord Camelford.* Boconnoc.

Lady Park. *Lord Eliot.* Liskeard.

Leskard is a large borough town, situate upon two hills; it has a fine old church, near which stood formerly a strong castle, now totally defaced and nothing left but the name. The members are elected by the burgesses and freemen, the mayor being the returning officer. Lord Elliot has now the interest. As this was St. Matthew's fair, of which they have three in the year, and three great markets, differing only in the latter being exempt from toll; we had an opportunity of observing it to advantage. The streets were mostly crowded with sheep and oxen; the former sold from £12 to £18 per score, the latter about £20 a pair, £4 lower than when the harvest, &c. render their use more requisite. From hence we passed over several large cultivated hills and through St. Ives, a small village with a good tower church. The country still continues more mountainous, interspersed with rich valleys, &c. About two miles from Kellington see a curious hill rising conically out of the winding vale, near a small river called Lemara; the woods on the left are very noble and beautiful.

St. Ives.

Lemara R.

Callington.

South Hill.

Kellington is a very old borough, with a good church and tolerable buildings; but is only a chapel of ease to South Hill. Here too the choice of a new mayor was joyfully expressed in ringing and festivity. The two members are here sent to parliament by the numerous votes of lease holders, &c. under the influence of the Earl of Orford and the government of a Portreeve, which was established in 1583. Not to mention every particular, and mode of conducting the 22 boroughs of this county; it may not be amiss to notice the present situation of Helstone, which sends two members to parliament by a single vote, an old cobbler, the only survivor of a considerable charter, which I believe has been renewed, but he will not give up his privilege; what an opportunity this is for providing for his family, &c. This interest belonged to the Godolphins. Grampound is in a similar situation. In the evening we proceeded over extensive heaths to Tavistock and crossed the river Tamar over an excellent bridge of six arches. About three miles down this river on the Devon side, at Bear-Alston, a borough of the Duke of Northumberland's, are some rich lead and silver mines, the property of Mr. Gallet, which have been lately renewed, and yield now three or four plates of silver per month.

*Earl of Orford.*

Helston.

*Godolphin.*
Grampound.

Beer Alston.
*Duke of Northumberland.*
*Gullet.*

After a long ascent up an immense hill we soon arrived at Tavistock, lowly situated on the river Tave, on a sandy ground pretty well cultivated. The present state of this town is considerable, consisting of several tolerable streets with a large old church, the body of which appears like three common parish churches united. The glory of this place formerly was its abbey; little now remains but a few old walls; a school was also erected here for preserving from oblivion the ancient Saxon language. The borough was never incorporated,[1] but is governed by a portreeve, annually chosen by freeholders at the lords-court.

Tavistock.
Tavy R.

Instead of pursuing the right road over Dartmore forest by Moreton to Exeter, we deviated round the north side of this vast heap of mountains to see Lydford waterfall. This being market day we met numbers of the people flocking hither with grain, a few sheep and an abundance of Michaelmas geese. The common vehicles of this country are panniers and horses; nor did we meet a single carriage the whole day. Pass over an extensive down, with fine prospects

Lydford
Waterfall.

[1] This is not correct, for a charter was granted in 1682 and revoked in 1688. See Mrs. G. H. Radford (now Lady Radford), " The Charter of Tavistock." (*Trans. Devon. Assoc.*., xlvi, 176-184.)

on our left and Dartmore on our right; this part of
the country is very coarse, moory and barren in its nature;
in some places productive of nothing but a dwarf kind of
furze; in others we see a considerable increase of tillage,
owing chiefly to the cultivation of potatoes; the soil is
mostly a stiff clay, which renders it unhealthy to sheep,
which are here of a small sort, and subject to the rot,
especially in wet seasons, which destroys them incredibly
fast.    In these parts which are too remote to obtain sea
sand, they shave off the turf, and by burning it, procure
excellent manure from its ashes, which mode of cultivation
being first used here, is called Devonshiring or Denshiring.

**Lyd R.**

The remarkable cataract of Lydford waterfall is formed
by a small stream running into the river Lyd, over a
romantic rock, sweetly clothed with wood.  Winding down
the rock, on a small path about half way, you are presented
with the finest milky streams imaginable, neither too perpendicular to be one confused heap, nor too much divided
to be ungraceful; but one continued silvery chain of 200
feet; towards the bottom the rock projects so favourably
as to fill the air with aqueous particles, and imitate the
effect of a real fountain, softly falling in a silver shower.
Descending beneath you look up to the whole with a similar
enchantment.  This surprising waterfall pleased me altogether
more than any in the North of England or Scotland, and
being a greater rarity in these parts it is more valuable
and striking.

**Lydford.**

Lydford, now reduced to a small village, was formerly
a town of note, which sent burgesses to parliament, but
for its poverty has long since been discharged of that
privilege; the ruins of a gaol-like castle are still visible.
From hence nothing occurs till we come to the village of

**Sourton.**

Sourton; whence opens a charming prospect towards the
west of a rich vale, &c. terminated by distant mountains.

**Okehampton.**

As we approach Okehampton, vulgarly called Ockington,
the beauties of the forest hang gracefully on the skirts of
Dartmore, but for this we are mostly indebted to the remains

**Earls of
Devon.**

of the old park, where once the Earls of Devonshire had
a noble castle, now quite in ruins, which till late belonged

**Courtenay**

to the Courtenays of Powderham castle, near Exeter, but
is now exchanged away to some part of the corporation.

The castle stands a little west of the centre of the county, and near the town of Okehampton.

This ancient borough stands in a vale on the river Oke, whence it has its name; at a mile distance from the parish church, beautifully situated on a hill amidst a thick grove. Here is a small manufacture similar to the rest of the towns of this county, but in the annals of history we find this place much more considerable than at present. The members of parliament are chosen by the freemen and freeholders, and the interest now rests with the Duke of Bedford. Here we dined and had our usual compliment so peculiar to this county of tarts and clotted cream, a composition to me more pleasing than any thing of the kind I had ever tasted. This essence of milk is gathered by scalding their whole quantity together in the state it comes from the cow, and letting it stand about a day, and then skimming off the top; by which means they have a greater quantity, but the milk is quite impoverished.

*Okement R.*

*Duke of Bedford.*

In the evening we proceeded to Crockern-well, the half-way house to Exeter; which, though not the most desirable inn, afforded us a comfortable repose. Here we overcame the difficulties of hills by an additional post horse, and moved with expedition amidst delightful scenery to the fair city we lately had passed through, and now breakfasted where we this day week had dined.

*Crockernwell.*

It now occurs to me to mention an idea of grandeur and opulence not to be found elsewhere in Great Britain, if on the whole face of the globe; (viz.) that by a more rapid abbreviation of this western tour, you might sleep twelve nights at twelve different cities, (viz.) London, Oxford, Worcester, Hereford, Gloucester, Bristol, Bath, Wells, Exeter, Salisbury, Winchester, and Westminster.

We now directed our course towards Dorchester. About half a mile from the city we pass the ancient and extensive pile of the laudable work-house or hospital before described; two miles beyond this is Heavitree gallows, with a square piece of ground inclosed by a strong wall, for the burial of sufferers; a plan I never remember to have seen before.[1] The road now in a more gravelly soil was excellent and

*Heavitree.*

---

[1] See pp. 83-4.

uninterrupted by tedious hills; the surrounding inclosures of arable and pasture, glowed with fertility; while the happy seedsman, scattering round his showers of grain, hailed the smiling season with the voice of melody.    Thus we journeyed on till we came within six miles of Honiton, from the brow of which hill we were presented with the sweetest scene of cultivation I ever beheld.    This may be called the garden of Devon, not only from its own intrinsic superiority, but the beauteous order in which it is disposed; a fine amphitheatre of meadow and arable enclosure gradually ascending towards the south, in the highest cultivation, up to its natural boundary of open hills, ranged in all the uniformity of a perfect wall; to the east and north appears a similar circular defence, but not so strongly marked.    Descending into this lovely vale, we saw on our left Escott, the seat of Sir George Yonge, a fine old place of good architecture and beautifully situated.[1]    A little farther the river Otter forms a sweet winding canal, where we pass a very picturesque scene of cots and ivy-mantled bridges.    This spot, now only a decayed village called Veniton, is famous for a battle fought against the Cornish rebels in the reign of Edward VI. We now met numbers of market people with panniers, crooks and gambades.[2]    Honiton is a neat market town situate on the river Otter; the country around it is beautiful. This town sends members to parliament, under the government of a portreeve, chosen annually at the court of the lord of the manor, who makes the return of the members elected by all the inhabitants, called burgage-holders.    The present condition of this town is indebted to a dreadful fire, which broke out on July 19th, 1747, and reduced three parts of it to ashes, to the great distress of several hundred industrious inhabitants.[3]    The houses now wear a pleasing aspect, and the principal street extending from east to west

---

[1] Built soon after 1680 by Sir George's grandfather, Sir Walter Yonge, and burnt to the ground in 1808. (Lysons, *Devon*, 469.) In note 4 on p. 179 this seat was incorrectly identified with the " Great House," Colyton.

[2] See p. 216.

[3] According to Lysons, this town had been visited by the destructive calamity of fire in 1672, 1747, 1757 and 1765; but it was the last-mentioned fire that was the most calamitous, 115 houses being burnt down, and the steeple of Allhallows Chapel, with the school and school-house, destroyed. (*Devon*, 281.)

is remarkably paved, forming a small channel well shouldered up on each side with pebbles and green turf, which holds a stream of clear water with a square dipping place opposite each door; a mark of cleanliness and convenience I never saw before. The first manufacture of serges was introduced into Devonshire at this town, but at present it is employed chiefly in making lace. After dining at an excellent inn, we proceeded over vast hills surrounded with beautiful vales; from the top of Honiton hill the landscape may vie with any part of this Kingdom.

Axminster, where we now arrived to repose, is a consider-able market town, situate on the river Axe, from whence, together with a minster erected here by King Athelstan, it has its name. This foundation was for seven priests, but afterwards reduced to two, for whom a portion of land was allotted, called priest-aller; which with the parsonage now belongs to two prebendaries of York, to pray for souls buried here, who were slain at the battle of Brunaburg, in a field, which is at present called King's-field.[1] The manufacture of this place is chiefly carpets, and esteemed superior to the Wilton, being worked by the pliant fingers of small children, from patterns and colours laid before them.[2] Thirteen shillings per yard is the lowest price, and from thence their value may be increased almost to any sum.

*Axminster.*

*King Athelstan.*

# OBSERVATIONS ON THE WESTERN COUNTIES OF ENGLAND By W. G. Maton 1794-6

Sidmouth being our next place of destination, on this day's journey we entered Devonshire. Not only another county, but a new scene, opened to us as we approached that town. Unlike the wide downs and frequent wastes, silent with desolation, in the county we had just left (Dorset), every part of the landscape now in view seemed, from the plenitude of its population, the extent of its cultivation and enclosures,

*Sidmouth.*

---

[1] See pp. 81-82.

[2] The manufacture was started in 1755 by Thomas Whitty, and lasted until 1835. See James Hine, "The Origin of Axminster Carpets." (*Trans. Devon. Assoc.*, xxi., 331-7.)

and the luxuriance of its vegetation, almost itself alive.  We quitted the high road about three miles from Sidmouth, and descended into the town by one of the lofty ridges that command it on each side and bound a most charming vale.

Sidmouth is situated close to the sea, which is reddened by reflecting the colour of the cliffs.  These are composed of sand, tinged by the red oxide of iron, and partly calcareous. Sand and pebbles have choked up the port, so that pleasure-boats and fishing-smacks are the only vessels that can touch at the shore.  It is much frequented in the bathing season, and many families continue their residence even during the winter.  The situation is certainly a very delightful one.

Taking leave of the coast for the present, we proceeded towards Exeter, through Ottery St. Mary.  This is a place of some trade, manufactories of flannel, serge, &c. having been lately established here,[1] through the laudable exertions of Sir George Younge,[2] and Sir John Duntze,[3] Barts.  The town has certainly much to recommend it to attention, particularly the church, which is a fine ancient fabric.  We did not view without interest an old mouldering turret, the only remains of a house once inhabited by the great Sir Walter Raleigh.[4]   There is another building deserving of notice just without the church-yard, where the old convention-room of Oliver Cromwell is shown to the traveller.[5]   The road to Exeter is a broad, flat, dusty turnpike, augmenting the glare of the sun's rays by the redness of its surface.  Clay now

*Ottery St. Mary.*

*Sir Geo. Yonge.*
*Sir John Duntze.*

*Sir W. Raleigh.*

*Oliver Cromwell.*

---

[1] Lysons (1822) says : " There was formerly a considerable manufacture of serges at Ottery, but it has much declined.  There is still a large manufactory for spinning wool." (*Devon*, 337.)

[2] Sir George Yonge, 5th bart., was born 1731, succeeded his father 1755, and died 1812.  At this date he was Master of the Mint.  His seat was at Escot, but it was sold in this year, 1794, to Sir John Kennaway, Bart. (Lysons, *Devon*, 469.)

[3] Sir John Duntze, Bart., lived at Rockbeare House.  He died 1795.

[4] The old house, which was the reputed residence of Sir Walter Raleigh, was situated in Mill Street.  There was, in 1793, one turret still existing, and the house had, altogether, a monasterial air. (Polwhele, *Devon*, ii., 240.)  It is very doubtful whether the tradition in this case is correct.

[5] The Chanter's House.  "Here came the Lord General Cromwell, and in 'the Great Parlour,' which seems afterwards to have been called 'the Convention Room,' Fairfax deputed Cromwell to take command of the forces in the West." (Coleridge, *Story of a Devonshire House*, 75.)

begins to preponderate in the soil, but a considerable portion of sand still remains mixed with it, so as to constitute a very rich loam, which seems to originate from the decomposition of a compact dark-coloured stone that lies very little below it.

We gazed in vain for a view of the capital of Devonshire until we arrived in the very suburbs, though the approach to it is in every direction on the ascent. The streets are extremely incommodious to those who pass them either on foot or on horseback, being very rough and filthy, and but partially paved.

The first object that arrested our attention in the city of Exeter was the Cathedral Church—a magnificent Gothic edifice, with two conspicuous Saxon towers. The altar-piece represents the inside of the church in perspective, and was executed in the reign of James I.

In an ancient building (which appears to have been originally a refectory for the college of prebendaries) now used as a school-room, near the church, we found an admirable portrait painted by an artist of the name of Gandy.[1] It is the head of a Dr. Langdon, who died in 1712.[2] One of the officers of the church informed us that Sir Joshua Reynolds used to contemplate this picture with new admiration as often as he came to Exeter, and he is said to have often declared that "had he painted that portrait, he should be more proud of it than of any of his performances."[3]

The city (with the suburbs) is about three miles in circumference, and contains sixteen churches within the walls and four without. Thirteen of these are said to have been exposed to sale by Oliver Cromwell, by the mouth of the common crier. It had formerly more convents than almost any place

*Exeter.*

*William Gandy.*
*Rev. Tobias Langdon.*
*Sir Joshua Reynolds.*

*Oliver Cromwell.*

[1] William Gandy was the son (or grandson) of James Gandy, who was a pupil of Vandyck.

[2] The Rev. Tobias Langdon, priest-vicar of the Cathedral, "a celebrated master of music." For the subsequent fate of this famous portrait, see G. Pycroft, *Art in Devonshire*, 47, where, however, it is wrongly assigned to *James* Gandy.

[3] Sir Godfrey Kneller, who was once at Exeter, by chance saw this picture, and with astonishment inquired who was the artist capable of having painted it, and when told it was by a painter of that city who was in great poverty, he exclaimed, "Good God! why does he bury his talent in the country when he might immediately come to London where his merit would soon be known and properly rewarded?" (Northcote, *Memoirs of Sir Joshua Reynolds*, 1813, p. 416.)

in the kingdom. There is a good quay, and the river is navigable for vessels of 150 tons burthen.

There was anciently a mint at Exeter, and indeed money was coined here as late as the reign of William III., some of whose coins I have seen distinguished by an E. under the bust.

The old walls remain in many places, and seem to have been originally exceedingly strong. An octagonal turret on the east side of the city, and the south gate continue very perfect. As Exeter is a place of great trade, particularly in articles of the woollen manufactory, we were not surprised to see shops and warehouses extending from one end of a street to the other. On the banks of the river there is a very large cotton manufactory, which employs three hundred men at a time. The exportation of serge, kerseys, &c. from this city has produced immense profits, the average value of it having been almost £600,000 per annum. The markets are Spain, Portugal, Germany, and Italy.

Thorverton.
Upton Pyne.

Having satisfied our curiosity in the city of Exeter, we visited the stone-quarries of Thorverton, and the manganese mine of Upton-Pyne. The latter is very productive,—at least what is dug at the upper part of the pit, and was used in the glass-houses formerly established at Exeter, but is now sent chiefly to London. The manufactory at Bristol undersold that of Exeter. The black oxide is used in glass-houses to take away the yellow, green, or blue tinge from glass intended to be of a clear white. Too large a proportion of it gives a violet colour.

Wood-sage grows in wonderful profusion here about. We were informed that the fruit of it is pretty generally used by the poor in the neighbourhood as a substitute for hops. It possesses the bitterness, and a good deal of the flavour of the latter.

Powderham
Cas.

We then passed along the banks of the Exe from Powderham Castle to Starcross. We were led to expect a noble situation for the castle, but how great was our disappointment to find it almost in a flat, very much exposed on the side towards the Channel, and with a broad marsh in front. It faces the river, but little pains have been taken to open the view to it with advantage, or to heighten the effect of those magnificent materials which nature has furnished. Some

part of the present castle is ancient, and gives an air of
grandeur to the whole, which however is by no means a
striking pile of building at any distance.

Though the Exe is very broad at its influx into the sea,
we saw Exmouth very distinctly across it, and perceived    Exmouth.
a similarity of soil on each side of the river. The town stands
very pleasantly, but is protected by nothing except a barred
haven. It had formerly a small castle.

The lands about Starcross were two years ago covered with    Starcross.
furze, but are now cultivated; they produce surprisingly well,
though so much exposed to the sea. We here saw women
employed at the plough, which they guided with as much
dexterity as the most robust men, and we were informed
that the practice is not uncommon in Devonshire, though I
question whether the failure of the loom would afford many
new hands to the farmer in other parts of the kingdom.

We came now again to the coast, and passed over several
bold cliffs, which rise quick from the shore, towards Teignmouth. In a pleasant valley, and close to a little creek, stands
Dawlish—a neat, new village not frequented by summer    Dawlish.
visitors until within the last two or three years.

Teignmouth is situated (as its name indeed implies) at the    Teignmouth.
mouth of the river Teign, which takes its rise on the moun-    Teign R.
tains about Chagford, and spreads a noble sheet of water
as it approaches the sea, though there is a large shoal of land
on the eastern side of the haven. On this latter spot, which
is covered by the sea at spring-tides, the view up the river
is extremely beautiful, the ground gradually rising on each side
into verdant hills, ornamented with wood, and cheerful with
cultivation. The cliffs overhanging the sea have a singular,
and, I think, very picturesque appearance. They are of a
deep red colour, (with the exception of a few broad patches
of verdure), and mount in rude irregular shapes, to the height
of 70 or 80 feet.

We proceeded from Teignmouth over a varied country
to Chudleigh, and remarked as we advanced that limestone    Chudleigh.
now began to prevail. The hills in the horizon exhibited
bolder forms than any we had lately seen. The ridge called
Haldon shut from our view the scenery about the Exe, and
made but a dreary feature in the landscape, though from
certain points its effect was not unpleasing.

Chudleigh is by no means an interesting place, being only a decent market-town, of small extent, yet it is agreeably situated. The neighbourhood is famous for cyder. An orchard of only three acres, very near Chudleigh, yielded in one year apples enough to make almost eighty hogsheads, at one guinea per hogshead. The cyder of this part of the country is of a most exquisite quality too.

There are some singular rocks (of a bluish limestone called Chudleigh marble) about half a mile west from the town, which from their romantic appearance and situation invite the steps of a traveller. The landscape that meets the eye from the highest part is uncommonly beautiful, and here and there the branches of a picturesque oak form a sort of natural canopy for the contemplative spectator. To the left are the fine woods of Ugbrook, the seat of Lord Clifford. One part of the rocks is upwards of 100 feet in height, and presents its broad front towards a charming vale terminated by the Teign. The Chudleigh limestone admits of a very good polish, and some of it is burnt into lime, by the aid of Bovey coal. It lies in strata five or six feet in thickness, which dip to the south-east.

Leaving the Ashburton road to the right, we proceeded through Bovey-Heathfield, in order to view some curious Coal-pits. We were surprised to find the coal in alternate strata with a whitish clay that constitutes the substance of the adjacent soil. These pits have been worked several years, and are of considerable service to a pottery close by, which is one of the largest in the west of England. The coal retains the vegetable structure, and has exactly the appearance of charred wood, being of a black, or blackish brown colour, extremely light and friable, separable into irregular laminæ, and strongly impregnated with bitumen. The pits are about eighty feet in depth; they are often filled with water to the height of forty feet, or more, and an engine is put in motion for carrying it off by an overshot wheel twenty-four feet in diameter, which works two levers with rods and buckets.

The borough of Ashburton stands on the banks of the river Dart, and is one of the four stannary towns of Devonshire. It is a great thoroughfare, being on the high-road from London to the Land's-end, and about half way between Exeter and Plymouth. The church has more the appearance

*Ugbrooke.*
*Lord Clifford.*

Bovey
Heathfield.

Ashburton.

of a collegiate than a parochial one, and has a very
handsome tower ninety feet high, with a small spire
covered with lead.   Adjoining to the church there is a chapel,
dedicated to St. Laurence, which, since the reformation, has
been used as a grammar-school.[1]   Ashburton is altogether a
neat, respectable town, and carries on a considerable manufactory of serge.   Once a week a market is held solely for
wool and yarn.

Proceeding from Ashburton to Totnes, we perceived that
the soil was now entirely shistose.   Wood and pasture lands
meet the eye more frequently than any other, but the scenery in
this part of Devon is altogether rich and interesting.   Dart-
ington-bridge is fortunately situated for affording a very
finished and romantic scene, in which a hill above, exuberantly
clothed with beech and oak, forms a noble feature.   On the
left appear fertile fields, coppices, and orchards, in a wide
range, pleasantly interspersed with numerous hamlets and
villages.

*Riverford Br.*

Totnes is built on the side of a steep hill, down which run
a tolerably good street, about three quarters of a mile in
length, and terminated by a bridge over the Dart.   It is one
of the most ancient towns in the kingdom, and was formerly
well fortified, being surrounded with walls and four gates, and
defended by a castle, which was erected by one of the Zouches,
once lords of the manor.    Only the southern gate now
remains.   A few fragments of the castle indeed may be seen
on a hill north-west of the town.[2]   The church, which is
spacious, was dedicated to the Virgin Mary, and has a tower
at the west end adorned with four handsome pinnacles.

*Totnes*

*Zouche.*

Berry-Pomeroy Castle is not more than a mile from Totnes.
The great gate, (with the walls of the south front) the north
wing of the court, or quadrangle, some apartments on the
west side, and a turret or two, are the principal remains of
the building, and they are so finely overhung with the branches
of trees and shrubs that grow close to the walls, so beautifully
mantled with ivy, and so richly incrusted with moss, that they

*Berry
Pomeroy.*

---

[1] A free school in connection with the chantry chapel of St.
Lawrence was founded by Bishop Stapeldon in 1314. (See *Six
Hundredth Anniversary of the Foundation of the Ashburton Grammar
School.*)

[2] See H. Michell Whitley, " Totnes Castle and Walled Town."
(*Trans. Devon. Assoc.*, xlviii., 189-198.)

constitute the most picturesque objects that can be imagined.
And when the surrounding scenery is taken into the account,
—the noble mass of wood fronting the gate, the bold ridges
rising in the horizon, and the fertile valley opening to the
east,—the ruins of Berry-Pomeroy Castle must be considered
as almost unparalleled in their effect.    The eastern tower is
accessible by a passage from the room over the gateway ; here,
we found, was the best point for surveying the environs of the
castle.    The interior part appears to be considerably more
modern than the gate and outer walls, the windows being
square or oblong, with linterns and cross bars of stone.    It is
going rapidly to decay, however, and the walls being composed
of slate might be entirely demolished with little trouble.
When perfect, these apartments must have been extremely
grand, and were decorated in a splendid manner, if one might
judge from the mouldings, columns, &c. which remain.    The
large room over the gateway is divided by a wall supported
by three pillars and circular arches, but it is not easy to
discover the use of it.    There was evidently a portcullis to
the gate, which is turretted and embattled, and over it the
arms of the family of Pomeroy are still to be seen.[1]

*Pomeroy.*

The face of the country, after we leave Berry-Pomeroy, is
rather insipid, a heath appearing to the right, and very little
wood, or irregularity of ground, in front.    At Torr-Abbey,
however, a delightful view of Torbay opens, with fine broad
swells to the north.

*Tor Abbey.*

Torr-Abbey originally belonged to a society of Canons
*Premonstratenses*, to whom the lands of Torr, the church of
St. Saviour that once stood there, fishing in the bay, and other
rights were given by William Briwer, or Bruer.    The Briwers
were a family of great note in the reigns of Richard I. and
John, and had a seat very near the abbey.    There are still
some remains of the old abbey of Torr, now converted into
out-houses, &c., close to a modern mansion, the seat of Mr.
Carey.    The situation is charming, and I must confess I
looked for a more striking object than the house as we rode
through the fine avenue, shaded by aged elm and oak.

*William
Brewer.*

*Carey.*

*Torquay.*

Torquay far exceeded our expectation in every respect.
Instead of the poor, uncomfortable village that we had

---

[1] See H. Michell Whitley, "Berry Pomeroy Castle." (*Trans.
Devon. Assoc.*, xlvii., 285-293.)

imagined, how great was our surprise at seeing a pretty range of neat, new buildings, fitted up for summer visitors, who may certainly here enjoy convenient bathing, retirement, and a most romantic situation.[1]    It commands a full view of Torbay, and is surrounded by a very bold amphitheatre of hills, from which the eye may command a prospect of astonishing grandeur and variety.

A singular cavern, called Kent's-hole, is considered as the greatest curiosity in this part of the county.[2]    It is about a mile distant from Torquay.    Two women, whose usual business it is, conducted us to the spot, provided with candles, tinder-boxes, and other necessaries for the expedition.    After pursuing rather an intricate track, we arrived at the mouth of the cavern, and soon saw there was some occasion for the assistance of guides, who presented each of us with a candle stuck in a piece of slitted stick.    The aperture was just large enough to admit us.    As we advanced, our guides fixed candles on the sides of the cavern, in order to give us as much light as possible, and to provide against the consequences of an extinction of those we held in our hands.    The chill we received after having entered is inconceivable, and our clothes were moistened by the continual dropping of water from the roof.    The lights, when viewed at a distance, gleaming through the gloomy vaults, and reflected by the pendant crystals, had a most singular effect.    We began to fancy ourselves in the abode of some magician, or (as our companions were two ancient females, and not the most comely of their years) in the clutches of some mischievous old witches, the representation of whose habitations in Shakespere's *Macbeth* we could for once persuade ourselves had its foundation in nature.    Kent's-hole is in no part more than twenty feet high, but the bottom of it is very irregular, being sometimes on an ascent, and sometimes on a descent, and the moisture of the stone on

Kent's Hole.

---

[1] Lysons (1822) says that "within a few years it has grown from a hamlet of a few scattered houses to a town of considerable population."    The population of the parish of Tor Mohun, in which Torquay was situated, increased from 838 in 1801 to 1925 in 1821. (*Devon*, xlviii, 525.)

[2] This was before it was systematically explored.    However, the cavern seems to have been known from time immemorial; and among the various inscriptions on its walls is seen "Robert Hedges, of Ireland, Feb. 20, 1688." (Murray, *Handbook for Devon*, 10th Ed., 159.)

which we trod rendered *both* not a little difficult and dangerous. The roof is in some places so low that we were obliged to advance on our knees. At length we reached the extremity of the cavern, which is full two hundred yards long, and, though it sometimes winds, seems to run for the most part in a southern direction. As no great elevation of ground appears on the outside, the declivity of it must be considerable.

The limestone of Torquay is of a hardish texture, and somewhat resembles that of the Bristol rocks in colour and fracture, but about Chudleigh and Ashburton, it is of a light blue, with veins of white, and takes so good a polish as to obtain the denomination of marble.

Torbay.

Torbay appeared in all its grandeur as we passed the more elevated part of its borders, in our way to Dartmouth. Here were the first myrtle hedges that I had seen; they were covered with a most delicious bloom, and surrounded many of the gardens by the road side. We could scarcely persuade ourselves that we were not on the south side of the British Channel. The bay appears to be about twelve miles in compass, and is reckoned one of the finest roads for ships our coast can boast of. It was the general station for the English fleet during the whole time of William III's war with France, and here it was that this monarch arrived, when Prince of Orange only, on the memorable fifth of November, 1688.

*William III.*

Dartmouth.

The country at some distance from Dartmouth has a very bold aspect, and the road curves round the feet of some lofty hills, which appearing in succession, and continually forming new lines and boundaries of sight, strike an admirer of picturesque effect extremely. We were in some measure prepared for the enchanting scene which our passage across the Dart opened to us. This river is almost half a mile wide between Kingswere (where we entered the ferry-boat) and Dartmouth. On our left appeared the castle, which stands at the mouth of the river, surrounded by a rich mass of oak, and the steeple of an adjoining church just peeps above the branches. Opposite to us was the town, situated on the declivity of a craggy hill, and extending, embosomed in trees, almost a mile along the water's edge. The quay and dock-yards project into the river, and cause an apparent curvature in its course which had an effect inexpressibly finished and beautiful.   Some ships of war, and several small vessels, floating in different parts of it, broke its uniformity.   The rocks on each side are composed of a glossy purple slate, and their summits fringed with a number of ornamental plants and shrubs.   Enraptured with so lovely a scene, we arrived insensibly at the quay of Dartmouth.

This town is very singularly built, the streets being one so much higher than another that it is almost possible to shake hands from without with a person at the window of an attic story.   The quay is large and convenient, and the trade of Dartmouth (by no means inconsiderable *now*) was *once* as extensive as that of any place in the county, Exeter excepted.

The walls of the old castle stand at the south end of the town, but do not give one an idea of its having been either strong or handsome.   It was of a circular form.   Red valerian grows in the crevices of the stone; this plant indeed is not uncommon in such situations along the western coast.

The present castle is full half a mile distant from the town, and, if not a warlike, is certainly a very picturesque building, but by no means spacious.   Adjoining to it there is a chapel, the stone tower and spire of which were built by the townsmen not many years ago.   It belongs to Stoke-Fleming Church, two miles off, and was erected in Edward III's time.

Stoke Fleming.

We felt the greatest reluctance to leave Dartmouth. The town itself indeed, and our accomodations were enough to drive us away at once, but the scenery about it delighted us more than any thing we had seen in the course of our tour.   Whether we were seated in the bow-window of our inn, which commanded an unobstructed view of the opposite banks of the Dart, or whether we rambled along the paths that divided in various directions about the rocks, there was a combination of features on which the eye gazed with inconceivable pleasure.   The scenery of Dartmouth certainly presents a most exquisite treat to a landscape painter.   The view towards the mouth of the harbour, in particular, exhibits such a happy assemblage of objects for a picture that it is perhaps scarcely to be exceeded.   A rocky knoll projecting from the shore makes an admirable foreground. One of the side-screens is formed by the picturesque castle with the adjoining church, just emerging from a fine wood which enriches the right-hand side; the other a high promontory, with a small fort at its feet; whilst the main sea appears in front through a narrow opening, and leaves nothing for the imagination to wish for in the composition.

A loose, bluish slate prevails almost the whole way to Ivy-bridge. This tract of country forms a part of what is generally known by the name of the South Hams, and is much celebrated for its richness and fertility. The eye, however, is offended, and the prospect obstructed too, by the fences, which are composed of high embankments topped with coppice wood. Square fields and strait hedge-rows, how profitable soever in an agricultural point of view, are really nuisances when considered as constituting a part of the scenery of a country.

Ivy-bridge is a small group of houses delightfully situated on the banks of the river Arme, which rushes with a loud roar over a bed of rocks; after a rainy season it forms quite a torrent, and brings down from the hills fragments of granite. The rocks which constitute its bed seem to have been torn and hurled, as it were, from their original situations by some paroxysm of nature. Close to the bridge stands one of the most comfortable and elegant inns in the west of England, and in the gardens belonging to it (which run along one side of the river) the bridge, the high grounds beyond it, the rocks, and the foaming current assume the most picturesque relations.

The Plymouth road now led us considerably to the left, and we passed through Plympton St. Mary. Here was formerly a college for a dean and four prebendaries, founded by one of the Saxon princes. A priory of regular canons was afterwards established, in the room of the former, who were displaced by Warlewast, Bishop of Exeter. The rigid prelate peremptorily inflicted this punishment upon them for not dismissing their wives, in obedience to the decrees of the synod of London, in 1102.[1]

Plympton-Earls is distant, but visible, from the high road. It was the birth-place of Sir Joshua Reynolds, whose father kept a grammar-school there. The castle, which was

South Hams.

Ivybridge.
Erme R.

Plympton
St. Mary.

*William
Warelwast.*

Plympton
Earle.
*Sir Joshua
Reynolds.*

---

[1] See p. 56.

anciently the seat of the family *de Ripariis*, is a conspicuous object at some distance. *Redvers or Rivers.*

Crossing the Plym, we were much struck by a view of Saltram, the seat of Lord Boringdon. The grounds extend along the banks of the river, and form a fine, decorated scene. The approach to the house lies through some well disposed groups of trees, on a gentle ascent to the left of it. There are several pleasing openings as you advance, and at length, on the summit of the hill, a noble and wide extent cf scenery unfolds itself. The house is built in a very plain, substantial manner, without any ornamental appendages whatever on the outside. After entering it, we were conducted through an elegant suite of apartments (on the ground floor) which are furnished with some charming pictures. Zuccarelli's best performances are in this collection. *Saltram. Ld. Boringdon.*

As we intended to visit Plymouth on our return out of Cornwall, we passed on without delay to Saltash. Opposite this place we found a commodious ferry-boat, which wafted us and our horses across the Tamar. *Tamar R. Saltash.*

Saltash is situated on the declivity of a very steep hill, which (through the principal street) it is not easy to ascend on horseback. The quay commands a fine view of the river down to Plymouth-dock, and of Maker-heights; on the left may be seen the mouth of the Tavy, and the bleak heaths of Roborough. Though a borough, Saltash is but a poor town, and yet the corporation are enriched by the anchorage and soilage of foreign vessels, the privilege of dragging for oysters, the ferry, &c. which, we were informed, produce considerable profits. The situation is not inviting, nor is there any thing picturesque in the appearance of the surrounding lands, which produce corn and pasturage, separated by uniform straight hedges. Towards St. Germain's the country assumes a more bold and ornamented aspect; some spots on the road are highly beautiful.

St. Germain's is a miserable borough town, where nothing could have detained us except the church, which is a very venerable, ancient fabric, said to have been founded by Athelstan. It was dedicated to St. Germaine, who, (if I recollect right) was Bishop of Auxerre, in France. The whole of the west front still remains, but the two towers (one of which is octagonal and the other square) do not *St. Germans.*

*King Athelstan.*

appear to be part of the original design.    The porch is
Saxon.    We soon perceived that the body of the church
was of no remote date, though the arches are turned on the
ancient Saxon pillars, which are uncommonly bulky, and their
capitals singularly ornamented.    The old chancel fell in,
with a great crash, in the year 1592, just after divine service.
The windows are in many places stained with the arms of
the diocese, and of several of its bishops, whose see was
fixed here after its removal from Bodmin, and before the
dioceses of Devon and Cornwall were united at Crediton.
There are vaults also of several ancient families, such as
the Scawens, Glanvills, and Eliots, over which are suspended
the pompous decorations of banners, escutcheons, &c.

*Scawen.*
*Glanvill.*
*Eliot.*

There was formerly a burial ground round the church,
but Lord Eliot, a few years ago, took it into his lawn, and
of course removed every sepulchral memorial, which occasioned no small murmur and complaint among the helpless
inhabitants of the town.    The parish is said to be twenty
miles in circumference, and to contain no less than fifteen
villages.

Within a few yards of the church, on the spot where a
priory formerly stood, the seat of Lord Eliot is situated,
from whose family the place takes the name of Port-Eliot.
The church lands came into the possession of the Eliots in
the reign of Elizabeth, from whom the borough received its
privileges.    Magnificence was wholly avoided in the exterior
of the mansion, and perhaps its simplicity is more correspondent to the scenery by which it is surrounded, and which is
rather to be called pleasing than picturesque or grand.

Port Eliot.

Lynher creek approaches within a small distance of the
spot, and is joined by the river Tidy, navigable from Tidiford.

Lynher Creek.
Tiddy R.
Tideford.

There are not more than fifty or sixty houses in St.
Germain's, which, however, would exercise its privileges just
as well were the number still less.    It is the property of
Lord Eliot, whose two sons are the present representatives.

After a ride of twelve miles on a rough, hilly, and intricate
road, which led through several villages we arrived at Looe.
There are two places indeed of that name, and they are so
called from the two rivers East and West Looe, which
unite just before they empty themselves into the sea, and
separate these towns.    One stream takes its rise a little

East and
West Looe.

north-west from Liskeard, and the other in the parish of St. Pennock. We were much struck by a view of the river as we descended into East Looe, which communicates with West Looe by a bridge of fifteen arches, built after a very ancient fashion. There was something more bold and of a grander effect with respect to the nearer objects than in any scene that had yet occurred. The river washes the bases of the mountainous swells of ground on both sides, and West Looe is flanked by a prodigious eminence that at a distance appears inaccessible, and in fact is one of the steepest spots in the county. Both towns are boroughs, though inconsiderable places, and supported chiefly by the pilchard fishery, which is a branch of business not very likely to recommend them to visitors.

We did not halt at Looe, but proceeded immediately     Fowey.
towards Fowey, our road stretching over the lofty hill just mentioned, and affording us an unobstructed prospect of land and sea. At the foot of some rocky, rising ground, at a short distance from Fowey, we had the satisfaction of seeing *Sibthorpia Europæa*, growing in great profusion.

Fowey is situated on the western bank of the river Fawy,     Fowey R.
along which it extends nearly a mile, and there is a ferry from the village of Polruan, immediately opposite. Scarcely any     Polruan.
wood appears, but the height of the rocks, the boldness of the neighbouring hills, and the wildness of the distant landscape have a grand effect as you cross the water.

Long before we landed at Fowey, our olfactory nerves were assailed by the effluvia of salted pilchards, astonishing stores of which are laid up in the town, and form a very productive article of trade. The very fields are strewed with the refuse of fish and salt, which no doubt makes excellent manure, and may be obtained, we were informed, at so small a price as nine pence, or one shilling per bushel, each bushel consisting of eighteen gallons. Many vessels being employed in the fishery at the time of our arrival, curiosity induced us to hire a boat, and go out to sea to observe their operations. The waves drove with such strength through the mouth of the river, that no small exertion was required to reach the distant fisher-boats, which are generally stationed in ten fathoms water and clear of all breakers. The slowness of our voyage, however, allowed us to contemplate at our leisure the fine shores between which we passed. Two square stone forts, one on each side of the river, stand between the mouth of it and the opposite quays of Polruan and Fowey. These were *Edward IV.* built by Edward IV. but are now suffered to run to decay, St. St. Catharine's Catharine's fort and the adjoining battery being thought Fort. a sufficient defence. Our boatmen informed us there was once a chain or boom, that might be extended from one fort to the other in case of an invasion. We were much struck with that of St. Catharine, as we passed under it. It stands on the summit of a steep and magnificent pile of rocks that form one of the jaws of the river, and becomes in many points of view a very picturesque object. There are some large pieces of cannon on the platform, of which the gunner seemed to be not a little proud. This honest fellow, who was entirely deprived of one of his eyes, and apparently of half the other, engaged to demolish any ship that offensively approached the harbour. I can certainly bear testimony to the *vigilance* of our friend the gunner, notwithstanding his deficiency of eyesight, for he spied one of my companions employed in drawing a view of his formidable fortress, and requested him forthwith to solicit the permission of the mayor. St. Catharine's fort (with the chapel which, we were told, once adjoined to it) was built by the townsmen in the reign of Henry VIII.

We were not fortunate enough to see the manner of drawing up the nets, or seines, but they were spread out, and a number of light sail-boats were coasting at a distance in order to give notice to the fishermen if a shoal should approach. Sometimes people are stationed on the rocks to watch the course of the fish, and are called *huers*, from their setting up a *hue* to the fishermen. One of the seines we saw stretched was two hundred fathoms in circumference, and eighteen in depth. Some are said to contain upwards of two hundred hogsheads, each hogshead including generally three thousand fishes. About twenty-eight thousand hogsheads were supposed to have been caught this season about the coast of Fowey, and even that number is not reckoned extraordinarily great. Ten years ago, however, the fish were so scarce that the families of the fishermen lived solely on limpets, which at other times they could not be prevailed upon to eat. The time at which the pilchards make their appearance on the Cornish coast is about the middle of July; at the latter end of

September they depart to the arctic regions, like the herring. Thirty or forty years back Christmas was the time of their departure. This alteration of their period is a very curious fact. Fishermen are never hired at present for a longer time than three months, or even six weeks, whereas formerly they were employed almost half a year.

Having waited some time for the appearance of a shoal, without success, we returned towards the town, and were struck more than ever with the sublime and picturesque effect of the coast. On our landing we found a great number of people collected at the quay, to whom a party of unfortunate fishermen just returned were exhibiting their torn nets. It was calculated that the profit of full forty pounds was lost, owing to an accident in hauling them up; without great steadiness and caution they are very apt to break. These fishermen had secured, however, some fine doree, turbot, and whiting-pollack, which (particularly the latter) are plentiful on the Fowey coast.

We now visited the store-houses for pilchard, the quantity of which, in one house alone, amounted to 390,000 fishes. The reader may judge of what importance the pilchard fishery is to this county, especially when he is informed that the cash paid for pilchards exported from the different ports of Cornwall has amounted, at a medium estimate, to the sum of nearly £50,000 annually. This sum includes the bounty allowed on exportation (which is 8s. 6d. per hogshead), and the oil made out of each. In the store-houses as well as in every cask, a portion of salt is spread between every layer of fish, and in the latter the fish are pressed as closely together as possible, so that the whole when turned out is quite in a compact state. The floor or pavement on which they are laid up is on a gentle declivity, that the deliquescent fat and salt may drain off and be preserved.

Fowey may be called a colony of fishermen; it is a large town, and contains many respectable inhabitants, most of whom, however, are concerned in the general trade. The church is a large, lofty, and handsome fabric, much ornamented with mouldings on the outside, and carved work within. Close to the burial ground, there is an eminence to which a flight of steps lead, and where a venerable old mansion called Treffry House stands. It is partly modern, and

*Trefry.*

originally belonged to the Treffry family.  In the roof of the hall appears the date, 1575.  The old gate-way remains, as well as the castellated aspect of the whole building, and there is a public walk near it, overlooking the town and harbour.

Menabilly.
*Rashleigh.*

We proceeded to Menabilly, the seat of Philip Rashleigh, Esq., M.P. for Fowey.[1]  It is situated about four miles west from Fowey, at a short distance from the sea, of which the front windows command an extensive view.  Under these windows myrtles flourish the whole year, and  perfume  with fragrance  the adjoining apartments.  Near  the  shore  Mr. Rashleigh built (a few years ago) a beautiful grotto, which is celebrated throughout the county, and not without reason. It stands at the extremity of a large grove, and is constructed with  the finest species  of marble  and serpentine,  brilliant crystals, pebbles, shells, &c.  A table, placed in the middle of it, contains specimens of thirty four species of granite, all collected in Cornwall.  Here are also some links of the chain (encrusted with shells, coral, &c.) which once extended across the Fawy.  They were taken up in the year 1776 by some fishermen.

From Menabilly we made excursions to the Poth stream-works of tin, Polgooth-mine, and Roche rocks.

Poth
Tin-works.

The Poth stream-works are about four miles from Fowey, contiguous to the shore of Trewardreth bay.  These works are some of the most considerable of the kind in Cornwall, and the ore is of the purest sort.  Without any other manage-ment than being pounded and washed on the spot, it is said to have brought thirteen parts for twenty at the smelting-house. The pebbles from which the metal is extracted are found imbedded in a bluish marl, mixed with sand, and containing various marine *exuviæ*.  The depth of the principal stratum is about twenty feet, and its thickness about six or seven. Great part of it had been worked before iron tools were used, for large pickaxes made of oak, holm, and box have been found here.  The pebbles run from the size of sand to that of a small egg, and are for the most part rounded evidently by attrition against each other.

---

[1] M.P. for Fowey from 1765 to 1802; known latterly as the 'Father of the House of Commons.'  Became F.S.A. and F.R.S. in 1788, and had great knowledge of Cornish minerals, of which he made a valuable collection. *(Dict. Nat. Biography.)*

Polgooth, one of the richest and largest tin-mines in the county, if not in the world, is situated about two miles south-west from St. Austle.   There are no less than fifty shafts; twenty-six are still in use, with as many horizontal wheels, or whims.   The depth of the engine-shaft is about 110 fathoms, and this machine draws up, at each stroke, a column of water thirty feet in height and fifteen inches in diameter.   There is also an excellent overshot water-engine with a wheel thirty-six feet in diameter.   Polgooth is said to have yielded a clear profit of £1,500 per month.   Upwards of £17,000 were expended, however, before the mine yielded one shilling.

North of St. Blazey there are considerable ridges, on which innumerable rills take their rise.   The particles of gold which are frequently found here about and especially at Castle Park, near Lestwythiel, and to the north of Probus, are probably washed down from the same rocky eminences.   The largest piece ever found in Cornwall was that which belonged to Mr. Lemon, grandfather of Sir William Lemon; it weighed fifteen penny-weights sixteen grains.

Roche-rocks, a pile of rocks starting abruptly out of a wide green surface, and covering some space with enormous fragments on which there are only a few vestiges of incipient vegetation, form a singular scene, exhibiting a kind of wild sublimity peculiar to itself.   Some of them are full sixty feet in height, and on a projection in one part stands a small Gothic building to all appearances very ancient, and tradition reports that it was once the cell of a hermit.[1]   A regular flight of steps lead to it.   Leaving Menabilly, we proceeded through St. Austle and Grampound to Truro.

On the downs between St. Blazey and St. Austle we remarked several barrows; in some places there were three, and in others as many as five, in a line.   We saw but few of these turf monuments in this county.

St. Austle, which is a small place, has nothing to recommend it to attention but the church, which is a fine, old fabric.   There is a large blowing-house for tin at the western extremity of the town.

Grampound, though a borough, cannot boast of much more extent, or respectability of appearance, than St. Austle. The river Fal, which takes its rise near St. Roche, runs

*Polgooth.*

*Lemon.*

*Roche Rocks.*

*St. Austell.*

*Grampound.*

*Fal R.*

[1] See p. 199.

through the place.  East of the Fal, above Grampound, the Cornish china-stone (as it is called) is principally procured. At Truro this substance has been manufactured into retorts and corcibles of so excellent a quality as to stand the fire with uncommon success, and it contains so small a quantity of iron, that the porcelain made from it in Worcestershire and Staffordshire is very little discoloured.

**Probus.**  We were much pleased with the tower of Probus church, which is a fine object, but without any accompaniment of agreeable scenery, or advantage of position.  In fact this part of the county is altogether insipid and unornamented, hills and vales succeeding each other with a tedious sameness.

**Truro.**  Truro stands in a vale at the conflux of two rivers, Kenwyn and St. Allen, which with the tide from Falmouth harbour, form a fine body of water, sufficient to bring up ships of full 100 tons.  It is unquestionably the handsomest town in Cornwall, the streets being regular and commodious, and the houses of a very neat appearance.  As it is a sort of central place with respect to the mines, adventurers generally hold their meetings there, and the tinners bring most of their tin hither to be coined, as it is called.  There are four other coinage towns, which are Liskeard, Lestwythiel, Helston, and Penzance.  To one of these places every block of tin that is to be sold must be brought, in order to be assayed and licenced by the officers of the Duchy of Cornwall, who take off a piece of about a pound weight from the bottom of the block, and, if they find it sufficiently pure, stamp the former with the Duke's arms.  For every hundred weight of tin so stamped he receives four shillings.  A stranger will be very much struck, at his first entrance into Truro, to see the blocks that lie in heaps about the streets.  Every block is worth ten or twelve guineas, weighing sometimes 320 pounds—a load too great for a thief to carry off without discovery.  More tin and copper are exported hence than from any port in the county.  The wharf is very large and convenient.

About one mile and a half from Truro, on the road to Falmouth, there is a large smelting-house for tin.  It contains ten reverberatory furnaces, which employ about twenty men.  Culm-coal is used as the flux, in the proportion of about one eighth to the ore.  They smelt within six hours six hundred weight of the latter, which yield about three hundred and fifty of tin. The furnaces are six feet in height, about as many in length, and three, or more, in breadth.

In our way to Falmouth we stopped at the stream-works of Carnon, which are very rich and extensive, the proprietors gaining at least £3000 per annum. The number of men and boys employed here amount to at least 150. Gold in minute grains is continually found.

The town of Penryn is finely situated. It carries on some trade and has a good custom-house and quay. A collegiate church for thirteen prebendaries was built here by Walter Bronescombe, Bishop of Exeter. The parish church is at Gluvias, a quarter of a mile or more from the town.

Falmouth is unquestionably one of the noblest ports in the kingdom, and so commodious that ships of the greatest burthen may come close to the quay. The harbour is said to be as large as that of Brundusium, and perhaps the whole English navy might ride within it. Its numerous creeks afford secure shelter to ships in the most tempestuous weather. The town itself is large and more populous than any three boroughs in the county, but does not return representatives to parliament. Many very opulent merchants reside here, and are concerned in a most extensive trade. The packet-boats to the West Indies, Spain, Portugal, and other countries depart hence.

About a mile from Falmouth, at the extremity of a peninsula which forms the south-west boundary of the bay, stands Pendennis Castle, a fine and extensive fortress. The works are nearly a mile in circumference, and from their elevated and commanding situation have a noble appearance from the town. This castle protects the entrance of Falmouth-harbour; it is considered as very strong, and was rendered so principally in the reign of Elizabeth, though some parts of the fortifications are as old as the time of Henry VIII.

On the opposite side of Falmouth harbour stands the Castle of St. Mawe's, which is far inferior in every respect to Pendennis. The adjoining village (I cannot call it a *town*) has sent members to parliament ever since the year 1562, though the inhabitants at present are merely a few fishermen, and the place itself is without church, chapel, or meeting-house.

*[marginal notes:]*

Carnon.

Penryn.

*Bronescombe.*
St. Gluvias.
Falmouth.

Pendennis Cas.

St. Mawes.

Gweek.
Helford R.
Mullion.

We were obliged to make a long circuit in order to get to the Lizard-point, by passing through Gweek, a village near the head of the Helford river, and thence to Mullion, which is the only place where any kind of accommodation can be obtained.

Mullion is a small village a little to the right of the road leading to the Lizard. The church tower may be seen, rising above some bleak hills, at a great distance, and we imagined that it must belong to something better than a group of wretched cottages.

We had proceeded about a mile from the village when we first saw *Erica vagans*, the most rare and beautiful of our English heaths. It grew in amazing profusion—indeed almost to the exclusion of every other plant. It is very singular that this beautiful plant should not have been discovered in any other part of England, and that it should grow in such wonderful profusion here. We lost it on a sudden, not a single straggling specimens being observed by us beyond a particular line, which was formed as nearly as we could guess, by the termination of the magnesian soil.

Kynance Cove.

Kynance cove is situated about a mile north-west from the Lizard-point, and is perhaps one of the most extraordinary spots on our coast. The descent to it is extremely steep, and overhung by large crags called in Cornwall *karns*. As to the cove itself, it is formed by huge black rocks, of an immense height, partly projecting into the sea, and so singularly disposed in one place as to open a fine natural arch into a sort of grotto. The rocks of Kynance cove are composed entirely of serpentine, varying much in colour internally, though the surface exhibits one uniform shade, being covered with a most beautiful sort of enamel, which seems to be chlorite. In colour is dark green, and there is a greasiness to the touch, which, with its other properties, render it the link, as it were, between talc and the more coarse, hard species of the mag. nesian class. The serpentine is a very beautiful stone, and would be very ornamental for chimney-pieces, slabs, &c., being scarcely distinguishable in appearance from marble.

The violence of the sea on this shore is so unfavourable to vegetation that not a single plant, of any kind, appears within a considerable distance. As we approached the top of the hill, however, above the cove, we saw *Geranium sanguineum* spreading itself in broad tufts.

Notwithstanding the persecution of the elements we continued our route to the Lizard-point, receiving this species of consolation from our guides—that there was no chance of better weather at any other time. They assured us that it rains at least seven months out of the twelve, and that a south-west wind almost always blows, in this part of the country. Wrecks happen near the Lizard continually. Foreign pilots, unacquainted with its perils seldom keep the necessary distance from it, and (what is the most melancholy circumstance) no kind of assistance can be afforded from the land. The cape is so steep and fenced with rocks, that no boat can come near and the wretched sufferers often perish in the sight of numerous spectators not more than a stone's throw distant! There are two lighthouses at the extremity of this Cornish *Chersonesus*, which is the southermost point of the whole coast of England.

Helston is situated on the banks of the Lo. It is a populous, decent town, and a borough, and its trade has long been good. Several tin-ships take their lading at the port, which is commodious and provided with a tolerable quay. There are four principal streets, intersecting each other at right angles. At Penrose, not far from Helston, are some lead-mines.

About four miles from Marazion, and half an one from the high road, towards the coast, stands Pengerswick Castle, of which a square stone tower, of three stories, with a smaller one annexed, and some fragments of walls are the only remains. The door, on the north, is machicolated. The different apartments are now used as granaries and hay-lofts, but the wainscoat, which is of oak, remains perfect. This wainscot is very curiously carved and painted, and there are several quaint pieces of poetry inscribed on the panels.[1] A winding stone stair-case leads to the top of the principal tower, which commands a good view of the surrounding country.

Our change of latitude began to be very sensible, or at least we imagined so, for we experienced a peculiar softness and salubrity in the air during our progress from Falmouth to the Land's-end.

Marazion, or Market-jeu (as it is sometimes called) is situated partly on a declivity, and partly on a flat beach that

Lizard Point.

Helston.
Cober R.
(Looe Pool.)

Penrose.

Pengersick
Cas.

Marazion.

[1] See H. R. Coulthard, *Story of an Ancient Parish, Breage with Germoe*, 127.

extends to Penzance.   It is sheltered by considerable elevation
of ground to the north.   We found an inn most conveniently
placed for a prospect of the Mount, which was only a quarter
of a mile distant, and exactly opposite us.   Never was there
a more beautiful spectacle!—the sea at this time surrounded
the broad craggy base of the Mount, the latter gradually
diminishing in size towards the top, and most admirably
terminated by the tower of a chapel, so as to form a complete
pyramid.   On the side opposite Marazion there are a few
houses, which, with the vessels at the pier, served to improve
the view.   From half ebb to half flood people may walk across
from the town on a fine pebbly path, so that St. Michael's
Mount is not always an island.   The rock of which it is
composed is entirely naked, and extremely steep and craggy.
The height from low-water mark to the top of the chapel-
tower is about 240 feet.   In circumference, at the base, the
mount measures about three quarters of a mile.   It consists
of a hard granite, in which transparent quartz is the prepon-
derating substance.

Before the invention of gunpowder St. Michael's Mount
must have been impregnable, and it is strange that on this
account it did not become a place of much greater importance
as a fortress.   Some of the old works remain, but in a ruinous
state, and the buildings have much more a monastic than a
martial appearance.   Indeed this rock was consecrated to
superstition many years ago, and its name in all probability
originated from a supposed appearance of the angel St.
Michael on it.

It belongs at present to Sir John St. Aubyn, Bart. who
resides on it some months every year, and has rendered the old
mansion extremly comfortable and commodious.   The old
taste is, in a great measure, retained, and very properly.   A
number of curious figures, escutcheons, emblems, and ciphers
occur in the different compartments.   The chapel does not
appear so ancient in the inside as without, but the stile is
by no means of a late period.   It is of the Gothic order,
and very spacious and lofty.   A narrow stone stair-case in one
of the angles leads to the top of the tower.   The prospect
hence is of so grand a kind as to defy description, and is
perhaps as striking as any that can occur to "mortal eye,"
at the same height.

*St. Michael's
Mount.*

*Sir John
St. Aubyn.*

In front of the house a strong battery has been erected, which commands the western part of the bay; the eastern is too shallow for the entrance of large vessels. As the monks enjoyed certain profits from the fisheries, they made a lantern for the guidance of the fishermen on one side of the tower, which is now vulgarly called St. Michael's Chair.

We were impatient to see the Wherry Mine, situated in the bay, about half a mile beyond Penzance. The opening of this mine was an astonishly adventurous undertaking. I have never heard of one similar to it in any other part of the world. Imagine the descent into a mine through the sea; the miners working at the depth of seventeen fathoms only below the waves; the rod of a steam-engine extending from the shore to the shaft,—a distance of nearly one hundred and twenty fathoms; and a great number of men momentarily menaced with an inundation of the sea, which continually drains in no small quantity through the roof of the mine, and roars loud enough to be distinctly heard in it! the descent is by means of a rope tied round the thighs, and you are let down in a manner exactly the same as a bucket is into a well; a well indeed it is, for the water is more than knee-deep in many parts of the mine. The upper part of the shaft resembles an immense iron chimney, elevated about twelve feet above the level of the sea, and a narrow platform leads to it from the beach: close to this is the engine-shaft, through which the water is brought up from below. Tin is the principal produce of the Wherry-mine; it is found dispersed (in small, indurated, glass-like lumps, of a blackish colour) in a substance resembling the elvan of Polgooth, but much more compact in texture, and of the nature of a porphyry. The ore is extremely rich.

*Wherry Mine.*

Penzance is a large and populous town, surrounded by a well cultivated and beautiful tract of country. Notwithstanding its exposure to the sea, the corn, and particularly wheat, seemed to be in a remarkably thriving state. The trade of this place consists chiefly in the exportation of pilchards and tin. There is a fine pier, along the eastern side of which vessels are very commodiously and safely anchored. The mildness of the air, the agreeableness of the situation, and the respectability of its inhabitants render Penzance particularly inviting to residence; and, with regard

*Penzance.*

to invalids, it may justly be considered as the Montpelier
of England. It stands partly on a declivity, open to the
sea, the Mount being a striking object as you look towards
the opposite coast, and a delightful landscape extends around
the whole of the bay.

Providing ourselves with a guide, we now started for
the Land's end.

We had the mortification to find the circle of stones
to which our guide conducted us very inferior in extent and
grandeur to what we had been taught to expect. The
appellation given to these stones by the vulgar is the Merry
Maidens, on account of a whimsical tradition that they were
no other than a circle of young women transformed into stone
for dancing on a sabbath day. There are two stones (one
about sixteen feet in height, the other about twenty), in a field
on the opposite side of the road; they seem to appertain
to the circle, the proper name of which I guess, from Borlase's
account to be Bolleit. In the course of our journey, some
time after having visited this part of the country, we were
informed that the stones which we ought to have seen were
at Boscawen-ûn, between St. Buryen's and Sancreed.

The country about St. Buryen's is extremly insipid and
uninteresting. We saw some pretty good fields of corn, but
the soil in general is far from being fruitful. The church-
tower of the village is a conspicuous object to a very great
distance, being situated on high ground, and the place is on
this account much exposed to tempestuous winds from the
ocean. Though now only a group of cottages, St. Buryen's
was once a town of great note and the seat of a college
of prebendaries. In the church are many curious relics of
antiquity, and it is a spacious building. We noticed a singular
monument, in the shape of a coffin, to the memory of Clarice,
wife of Geoffrey de Bolleit, who in Henry III.'s time enjoyed
a manor in this parish. The doors of the pews, and even
the seats themselves, have a good deal of rude ornament
about them, and are probably coeval with the foundation of
the church. Opposite the great door (in the church-yard)
stands a very ancient cross, on one side of which are five
balls, and on the other is a rude figure representing our
Saviour. Another cross, somewhat similar, faces the entrance
into the church-yard. The remains of the college are said

Merry
Maidens.

Nine Maidens.
St. Buryan.

*Bolleit.*

to have been wantonly demolished in Cromwell's time by one
Shrubshall, Governor of Pendennis Castle.

    After crossing some rocks, which we at first conceived to
be the final barriers to our progress westward, we came to
the grand promontory that projects into the Atlantic farther
than any other part of the Cornish coast.   This is the
Land's-end—a very striking spot both on account of the
vastness of the objects it presents, and the convulsed features
of the surrounding country.   There is a cavern underneath,
and here the waves of the ocean burst and bellow with a
tremendous fury.   The huge detached piles of rocks lying
just off the land must have once adjoined to it, and we may
imagine the latter to have been once connected with the distant
isles of Scilly.   These isles, though nine leagues from us,
were visible to the south-west, appearing like a cluster of
cliffs, round which the Atlantic rolled in a mighty horizontal
wave.   Just off the Land's-end, on a large rock called the
Armed Knight, stands a light-house, the windows of which,
though almost one hundred feet in height, have often been
broken by spray in a tempest!

    The sea between Cornwall and the Scilly Islands is said
to be of an equal depth the whole way;  yet there are many
rocks like those near the Land's-end, which are well known
to fishermen, and which seem to be memorials of the
abridgement of the main land.   The rocks at the Land's-end,
and in most parts of this district of Cornwall, consist of a
very close species of granite, that takes a good polish and is
applied to a variety of useful purposes.   It is that to which
the Cornish name of moorstone seems more immediately
applicable, forming not only the basis, as it were, of that
part of the county west of Penzance and St. Ives, but of a
chain of mountains that may be traced, in a direction
nearly east by north, to Dartmoor.

    We had now completed our survey of the southern coast.
Our attention was hereafter to be turned to the mining
country, in the vicinity of the northern shore, so that St. Ives,
Camborne, Redruth, and St. Agnes seemed to mark out the
line of our route.

    At the extremity of a high ridge, overlooking the surfy
recess of White-sand Bay, stand the lonely ruins of the
Chapel Karn-breh.   They scarcely form the skeleton of the

*Shrubshall.*

Land's End.

Scilly Is.

Armed
Knight.

Whitesand
Bay.
Carn Brea.

original building, which appears to have been a chantry, erected for the same purpose as several others on our coast— the performance of religious service for the safety of mariners.

St. Just.

Leaving the chapel on the left, we came to St. Just, a sad, dismal place, situated in a most inhospitable and cheerless corner of the county.

With a rugged, barren ridge of moorstone hills on the right, and the sea at no great distance on the left, the road to St. Ives passes near numerous pits and deserted shafts of mines, which render a journey over this part of the county by night extremely dangerous. The moorstone lies dispersed in detached blocks, many of them huge enough for another Stonehenge. Scarcely a shrub appears to diversify the prospect, and the only living beings that inhabit the mountainous parts are the goats which browze their scanty herbage.

Chun Cas.

We went about two miles out of the high road, to the right, to view Castle Chun, and a large cromlech near it called the Giant's-coit. The former is a specimen of rude military architecture, and must be ascribed to a very early period. It occupied a considerable space, but, though the plan may soon be traced, it appears at first to consist of unmeaning heaps of stones. There seem to have been two regular *ballia*, or wards, and the ramparts are of a circular form, corresponding in some degree to the nature of the eminence on which they are situated. The Giant's Coit consists of four stones, the upper one (which is very ponderous) resting on the other three. These last are not placed erect, but inclined considerably.

Giant's Coit.

St. Ives.

In the midst of mines, and open to a very fine bay bounded by bold rocks of black killas, stands the town of St. Ives, a populous sea-port and borough. The harbour, however, is in many places choked up with sand, brought by north-west winds; the other ports on this coast suffer the same inconvenience. Pilchards and slate are the principal articles of exportation, the former being in most seasons very plentiful in the bay. At the time of large draughts it is usual for all the inhabitants to contribute their assistance;—shops are deserted, and, if it should be Sunday, even the churches. The stench arising from the stores, and from the putrid *rejectamenta* lying about the town, is to strangers almost intolerable.

The day after our arrival at St. Ives, we set out to visit the large smelting-houses at Hale, and the neighbouring copper-mills. Hale is situated on the eastern side of the river of the same name, which rises near Crowan, and falls into St. Ives bay about three miles from that town. This river is navigable below St. Erth, spreading an area of sand nearly half a mile wide at a medium, and more than two miles long. Near the church of Phillack, there is a branch of the haven which admits ships of some burthen at the height of a spring tide, but the bed of it has been so much raised by the sand from the sea that the tide enters only six hours in the twelve. Not far from Lelant the Hale is fordable, at particular hours of the day. I ought to mention however, that, as some of the sands are quick, it is not prudent to cross without the assistance of a guide. A great trade is carried on at Hale, especially in iron and Welch coal for the steam-engines and smelting-houses, Bristol wares, and limestone from Glamorganshire. The coal is conveyed to its places of destination on horses' backs. A prodigious number of these animals therefore travel together in this part of the county, which from its rocky and mountainous nature is not easy to be traversed by carts or waggons. In some parts of Devonshire, indeed, these species of conveyance are as frequent, and troops of horses are seen carrying wood, fuel, &c. from one place to another. Some of them appear like moving coppices at a distance, being so covered with boughs and branches of trees that they are scarcely able to see their way. In narrow lanes we were often incommoded by these unceremonious travellers.

The smelting-houses of Hale are chiefly for the copper brought from the Camborne and Gwennap mines. Nothing can be more shocking than the appearance which the work-men exhibit. So dreadfully deleterious are the fumes of arsenic constantly impregnating the air of these places, and so profuse in the perspiration occasioned by the heat of the furnaces, that those who have been employed at them but a few months become most emaciated figures, and in the course of a few years are generally laid in their graves.

About three miles from Hale, higher up the river, are the copper-mills, or pounding-houses as they are more frequently called. Blocks, or bars, of copper are here reduced into flat

Hayle.

Hayle R.
Crowan.

St. Erth.

Phillack.

Lelant.

sheets of any thickness, by being heated by the reverberation of flame in a furnace constructed for the purpose, and then immediately applied between large iron rollers turned by a water wheel.

The country around Hale is entirely covered with sand, which is blown about by every blast, and renders its appearance truly dismal. Between Hale and Redruth there is a regular line of copper-mines, which seem to be the richest in Cornwall. Huel-Gons, near Camborne, is perhaps one of the *deepest* in the county, being 140 fathoms below the surface of the ground. At a short distance eastward lies Dolcooth, which besides copper has yielded cobalt to the amount of several tons. The depth of the engine-shaft is 174 fathoms.

We now come to the famous copper-mine called Cook's kitchen, which employs an amazing number of hands, and yields an immense profit. From 300 to 350 tons of ore have been raised here in a month, and within the last ten years this mine has yielded a profit of £100,000, exclusive of the lord's portion and all other expenses whatever. No less than 340 persons are employed; and, in short, the attendance and apparatus at Cook's-kitchen render it perhaps one of the most remarkable mines in the world.

Tincroft is the last, or easternmost mine of this range, and the principal lode is probably only a continuation of one of those in Cook's-kitchen. The steam-engine we found to be on Hornblower's principle.

A little south-west from Redruth the ridge abruptly terminates, and just at the extremity of it, surrounded by rock-basins, altars, cromlechs, and other druidical relics, stands Castle Karn-breh. The foundation of this building is laid on a rude heap of rocks, which not being all contiguous, arches are turned over the cavities. One part of it is supposed to have been British work; the other is certainly modern, and, from the style, must have been added to the former merely as a sort of prospect-house. The ancient part is pierced with loop-holes, but the other has Gothic windows. A flight of steps lead to the door, which is not in the old wall, nor is it easy to discover how far the latter extended. There were formerly some outworks to the north-west. This building appears to have consisted originally of three stories, but the lowermost only is kept

*Camborne.*

*Dolcoath.*

*Cook's Kitchen.*

*Tincroft.*

*Carn Brea Cas.*

in repair. It commands a vast horizon, and the prospect has at the same time a very peculiar complexion. The bold and stupendous monuments which lie scattered on all sides; the silence and desolation of the spot; and, above all, the awful vestiges of convulsion which the hills exhibit, awaken sublime ideas in a spectator. From the numerous coins, celts, &c. of remote antiquity, that have been found here, one may conjecture that it was of great note with the early inhabitants of our island.

The town of Redruth is situated in the very heart of the mining country, and of course occupies a bleak, exposed spot. We found nothing interesting to us here, except an extensive collection of minerals. Redruth.

The Gwennap mines are to the south-east of Redruth, and to the right of the high-road to Truro. The principal are Huel-Virgin, Caharrack, and Poldice. The North-Down mines (nine in number) occupy an extent of ground about two miles in length and one mile in width, lying to the left of the high road to Truro. St. Agnes is situated on the north coast, surrounded by several rich tin-mines. It cannot be considered as a port, for, though a quay has been more than once erected for the accommodation of vessels, the violence of the sea has always soon demolished it; and the harbour is choked up with sand. On the left is a remarkable eminence called St. Agnes' beacon, 500 feet above the level of the water. Gwennap. St. Agnes. St. Agnes Beacon.

The only silver-mine in this county is Huel-Mexico, situated to the left of the road leading from St. Agnes to St. Michael, and not far from the sea, the sand of which covers all the adjacent country. It is about ten years since the mine was first worked, and the depth is now nearly twenty-four fathoms. I found it very dangerous to descend, on account of the ladders continuing quite straight to the bottom, and there being no resting place except a niche cut on one side in the earth. Should one unfortunately miss one's hold of the ladder in this shaft, there is nothing to prevent a fall to the very floor of the mine.

We passed over a dismal country to St. Michael, or (as it is vulgarly called) Mitchell. Though a borough, this is a sad, mean place, and did not offer any thing worthy of notice. It cannot boast even of a church. Mitchell.

St. Columb
Major.

St. Columb (which is also a borough) has the advantage of a decent, paved street, and is a church-town, but not more likely to detain a traveller than St. Michael. There are some stream-works in the neighbourhood, which produce the wood-tin. The soil seems encouraging to cultivation in some spots, but towards St. Roche a wild, extensive heath spreads itself, and the road to Bodmin presents a barren scene until it approaches pretty near to that place, when it becomes bordered (and not sparingly) with wood.

Bodmin.

Bodmin is screened on all sides by rising ground, and was invisible to us until we were almost in the streets. It must have been formerly a very flourishing, extensive place, and was famous for its manufactories. Indeed it is still a large town, and has one fine, wide street, inferior to none in the county. A manufactory of yarn too continues, but is said to be much on the decline. The assizes are holden here once in the year, and the county-gaol, built very lately, stands in a healthy spot just without the town. This building is laid out nearly on the plan recommended by

*Howard.*

Mr. Howard, and struck us as a model for all places of confinement. A little to the east we observed some ruinous walls, which are said to be the remains of a hospital for lepers, dedicated to St. Lazarus. The church of Bodmin is very spacious, and a venerable old pile. Before the see was removed to St. Germain's this was the Cathedral of the diocese, and it belonged, as the conventual church, to the adjoining monastery of St. Petroc. Its spire was blown down by a violent hurricane in the year 1699. The monastery belonged to the Benedictines, but being plundered by the Danes in 981, and the Monks dispersed, its revenues were enjoyed principally by the Earl of Morton and Cornwall, and afterwards devolved to the crown. A little before the dissolution, however, we find that a prior and canons possessed the monastery. In the church-yard there appear to be some remains of the priory.

From Bodmin we returned to the northern coast, passing through Wadebridge and Camelford. Between Bodmin and

Wadebridge.

Wadebridge the country is somewhat varied, and there is a vale pleasingly wooded, and (what is not very common in Cornwall) interspersed with orchards; but as we approach

Camelford.

Camelford, the prospect ceases to be in the least interesting, except on account of its wildness, and perhaps is more insipid than in any part we had visited. There are quarries, called Denyball slate-quarries, to the left of the Camelford road that produce an excellent slate for roofs, equal perhaps to any in the kingdom. Its colour is a greyish blue. The rough masses are raised from their beds by wedges, driven by bars of iron, and are split by means of a strong, broad chisel, and a mallet. *Delabole.*

Wadebridge and Camelford are both inconsiderable places, and with regard to the situation of the latter, none can possibly be more dismal. The river Camel makes a long circuit before it arrives at Wadebridge, (where it is crossed by a fine bridge of seventeen arches), and empties itself into Padstow-harbour. This harbour is so much obstructed by sand that navigation is difficult, except in its very channel, where the water is deep enough to support ships of great burthen. Camelford is a place of great antiquity and a borough, but we found nothing within its precincts that deserved attention. *Camel R.*

Between Padstow-harbour and Camelford, antimony mines have been worked with some success.

One of our objects in returning to the northern coast was a view of the remains of a remarkable fortress called King Arthur's Castle at Tintagel. Enough of the works remain to show that Tintagel Castle was very strong and spacious, though I doubt whether much of what is now standing is of so early a date as the British times. The situation is a bold slaty promontory, part of it almost separated from the main land by an immense chasm, and, unless this chasm has been formed since the dilapidation of the Castle, accessible only by means of a drawbridge. It is evident that the rocks have been rent in *one* place, at least, subsequently to the erection of the walls, for a long fissure can be traced through both them and their foundation. What remains on the peninsular part is a circular, garretted wall, inclosing some traces of buildings : here was probably the keep. Underneath, is a cavern, or subterraneous passage, through which boats could once sail from one side of the rocks to the other at full tide, but, some masses having fallen down from above, it is now in some measure blocked up. The walls on the other side of the chasm *Tintagel.*

inclose two narrow courts, and at the highest part of the fortress there are several steps leading to the parapet. The whole is constructed with slate, which is pierced with holes for discharging arrows, &c. On the side towards the sea the precipice is truly terrific; the whole circumference, indeed, has great advantages from nature.

Whilst we were contemplating this remarkable spot, our guide pointed out to us some choughs flying beneath us. These were the first we had seen, in a wild state, in Cornwall, though the bird is so common on its coasts that it is generally known by the name of the Cornish daw. The natives are so much attached to them that it is very common to see tame ones in their gardens. The chough may be immediately distinguished from the common crow by its red legs and bill; besides, the colour is a sort of violaceous black. Ruined towers by the sea side, and sequestered, craggy rocks being its favourite haunts, about Tintagel there are considerable numbers.

Trevena.
Bossiney.

A little to the east of King Arthur's Castle stands the borough of Tintagel, known also by the name of Trevena and Bossiney—a most miserable, shabby group of cottages, without even a public-house. The country around it is bleak and rugged, and the whole formed such a dismal picture of desolation that we began to imagine ourselves removed by enchantment out of the region of civilization. There are about twenty houses within the borough, but the number of voters is seldom so great. At this time there are five or six only. Their qualifications consist in living in the parish, and having land in the borough.

Boscastle.

From Tintagel we proceeded over a rocky road to Boscastle, a village not far from the former, and in a highly romantic situation. The cottages are all in a deep valley washed by a small inlet of the sea, whilst fine mountainous eminences crowd round them on all sides, cut by craggy gaps, and clad with brushwood. This place was once

Bottreaux.

famous for a castle, built by one of the Botereaux family, but there are no fragments remaining.

Launceston.

At the distance of five or six miles from Boscastle we had the same insipid scenery that appears about Camelford, and it continued until we came near Launceston, the castle of which was a forlorn, indistinct object on our left a long way. A screen of mountain-ash, elm, and oak on each side of the road forms an avenue to the town and a most agreeable contrast to the country we leave behind. To ride under the shade of a hedge-row was a real luxury to us.

Launceston is situated on the borders of a pleasing and cultivated country, partly on an eminence, and partly on a sharp declivity to the north. In entering the town, we passed under the mouldering walls of its ancient castle, which even now retains a threatening aspect, and must have been once a very strong and important fortress. The keep stands on an elevated knoll that appears to be partly artificial and is said to have extended originally farther into the town. The principal entrance is to the north-east, where stood the great gate, which is in an imperfect state, but some walls still adjoin to it. After crossing a considerable area we mount a flight of steps, rising very quick, to the keep. The latter is surrounded by a circular wall, intended probably for a sort of covered way; about six feet within it there is a second wall, twelve feet in thickness, through which a staircase leads to the top. The whole diameter of the keep is 93 feet, and the height of the parapet above the base-court 104 feet.

Including the borough of Newport, which joins close to Launceston, this is a very populous and extensive place. The church belonging to the former was once a conventual one, dedicated to St. Stephen; hence the parish has sometimes the same appellation. A prior and canons, of the order of St. Augustine, placed here by Warlewast, Bishop of Exeter, inhabited at first a spot near the castle, but were afterwards removed to the other side of the river Kensey, which runs under the hill. The church of St. Thomas occupies a pleasant, rural situation near the foot of the latter. In the heart of the town stands that of St. Mary Magdalen, a handsome fabric, in a rich style of the Gothic order, but much obscured by other buildings. There are two fine Gothic gates still standing. At the entrance to the White-hart inn we observed a noble Saxon arch; so that it is not improbable that on the site of it stood the monastery mentioned above. Launceston has altogether a very respectable appearance. The assizes are holden here

*Newport.*

*Wm. Warlewast.*

*Kensey R.*

alternately with Bodmin, and it is considered as the chief town in the county.

Our nearest way to Plymouth lay through Callington and Saltash. The face of the country becomes now both varied and fertile, and formed a pleasing preparation to our return into the delightful county of Devon. We frequently discovered the Tamar gliding through a succession of cultivated lands and enclosures. Sometimes an immense landscape opened to our view. On the left a range of mountains, the harshness of their outline mellowed by distance, seemed to advance in a north-east direction. Near these are the huge monuments called the Hurlers, and also the Cheese-rings, as they are vulgarly named. The Cheese-rings were probably constructed by nature herself, in one of her whimsical moments. The Hurlers are three singular and large circles of stone which intersect each other, the centres being in a right line; the name is derived from a ridiculous tradition that they were once people amusing themselves at hurling, a favourite sport with the Cornishmen.

Before we came to Callington we perceived some mines on the right. St. Kitt's hill (on the left) consists entirely of granite, and, at the very top, a shaft has been sunk for digging tin. The prospect from the summit embraces a vast tract of country, and brings both banks of the Tamar under the same natural district, by showing a perfect similarity in their agricultural, as well as their geological aspect.

Callington has nothing to boast of but its church, a spacious, towering fabric. Though a shabby place, it may justly claim a superiority in rank to many other of the Cornish boroughs. Its manufactory of cloth is as brisk as any carried on in the county, but this is a branch of business which seems to be migrating very fast from the more western part of the kingdom.

As we came nearer to the Tamar, our views gradually improved, and the vicinity of Pentilly Castle, which stands on·its edge, is highly beautiful and luxuriant. This is a modern building, and has the appellation of a castle, I imagine, only from its embattled form.

The day after our arrival at Saltash, we went up the Tavey to visit the lead mines of Bere-Alston. There is a

Cheesewring.

Hurlers.

Kit Hill.

Callington.

Pentillie Cas.

Bere Alston.

profusion of wood in the vicinity of the mines, and the space comprehended between the Tamar and the Tavey towards their confluence presented a great number of very lovely landscapes. Bere-Alston, though a borough, is quite a mean village, and we were informed that not a single voter resides in it.

The town of Plymouth is large, but an ill-built, disagreeable place, infested with all the filthiness so frequent in sea-ports. It carries on a very extensive trade, and there is a great exportation of pilchards to Italy and other catholic countries. The fishery does not extend farther eastward than this harbour. The new quay lies on the west side of Suttonpool, where vessels are pretty safe, when those in the Sound, and even in Catwater, run great risks from the high sea which a south wind generally brings. Wrecks often happen under Mount Batten, and other eminences near the town. A citadel, built on a noble scale, protects the Sound; yet the entrance of the latter does not seem sufficiently guarded, and (if the security of Plymouth be of importance to the kingdom) it is not easy to account for the plan proposed some years ago by the Duke of Richmond being rejected. Without some stronger works, his Grace thought the place very far from being impregnable. Hamoaze (the mouth of the Tamar) is commanded by the works on St. Nicholas's isle,—a spot about two acres in extent, on the north-west side of the Sound. The citadel has five regular bastions, a large storehouse, and many fine pieces of cannon, and was erected in the reign of Charles II. At a little distance west from the town are the marine barracks, which occupy a considerable extent of ground, and have more the appearance of a college, than of a building for the accommodation of soldiers.

Two miles from Plymouth, on the eastern side of the Tamar, stands the town of Plymouth-Dock, almost united to the former by the village of Stonehouse and the numerous houses that extend along the road. From the bustle and continual passing of people we could fancy ourselves in the outskirts of London. The Royal hospital is situated on the right, enjoying a fine, elevated spot that seems peculiarly favourable to a supply of wholesome air. On the left appears the governor of Plymouth's house, overlooking the Sound, Hamoaze, and Stonehouse-pool from a rocky eminence which

*Marginal notes:*

Plymouth.

Sutton Pool.

Catwater.

Mount Batten.

*Duke of Richmond.*

Hamoaze.
Drake's Is.

Citadel.

Devonport.
Stonehouse.

borders the latter, and which is fortified with some regular works for the defence of the dock-yards.

The levelling of so large a space of ground as the dock-yards occupy must have been attended with prodigious labour, particularly the gun-wharf, which was hewn out of some schistose rocks to the depth of thirty feet, or more. The docks and basins are constructed on a spacious and magnificent scale, and the different offices and work-shops are extremely commodious and complete. The wet dock is formed to contain five first-rates at a time, and there is a basin 200 feet square. The rope-house is longer by twenty fathoms than that of Portsmouth, the whole length of it being 400 fathoms. Those who have never seen similar scenes cannot form any conception of the activity and variety of employments exhibited here, nor is any spectacle better calculated to enable one to make a proper estimate of human ingenuity, than the gradual growth of a few rude pieces of timber into the majestic, wonderful structure that encounters the winds and waves.

**Tavistock.**

We migrated a little from the high road to Tavistock, to enjoy the beautiful scenery of Plym Wood. Tavistock still preserves many fine remains of its abbey, which must once have been no less splendid in its construction than spacious in extent. Its revenues were princely, and its abbots were lords of parliament and mitred. There were thirty-six stalls in the old conventual church, no part of which is standing, but there are several buildings that seem to have belonged to the abbey; they are now used for warehouses and other purposes. Adjoining to the principal inn is a large handsome Gothic gate, adorned with lofty pinnacles, as are also the contiguous remains.

The town of Tavistock is populous and very charmingly situated, but the streets are narrow and the buildings mean. Its supply of every species of provision is abundant, particularly in the article of fish; this results from its proximity to Plymouth. The church has a venerable air, and contains several monuments deserving of notice.

**Okehampton.**

From Tavistock we proceeded to Okehampton. To the right of the road, within the precincts of Dartmoor, some mines drew our attention, and farther on to the left there is a very remarkable water-fall, which also led us from the high road.

We came first to a copper-mine, called Huel-Friendship, situated in a valley about five miles from Tavistock. About a mile east-ward from the copper mine, we saw two tin mines, Huel-Jewel, and Huel-Unity.

The Devonshire tinners became a separate body from those of Cornwall in the time of Edward I. Before this prince's reign the tinners of both counties enjoyed one common corporate capacity, and held a common parliament on Hengstone-hill, but the Devonshire tinners have since assembled on Crockern-torr. Their laws, with regard to mining, seem to have never been so well defined, or so equitable, as those which respect the Cornishmen, but both being included within the Duchy of Cornwall, are under the same general constitution. One general warden, called the Lord Warden of the Stannaries, either by himself or his deputy, has the supreme decision in matters both of law and equity, relative to the tin mines of the duchy. A court is generally holden once a month by the sub-warden, who receives appeals from inferior courts, wherein other officers preside, but a jury is impanelled on all occasions. No laws are valid unless regularly passed in a stannary parliament, to which every stannary town sends six representatives, who in Cornwall are styled Stannators, in Devonshire Jurats. Every act must be signed by these representatives, the Lord Warden, or his deputy, and lastly by the Duke himself (in his privy council) or the sovereign, and has then all the authority, with regard to tin affairs, of an act of the supreme legislature of England. There are only four stannary towns in Devonshire, viz. Plympton, Tavistock, Ashburton, and Chagford.

I have never seen a more dreary tract than that over which we passed from the tin mines towards Lidford. The soil is exceedingly swampy and moist, and covered with bog-moss (*Sphagnum palustre*), through which our horses' legs penetrated knee-deep at every step. If we had not been accompanied by the captain of the mines, who seemed to be well acquainted with the country, we should have been in unceasing apprehension of sinking deeper than our heads. Though it may naturally be imagined that so wet,

Hingston
Down.
Crockern Tor.

exposed, and uncomfortable a district must be unhealthy, we were informed that the inhabitants live to an extraordinary age. They reckon themselves middle-aged only when arrived at sixty, and "it is no very uncommon thing (said our guide) to hear the death of a man of seventy years of age spoken of as if premature!" The principal cause, I believe, of this longevity is the absence of temptations to intemperance.

Lydford.

Lidford is a place of some antiquity, and was once a borough. There is a castle, which has been used as a prison for offenders against the stannary laws. It is a square building of an unmeaning appearance, being without strength or ornament. The burgesses were excused from sending representatives to parliament *propter paupertatem*—a plea which the present appearance of it seems to have fairly justified them in making, for it is dwindled into a small, shabby village.

Okehampton.

As we approached Okehampton, a fine valley opened to the south, and the ruins of the castle appeared on a lofty knoll in the midst of a rich mass of wood, which covers also the eminences around it. The church stands to the left of the road, and there is a gradual descent of almost a mile from it down into the town.

Okement R.

Okehampton, or Ockington (as it is generally called in Devonshire) is situated very nearly in the centre of the county. It takes its name from the river Oke running through it. There is only one large street, and that without the advantage of good buildings. The principal trade consists in a manufactory of serge, which, however, is on the decline, and the chief support of the place seems to be the turnpike-road running through it from Exeter to Launceston. We did not find any building worthy of notice, except a ruinous chapel apparently of some antiquity.

Okehampton Castle is distant about a mile from the town. It stands on a natural eminence rising out of some verdant meadows, which are watered by a beautiful, clear stream, and enclosed by well wooded acclivities. Nothing can be more pleasing than the whole scenery, which, with the ivy-clad ruins of the Castle, its mouldering turrets, and crumbling walls, conspires to form a most picturesque landscape. Enough of the Castle remains to show that it was originally a place of splendour and consequence, and very strongly built.    The river served as a moat to it on one side, and the back part of it is rendered inaccessible by the steepness of its acclivity.    The gate, which is overhung with foliage, stands on the side towards the town.

The country improved extremely in fertility and richness as we approached Exeter; neither is it destitute of boldness, though we had now lost the grand lines of the granite mountains, which finally terminate a few miles beyond Okehampton.

Quite to Honiton the landscape continues uninterruptedly rich, and some of the highest hills are decorated to their summits with wood and luxuriant verdure.    Arable, meadow, and pasture lands seemed to be in pretty equal proportions. Separation of property is made by hedge-rows, from which rise tall, slender elms pared almost to mere poles, it being the practice to strip them of their branches to a great part of their height.    The multitude of villages scattered on all sides conspire with this sweet scene of cultivation to produce on the mind the most pleasing impressions imaginable. *Honiton.*

Honiton is situated in a delightful vale watered by numberless streams and brooks.    The river Otter flows through the town, which consists of a broad, handsome street running from east to west, and well paved.    The parish church is half a mile distant, but there is a chapel, called Allhallows, within the place.    A manufactory of lace is the only flourishing business, yet Honiton is by no means deficient in population.    It is a borough by prescription, and all the inhabitants who pay scot and lot are entitled to votes. *Otter R.*

Axminster enjoys equal conveniences, in regard to water, with Honiton, the River Axe (from which it takes its name) running through the middle of the parish.    The high road to Dorchester led us through this neat, healthy town.    From the reported antiquity of its foundation, we felt some curiosity to view the church, which is a heavy, but venerable structure, and has undergone various alterations at very different periods, as is evident from the various styles of architecture which it exhibits;  no part of it, however, can be of so early a date as the reign of (its supposed founder) Athelstan. *Axminster.* *Axe R.*

Axminster is famous for a manufactory of carpets, the

process of weaving which is very different from any other that I have seen.    They are woven in one entire piece, several hands being employed in conjunction at the same loom.

The soil for some miles between Wellington and Columbton is gravelly, and abounds with large, rounded pebbles.    A part of it assumes a heathy appearance, and yields little by cultivation.    Towards the latter place we again find the red loam, and its attendant fertility.

Cullompton.

Culm R.

The situation of Columbton is singularly agreeable, being surrounded by luxuriant scenery, and cultivation.    Here is a bridge over the Columb, which takes its rise, apparently, on the Blackdown hills, and joins the Ex near the village of Hucksham.

Bradninch.

Nearer to Exeter stands Bradnich, at the foot of a very long, steep hill, by the draining foot of which the place is rendered constantly wet and muddy.    Frequent swells, of some boldness, mark the neighbouring country to the south. Our return to this region of fertility seemed welcomed by the feathered tribe, for we were chanted through the woods by a choir of nightingales.

Upton Pyne.
Newton
St. Cyres.
Crediton.

The only additional information we obtained on this (our third) visit to Exeter was, that the manganese mine of Upton-Pyne had been filled up, and another opened at Newton St. Cyres.    In the direction of Crediton (pronounced by contraction Kirton), the country appears crowded with villages, and abounds with corn, pasture, and timber. Crediton is one of the most ancient towns of the county, and was once perhaps one of the most respectable, having been some time an episcopal see, and represented in parliament.    The old church, Leland says, was situated on the spot now occupied by houses on one side of the present burial-ground.    There are no more remains of it, nor of the bishop's palace, than if such buildings had never existed. The college of prebendaries too has been long since dissolved. Crediton continued to flourish, however, until a great fire happened (on 14 Aug., 1743) which destroyed upwards of 450 houses.    A second fire unfortunately broke out in May, 1772, when the town was reduced still more, so that it is now of very small extent.    The church is large and has quite a collegiate appearance.

Continuing our course to the north-west, we came to Bow,—a most wretched place, unable to afford the smallest accommodation of a decent kind,—and afterwards to North-Tawton, where the few travellers that pass may not perhaps apply in vain for a bed; the appearance of this village is infinitely more in its favour than that of the former.

A very fertile soil runs eastward from Bow, and from its deep red surface, is generally distinguished by the appellation of the *red land*. It is a deep loam, containing a large proportion of clay. The red land is let in many instances at as high a price as three pounds per acre, but this richer soil does not extend more than three miles, at the utmost, in breadth.

About Hunichurch, the country assumes a more irregular, heathy, and open aspect, and the gritstone, which forms the basis of the loamy soil, passes into siliceous slate. After this we soon came to an argillaceous species that extends along the more northern district of Cornwall. This sort of soil is so miserably unproductive about Stratton and Kilkhampton, that 400 acres of land will not let for £80.

Torrington enjoys a proud, elevated site. A spot called the bowling-green, on the south side of the town, is an advantageous point for viewing the river, which is here seen to flow in a graceful current along a narrow valley, enclosed by grand sloping ridges. Some of the distant precipices are very beautifully wooded.

Torrington is a very long town, and contains a great number of inhabitants, who are employed principally in the woollen manufacture. It had formerly a castle overlooking the river; some remains are still visible. There are two churches, one of which is furnished with a library.

From Torrington we went to Frithelstoke to view the remains of its priory. These adjoin to the parish church, and point out the form of the ancient conventual one, besides which there are the walls of two or three apartments that belonged probably to the prior. The west window of the old church continues perfect, fronting what was, to all appearance, once the grand court of the monastery, but is now a farm-yard. The great gate stands in a line with the south wall of the present burial ground.

**Torridge R.**
**Bideford.**

The river Towridge, when it arrives at Biddeford forms (with the addition of the tide) a very broad sheet of water. Biddeford has to boast of a noble bridge, a most commodious wharf (situated in the heart of the town) and a body of water sufficient to bring up to it vessels of 500 tons, except at the ebb tide, when almost half the channel of the river is left dry. From standing quite on a declivity, this town is much cleaner than sea-ports usually are, and many of the streets are spacious and the abode of opulence. As to the business of the port, it appears to consist principally in the landing of wool from Ireland, fish from Newfoundland, and rock-salt (by a preparation of which they cure their herrings) from Liverpool and Warrington. Lime-burning is a considerable article of trade at Biddeford, one hundred tons of Welsh limestone being often burned in a day. And here is a large pottery, the clay of which is brought from Fremington. A stratum of a fine reddish sort has been worked to the depth of more than twenty feet. It is procured at as easy a price as half-a-crown per ton.

**Fremington.**

**Clovelly.**

At Clovelly is a little pier for vessels, and the harbour is noted for the herring-fishery. The land, as it juts out into the promontory of Hartland, is by no means remarkable for fertility, nor is it either novel, or varied enough to be pleasing to the eye.

**Hartland.**

Hartland has the advantage of a market, but exhibits an air of poverty that depresses it to a level with a Cornish borough. We were very little prepared for the finished scenery that opened as we descended the road to the Priory, which is situated in so deep a dell that it is overlooked by the eye from Hartland. Every advantage has been taken of the spot to create a picturesque and agreeable scene, the slopes on each side being planted very judiciously, and the intermediate lawn opened to a little bridge that crosses a swift, bubbling brook. On the left, as we approach the grounds, there is a charming drive passing close under a hanging thicket of great beauty. Though built in a monastic fashion, with Gothic windows, the Priory is wholly modern, no remains of the old structure being left. It is at present the residence of Colonel Orchard.[1]

[1] The Abbey was rebuilt by Colonel Paul Orchard in 1779.

Hartland-quay consists of about a dozen decent cottages, and has a commodious little pier, at which commodities of various kinds, for the supply of this part of the country, are landed from Biddeford and Barnstaple; and here the fishermen and coasters find good shelter against the south-westerly winds, by mooring under the eminences.

The river Taw, from being joined by a great number    Taw R.
of brooks, acquires a considerable breadth, though as a haven it is become too shallow, not being able to support ships of more than two hundred tons in burthen. The great increase of sand in its channel occasions the neighbouring fields being overflowed at spring tides. Few towns have a more neat and comfortable appearance than Barn-    Barnstaple.
staple. It contains at least four thousand inhabitants.[1] There are prosperous manufactories of waistcoats, silk stockings, &c. and a variety of articles are exported. None of the works belonging to the castle are now to be found, except the mount, which might still serve to erect a battery upon.

A very barren, uninteresting tract soon succeeds the cultivation and beauty so conspicuous in the environs of Barnstaple. Towards Ilfracombe, however, the country    Ilfracombe.
assumes a very peculiar and distorted aspect, being broken into vast knolls, steep precipices, and irregular hollows.

The situation of Ilfracombe is truly romantic. The port is a beautiful natural basin, sheltered by craggy heights that are overspread with foliage. Ships find safety here when it is dangerous to run into the mouth of the Taw, and they have the convenience of an excellent pier and quay, which together form three sides of a square. The town consists chiefly of one street, full a mile long. It has a neat, healthy appearance, and is said to contain about two thousand inhabitants. The church stands at the upper part of the town; and there is a chapel, on a sort of knoll which may be called St. Michael's Mount in miniature, being joined to the main land only by a narrow neck.

Before we proceeded to Linton we resolved to visit Combe-Martin, a village surrounded by lodes of iron    Combe Martin.

---

[1] The population of Barnstaple in 1801 was 3,748, and in 1821 it was 5,079. (Lysons, *Devon*, xl.)

and lead.   Our road conducted us through a bold mountainous country abounding with spots most highly picturesque.
Berrynarbor.   A village-church, about a mile from Combe-Martin, is
situated to peculiar advantage, and overlooks a valley
in which the projecting declivities form various fine lines,
and becomes excellent materials for the employment of the
pencil.

We found Combe-Martin placed in a dale, along which
it extends at least a mile from the sea-shore.   The scenery
of the latter is really magnificent: its more prominent parts
are singularly striking, and have the happiest accompaniments
imaginable.   The sea enters a little cove at Combe-Martin,
commodious for the mooring of small vessels; and here
the produce of the mines is shipped for Wales and Bristol.
There is no curiosity, in way of antiquities, except an old
manor-house.   The building, by its ruinous aspect, freshens
the melancholy with which we are accustomed to reflect
on the decline of the honest hospitality of our fore-fathers.
The mansion has long been deserted by its proprietors,
and, though still tenanted by a farmer, approaches the last
stage of decay.[1]

# THE RURAL ECONOMY OF THE WEST OF ENGLAND   By William Marshall 1796

The chief town of the district of West Devonshire is
Plymouth.   Plymouth, which, with the new town adjoining to the
Devonport.   dockyard, and familiarly called Dock, together with the
Stonehouse.   village of Stonehouse, which now nearly unites the new and
the old towns, may be said to form, at once, the port and
the market of the district.

Tavistock.   Tavistock, however, in point of situation, and heretofore,
perhaps, in that of respectability, might rank high among
the market towns of the kingdom.   It is situated in the
northern quarter of the district, among its richest lands
(though beset with wild mountain scenery), and was formerly

---

[1] In Lyson's time (1822) it was occupied by a labourer.
(*Devon*, 137.)

famous for its monastery. At present, though meanly
built, it is a tolerable market town; and it is the only
inland town in the district now immediately under survey.

The villages of west Devonshire are few and small; farm
houses, and many cottages, being happily scattered over
the arrears of the townships. Nevertheless, near most of
the churches, groups of houses occur; with here and there
a hamlet.

Within one of its townships are found the remains of
a borough—Beer-Alston: in which, however, not a single
voter at present resides.

Bere Alston.

The natives of Devonshire are mostly of good person;
tall, straight, and well featured. Many of the women are of
elegant figure.

In the habitudes and manners of the middle class we
find little which marks the inhabitants of this Western
extremity of the Island, from those of the more central parts
of it; except what arises from an over-rated estimate of
themselves.

The habitations of the district immediately under notice
are superior to those of most other parts of the Island;
owing chiefly, perhaps, to the materials of building being
plentiful and good. Stone is almost everywhere abundant;
and slates of the first quality for covering are procurable
at a small expense; and lime for cement is also a cheap
article. Even the cottages are mostly comfortable, and
sometimes neat. The farm buildings are generally substantial and commodious, compared with those of many
districts, for farms of similar size.

The food of working people is somewhat below par.
Barley bread, skim-milk cheese, and potatoes, are principal
articles of food among labourers and small working farmers.
Formerly, barley bread was prevalent at the tables of the
middle classes of society. The beverage is chiefly cider; or
during a scarcity of this, beer; the liquors are a base kind
of spirit drawn from the lees of cider, and smuggled French
brandy.

The fuel of farmers and cottagers, in the enclosed country,
is invariably wood; on the skirts of the mountains, peat or
turf is in use. Lime is burnt chiefly or wholly with Welch
culm, and Plymouth has a supply of Newcastle coals.

The employments of the district are chiefly those of husbandry. The little mining which has lately been done, has been carried on chiefly, I believe, with miners from the western parts of Cornwall. At Tavistock is a serge manufactory, but not, I believe, of any great extent,[1] and the spinning of worsted employs, of course, some of the female villagers in its neighbourhood. Much worsted yarn, however, is sent out of Cornwall, to be woven in Devonshire; where women are employed in the weaving of serges.

Provident Societies, or Box Clubs, were introduced into this district about thirty years ago. In Tavistock and its neighbourhood there is one or more, I understand, for single women (mostly serge weavers); and some of the men's clubs, I am told, make a provision for widows.

Public corn mills are usually supplied with water by means of leats. These most ancient of public works still remain, here, in their pristine state. The poor take their own corn to the mill, and there dress it, themselves; the miller finding them dressing sieves; and the farmer of whom it is purchased, a horse, to take it and the female who dresses it, to the mill.

The roads of West Devonshire are, at present, most remarkable for their steepness. Less than half a century ago, they were mere gullies, worn by torrents in the rocks; which appeared in steps, as staircases, with fragments lying loose in the indentures. Speaking with little if any latitude, there was not, then, a wheel carriage in the district; nor, fortunately for the necks of travellers, any horses but those which were natives of the country.

At length, however, good turnpike roads are formed, between town and town, throughout this quarter of the Island; and most of the villagers have carriage roads opened to them; though many of these by-roads, as yet, are narrow, and abound with steeps. In Devonshire, as in other mountainous countries, the first inhabitants crossed the hills, on foot, in straight forward paths. When horses came into use, the same tracks were pursued; and some of them have been continued in use to the present time.

---

[1] Lysons (1822) says: "This town had formerly a very extensive manufactory of coarse serges. It is now on the decline." (*Devon*, 472-3.)

This district has no traces of common fields. The cultivated lands are all enclosed; mostly in well sized enclosures; generally large in proportion to the sizes of farms. They have every appearance of having been formed from a state of common pasture; in which state some considerable part of the district still remains; and what is observable, the better parts of those open commons have evidently heretofore been in a state of aration; lying in obvious ridges and furrows; with generally the remains of hedgebanks, corresponding with the ridges; and with faint traces of buildings.

The market of Plymouth has long, I believe, been esteemed the first in the Island, for the abundance, variety, and excellency of its sea fish. Of late years, however, this market has been the worse supplied, as the prime fish, caught by the fishermen in its vicinity, have been contracted for, by dealers, for that of Bath. And some share of the finny treasure, which these shores produce, is sent, I understand, to the London market.

Plymouth.

In a political view, however, the pilchard fishery of Cornwall is the most worthy of attention. In some seasons the quantities that are said to be caught are almost incredible employing many vessels and men in taking and curing them; and affording an article of foreign traffic, of no mean consideration.

The produce of the rivers of the district is chiefly salmon, which resort to them in great abundance.

Possessory right, or landed property, puts on an appearance, here, very different from that which it wears in other parts of the Kingdom. The fee simple is principally in the possession of men of large property. But instead of letting out their lands to tenants, at an annual rent equivalent to their value, they are sold, in small parcels or farms, generally for three lives named by the purchaser, or ninety-nine years, provided any one of the parties named survives that period: reserving, however, a small annual rent, together with a heriot or other forfeiture, on the death of each nominee, similar to those attached to the copyhold tenure; which this species of tenancy, or tenure, very much resembles: it being usual to put in fresh lives, as the preceding ones drop off; receiving a fine or adequate purchase, for the addition of a fresh life, or lives. This state of landed property, which is common to the west of England, forms one of the many striking features which rural economy at present exhibits in this part of the Island.

It is, I believe, the universal practice, in the district under survey, for the rector, whether lay or clerical, to send valuers over his parish presently before harvest, to estimate the value of his tithes. If the owner of the crop approves of the valuation, he reaps the whole of it: if not, the rector gathers his tithe in kind: a circumstance, however, which, I understand, seldom takes place.

The labourers of the district are below par: many of them drunken, idle fellows; and not a few of them may be said to be honestly dishonest; declaring, without reserve, that a poor man cannot bring up a family on six shillings a week and honesty. In addition, however, to these low wages, it is pretty common for farmers to let their constant labourers have corn at a fixed price; and endeavour to give them piece-work—to be paid for, by measurement, or in gross.

The wages of servants, as those of labourers, are low, compared with those of most other districts. The yearly wages of men run from six to eight pounds; of women three pounds or three guineas.

It is a universal and common practice, throughout Devonshire, and, I believe, the West of England in general, to put out the children of paupers, boys more particularly, at the age of seven or eight years, to farmers and others; and to bind them, as apprentices, until they be twenty-one years of age; and formerly until they were twenty four! on condition of the master's finding them with every necessary during the term of apprenticeship.

Formerly, carriage of every kind was done entirely on the backs of horses; except in harvest, when sledges, drawn by oxen, were sometimes used; also heaps of manure in the field were dragged abroad in small cart sledges, either by oxen or horses. Twenty years ago there was not a " pair of wheels " in the country; at least not upon a farm; and nearly the same may be said at present. Hay, corn, straw, fuel, stones, dung, lime, &c. are, in the ordinary practice of the district, still carried on horseback.

Oxen have ever been the plough team of the district:

sometimes with horses before them; but more generally alone: four aged oxen, or six growing steers, are the usual "plough" of the district.

Oxen are universally worked in yoke; yet are remarkably tractable; and step out with a pace which a Kentish clown would think a hardship to follow, with his high-fed horse team.

The style of driving an ox team, here, is observable; indeed, cannot pass unnoticed by a stranger. The language, though in a great degree peculiar to the country, does not arrest the attention; but the tone or rather tune, in which it is delivered. It resembles, with great exactness, the chantings, or recitative of the Cathedral service. The plough boy chants the counter tenor, with unabated ardour through the day; the plough man throwing in, at intervals, his hoarser notes. It is understood that this chanting march, which may sometimes be heard to a considerable distance, encourages and animates the team, as the music of a marching army, or the song of the rowers. Let this be as it may, I have never seen so much cheerfulness attending the operation of ploughing, anywhere, as in Devonshire.

Cart horses, since the introduction of wheel carriages, are beginning to creep into the district. They are mostly of the black, heavy-heeled, unprofitable breed. But, in a country where draught oxen are of so excellent a quality, and where the drivers of ox teams are so expert, and at present so partial to them, it were pity almost to introduce any other animal of draught; unless under particular circumstances. It would be as direct an affront to a steady good servant, in this district, to "ordain" him to go with a team of horses, as it would be to a Kentish ploughman, to order him to take charge of a team of oxen; and it might be a crime to do away so valuable a prejudice.

The furniture of pack horses varies with the load to be carried. Hay, corn, straw, faggots, and other comparatively light articles of burden, are loaded between "crooks"; formed of willow poles, about the thickness of scythe handles; and seven or eight feet long; bent as ox-bows; but with one end much longer than the other. These are joined in pairs, with slight cross bars, eighteen inches to two feet long; and each horse is furnished with two pairs of these crooks; slung together, so as that the shorter and stronger ends shall lie easy and firmly against the pack saddle; the longer and lighter ends rising, perhaps, fifteen or more inches, above the horse's back, and standing four or five feet from each other. Within, and between, these crooks, the load is piled, and bound fast together, with that simplicity and dispatch, which long practice seldom fails of striking out.

Cordwood, large stones, and other heavy articles are carried between "short crooks"; made of four natural bends or knees; both ends being nearly of the same length; and, in use, the points stand nearly level with the ridge of the pack saddle.

Dung, sand, materials of buildings, roads, &c., &c. are carried in "pots"; or strong coarse panniers; slung together, like the crooks; and as panniers are usually slung; the dung, especially if long and light, being ridged up, over the saddle. The bottom of each pot is a falling door, on a strong and simple construction. The place of delivery being reached, the trap is unlatched, and the load released.

Lime is universally carried in narrow bags; two or three of them being thrown across a pack saddle; which is of wood, and of the ordinary construction.

The shovel is pointed, in the manner of the hay spade of the North of England; resembling the marks on the suit of spades, in playing cards: a circumstantial evidence, this, that the tool under notice was once the common spade or shovel of the Island at large. In this part of it, it still supplies the place of both spade and shovel.

About twenty years ago the cultivation of the potatoe was introduced into this district; and turnips have been more or less cultivated for a much longer time; but not in a manner which redounds any honour on their cultivators.

Everything is sown broadcast. A modern drill made its appearance some years ago; but it has been laid aside.

Farmers of every class (some few excepted) carry their corn into the field on horseback, perhaps a quarter of a mile from the barn, to the summit of some airy swell; where it is winnowed, by women! the mistress of the farm, perhaps, being exposed in the severest weather, to the cutting winds of winter, in this slavish and truly barbarous employment.    The machine fan, however, is at length making its way into the Western extremity of the Island.

It is not more than twenty-five years, if so much, since the entire country, including, I believe the markets of Plymouth, was supplied with potatoes from the neighbourhood of Moretonhampstead, at the opposite end of Dartmoor, and at not less than twenty miles distance from the centre of this district, nor less than thirty miles from Plymouth and its dockyard!    The film of prejudice, however, being at length seen through, potatoes were found to grow, and to produce their kind, at the West end, as well as at the East end, of Dartmoor.

Moreton-
hampstead.

For the fruit markets, cherries, pears, and walnuts are raised in great abundance; especially in the township of Beer Ferrers; which is said to send out of it a thousand pounds worth of fruit (including strawberries) annually.

Bere Ferrers.

The mistleto is not known to this district, nor, I believe, to any part of Devonshire or Cornwall.

An excursion into Cornwall.    In passing by Callington and Liskard to Bodmin, some very high hills are seen to the North of the road:—"Hinkstone," a depressed cone, with a Prospect House on the top, is seen at great distances; but a hill westward of it, overlooking Callington, is said to be the highest land in the county.    Many ragged tors, of the true mountain cast, are seen in this ride.

Hingston
Down.

The roads are of stone, and in some parts extremely well kept.    The gates few, and the tolls moderate.    Toll roads are now formed between most or all of the market towns.    The roads of Cornwall were formerly very rough and dangerous; especially across the open heaths, among the mines! yet, at the first introduction of them in this country, obstinate riots took place.

There are some mines, but not many, in this ride; they are now, I understand, confined to the Western parts of the County.

The manufacture of the district, I believe, is principally woollen yarn, for the Devonshire sergemakers and clothiers.

The townships appear to be large,—with numerous hamlets.    Towards the mountains, turf (provincially "vags") and peat (provincially "turf") are used as fuel.    But little of the peat of these hills is firm enough, it seems, to be charred (as on Dartmoor), for the use of blacksmiths.

The mountains and their skirts are open; the lower lands all enclosed. The fields are well sized and well formed. The banks are thinner and lower than in West Devonshire, but of the same form. The buildings are mostly of stone and slate; some "cob"—or mudwall.

The crops are wheat and barley, with some oats and turnips (unhoed), with a little clover and upland ley. But not a bean nor a pea (unless harvested), in this ride!

Some oxen and horses in carriages. But packhorses seem still to be much in use. A singular kind of two-wheel carriage, for horses or oxen, is here in common use; especially, I believe, to carry harvest produce upon. It is called a "wain"; and it is a hay cart, or wain, without sides: having only two arches bending over the wheels, to keep the load from bearing upon them! with a wince behind. How simple; and, being low, how easily loaded! I met two on the road, laden with wool; each with two oxen at the pole, and two horses before them.

**Liskeard.** The tillage is apparently better here than in Devonshire. About Liskard the land appears to be in a good state of cultivation. Orchards evidently diminish with the distance westwards.

The views are frequently picturable, and sometimes grand: but they cloy, through a frequency of repetition and a degree of sameness.

There are two distinct species, or varieties, of furze now in full blow. The lower skirts of the uncultivated hills are gilded with them. One of them is the creeping sort, which is common to the southern counties; the other **Tavistock.** is called the "French furze"; and Tavistock, I understand, has long been a market for furze seed.

**Callington.** Callington is a small market town, and a borough. **Liskeard.** Liskard is a large, populous, decent-looking place, and would appear respectable in any part of the Kingdom; it is **Bodmin.** likewise a borough. Bodmin, though one of the County towns, is much inferior in size and respectability; this, too, is a borough.

**Five Lanes.** The elevation of the country is very great, between **Bodmin Moor.** Bodmin and Five Lanes, over Bodmin Down, and Temple

Moor. Some very high points of view are reached. Saw
the cliff and the estuary of Padstow. In a clear day both
seas are observable (near Fowey and Padstow). Some
remarkable rugged mountains are seen towards the North
coast. Passed Dosmary Pool, a small lakelet, about a mile
in circumference, upon the higher parts of these heaths;
and crossed a quaking bog; which has formerly, no doubt,
been a lake. From the elevations surmounted in this ride,
and from the top of the castle of Launceston, perhaps half
of Cornwall, and a very large portion of Devonshire are
seen over: the whole a strongly featured country.

About Launceston are some well-soiled but very steep
hills. At Milton Abbot's is a plot of the finest grass-land
in the kingdom! Also about Lamerton and Tavistock is
some good grazing land.

The road in general is good. For a considerable way
the stones are covered with a kind of rough sand, or small
gravel, apparently the loose materials of which granite is
composed; making an admirable road. The moors are
open: except some small enclosures about Temple, &c.
Cultivated lands are everywhere enclosed.

The buildings are of stone and slate. At Launceston
the houses are mostly faced with slates: some of them three
or four feet square. The church is of moorstone, deeply and
richly sculptured! Substantial and beautiful, as a Gothic
building: the workmanship must have been immensely
great, seeing the hardness of the materials—a shining granite.

Saw several goats browzing on furze. I was told that
numbers are kept in Cornwall, for milking; some herds
consisting of a hundred head; and that goats' and kids'
flesh are not uncommon in the Cornish markets.

Temple is a deserted village! The only one I have
ever seen. Some years ago, not a single person lived in
the township! (a curacy appendant to Blisland) and only
one little farmhouse is now inhabited:—the ruins of half a
dozen or more; the body of the church down; the chancel
remains. Goldsmith, surely, must have travelled this road!

Launceston—provincially, and universally throughout the
country, "Laanson," is a genteel looking place, but
awkwardly situated, on the brink and side of a very steep
hill. The street leading to Newport is as steep, almost, as

Temple Moor.
Padstow.

Dozmary Pool.

Launceston.

Milton Abbot.
Lamerton.
Tavistock.

Temple.

Launceston.

Temple.

Blisland.

Launceston.

Newport.

the roof of a house.    The castle, which has been a very
strong fortress, commands some charming views.    Newport,
a paltry borough—a mean looking hamlet—belonging to
**St. Stephen's.** the parish of St. Stephen's, a village which stands opposite
**Milton Abbot.** to Launceston.    Milton Abbot's a charming situation—the
Abbots were admirable judges of soils and situations.
**Tavistock.** Tavistock is also well situated; and was heretofore famous
for its abbotry.

I am agreeably disappointed with respect to Cornwall.
From what I had seen on the banks of the Tamar, I
expected to have found, as I went further westward, a
wretched country, wretched roads, wretched towns, wretched
accommodations, and wretched inhabitants.    On the contrary,
the country, whether in point of soil or cultivation,—except
the higher mountains, and they are good in their kind,—is
above mediocrity.    The roads, their unlevelness apart, are
among the best in the kingdom.    The towns, substantial
and neat.    The accommodations, equal to anything met with,
out of the great roads.    The inhabitants, intelligent, civil,
are said to be extremely hospitable, are affable, clean in
appearance, and handsome in their persons.    What most
disgusts a stranger, in travelling through Cornwall, is the
inordinate number of its boroughs; and this impropriety
lies not with the people of Cornwall.    There are none,
indeed, so sensible of it, as the inhabitants themselves.

**Okehampton.** The town of Okehampton, well sized and respectable,
considering the recluseness of its situation, is seated in a deep
basin, broken into three parts, by the narrow wooded valleys
**Okement.** of the Oke and its two principal branches: the former
winding towards the North, the latter spreading wide to
the East and West; and embracing, as with arms, the
Northern point of the Dartmoor mountain; which here
forms a flattened stage of considerable extent and elevation;
overlooking the town, and forming one side of the basin
in which it is situated.    The face of the steep is finely
hung with wood—mostly large full-headed oaks; being part
of the ancient demesne lands belonging to the Castle of
Okehampton, whose ruins still occupy a peninsular hillock
that faces this bold woody steep; being divided from it
by the Western branch of the Oke.    The scenery is truly
alpine.

Upon this eminence, and on the Western brink of the basin, stands the principal Church of Okehampton: proudly situated; and forming a 'good object from the opposite height; making one feature of a fine landscape.

The entire environs, and the views from them are rich and beautiful; but the scale is small. A truly monastic situation,—rich and recluse—yet, I believe, without the vestige of a monastery!

Hatherleigh is a mean market town, mostly or wholly built with red earth and thatch. Some of the houses white-washed, others rough-cast.   *Hatherleigh.*

Four oxen, two horses, two men, and a boy, at plough!

A charming broad wooded basin opens to the west, between Hatherleigh and Sheepwash.   *Sheepwash.*

A wide flat of marshes to the right; apparently in a wild, neglected, unproductive state. Hewish, Sir James Norcliff's,[1] appears on the opposite banks of these marsh lands.   *Huish.*
*Norcliffe-Innes.*

A bad turnpike road traces a high ridge of cold white clay,—commanding a strongly featured country.

Ascend Padstow Hill: an insulated eminence commanding a fine circle of views. To the South, the mountain of Dartmoor rising bold to the view, and forming a remarkably strong feature from this point. To the East, the rising banks of the Oke and the Taw; apparently, well soiled, and well cultivated; the foreground of this view, the Valley of Marland—or Marshland, in a state of neglect,—much of it occupied by furze; to appearance, highly improvable. To the North, a ridge of well soiled arable upland. To the West, a well wooded district.   *Petrockstow (?)*
*Okement R.*
*Taw R.*
*Peter's*
*Marland.*

Passed the first cart: drawn in the Cleveland manner! three horses; one in the shafts, the other two abreast, and guided by reins: loaded with bark, for the port of Bideford; to be there shipped for Ireland.

Cross a well timbered hollow. Much valuable ship timber in this district. Close woody lanes,—how tantalizing to a traveller!

---

[1] Sir James Norcliffe Innes, bart., afterwards Duke of Roxburgh, bought the estate in 1782, and built a new house there for his residence, called Innes House. It is now the property and seat of Lord Clinton. (Lysons, *Devon*, 285.)

Winscott.

A box—Winscot—the first house I have passed in this stage.[1]  Observe several good horses.  Query, bred in this district?  Meet a string of lime horses from Bideford; eight or ten miles.  Lime here a prevailing manure.

Instance of a cropt hedge.  What a loss to the traveller, that the practice is not prevalent.

Torrington.

A fine view of the Valley of Torrington bursts upon the eye.  Dip down to the Bridge of Torrington.

The townships in this stage appear to be of the middle size.  The churches in general tall and conspicuous.  Of the state of enclosure, it may be said that about half the lands, which fall immediately under the eye, are enclosed; the rest, in coarse furzy commons, capable of great improvement.  The state of husbandry, on the whole, is considerably below par.

Torridge R.

The town of Torrington is proudly situated on the brink, and partly hanging on the brow, of the eastern bank of the Oke.  It is a large inland market town; but has no thoroughfare to support it.  There is no posting inn in the place!  and only one chaise kept for hire.  Nevertheless, the town is neat, and the people alive.  Circumstances to be accounted for only in the many family residences which appear in the neighbourhood, and which seldom fail to meliorate the manners of every class of those who fall within the sphere of their influence.

The view from the site of the Castle—now a bowling green—is uncommonly fine.  A wooded amphitheatre, richly diversified: with a lengthened bend of water in the middle ground:—and with fox-hounds in the woods!

A well soiled common near the town; stocked with small neat sheep.  Pass between well soiled enclosures: a rich and beautiful country.  Cross a lovely wooded valley: thriving oak timber; well thinned and set out.  The surface broken, abruptly, into hill and dale: a truly Danmonian passage.  Reach the summit of the ridge: a furze-grown waste.  A broad view of the Bristol Channel meets the eye; with extensive land views on either side.  On the one hand, Hartland Point is a prominent and striking feature; on the other, Exmoor rises boldly to the view.

[1] In the parish-church of Peters Marland are several memorials of the family of Stevens of Winscott. (Lysons, *Devon*, 386).

Descend towards Bideford.  Meet strings of lime horses, Bideford.
with pack-saddles and bags of lime.  Also two-horse carts,
with lime and sea sand.

The town of Bideford is remarkably forbidding.  Meanly
built houses (timber, brick, or mud, covered with bad slate
or thatch), stuck against a steep hill.  The streets, of course,
are awkward; and most of them are narrow.  In the
vacant spaces between the streets, immense piles of furze
faggots rise, in the shape of houses, and make the houses
themselves appear more like hovels than they really are.

These dangerous piles of fuel are for the use of the
pottery, for which only, I believe, this town is celebrated:
chiefly, or wholly, the coarser kinds of earthenware.

The Bridge of Bideford is an extraordinary erection:
a high thick wall, run across the river or narrowed estuary;
with Gothic gateways, here and there, to let the water pass.

The tide out: many men employed in loading packhorses with sand, left in the bed of the river: and, in every
vacant corner about the town, composts of earth, mud,
ashes, &c., are seen.  Shell sand is said to be plentiful on
the coast; but little, if any of it, is brought up this river.

On the shore of the estuary, opposite to the town, are
several limekilns, now in full work.  Numbers of packhorses, and a few carts, loading, or waiting for loads.  The
stone, chiefly, and the culm with which it is burnt, wholly,
brought across the channel from the coast of Wales.  The
kilns are similar to those in West Devonshire.  The lime
is carried fourteen or fifteen miles; chiefly on horseback.

The whole country is enclosed; mostly in large fields,
with coppice fences—cut down by the wind: a circumstance
more favourable to the admirers of natural landscape, than
to the husbandman.

No hedgerow timber: but a few groups of trees are
scattered on the hills.  The steep banks of the Oke are Torridge R.
chiefly hung with coppice wood.

Bideford Market: A few fat, and some store cattle; with
three or four heifers and calves.  The heifers somewhat
small; but neat; and with remarkably fine bags! the most
promising appearance of milk that I have observed in the
Devonshire breed of cattle.  A few sheep, and two or three
colts (weaned foals) in halters.  The corn market well filled

with long two-bushel bags ; chiefly of wheat.   The shambles full of good mutton ;—with a scanty show of beef.   Salmon in considerable plenty ; but no sea fish !   The women's market well supplied.   Cart loads of country bread, exposed in the market place, for sale.   A market article, this, which I have not before observed.   Upon the whole, the market of Bideford may be set down as very respectable.

Stroll upon the rising grounds on the North side of the town.   These grounds are separated from the hill on which the town is situated, by a creek of marshland, in its natural state, as formed by the tide ; excepting a plot of seven or eight acres, which is now embanking : an operation which, if it were carried on with proper exertion, could not fail to pay threefold for the money expended.   If the men who are employed upon it, may be considered a sample of the labourers of North Devon, they exceed in idleness their countrymen of the West.

A low bank, thrown up across these marshlands, furnishes, at once, a safe road, and gives effect to a tide mill, situated near one end of it.

A rich loamy soil to the very summit of this hill : a narrow ridge.   A good view of the Bay of Barnstaple, and its finely diversified coast : here, a flat shore ; there, steep lofty cliffs.   Some charming near views are seen from these grounds.   Tapley (Mr. Cleveland's) a fine situation, is seen with advantage.[1]

Tapeley.
Clevland.

The entire environs are studded with *houses* : some of them substantial ; others neat.   Yet still we find the town itself a contrast to Torrington.   The influence even of half a score families is not sufficient to burnish the appearance and manners of a small seaport town, in a remote situation.

On a general view of the district, at this season (September), it resembles South Devonshire so much, with respect to natural characters and farm management, that, in a register of their rural economy, they might well be considered as one and the same district ; excepting an observable superiority in the breeds of cattle and horses in

[1] Tapeley, in the parish of Westleigh, was bought by William Clevland, Esq., from the Giffards, about the beginning of the 18th century.   John Clevland, Esq., M.P., died in 1817.   (Lysons, *Devon*, 553.)

this part of the County; and except a somewhat freer use of wheel carriages, here, than in the South Hams and West Devonshire.

From Bideford to Barnstaple is another broken billowy district: high rotund swells, separated by deep narrow valleys.

Creeks of marshland branch out of the estuary of the Taw: the soil of these marshlets is somewhat reddish. **Taw R.** Now stocked with cattle. But they are at present in a rough unreclaimed state, and appear to be highly improvable.

The road of stone, and remarkably good.

The timber trees, on this side of the County, are remarkably shorn with the North West wind.[1]

The wide valley of the Taw opens to the view,—and the nature of the country changes, from clean sound land, to a cold aquatic soil: alder swamps, rushy enclosures, and rough furze grounds; with much oak wood. The coppices in general healthy; but the timber much injured by the coldness of the substratum, and the winds from the sea. One wood completely stag-headed: a waste of property to let it stand.

Met several flocks of Exmoor lambs; many hundreds, invariably horned, and, mostly, even in carcase; on their way to the North West of Devonshire, and the North of Cornwall, to their winter pasture.

Enter on the descent into the vale, or valley, of Barnstaple. Towards the foot of the hill the land improves. **Barnstaple.** A broad flat of meadows and marshlands. Some large houses are seen, among the fine scenery, on the opposite banks of the valley.

The bridge of Barnstaple is similar to that of Bideford.

No sheep observed in the enclosures; nor wheel carriages on the road.

The town of Barnstaple is respectable. The streets are wider and better laid out, than those of old towns generally are. Many of the houses are substantially built of brick. But the covering here is of the same mean-looking slate as that which is in use at Bideford.

Leith carts and Highland sledges (or implements very much resembling them!) are seen in the streets of Barnstaple.

---

[1] Should be *South* West wind.

Some small craft in the river, and in a creek which washes one side of the town.   And two small vessels on the stocks.

Pilton, a pleasant village, adjoins to Barnstaple.

**Pilton.**

**Codden Hill.**

A bold promontory, which rises abruptly in the centre of the broad valley, above the town,—severing the Taw from the brook of Pilton and its sweetly winding woody dell,—forms a striking feature among the assemblage of picturáble scenes, which the environs of Barnstaple appear, even through the dim medium of rain, to be capable of affording.

A rich flat of meadows and marshlands above the town, nearly a mile wide, evidently formed by the tide and floods. The country on either side picturably broken and well wooded.   Pass through Newport, a large village; the buildings chiefly earth and thatch, but some brick, stone, slate, and pantile, in use.

**Newport.**

The day is set in for rain; yet the appearance of the country is delightful beyond description.   Perhaps rain, as varnish, mellows the views.

The roads in a shameful state: evidently injured by the hedges.   Why is not the law enforced?   In this country, where woodlands abound, and where coals may be had at a reasonable rate, no serious evil could arise were all the hedges in it shorn to their mounds.

Get a broad view of the rich and beautiful valley of Swimbridge.   A fine back view of the Estuary and its banks: broad, but grand, and picturable.

**Swimbridge.**

Meet a pair of wheels: the first from Bideford.

A sweet country, but most difficult to be seen!   Black limestone road, tolerably good.

Filleigh, Lord Fortescue's noble place, breaks at once upon the eye: a finely wooded basin.   The timber abundant, and seemingly well set out.   A herd of young cattle, and a flock of sheep, in the grounds about the house.   The farmery large; bespeaking a suitable portion of demesne in hand.

**Castle Hill (Filleigh).**
*Fortescue.*

A very deep quarry of black limestone, similar in appearance to the Chudleigh marble, but the colour is less bright.   This capacious quarry is not less than fifty feet deep. The stones are brought up from the lower depths on horseback, and the water raised by a horse pump.

Pass a string of two-horse carts, guided with reins, in the Cleveland manner! Has a colony of Clevelanders formerly settled in North Devonshire, and brought with them their carts and horses?

Vile roads again: and in the neighbourhood of a great man's residence! But, perhaps, his lordship's lime work is the principal cause of the evil. The colour of the materials, and the state in which they at present lie, give them every appearance of roads to coal pits.

Mount a rich well turned swell, and enter the town of South Molton.

South Molton.

The town, which consists of a spacious well built market place, surrounded with inferior streets, caps a rotund hillock, situated among other hillocks of a similar nature, and wearing similar appearances; rich and beautiful in a superior degree.

Some wood in the valleys, but not one acre of unproductive land to be seen in the neighbourhood. One of the finest farming districts in the Kingdom.

Walked towards the Barton of Great Hill to view Mr. Triggs' breed of cattle, which is reckoned one of the first in this neighbourhood; and the district of South Molton is spoken of as the first for the North Devonshire breed. They are evidently a superior variety of the middle-horned breed, and are, of course, one of the first breeds of cattle in the Island.

Great Hill.
*Trigg.*

At less than two miles from the town, leave its fertile environs. A pretty but unproductive valley to the left: alders, rushes, and rough grounds.

Meet a drove of cart horses, and a string of saddle horses, on their way to the Fair of Barnstaple—the property of a Dorsetshire dealer.

Mount a rough furze-grown height, an extensive common, —and catch a broad view to the South: apparently, a cold infertile district.

Bend to the left, from the Tiverton road; and enter narrow woody lanes, barely pervious by a carriage.

Break out of this pass, into other commons; and nearly approach the heaths of Exmoor, a narrow valley only intervening.

Exmoor.

Exmoor, in this point of view, is without feature; appears as a flat, or at most, a tamely billowy heath. Its hills scarcely rise above the cultivated swells that environ them. This side of it, at least, has not a trait of the mountain character.

Enter and skirt a wide fern-grown common; large plots of fern now in swath. Also dwarf furze, and some heath. The soil deep and culturable.

The valley widens, and breaks into well soiled hillocks.
**East and West Anstey.** The two parishes of East and West Anstey appear to be in a good state of culture.

Meet strings of lime horses, from Bampton lime works.

Lose sight of the Exmoor hills, but still keep the brink of the valley, having enjoyed a tolerably level road for seven or eight miles!

Leave the high ground, and descend into the valley. Stirring wheat fallows, with four oxen; the first oxen, and the first plough, I have seen at work in North Devonshire! Instance of watering grassland: the first I have observed in North Devonshire.

**Dulverton.** Approach Dulverton, by another Gothic bridge. This small market town is situated in a deep narrow valley, and
**Pixton.** immediately below the town is a small place, Pixton, belong-
*Acland.* ing to the Acland family.

Proceeding towards Bampton, see the Exe, at some distance, winding at the foot of a tall steep woody bank; a passage of natural scenery,—sketched with a broad free pencil.

Descend precipitously into another fertile and recluse
**Bampton.** plot of country—the beautiful environs of Bampton.

Bampton—a small mean market town; overlooked by an extensive limework, whose ragged excavations and heaps of rubbish seem to conspire with the town to disfigure this sweetly designed passage of Nature. But the face of a country cannot be disfigured to a better purpose, than that of contributing to its improvement. These works are said to have been carried on, time immemorial, for the purposes of husbandry.

The rubbish of the quarries is carried out on horseback; and the stone is drawn up to the kilns in three-wheeled horse barrows, which an old labourer tells me, have been used in this country beyond memory. The fuel of these limeworks is Welch culm, fetched by land from Watchet, sixteen miles.

The price of stone lime, three shillings the hogshead; of the ashes, two shillings, for the use of the mason!

Several orchard grounds in the neighbourhood of Bampton.

Reach a rough, improvable, red-soiled height, from which Dartmoor, for the first time, is seen rising to the view.

Pass between beechen coppice-hedges.

The Vale of Exeter bursts open, with fine effect. Also a broad view of the more Eastern confines of Devonshire presents itself. Now, a rich vale view, of the Bradninch quarter of the Vale of Exeter, is spread under the eye.

Descend, by a long broken steep, to Tiverton.                    Tiverton.

The inhabitants of North Devonshire, throughout, appear to be civilized and intelligent; the lower class differing much, in these respects, from those of the mining country. Their fuel—wood and Welch coals. Their employments—husbandry and the worsted manufactory.

The farmers appear to be of the middle and lower classes: mostly, plain, decent-looking, working husbandmen, of twenty to fifty or a hundred pounds a year. I saw few, if any, which appeared to be of the superior order of farmers.

No rabbit warren fell under the eye; indeed the lands passed through are in general too good for that application. To apiaries, however, the goodness of the lands cannot be an objection; yet I observed few, if any bees, in this large tract of country.

The state of husbandry, from this cursory view of it, appears to be superior to that of South Devonshire, and on a par with that of the Kingdom at large. In the management of live stock, especially horses, cattle, and swine, North Devonshire, it is probable, has, for some length of time, paid more than ordinary attention.

Of the face of this fair country it were impossible to say too many fine things. But, as its goodly features might lose much of their force in my own description, I will briefly set it down at what its happy inhabitants believe and assert it to be—"the richest finest country in the world."

## LETTERS FROM ENGLAND     By Don Manuel Alvarez Espriella (Robert Southey) 1802

Wednesday, April 21, 1802.

I write to you from English ground. On the twelfth morning after our departure from Lisbon we came in sight of the Lizard, two light-houses on the rocks near the Land's End, which mark a dangerous shore. The day was clear, and showed us the whole coast to advantage; but if these be the white cliffs of England, they have been strangely magnified by report: their forms are uninteresting, and their heights diminutive; if a score such were piled under Cape Finisterre, they would look like a flight of stairs to the Spanish mountain. I made this observation to J——, who could not help acknowledging the truth, but he bade me look at the green fields. The verdure was certainly very delightful, and that not merely because our eyes were wearied with the gray sea: the appearance was like green corn, though approaching nearer I perceived that the colour never changed; for the herb, being kept short by the cattle, does not move with the wind.

We passed in sight of St. Maurs, a little fishing-town on the east of the bay, and anchored about noon at Falmouth. There is a man always on the look-out for the packets; he makes a signal as soon as one is seen, and every woman who has a husband on board gives him a shilling for the intelligence. I went through some troublesome forms upon landing, in consequence of the inhospitable laws enacted at the beginning of the war. There were then the vexatious ceremonies of the custom house to be performed, where double fees were exacted for passing our baggage at extraordinary hours. J—— bade me not judge of his countrymen by their sea-ports: it is a proverb, said he, "that the people at these places are all either birds of passage, or birds of prey;" it is their business to fleece us, and ours to be silent.—Patience where there is no remedy!— our own aphorism, I find, is as needful abroad as at home. But if ever some new Cervantes should arise to write a

*Lizard Point.*

*St. Mawes.*
*Falmouth.*

mock heroic, let him make his hero pass through a custom house on his descent to the infernal regions.

The inn appeared magnificent to me; my friend complained that it was dirty and uncomfortable. I cannot relish their food: they eat their meat half raw; the vegetables are never boiled enough to be soft; and everything is insipid except the bread, which is salt, bitter, and disagreeable. Their beer is far better in Spain, the voyage and the climate ripen it. The cheese and butter were more to my taste; *manteca* indeed is not butter, and the Englishman who wanted to call it so at Cadiz was as inaccurate in his palate as in his ideas. Generous wines are inordinately dear, and no others are to be procured; about a dollar a bottle is the price. What you find at the inns is in general miserably bad; they know this, and yet drink that the host may be satisfied with their expenses; our custom of paying for the house-room is more economical, and better.

Falmouth stands on the western side of the bay, and consists of one long narrow street which exhibits no favourable specimen, either of the boasted cleanliness or wealth of the English towns. The wealthier merchants dwell a little out of the town upon the shore, or on the opposite side of the bay at a little place called Flushing. The harbour, which is very fine, is commanded by the castle of Pendennis; near its mouth there is a single rock, on which Pendennis Cas. a pool is erected because it is covered at high tide. A madman not many years ago carried his wife here at low water, landed her on the rock, and rowed away in sport; nor did he return till her danger as well as fear had become extreme.

Some time since the priest of this place was applied to to bury a certain person from the adjoining country. "Why, John," said he to the sexton, "we buried this man a dozen years ago:" and in fact it appeared on referring to the books of the church that his funeral had been registered ten years back. He had been bed-ridden and in a state of dotage during all that time; and his heirs had made a mock burial, to avoid certain legal forms and expenses which would else have been necessary to enable them to receive and dispose of his rents. I was also told another anecdote of an inhabitant of this town, not unworthy of a stoic:—

His house was on fire; it contained his whole property; and when he found it was in vain to attempt saving any thing, he went upon the nearest hill and made a drawing of the conflagration :—an admirable instance of English phlegm!

The perpetual stir and bustle in this inn is as surprising as it is wearisome. Doors opening and shutting, bells ringing, voices calling to the waiter from every quarter, while he cries "coming," to one room, and hurries away to another. Every body is in a hurry here; either they are going off in packets, and are hastening their preparations to embark; or they have just arrived, and are impatient to be on the road homeward. Every now-and-then a carriage rattles up to the door with a rapidity which makes the very house shake. The man who cleans the boots is running in one direction, the barber with his powder-bag in another; here goes the barber's boy with his hot water and razors; there comes the clean linen from the washer-woman; and the hall is full of porters and sailors bringing in luggage, or bearing it away; now you hear a horn blow because the post is coming in, and in the middle of the night you are awakened by another because it is going out. Nothing is done in England without a noise, and yet noise is the only thing they forget in the bill!

Thursday, April 22.

Early in the morning our chaise was at the door, a four-wheeled carriage which conveniently carries three persons. It has glass in front and at the sides, instead of being closed with curtains, so that you at once see the country and are sheltered from the weather. Two horses drew us at the rate of a league and a half in the hour; such is the rapidity with which the English travel. Half a league from Falmouth is the little town of Penryn, whose ill-built and narrow streets seem to have been contrived to make as many acute angles in the road, and take the traveller up and down as many steep declivities as possible in a given distance. In two hours we reached Truro, where we breakfasted: this meal is completely spoilt by the abominable bitterness of the bread, to which I shall not soon be able to reconcile myself. The town is clean and opulent; its main street broad, with superb shops, and a little gutter stream running through it. All the shops have windows

Penryn.

Truro.

to them; the climate is so inclement that it would be impossible to live without them. J—— showed me where some traveller had left the expression of his impatience written upon the wainscot with a pencil—'Thanks to the Gods another stage is past'—for all travellers are in haste here, either on their way home, or to be in time for the packet. When we proceeded the day had become dark and overclouded;—quite English weather:—I could scarcely keep myself warm in my cloak: the trees have hardly a tinge of green, though it is now so late in April. Every thing has a coarse and cold appearance: the heath looks nipt in its growth, and the hedge-plants are all mean and insignificant: nettles, and thistles, and thorns; instead of the aloe, and the acanthus, and the arbutus, and the vine. We soon entered upon a track as dreary as any in Estremadura; mile after mile the road lay straight before us; up and down long hills, whose heights only served to show how extensive was the waste.

Mitchel-Dean, the next place to which we came, is as miserable as any of our most decayed towns; it is what they call a rotten borough: that is, it has the privilege of returning two members to Parliament, who purchase the votes of their constituents, and the place has no other trade:— it has indeed a very rotten appearance. Even the poorest houses in this country are glazed: this, however, proves rather the inclemency of the climate than the wealth of the people. Our second stage was to a single house called the Indian Queens, which is rather a post-house than an inn. These places are not distinguished by a bush, though that was once the custom here also, but by a large painting swung from a sort of gallows before the door, or nailed above it, and the house takes its name from the sign. Lambs, horses, bulls, and stags, are common; sometimes they have red lions, green dragons, or blue boars, or the head of the king or queen, or the arms of the nearest nobleman. One inconvenience attends their mode of travelling, which is, that at every stage the chaise is changed, and of course there is the trouble of removing all the baggage.

The same dreary country still lay before us; on the right there was a wild rock rising at once from the plain, with a ruin upon its summit. Nothing can be more desolate

*Mitchell.*

*Indian Queens.*

than the appearance of this province, where most of the inhabitants live in the mines. " I never see the greater part of my parishioners," said a clergyman here, " till they come up to be buried." We dined at Bodmin, an old town which was once the chief seat of religion in the district, but has materially suffered since the schism; ill-built, yet not worse built than situated, being shadowed by a hill to the south; and to complete the list of ill contrivances, their water is brought through the common burial-place. They burn earth-coal every where; it is a black shining stone, very brittle, which kindles slowly, making much smoke, and much ashes: but as all the houses are built with chimneys it is neither unwholesome nor disagreeable. An Englishman's delight is to stir the fire: and I believe I shall soon acquire this part of their manners, as a means of self-defence against their raw and chilly atmosphere. The hearth is furnished with a round bar to move the coals, a sort of forceps to arrange them, and a small shovel for the cinders; all of iron, and so shaped and polished as to be ornamental. Besides these, there is what they call the fender, which is a little movable barrier, either of brass or polished steel, or sometimes of wire painted green and capt with brass, to prevent the live embers from falling upon the floor. The grates which confine the fire are often very costly and beautiful, every thing being designed to display the wealth of the people; even the bars, though they are necessarily blackened every day by the smoke, are regularly brightened in the morning, and this work is performed by women. In good houses the chimneys have a marble frontal, upon the top of which vases of alabaster or spar, mandarins from China, flower-stands, or other ornaments are arranged.

After dinner we proceeded to Launceston; the country improved upon us, and the situation of the place as we approached, standing upon a hill, with the ruins of the castle which had once commanded it, reminded me of our Moorish towns. We arrived just as the evening was closing; our chaise wheeled under the gateway with a clangor that made the roof ring; the waiter was at the door in an instant; by the time we could let down the glass, he had opened the door and let the steps down. We were shown into a

*Bodmin.*

*Launceston.*

comfortable room; lights were brought, the twilight shut out, the curtains let down, the fires replenished. Instead of oil, they burn candles made of tallow, which in this climate is not offensive; wax is so dear that it is used by only the highest ranks.

Here we have taken our tea; and in the interval between that and supper, J—— is reading the newspaper, and I am minuting down the recollections of the day. What a country for travelling is this! such rapidity on the roads! such accommodation at the resting-places! We have advanced fourteen leagues today without fatigue or exertion. When we arrive at the inn there is no apprehension lest the apartments should be preoccupied; we are not liable to any unpleasant company; we have not to send abroad to pur-chase wine and seek for provisions; every thing is ready; the larder stored, the fire burning, the beds prepared; and the people of the house, instead of idly looking on, or altogether neglecting us, are asking our orders and solicitous to please. I no longer wonder at the ill-humour and fastidiousness of Englishmen in Spain.

Friday, April 23.

Launceston castle was formerly used as a state prison. There were lazar-houses here and at Bodmin when leprosy was common in England. They attributed this disease to the habit of eating fish, and especially the livers; the fresher they were the more unwholesome they were thought. Whatever has been the cause, whether change of diet, or change of dress, it has totally disappeared.

The Tamar, a clear shallow and rapid stream, flows by Launceston, and divides Cornwall from Devonshire. The mountainous character of the river, the situation of the town rising behind it, its ancient appearance, and its castle towering above all, made so Spanish a scene, that perhaps it pleased me more for the resemblance; and I would willingly for a while have exchanged the chaise for a mule, that I might have loitered to enjoy it at leasure. The English mode of travelling is excellently adapted for every thing, except for seeing the country.

We met a stage-waggon, the vehicle in which baggage is transported, for sumpter-beasts are not in use. I could not imagine what this could be; a huge carriage upon four

**Tamar R.**

wheels of prodigious breadth, very wide and very long, and arched over with cloth, like a bower, at a considerable height: this monstrous machine was drawn by eight large horses, whose neck-bells were heard far off as they approached; the carrier walked beside them, with a long whip upon his shoulder, as tall again as himself, which he sometimes cracked in the air, seeming to have no occasion to exercise it in any other manner: his dress was different from any that I had yet seen, it was a sort of tunic of coarse linen, and is peculiar to this class of men. Here would be an adventure for Don Quixote! Carrying is here a very considerable trade: these waggons are day and night upon their way, and are oddly enough called flying waggons, though of all machines they travel the slowest, slower than even a travelling funeral. The breadth of the wheels is regulated by law, on account of the roads, to which great attention is paid, and which are deservedly esteemed objects of national importance. At certain distances gates are erected and toll-houses beside them, where a regular tax is paid for every kind of conveyance in proportion to the number of horses and wheels; horsemen and cattle also are subject to this duty. These gates are rented by auction; they are few or frequent, as the nature of the soil occasions more or less expense in repairs: no tax can be levied more fairly, and no public money is more fairly applied. Another useful peculiarity here is, that where roads cross or branch off, a directing post is set up, which might sometimes be mistaken for a cross, were it in a Catholic country. The distances are measured by the mile, which is the fourth of a league, and stones to mark them are set by the way-side, though they are often too much defaced by time or by mischievous travellers to be of any use.

The dresses of the peasantry are far less interesting than they are in our own land; they are neither gay in colour, nor graceful in shape; that of the men differs little in make from what the higher orders wear. I have seen no goats; they are not common, for neither their flesh nor their milk is in use; the people seem not to know how excellent the milk is, and how excellent a cheese may be made from it. All the sheep are white, and these also are never milked. Here are no aqueducts, no fountains by the way-side.

Okehampton, which we next came to, stands in the county of Devonshire; here also is a ruined castle on its hill, beautifully ivied, and standing above a delightful stream. There was in our room a series of prints, which, as they represented a sport peculiar to England, interested me much: it was the hunting the hare. The first displayed the sportsmen assembled on horseback, and the dogs searching the cover: in the second they were in chace, men and dogs full speed, horse and horseman together leaping over a high gate,—a thing which I thought impossible, but J—— assured me that it was commonly practised in this perilous amusement: in the third they were at fault, while the poor hare was stealing away at a distance: the last was the death of the hare, the huntsman holding her up and winding his horn, while the dogs are leaping round him.

This province appears far more fertile than the one we have quitted; the wealth of which lies under ground. The beauty of the country is much injured by inclosures, which intercept the view, or cut it into patches; it is not, however, quite fair to judge of them in their present leafless state. The road was very hilly, a thick small rain came on, and prevented us from seeing any thing. Wet as is the climate of the whole island, these two western provinces are particularly subject to rain; for they run out between the English and Bristol channels, like a peninsula: in other respects their climate is better, the temperature being considerably warmer; so that sickly persons are sent to winter here upon the south coast. Much cyder is made here: it is a far pleasanter liquor than their beer, and may indeed be considered as an excellent beverage by a people to whom nature has denied the grape. I ought, perhaps, to say, that it is even better than our country wines; but what we drank was generous cyder, and at a price exceeding that which generous wine bears with us; so that the advantage is still ours.

We only stopped to change chaises at our next stage; the inn was not inviting in its appearance, and we had resolved to reach Exeter to a late dinner. There were two busts in porcelain upon the chimney-piece, one of Bonaparte, the other of John Wesley, the founder of a numerous sect in this land of schismatics; and between them a whole-length

figure of Shakespere, their famous dramatist. When J——
had explained them to me, I asked him which of the
three worthies was the most popular. "Perhaps," said he,
"the Corsican just at present; but his is a transient
popularity; he is only the first political actor of the day,
and, like all other stage-players, must one day give way to
his successors, as his predecessors have given way to him.
Moreover, he is rather notorious than popular; the king
of Prussia was a favourite with the people, and they hung
up his picture as an alehouse sign, as they had done prince
Eugene before him, and many a fellow gets drunk under
them still; but no one will set up Bonaparte's head as an
invitation. Wesley, on the contrary, is a saint with his
followers, and indeed with almost all the lower classes. As
for Shakespere, these people know nothing of him but his
name; he is famous in the strictest sense of the word, and
his fame will last as long as the English language; which
by God's blessing will be as long as the habitable world
itself." "He is your saint!" said I, smiling at the warmth
with which he spake.

At length we crossed the river Exe by a respectable
bridge, and immediately entered the city of Exeter, and
drove up a long street to an inn as large as a large convent.
Is it possible, I asked, that this immense house can ever be
filled by travellers? He told me in reply, that there were
two other inns in the city nearly as large, besides many
smaller ones; and yet, that the last time he passed through
Exeter, they were obliged to procure a bed for him in a
private dwelling, not having one unoccupied in the house.

Saturday, April 24.

If the outside of this New London Inn, as it is called,
surprised me, I was far more surprised at the interior.
Excellent as the houses appeared at which we had already
halted, they were mean and insignificant compared with this.
There was a sofa in our apartment, and the sideboard was
set forth with china and plate. Surely, however, these
articles of luxury are misplaced, as they are not in the
slightest degree necessary to the accommodation of a
traveller, and must be considered in his bill.

Exeter is an ancient city, and has been so slow in adopting
modern improvements that it has the unsavoury odour of

**Exeter.**

Lisbon. One great street runs through the city from east to west; the rest consists of dirty lanes. As you cross the bridge, you look down upon a part of the town below, intersected by little channels of water. The cathedral is a fine object from those situations where both towers can be seen, and only half the body of the building, rising above the city. It cannot be compared with Seville, or Cordova, or Burgos; yet certainly it is a noble pile. Even the heretics confess that the arches, and arched windows, and avenues of columns, the old monuments, the painted altar, and the coloured glass, impress them with a feeling favourable to religion. For myself, I felt that I stood upon ground which, desecrated as it was, had once been holy.

Close to our inn is the entrance of the Norney or public walk. The trees are elms, and have attained their full growth: indeed, I have never seen a finer walk; but every town has not its Norney as with us its *alameda*. I was shown a garden, unique in its kind, which has been made in the old castle ditch. The banks rise steeply on each side; one of the finest poplars in the country grows in the bottom, and scarcely overtops the ruined wall. Jackson, one of the most accomplished men of his age, directed these improvements; and never was accident more happily improved. He was chiefly celebrated as a musician; but as a man of letters, his reputation is considerable; and he was also a painter: few men, if any, have succeeded so well in so many of the fine arts.[1] Of the castle itself there are but few remains; it was named Rougemont from the colour of the red sandy eminence on which it stands, and for the same reason the city itself was called by the Britons the red city.

In most of the English towns they have what they call circulating libraries: the subscribers, for an annual or quarterly payment, have two or more volumes at a time, according to the terms; and strangers may be accommodated on depositing the value of the book they choose. There are several of these in Exeter, one of which, I was told, was considered as remarkably good, the bookseller being himself a man of considerable learning and ability. Here was also a literary society of some celebrity, till the French

*Northernhay.*

*Jackson.*

---

[1] William Jackson, born 1730, died 1803. (Townsend, *Trans. Devon. Assoc.*, xiv, 695-701.)

revolution, which seems to have disturbed every town, village, and almost every family in the kingdom, broke it up.[1]   The inhabitants in general are behind-hand with their countrymen in information and refinement.   The streets are not flagged, neither are they regularly cleaned, as in other parts of the kingdom; the corporation used to compel the townspeople to keep their doors clean, as is usual in every English town; but some little while ago it was discovered, that, by the laws of the city, they had no authority to insist upon this; and now the people will not remove the dirt from their own doors, because they say they cannot be forced to do it. Their politics are as little progressive as their police : to this day, when they speak of the Americans, they call them the rebels.   Everywhere else, this feeling is extinguished among the people, though it still remains in another quarter. When Washington died his will was published in the newspapers; but in those which are immediately under ministerial influence, it was suppressed by high authority.   It was not thought fitting that any respect should be paid to to the memory of a man whom the Sovereign considered as a rebel and a traitor.

The celebrated Priestley[2] met with a singular instance of popular hatred in this place.   A barber who was shaving him heard his name in the midst of the operation;—he dropt his razor immediately, and ran out of the room exclaiming, 'that he had seen his cloven foot.'

I bought here a map of England, folded for the pocket, with the roads and distances all marked upon it.   I purchased also a book of the roads, in which not only the distance of every place in the kingdom from London, and from each other, is set down, but also the best inn at each place is pointed out, the name mentioned of every gentleman's seat near the road, and the objects which are most worthy a traveller's notice.   Every thing that can possibly facilitate travelling seems to have been produced by the commercial spirit of this people.

---

[1] The society was known as "A Society of Gentlemen in Exeter," and published a volume of essays in 1796. (Townsend, *Trans. Devon. Assoc.*, xiv, 700.)

[2] Joseph Priestley, the famous chemist and man of science, born 1733, died 1804, was also famous as a theologian.

As the chief trade of Exeter lies with Spain, few places have suffered so much by the late war. We departed about noon the next day; and as we ascended the first hill looked down upon the city and its cathedral towers to great advantage. Our stage was four leagues, along a road which, a century ago, when there was little travelling, and no care was taken of the public ways, was remarkable as the best in the West of England. The vale of Honiton, which we overlooked on the way, is considered as one of the richest landscapes in the kingdom: it is indeed a prodigious extent of highly cultivated country, set thickly with hedges and hedge-row trees; and had we seen it either in its full summer green, or with the richer colouring of autumn, perhaps I might not have been disappointed. Yet I should think the English landscape can never appear rich to a southern eye: the verdure is indeed beautiful and refreshing, but green fields and timber trees have neither the variety nor the luxuriance of happier climates. England seems to be the paradise of sheep and cattle; Valencia of the human race.

Honiton, the town where we changed chaises, has nothing either interesting or remarkable in its appearance, except that here, as at Truro, a little stream flows along the street, and little cisterns or basins, for dipping places are made before every door. Lace is manufactured here in imitation of the Flanders lace, to which it is inferior because it thickens in washing; the fault is in the thread. I have reason to remember this town, as our lives were endangered here by the misconduct of the innkeeper. There was a demur about procuring horses for us; a pair were fetched from the field, as we afterwards discovered, who had either never been in harness before, or so long out of it as to have become completely unmanageable. As soon as we were shut in, and the driver shook the reins, they ran off— a danger which had been apprehended; for a number of persons had collected round the inn door to see what would be the issue. The driver, who deserved whatever harm could happen to him, for having exposed himself and us to so much danger, had no command whatever over the frightened beasts; he lost his seat presently, and was thrown upon the pole between the horses; still he kept the reins, and almost miraculously prevented himself from falling

*Honiton.*

under the wheels, till the horses were stopped at a time when we momently expected that he would be run over and the chaise overturned. As I saw nothing but ill at this place, so I heard nothing that is good of it: the borough is notoriously venal; and since it has become so the manners of the people have undergone a marked and correspondent alteration.

This adventure occasioned considerable delay. At length a chaise arrived; and the poor horses, instead of being suffered to rest, weary as they were, for they had just returned from Exeter, were immediately put to for another journey. One of them had been rubbed raw by the harness. I was in pain all the way, and could not but consider myself as accessory to an act of cruelty: at every stroke of the whip my conscience upbraided me, and the driver was not sparing with it. It was luckily a short stage of only two leagues and a quarter. English travelling, you see, has its evils and its dangers. The life of a post-horse is truly wretched:—there will be cruel individuals in all countries, but cruelty here is a matter of calculation: the postmasters find it more profitable to overwork their beasts and kill them by hard labour in two or three years, than to let them do half the work and live out their natural length of life. In commerce, even more than in war, both men and beasts are considered merely as machines, and sacrificed with even less compunction.

**Axminster.**    There is a great fabric of carpets at Axminster, which are woven in one entire piece. We were not detained here many minutes, and here we left the county of Devonshire, which in climate and fertility and beauty is said to exceed most parts of England: if it be indeed so, England has little to boast of. Both their famous pirates, the Drake and the Raleigh, were natives of this province; so also was Oxenham, another of these early buccaneers, of whose family it is still reported, that before any one dies a bird with a white breast flutters about the bed of the sick person, and vanishes when he expires.

# INDEX

Athelstan, King, 3, 4, 16, 18, 25-
6, 50, 82, 84, 109, 140, 142,
179-81, 189, 202, 217, 233, 245,
273
Athelstan's Palace, 142
Atry Stone, 14
Attorneys, 170
Audley, Lords, 3
Augustinian Canons. *See* Bod-
min, Exeter, Frithelstock,
Hartland, Launcells, Launces-
ton, Marsh, Plympton, St.
Anthony, St. Germans
Augustinian Nuns. *See* Corn-
worthy
Austell, Saint, 40
Autre. *See* Ottery St. Mary
Autre R. *See* Otter
Avon (Aume, Awne) R., 60,
163-4, 186
Axe Bay. *See* Seaton Bay
Axe Br., 80, 82, 137, 144
Axe R., 80-3, 137, 143, 178, 233,
273
Axminster, 81-3, 110-11, 137,
144-5, 178, 233, 273, 310
Axmouth, 80-1
Axmouth Cell (Benedictine), 81

BAILIFFS, Exeter, 104, 109-10
Bailiffs or Portreeves. *See* Port-
reeves
Baize. *See* Cloth Manufacture
Bake-houses, 188
Baldwin the Sheriff, 67, 140, 211.
*See also* Redvers
Balingers, 22
Balle, a Tin-work, 191
Balle, Thomas, 183
Balliol College, Oxford, 177, 214
Bampfylde(Bamfeild), Sir Amias,
86 ; Sir Copleston, 103 ; Hugh,
103
Bampton, 4, 148, 180, 296
Bampton, Oxf., 140
Barbadoes. *See* West Indies
Barges, 46
Bark Exported, 289
Barnstaple (Barnstable, Bas-
table, Beardastapole, Berde-
nestaple, Berstaple), 1-4, 134,
167, 171-4, 176, 212, 277, 293
Barnstaple Bay, 171
Barnstaple Br., 2, 174, 293
Barnstaple Priory (Cluniac), 2-4
Barnstaple Water. *See* Taw
Baronies. *See* Honours

Barracks, 188, 269
Barret, Mr., 43
Barrett, Mrs. Elizabeth, 87 ;
John, 87
Barrows, Sepulchral, 1, 39, 197,
200, 251
Bars, Pebble. *See* Pebble Ridges
Bars, Sand. *See* Sand Bars
Bartholomew, Bp., 87
Bartholomew Trout. *See* Trout
Bartholomew Yard, Exeter, 70
Bartlet, William, 172
Basill, 12
Basset, 12, 21 ; Francis, 193 ;
Sir John, 21 ; Ralph, 21 ;
William, 21
Bastable. See Barnstaple
Bath, Earls of. *See* Bourchier,
Grenville
Bath, Trade with, 281
Batteries. *See* Guns
Battery Ware. *See* Brass
Battle Abbey, 70, 141
Battle-axes. *See* Weapons
Bayly (Baly), William, 112
Bay Trees, 221
Beam, 105
Beardastapole. *See* Barnstaple
Bear Inn, Exeter, 141
Beauchamp, Robert, 7
Beaulieu (Bewle) Abbey, 32
Bec Abbey, 140
Becket Family, 50
Bedeford. *See* Bideford
Bedford Chapel, Exeter, 71
Bedford Circus (House), Exeter,
71, 91, 141-2
Bedford, Duke and Earl of. *See*
Russell
Bedlow. *See* Bellew
Beech, 297
Beer (Berewood), 80
Beer or Ale. *See* Ale
Bekelly (Bokelley), 15
Bellever (Belliford), 211
Bellew (Bedlow), 6 ; Henry, 6 ;
John, 6 ; Patrick, 6
Bells, Church, 61, 84, 111, 140
Bench Ends, Church, 258
Benedictine Houses. *See* Ax-
mouth, Bodmin, Cowick,
Exeter, Modbury, Otterton,
Pilton, Polslo, Sidmouth, Tavi-
stock, Trescow
Berdenestaple. *See* Barnstaple
Bere Alston, 229, 268-9, 279
Bere Ferrers, 42, 52-3, 59, 285

CABER (Cober), R., 164, 255
Cablan R. *See* Camel
Caharrack Mine, 263
Cairdine. *See* Kerthen
Cairns, 137
Calamansack (Calmansake, Cheilow) Cr., 33
Calendar Brothers. *See* Kalendars
Callington (Kellington), 205, 228, 268, 286
Calstock, 47, 205
Calstock (Caulstoke) Br., 8, 52
Camborne, 261-2
Camel (Allen, Cablan) R., 14-16, 158, 200-2, 265
Camelford (Comblefford), 14, 133, 201, 265
Camelford, Lord. *See* Pitt
Camera Obscura, 189
Campernulph. *See* Champernowne
Camps. *See* Earthworks
Canal, Proposed, 193
Canary Is., Trade with, 102
Candles, Tallow, 303
Canelles or Canelys. *See* Goonhillies
Canons, Augustinian or Regular. *See* Augustinian Canons
Canons, Secular. *See* Collegiate Churches
Cantilupe Family, 61
Cantuary Priests. *See* Vicars Choral
Canute, King, 50, 181
Cape Cornwall, 193, 195
Cap of Maintenance, 90, 110
Capstans for Hauling Boats, 25
Cardinham Cas., Honour, and Manor, 20, 45
Cardinham (Caridinham), 40, 42, 44-5; Isolda de, 40; Robert de, 42, 44. *See also* Dynham
Caregroyne Rock, 34
Carew (Carey, Carow), 67; Sir Gawen, 11, 87; Sir George, Baron Carew of Clopton, 64-5, 77, 87-8; George, 87; Sir John, 78, 214; John, 78; Sir Nicholas, Baron, 45, 67, 78; Odo, 78; Sir Peter, 77, 87-8; Sir Philip, 77; Sir William, 77
Cargreen (Caregrin), 52
Cargurrell, 39
Caricause in Cous (St. Michael's Mount), 195

Carlion, Mr., 225
Carmelite Houses. *See* Plymouth
Carnary Chapel, Exeter, 70
Carhangives (Carnhangives) Earthworks, 20
Carnbrea (Carnbray, Karn-breh), 21, 192, 259, 262-3
Carne Godolcan or Godolghan. *See* Godolphin Hill
Carnon, 253
Carnsew (Carniovies, Carnsey), Mr., 15
Carpet Manufacture, 233, 273-4, 310
Carriages and Carts, 209, 224, 280, 282, 286, 289-91, 293-6, 300, 303-4
Carrick Roads (Caryk Road), 34
Carteis, Mr., 43
Carteret, Mr., 198
Cart-horses, 283, 289, 295, 304
Cartuther (Cortyder), 50
Carvings, Stone, 84, 107-8, 116, 131, 140, 169, 191, 206, 214, 287. *See also* Monuments
Carvings, Wood, 89, 116, 186, 255, 258. *See also* Bishop's Throne
Cary (Carey, Caryl), Mr., 240; Robert, 6; Valentine, Bp., 86
Casewater. *See* Chacewater
Castiglione, Signor, 98, 105
Castle-an-Dinas (Castellan Danis, Castelle Endinas), 18, 19
Castle Cart Earthworks, 203
Castle Dour, 45
Castle Downs or Danes Earthworks, 199
Castleguard Tenure, 9, 61. *See also* Knights' Fees
Castle Hill, Filleigh, 294
Castle Horneck, 195
Castle Park, Lostwithiel, 251
Castle Point, Falmouth. *See* Pendinas
CASTLES : Barnstaple, 1, 2, 277; Berry Pomeroy, 62, 239-40; Bodrugan, 39; Boscastle, 11, 266; Bryer, 95; Cardinham, 45; Carhangives, 20; Carnbrea, 21, 192, 262; Cayle, 21; Chun, 260; Colcombe, 79; Combe, 21; Dartmouth, 64, 78, 242-3; Dingerein, 39; Dour, 45; Exeter (Rougemont), 69, 91, 106, 109, 114, 139, 148, 180, 182, 216, 307; Exmouth,

Exeter Cathedral, 69, 71-5, 84-9, 105-9, 116, 140, 148, 180-1, 217, 235, 307; Cath. Officers in 1635, 84
Exeter College, Oxford, 50, 181, 205
Exeter, Duke of. *See* Holland
Exeter, Marquis of. *See* Courtenay
Exeter People, 138, 308
Exeter Religious Houses: Abbey (Benedictine), 74, 140, 181, 217; Black Friars (Dominican), 71, 141; Crossed Brethren, 72; Grey Friars (Franciscan), 70, 141, 182; Nunnery, 140; Priory of St. James (Cluniac), 141; Priory of St. John (Augustinian Canons), 70, 72, 141; Priory of St. Nicholas, 70, 141
Exminster, 69
Exmoor, 1, 62, 90, 176, 181, 290, 295-6
Exmoor Lambs, 293
Exmouth, 68-9, 182, 237
Exports: Bark, 289; China Stone, 197; Cloth, 107, 112, 114, 136, 236; Copper, 162, 192, 252; Corn, 197-8; Herrings, 171; Lead, 102; Pilchards, 151, 163-4, 194-5, 198, 226, 249, 257, 260, 269, 281; Slate, 134, 201, 260; Tin, 102, 198, 252, 257

FAIRFAX, General, 234
Fairmile, 179
Fairs: Barnstaple, 3, 295; Bideford, 5; Chagford, 68; Fowey, 41; Helston, 30; Liskeard, 49, 228; Looe, East, 48; Marazion, 27; Mousehole, 26; Penryn, 35; Penzance, 27; Plympton, 57; Torrington, 6; Tregoney, 36
Fal (Fala, Vale) R., 36-7, 197, 199, 251
Fallopit, 168
Falmouth (Falamuth), 33-4, 37-8, 40, 160-1, 167, 197, 253, 298-9
Fanshawe, Lady, 226
Fats (Tin-works), 199
Feasts, Parish, 210
Feniton (Veniton), 232
Fenny (Venne, Veniton) Bridges, 77, 179, 232

Ferns, 296
Ferrers Family, 23, 29
Ferries, 15, 20, 51, 53, 122-3, 155, 188, 197, 222-3, 242, 245, 247
Fiennes, William, Viscount Say and Sele, 134
Filleigh, 294
Finn, Mr., 224
Fire-engines. *See* Steam-engines
Fire-places and Fire-irons, Domestic, 302
Fires, Towns suffering from: Crediton, 212-13, 274; Honiton, 179, 232; Marazion, 28; Tiverton, 214
Firs, 183, 189
Fisacre, Mr., 66
Fishing Methods, 148-51, 198, 248
Fishing Rights, 240
Fishing Towns and Villages. *See seperate names*
Fishing Trade (*kind not specified*), 16, 130, 160, 166, 196, 281. *See also* Exports
Fish, Kinds of. *See* Doree, Eels, Herrings, Mackerel, Pilchards, Salmon, Salmon Peal, Trout, Turbot, Whiting-Pollack
Fitzgerald, William, 78
Fitz Hibben, *alias* Phibben, 191
Fitzmatthew, Peter, 66
Fitzralph, John, 17
Fitz-Richard Family, 42
Fitzwarren, Lord. *See* Bourchier
Fitzwilliam, 42; Robert, 40; William, Earl of Southampton, 5, 7
Five Barrows (The Tourres), 1
Five Lanes, 286
Flannel Manufatcure. *See* Cloth Manufacture
Flavel, John, 152
Flax Spinning. *See* Yarn Manufacture
Fleming, 78; Alan, 78; Barons of Slane, 3, 6
Flight Shot. *See* Arrow Shot
Floods, 135-6, 294
Flushing, Falmouth, 299
Font, 120
Food in General, 279, 299
Fooly, Capt., 98
Force (Fortification), 39, 47
Force, Henry, 29
Ford Abbey (Cistercian), 81
Ford, Sir Henry, 106

261 ; Salt, 173, 276 ; Timber,
198 ; Wine, 102, 174 ; Wool,
174, 276
Indian Queens Post-house, 301
Iniscaw. *See* Trescow
Inishaw (Innisschawe), 24
Inispriven, 31
Innes House, 289
Innes, Sir James Norcliffe-,
afterwards Duke of Roxburgh,
289
Inns, 54, 83, 103-4, 117, 135, 141,
144, 149, 203, 219, 223, 225,
231, 233, 243-4, 256, 267, 270,
299, 301-3, 305-6, 309
Ireland, Trade with, 16, 167, 174,
176, 201, 276, 289
Iron Imported, 198, 261
Iron, Occurrence of, 277
Irrigation, 296
Isca, 137, 142, 176
Iscanus, Josephus. *See* Joseph
of Exeter
Isleston. *See* Shag Rock
Italy, Trade with, 107, 147, 151,
155, 226, 236, 269
Ivybridge, 58, 219, 244

Jä. *See* Hia
Jackson, William, 307
Jagford. *See* Chagford
James II (Duke of York), 188
Janowick, Col., 94
Jay, Cornish. *See* Chough
Jenings, Mr., 97
Jersey I., 198
Jewellers, 102
John, King, 30, 37, 61, 64, 146,
186, 211
John, Treasurer of Exeter Cath.,
70
Joseph of Exeter (Josephus
Iscanus), 182
Juhel (Johelus) de Totenes. *See*
Totnes, Joel de
Jurats, 271

KALENDARS, Fraternity of, 72
Karns, 254
Keke, Mr., 190
Kellington. *See* Callington
Kelly, 205
Kenn R., 182
Kendall (Kendale), Mr., 49
Kennaway, Sir John, 234
Kenning, 23, 39, 65
Kenor. *See* Connerton

Kensey R., 267
Kenton, 68-9
Kent's Hole, 241-2
Kenwith (Kennith) Cas., 176
Kenwyn R., 252
Kenwyn (Kenwen) Street, Truro,
36
Kerris, 27
Kerseys. *See* Cloth
Kerthen (Cairdine), 29
Kerton. *See* Crediton
Keyham (Kaine Place), 53
Kilkhampton, 275
Killet, Dr., 84
Killigrew (Keligrew, Kiligrew,
Kylligrin), 30, 33-4, 38, 198 ;
John, 33-4 ; Thomas, 18, 198
Killigrew, St. Erme, 33
Kilmington, 82
Kingsand (Kingston), 221-2
Kingsbridge, 65
King's College, Cambridge, 28-
9, 213
Kingsfield (Kingsmead), 82, 178,
233
Kingsteignton, 68
Kingswear, 65, 242
Kirkham (Kirkam), Mr., 106-7,
110
Kirton. *See* Crediton
Kismeldon (Kissington) Br., 8
Kit Hill, 205, 268
Kiwartun Family. *See* Chiverton
Kneller, Sir Godfrey, 235
Knights' Fees, 45, 175
Kynance Cove, 254

LABOURERS, 282
Lace-making, 107, 136, 233, 273,
309
Lacy (Lacey), Edmund, Bp., 2,
11, 18, 22, 54, 61, 72-4, 88, 140,
181
Ladock, 33
Lady Park, 228
La Fontaine, M. de, 19
La Hay, William de, 41
Lamber R., 205
Lambert, General, 154, 188
Lamelin, 47
Lamelin Family, 47
Lamerton, 205-6, 287
Lamorran (La Moran, Lan
Moran) Cr., 36
Lanant. *See* Lelant
Land Gained from the Sea, 143
Landkey, 74

Land's End, 22, 96, 129-30, 165-
6, 193, 195, 259, 298
Land Submerged by the Sea, 27,
29, 67, 195, 223
Land Tenure, 10, 25, 281
Lanes, 117-18, 122, 289
Langdon, Rev. Tobias, 235
Lanherne (Lanheran), 19, 200
Lanhydrock, 167
Lanihorne (Lanyhorne), 37
Lanlivery, 203
Lanstephan. *See* Launceston
Lanteglos, 47
Lantinny, 32
Lantyan (Lantian, Lantient)
Honour or Manor, 43
Lantyan Pill, 43
Lapper-stones, 137
Laprin Br. *See* Resprin
Larkbear (Lathbier) Religious
House, 141
Latin Inscriptions, 40, 45, 71, 73-
4, 204
Launcels, 12
Launcels Cell (Augustinian
Canons), 12
Launceston (Laanson, Lanstoun,
Lanstephan, Lostephan), 8-11,
18, 49, 131, 134-5, 169, 206,
208, 266-7, 287-8, 302-3
Launceston Collegiate Church
(St. Stephen's), 10, 11, 267
Launceston Priory (Augustinian
Canons), 10, 11, 267
Laurels, 228
Laurustinus, 189, 221
Lazars. *See* Lepers
Lead Mines, 99, 159, 178, 197,
229, 255, 268
Lead, Occurrence of, 13, 165,
167, 278
Lead Trade, 102
League, Great, 67
Leather Trade, 157, 192
Le Bon (Delabont), Walter, 62
Lee Mill Br. (Le Br.), 57
Legends, Church, 72
Lelant (Lanant, Lannant), 20, 22,
193, 261
Lemara R., 228
Lemon, Mr., 251 ; Sir William,
251
Lemon R. (Leman Water), 68
Leofric, Bp., 51, 71, 84, 88-9, 140,
217
Lepers, 18, 61, 70, 199, 264, 303
Lergen Br., 45

Lerryn (Lerine), 46
Levant, Trade with, 107
Levelis, Thomas, 26
Levine Prisklo, *alias* Levine
Pole. *See* Swan Pool
Libraries, 89, 116, 139-40, 148,
200, 214, 217, 275, 307
Lidford. *See* Lydford
Lieutenants, County, 109
Lighthouses, 23, 102, 121,
128, 143, 153, 255, 257, 259,
298
Limestone and Lime, 186, 200,
209, 215, 218, 237-8, 242, 261,
276, 279, 290-1, 294, 296-7
Lime Trees, 221
Lincoln, Theophilus Clinton,
Earl of, 126
Limpets, 248
Lipsius, 187
Lisbon. *See* Portugal
Lisburne, Earl of. *See* Vaughan
Liskeard (Leskard, Liscard), 49,
156, 158, 168, 198, 203, 223,
228, 247, 286
Lisle, Alice de, 26-7
Literary Society, 308
Liverpool, Trade with, 173, 276
Livery Dole, 83
Living, Bp., 50-1
Lizard (Lyzart) Pt., 31, 129-30,
189, 197, 255, 298
Loadstone, 99, 102
Lobsters, 151
Lodenek, 16
Logan Stone, 25
London, Trade with, 134, 136,
164, 236, 281
Long, Gilbert, 70 ; John, 70
Longevity, 272
Longships, 195
Looe (Lonn, Loow, Lowe), East
and West, 47-8, 122, 159-60,
224, 246-7
Looe Br., 48, 122, 160, 225, 247
Looe I., 221, 224
Looe (Loo, Lo), Pool, 30-1, 196,
255
Loosemoore, John, 85, 106
Lord's Meadow, Crediton, 212
Lostephan. *See* Launceston
Lostwithiel (Lestwithiel), 43-6,
159, 168, 198, 203, 208, 225,
227, 251
Lostwithiel Br., 45-6
Loudham, Mr., 142
Lovibond (Lovebone), John, 15

# ADDENDA AND CORRIGENDA

Page   1, note 1. According to Prof. Skeat, the word "staple," in the sense of a market, is of French origin, and has nothing to do with place-names. The Anglo-Saxon *stapol* meant a post or pillar, so " Beardastapole " is " Beard's post or pillar."

   ,,   10, note 3. Since Dr. Oliver's time considerable remains of the foundations of Launceston Priory have been unearthed. (See Kelly's *Directory*, 1914.)

   ,,   13, line 33. "False braye" is an advanced parapet surrounding the main rampart. The earliest example of the use of this term given in the *New English Dict.* is 1645.

   ,,   30, margin. For " Love Pool" *read* " Looe Pool."

   ,,   111, heading. For " 1695 " *read* " 1699."

   ,,   114, lines 20, 22. " Bow-dye " was a scarlet dye prepared from tin, and was so named from Bow, near Stratford in Essex, where dyers particularly carried on their work in the seventeenth century. (*New English Dict.*) The word " changeable " agrees with the text, but is probably a misprint for " chargeable," that is, costly.

   ,,   126, note 1. For " Theophilus Clinton, Esq., of Lincoln," *read* " Theophilus Clinton, Earl of Lincoln and Baron Clinton."

   ,,   179, note 4. For " The ' Great House' at Colyton " *read* " Escot."

   ,,   203, line 4. For " grand " *read* " guard."

   ,,   205, note 1. For " Kent." *read* " Knt."

   ,,   252, line 4. For " corcibles " *read* " crucibles."